Film
Review
2009-2010

Film Review
2009-2010

Michael Darvell and Mansel Stimpson

Founding Father:
F. Maurice Speed 1911-1998

Oscar-winner
Kate Winslet in
The Reader.

Reynolds & Hearn Ltd
London

To Ann Barker, a lifelong friend and cinema companion – MD

To Roy Galloway, proprietor of the Curzon Cinema, Eastbourne, a surviving example of
the independent owner whose cinema is welcoming and has an individual atmosphere
that reflects his great love of films – MS

Acknowledgements

The Editors would like to thank the following, without whose help this book
might not have appeared: Carol Allen, Clive Baxter, Alex Buchan,
James Cameron-Wilson, Jeremy Clarke, Marcus Hearn, Kiran P Joshi,
Marshall Julius, Dee Pilgrim, David Pratt, Carolynn Reynolds,
Richard Reynolds, Jonathan Rigby, George Savvides and Derek Winnert.

In Memoriam pictures supplied by The Tony Hillman Collection.

First published in 2009 by
Reynolds & Hearn Ltd
61a Priory Road
Kew Gardens
Richmond
Surrey TW9 3DH

A CIP catalogue record for this book is
available from the British Library.

ISBN 978 1 904674 07 8

Designed by James King.
Jacket designed by Peri Godbold.

Printed and bound in Malta by Progress Press Co. Ltd.

Contents

Nicole Kidman
and Hugh
Jackman clinch
the romantic
deal in *Australia*.

Introduction

In the period under review in this volume (July 2008 to June 2009) some 440 films were released in the United Kingdom. We have covered over 400 of them in our Film Releases section. The remaining few are some specialist films that received only rare screenings in Britain, mainly at club cinemas for a limited run, films that came and went so quickly that hardly anybody had a chance to review them, some older titles that appeared years after their production date, a number of new Bollywood films which are still not promoted as widely as other releases and also some films that distributors decided not to screen for the press so that our reviewers had no chance to see them.

The worth of film critics is being questioned now that many UK national and local newspapers are cutting back on staff because of the slump in advertising revenue. Some papers are restricting their film reviews to the main releases of the week and ignoring the independent and foreign films, movies that in fact that need promotion more than the Hollywood blockbusters. In future years print reviewers on all subjects, be it film, theatre, music, art etc, may well be history as so many publishers now prefer to fill their pages and websites with their own readers' blogs.

Everybody is entitled to have an opinion, but then that's why publications have a 'Letters to the Editor' page. Amateurism is now rearing its small-time head and the well-turned phrase of your favourite professional film critic could well be a thing of the past, as we remember the halcyon days of, say, Pauline Kael, Kenneth Tynan, Dilys Powell and all the Penelopes (Gilliatt, Mortimer, Houston) who used to write on films and whose weekly or quarterly contributions were something to look forward to with some excitement. Although we do have some very good younger film critics writing today, Philip French of *The Observer* and Derek Malcolm of the London *Evening Standard* are the sole survivors of the old school of critics still reviewing with an expert film knowledge and a deep passion for the job. In future nobody is going to look forward with any anticipation to Joe or Jill Bloggs and their twopennyworth of ill-considered thoughts on the latest releases. Films are made by professionals and they should be reviewed by professional writers with experience and a love of cinema.

Young people are noted for knowing absolutely nothing about anything. You only have to tune in to *University Challenge* any week to see how ignorant contestants are on the history of any art form except, of course, pop music. When it comes to the arts most young people can only appreciate the brand new because they have no interest or knowledge of the history of film or theatre or music. They only know films through what's presented to them week in and week out at their local Odeon or Cineworld or what turns out to be the newest big West End musical or whatever tracks have just hit the pop charts. The back story of their chosen art form seems to be of no interest to them. I have always found that old films are generally more interesting than many of the new releases. Most new films will be forgotten in a few weeks, months or years but the best of them, a small percentage, no doubt, will survive to become classics in their own right.

These days there are virtually no UK outlets for

the revival of old films. A few film societies remain but, apart from the British Film Institute's National Film Theatre, repertory cinemas have all but disappeared from the UK film scene. The sole remaining one in London, since the Hampstead Everyman went straight (ie new, mainstream releases only) is the Riverside Studios in Hammersmith where, at the time of writing, you could see double-bills of Ken Loach (one old film, one new), Buñuel and Polanski, Tati's *Jour de Fête* and *Monsieur Hulot's Holiday*, and a double-bill of *Room at the Top* and *Look Back in Anger*, all showing in rep with the more current releases.

As a teenager, long before I worked for the listings magazine *What's On In London*, I would scour its pages every week and seek out the best double-bills of revivals often showing at the Classic cinemas in Kilburn, Stockwell, Tooting and Hampstead or catch up with vintage films at the Ionic Golders Green, the Paris Pullman in Chelsea, the Globe in Putney or the Empire in Watford. Then the Everyman was noted for its Bergman seasons and those were also the days of the Starlight, the film club at the Mayfair Hotel, where you could take your gin and tonic into the cinema and nosh on the free sausage rolls while viewing revivals of MGM musicals. And if you were really desperate to catch up with a film, there was always the Biograph at Victoria and the Tolmer at Euston (seats from the pre-decimal price of one and threepence). All have now gone and in the process going to the pictures has lost something valuable and sadly all too irretrievable.

To catch up with old films you now have to turn to television or DVD, even if watching movies at home is not the best way to enjoy cinema, as it has always existed as a collective entertainment experience. Sadly, terrestrial television has given up on showing many very old black and white films, preferring instead to screen more recent movies, many of which did no business at the cinema or went straight to video. News also comes that, because sales of vintage films on DVD are dropping, distributors will in future concentrate on marketing the more recent films. However, all is not lost, as the British Film Institute's programme of re-releases ensures that some classics of the seventh art are still available to see at your local cinema or arts centre.

If you read Peter Bradshaw's film reviews in *The Guardian*, it is invariably the re-issue that is the best film of the week and often the only one to be awarded five stars. Mainly these come from the BFI's ongoing policy of re-releasing new prints of films that have not been seen in cinemas for decades. The BFI's re-issues for the period 2008 and 2009 include such titles as Kurosawa's *Ikiru*, Truffaut's *Jules et Jim* and *Les Quatre Cents Coups*, David Lean's *Passionate Friends*, Michael Powell's *A Matter of Life and Death*, Elia Kazan's *A Streetcar Named Desire*, Terrence Malick's *Badlands*, Joseph Losey's *Accident*, Joseph Lewis' *Gun Crazy*, Jacques Demy's *Les Demoiselles de Rochefort*, Hitchcock's *North by Northwest* and *Notorious*, Godard's *Pierrot le Fou*, Oshima's *In the Realm of the Senses*, Sergio Leone's *Once Upon a Time in the West*, and Orson Welles' *Citizen Kane*. These titles represent a pretty wide view of world cinema. Could anything that opened in the past year be a match for any of these films? I suppose we won't know until, say, in 20 years' time we are labelling some of the current output as classics.

For the past six years Park Circus, the distributor of classic and back catalogue films, has made over ten thousand titles available for the big screen. They are exhibited through repertory and festival bookings, making it simple for the rights owners of the films to offer their back catalogues for theatrical distribution. They are also re-issuing a number of films themselves and those that will be seen between now and May 2010 include *The Godfather*, *The Red Shoes*, *Gentlemen Prefer Blondes*, John Frankenheimer's *The Manchurian Candidate* and *Pandora and the Flying Dutchman*. Other titles on their books include *Pretty Woman* and *Withnail and I*, while they also release such popular and more current titles as *Hannah Montana* and *High School Musical 3*. From their list of bookings for screenings at mainly UK arts centres rather than dedicated cinemas, are *The Red Balloon*, *Paths of Glory*, *Cinema Paradiso*, *Genevieve*, *Bicycle Thieves*, *The General*, *This Sporting Life* and Hitchcock's *The Lady Vanishes*, again another list that covers classics of world cinema that are now seldom seen theatrically. One to catch before Christmas 2009 is Serge Bromberg's documentary of Henri-Georges Clouzot's unfinished 1964 film *Inferno*, which appears to be a scoop for Park Circus.

Film producers are always looking for new ways to raise money, getting people to back their product even before it has seen the light of any day. This year a new British film was made through the auspices of the MySpace website. It all started two years ago when would-be film-makers were asked to submit short film entries as audition pieces with a £1 million budget as the prize. Over 800 applicants were cut down to a short list of just a dozen by the backers, MySpace, Film4 and Vertigo Films, from which a panel of film celebrities then chose just three. Following an online sales pitch, MySpace viewers chose Vito Rocco's *Faintheart*, a comedy about an ordinary man who takes part in weekend Viking battle reconstructions and in the process loses his wife to a PE instructor.

David Lemon's screenplay was then scrutinised by MySpace users who were asked to provide lines for three scenes, but waiving any rights should they appear in the finished film. Casting the film was done through MySpace auditions and some 1,400 applications were received from which ten minor roles were filled, although the main parts went to experienced professional actors including Eddie Marsan, Ewen Bremner, Jessica Hynes, Anne Reid, Tim Healy and Paul Nicholls etc. However, MySpace users did provide some of the music on the soundtrack. Shown at the Edinburgh Festival in 2008, *Faintheart* proved to be just an interesting experiment but nothing more than an average British comedy. It didn't seem to get a very wide UK release, despite its taglines of "May the Norse be with you" and "A zero will rise", but it is now available on DVD.

Zac Efron and Vanessa Hudgens are no Fred and Ginger but teenies will still love *High School Musical 3: Senior Year*.

Another and still ongoing method of raising money for making films is through Buyacredit.com. Schoolboys Adrian Bliss, Tony Stubbs and Ben Robbins plan to film *Clovis Dardenter*, a forgotten novel by Jules Verne. To raise the necessary finance, £1 million, they are selling the end credits of the film at a minimum of £1 each (and presumably a maximum of £1 million?). To promote the scheme they have also made a short film called *Jam* with a celebrity cast including Lynda Bellingham, Patricia Hodge, Annette Badland, Frank Skinner, Phillip Schofield, Paul Daniels and Debbie McGee. We await the results with curiosity and especially look forward to reading the credits which, apparently, will last about thirty minutes and form an integral part of the finished film.

However, once you have made your film, how do you then find adequate distribution? Apart from its regular policy of partial financing of films, the UK Film Council also helps in the distribution of new films through its Prints and Advertising Fund, thus enabling independent films to achieve a wider showing. For instance, Artificial Eye has received £70,000 for *Fish Tank*, Andrea Arnold's Cannes award-winning film about a teenage girl coming to a moment of decision in her life, which doubled the number of screens for the film's release from 20 to 40. Adventure Pictures were given £67,050 for Sally Potter's *Rage*, a scathing look at the fashion industry, and Pathé Productions had £125,000 for Pedro Almodóvar's film noir *Broken Embraces* with Penélope Cruz, so that it could expand its distribution from 40 to 90 screens. There are further examples of both small and large amounts of money from the UKFC helping British films to get shown. Let's hope that the Council will be able to continue this policy if and when it merges with the British Film Institute, an idea proposed by the Department of Culture, Media and Sport in an effort to co-ordinate two publicly funded UK film organisations into one.

One film that may not need any extra promotion is *Colin*, the latest British zombie film that was the talk of the 2009 Cannes Film Festival where it was seen in the Cannes Lions section presentation of new directors. The reason for the interest is that it cost all of £45 to make. It is very much a one-man band production as it is written, directed, photographed, recorded and edited by Marc Vincent Price (check out that name!) who also did the sound design, visual effects, mixing and grading using a camcorder and his college software. The cast were assembled via Facebook and MySpace and *Colin* received its London premiere in the tenth anniversary season of FrightFest, in itself a fact that proves those zombies and vampires will never lie down. It went on general release on 31 October, 2009. The spirit of Roger Corman and Robert Rodriguez lives on. Is this then the future of filmmaking…?

Does the cinema even have a future? You may well ask. Even in these dark days of credit crunches and cutbacks the answer in the UK would appear to be a resounding yes. Despite rising prices more and more people are going to the cinema, if the pattern set by Cineworld patrons is anything to go by. The UK cinema chain has seen an increase in revenue of 18 per cent in the first three months of the financial year 2009-10. Global blockbusters such as *Mamma Mia!, Slumdog Millionaire* and *Star Trek* have contributed to the recent increase, plus Cineworld's commitment to both 3D technology and Bollywood product as well as their special deals such as Bargain Tuesdays and Orange Wednesdays. Could the rise in prices and

the special offers be in any way connected, as an indication of the direction in which the cinema should be going? Perhaps more cheaper seats and special offers might raise the profits even further. There's a thought in these troubled times. Meanwhile we have James Cameron's *Avatar* to look forward to in December 2009 which may be the Christmas present every cinema exhibitor has been waiting for. Advance speculation predicts that this 3D spectacle could be even bigger than *Titanic*. Now there's another thought…

Michael Darvell

This being the third edition of the *Film Review* annual under the aegis of Michael Darvell and myself, it is my hope that we have settled in. I trust that we have done so in such a way that we are leaving our own imprint on the annual while also remaining faithful to what readers have come to expect of it over the years. In a work such as this, which is now reaching its 65th year, one is very conscious of what was achieved by both the late F Maurice Speed as its founder and by James Cameron-Wilson, for whom Speed was a mentor and who happily remains a contributor to this day. Following in their footsteps, Michael and I seek to maintain their standards but, since all good writing reflects the personality of the author, certain changes of tone have obviously emerged.

If, to some extent, the sales figures confirm that our endeavours have been successful, the fact remains that my own experience both as a critic and as one who writes up interviews (the latter now mainly centred on opera rather than on film) is that one gets very little direct feedback. During the years when I wrote for *What's On In London* I did on occasion receive a letter. Indeed, I treasure to this day one or two from people who felt that they had to write because they had been overwhelmed by some film that I had recommended and which they might not have seen but for my words. There have also been a few times when filmmakers have contacted me with thanks for some article or review, but, in an age when letter-writing is

going out of fashion, this gets ever rarer.

In the circumstances I have not been surprised by the absence of any letters about recent editions of the annual. However, in many ways the internet has taken over, both as the means by which books are ordered and as a place where the public can express their opinions. It's apt enough, then, that the one example of feedback that has caught my eye consists of a comment by Mr M Catchpool of Burton-on-Trent posted by him on the Amazon website. Referring to the 64th edition, he gives it a rating of four stars out of five and describes it as "still the best film year book". I am appreciative of his taking the trouble to make his approval known since such remarks may well encourage others to buy the annual.

Quoting Mr Catchpool also gives me the opportunity to clarify a point regarding the reviews. The one criticism made by him is that in the old days James Cameron-Wilson's reviews would give more storyline details than ours do, thus helping readers to decide whether or not to seek out some particular film. I understand the point he is making, but the fact is that the annual has always aimed at covering all the releases in the UK and in recent years the number has increased significantly. To write reviews of the same length as of old would substantially increase the length of the book – which would be fine, but for the fact that it would also inevitably increase the price. Consequently, the reviews have to be more succinct, but, especially with the titles that I recommend, I hope that within the smaller space I am still able to convey enough about the nature and character of the film to evoke a response from the reader. It may be an imperfect world, but I sincerely hope that Mr Catchpool will like this edition of the annual no less than he did the last one, and that he will not be alone in doing so.

Mansel Stimpson

Who wants to be an international star then? Meet Dev Patel in *Slumdog Millionaire.*

Top 20 UK
Box-Office Hits

31 August 2008 – 12 July 2009

1. Mamma Mia!
2. The Dark Knight
3. Quantum of Solace
4. Slumdog Millionaire
5. Wall.E
6. Transformers: Revenge of the Fallen
7. Madagascar: Escape 2 Africa
8. Star Trek
9. Monsters vs Aliens
10. High School Musical 3: Senior Year
11. Night at the Museum 2: Battle of the Smithsonian
12. Angels & Demons
13. X-Men Origins: Wolverine
14. Bolt
15. The Hangover
16. Ice Age: Dawn of the Dinosaurs
17. Marley and Me
18. Terminator Salvation
19. The Chronicles of Narnia: Prince Caspian
20. The Mummy: Tomb of the Dragon Emperor

Top 10
Box-Office Stars

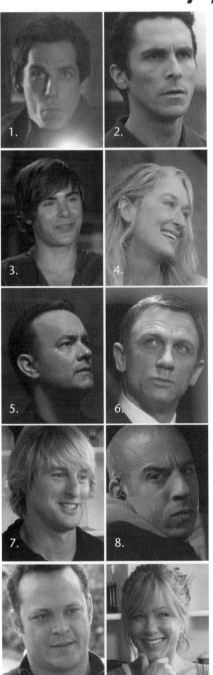

1.
2.
3.
4.
5.
6.
7.
8.
9.
10.

STAR OF THE YEAR: BEN STILLER

2. Christian Bale
3. Zac Efron
4. Meryl Streep
5. Tom Hanks
6. Daniel Craig
7. Owen Wilson
8. Vin Diesel
9. Vince Vaughn
10. Jennifer Aniston

In spite of, or perhaps *because* of, the economic crisis, audiences flocked to the cinema in unforeseen numbers. *Mamma Mia!* knocked *Titanic* off its pedestal as the highest-grossing film in UK cinemas – ever. Who would have thought that the little-known theatre director Phyllida Lloyd, with her first film, would see herself replace James Cameron as the skipper of Britain's most favoured cinematic event? But in spite of a stellar cast, the real attraction of *Mamma Mia!* was ABBA, a vanilla quartet at one time regarded *infra dig* in cultural circles. In times of hardship popularism will find its tapping feet. As for *bona fide* box-office stars, they had a tough time competing against the continuing appeal of computer animation and special effects, with the likes of Ben Stiller, Reese Witherspoon and John Travolta finding their true voice hidden behind a CGI creation. However, only Stiller proved that he was as popular in the flesh as his leonine alter ego in *Madagascar: Escape 2 Africa*. With Stiller's phenomenal success in *Night at the Museum 2: Battle of the Smithsonian* and *Tropic Thunder*, there was nobody else to match him. On the home front, the Pembrokeshire-born Christian Bale found himself in two whopping hits, *The Dark Knight* and *Terminator Salvation*, a little commercial compensation for his masochistic duty on the little-seen *The Machinist* and *Rescue Dawn*. Runners-up include Reese Witherspoon, Miley Cyrus, Jim Carrey, Adam Sandler, Robert Downey Jr, George Clooney, Simon Pegg and Clint Eastwood.

James Cameron-Wilson

Releases of

This section contains details of all the films released in the UK between 1 July, 2008 and 30 June, 2009, the period covered by all the reference features in this volume.

The film reviews are followed by the main credits for the film, beginning with names of the leading actors, then the Director, Producer (s), Screenplay Writer, Cinematographer, Production Designer or Art Director, Editor, Soundtrack Composer and Costume Designer.

For technical credits the normal abbreviations operate and are as follows: Dir – for Director; Pro – for Producer; Ph – for Cinematographer; Pro Des – for Production Designer; Art Dir – for Art Director; M – for Composer; and Cos – for Costume Designer. The production companies involved are listed with the final name in the list being the distributor. The credits end with the film's running time, the country or countries of origin, the year of production, the UK release date and the British Board of Film Classification's certificate.

Reviewers: Carol Allen (CA); Clive Baxter (CB); James Cameron-Wilson (JC-W); Jeremy Clarke (JC); Michael Darvell (MHD); Marshall Julius (MJ); Dee Pilgrim (DP); Richard Reynolds (RR); George Savvides (GS); Mansel Stimpson (MS); and Derek Winnert (DW).

Star Ratings

★ ★ ★ ★ ★ **Exceptional**
★ ★ ★ ★ **Very Good**
★ ★ ★ **Good**
★ ★ **Mediocre**
★ **Insulting**

Zac Efron keeps his finger on the pulse in the change of life comedy 17 Again.

12 Rounds ★ ★ ★

After Miles Jackson (Aidan Gillen) escapes from prison in New Orleans he seeks revenge on the man who put him there and also killed his girlfriend. So he kidnaps the girlfriend of detective Danny Fisher (John Cena) and forces him into twelve rounds of dangerous games. World Wrestling Entertainment champion Cena is a strong but rather humourless presence, so it's left to Gillen to inject some sinister mischief into this efficient but old-fashioned thriller. GS

❯ John Cena, Aiden Gillen, Ashley Scott, Steve Harris, Brian J White.
❯ *Dir* Renny Harlin, *Pro* Harlin, Mark Gordon and Mike Lake etc, *Screenplay* Daniel Kunka, *Ph* David Boyd, *Pro Des* Nicholas Lundy, *Ed* Brian Berdan, *M* Trevor Rabin, *Cos* Jill Newell.

Mark Gordon Company/Midnight Sun PicturesFilms/WWE Studios- 20th Century Fox. 108 mins. USA. 2009. Rel: 27 May 2009. Cert 12A.

17 Again ★ ★ ★ ★

Mike O'Donnell (Matthew Perry) is a bitter 37- year-old man who is unhappy both at work and at home. Surprisingly he becomes 17 again when his wish to be young becomes a reality. Zac Efron plays the young Mike and he effortlessly demonstrates both the innocence as well as the maturity of his character. The scenes where he flirts with his much older wife (Leslie Mann) or where he supports his children as one of their schoolmates are beautifully handled. Enjoy! GS

❯ Zac Efron, Leslie Mann, Thomas Lennon, Matthew Perry, Tyler Steelman, Alison Miller.
❯ *Dir* Burr Steers, *Pro* Jennifer Gibgot and Adam Shankman, *Screenplay* Jason Filardi, *Ph* Tim Suhrstedt, *Pro Des* Garreth Stover, *Ed* Padraic McKinley, *M* Rolfe Kent, *Cos* Pamela Withers-Chilton.

New Line Cinema/ Offspring Entertainment-New Line Cinema. 102 mins. USA. 2009. Rel: 10 Apr 2009. Cert 12A.

the Year

88 Minutes ★ ★ ½

Dr Gramm (Al Pacino), a college professor and forensic psychiatrist for the FBI, receives a threat: he will die in 88 minutes. Serial killer Forster (Neal McDonough) who has been convicted on Gramm's testimony is awaiting execution but a new copycat killer is on the loose. Pacino is more restrained than usual in a role that he could do in his sleep. Thompson's script uses all the tricks of the genre and Avnet keeps the pace going but the twist is easily spotted well before the climax. GS

▶ Al Pacino, Alicia Witt, Veelee Sobieski, Amy Brennerman, William Forsythe, Neal McDonough.
▶ *Dir* Jon Avnet, *Pro* Avnet, Randell Emmett, Avi Lerner and Gary Scott Thompson, *Screenplay* Thompson, *Ph* Denis Lenoir, *Pro Des* Tracy Gallacher, *Ed* Peter Berger, *M* Edward Shearmur, *Cos* Mary McLeod.

Millennium Films/Emmett/Furla Films/ Brightlight Pictures/Brooklyn Films etc- Warner Bros.
108 mins. Germany/USA. 2007. Rel: 3 Aug 2008. Cert 15.

Afghan Star ★ ★ ★

The title comes from a TV series in the *Pop Idol* mode which is highly popular in Afghanistan. Four contestants are central to this documentary but the real interest lies in this being a country reacting against the ban on popular music enforced by the Taliban between 1996 and 2001. Even now female participants find themselves threatened thus proving how firmly traditional attitudes are entrenched. The film would be stronger had director Havana Marking opted for investigation rather than routine reporting. MS

▶ With Rafi Naabzada, Lema Sehar, Hameed Sakhizada, Setara Hussainzada, Daoud Sediqi.
▶ *Dir* and *Pro* Havana Marking, *Ph* Phil Stebbing, *Ed* Ash Jenkins, *M* Simon Russell.

A Redstart Media, Roast Beef Productions, Aria Productions production etc-

Roast Beef Productions
87 mins. UK/Afghanistan. 2008.
Rel: 27 March 2009. No Cert.

The Age of Stupid ★ ★ ★ ½

Stupid is indeed the word for this film's choice of title for it suggests a nerdish American teen comedy rather than a companion piece to Al Gore's *An Inconvenient Truth*. Its structure, six documentary threads linked by Pete Postlethwaite as a future survivor looking back on what we did – or, rather, failed to do – in 2009, is sometimes heavy-handed. Nevertheless this is a passionate warning about the need to act to confront climate change now. MS

▶ Pete Postlethwaite, Jeh Wadia, Piers Guy, Fernand Pareau, Alvin DuVernay III, Layefa Malemi.
▶ *Dir* and *Written by* Franny Armstrong, *Pro* Lizzie Gillett, *Ph* Armstrong and Lawrence Gardner, *Pro Des* David Bryan, *Ed* David G. Hill, *M* Chris Brierley, *Cos* Heidi Miller.

Spanner Films/Passion Pictures etc.- Dogwoof Pictures.
92 mins. UK. 2008. Rel: 20 March 2009. Cert 12A.

Alexandra ★ ★ ★

A remarkable presence graces this film, that of the singer Galina Vishnevskaya now an octogenarian. She totally inhabits her role as a general's widow visiting her grandson who is doing military service. Vishnevskaya is clearly committed to the film's anti-military stance but Alexander Sokurov's film is minimalistic in its story-telling and conveys all too well the boredom of a soldier's life. Lacking any wider appeal the film is likely to end up preaching to the converted. MS

▶ Galina Vishnevskaya, Vasily Shevtsov, Raisa Gicheva.
▶ *Dir* and *Written by* Alexander Sokurov, *Pro* and *M* Andrei Sigle, *Ph* Alexander Burov, *Art Dir* Dmitri Malich-Konkov, *Ed* Sergei Ivanov, *Cos* Lydia Krykova.

Proline-film/Rezo Productions etc.-
Artificial Eye Film Company.
95 mins. Russia (Republic)/France. 2007.
Rel: 26 Sept 2008. Cert PG.

American Teen ★ ★ ★ ½

Warsaw, Indiana, is the place and Nanette
Burstein's documentary portraying
contemporary American youth focuses on
five students in the High School there. Her
film is not without interest and it strives to
be different, but paradoxically the elements
designed to enhance its appeal count against
it. The glossy look of the piece, the songs on
the soundtrack and touches of animation
combine to smack more of fiction than of
rough and ready reality and thus undermine
its effectiveness. MS

▶ With Hannah Bailey, Megan Krizmanich,
Jake Tusing, Colin Clemens, Mitch Reinholt.
▶ *Dir* Nanette Burstein, *Pro* Burstein, Jordan
Roberts and others, *Ph* Laela Kilbourn,
Wolfgang Held and Robert Hanna, *Ed* Mary
Manhardt, Tom Haneke and Burstein,
M Michael Penn, *Animation* Blacklist etc.

**Paramount Vantage/A&E IndieFilms/
Firehouse Films etc.-Optimum Releasing.**

102 mins. USA, 2008. Rel: 6 March 2009.
Cert 15.

Angel ★

François Ozon comes a cropper with this his
first English-language feature. In adapting
Elizabeth Taylor's novel, he never finds a
tone suitable for this tale of an early 20th
century writer (Romola Garai) whose lack of
talent doesn't prevent her from achieving
popular success. You can't really blame the
players, although Garai's constant emoting
as the insufferably cocksure heroine doesn't
help. It's a film that moves from satire to
melodrama without ever becoming engaging,
involving or credible. MS

▶ Romola Garai, Sam Neill, Charlotte
Rampling, Lucy Russell, Michael Fassbender.
▶ *Dir* and *Written by* François Ozon from
Elizabeth Taylor's novel, *Pro* Olivier Delbosc
and Marc Missonnier, *Ph* Denis Lenoir, *Pro
Des* Katia Wyszkop, *Ed* Muriel Breton, *M*
Philippe Rombi, *Cos* Pascaline Chavanne.

**Fidélité/Poisson Rouge Pictures/C. Granier-
Deferre/Scope Pictures/G. Lernal etc.-Lionsgate.**
120 mins. France/UK/Belgium. 2006.
Rel: 29 Aug 2008. Cert 15.

Michael;
Fassbender and
Lucy Russell
seem at a loss
for words in
Angel.

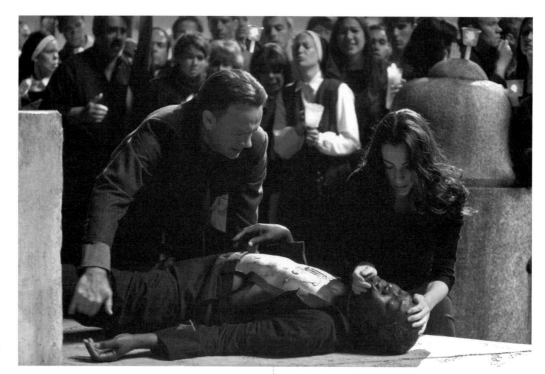

Angels and Demons: Tom Hanks as the Harvard symbologist looking for trouble in the Vatican.

Angels and Demons ★★½

Before Dan Brown wrote *The Da Vinci Code* he penned *Angels and Demons.* Cashing in on the $758m take of the latter, Ron Howard, Akiva Goldsman, Uncle Tom Hanks and all return to the world of ancient secrets, arcane symbols and underground crypts. Here, Harvard symbologist Robert Langdon (Hanks) is called to the Vatican following the death of the Pope and the kidnapping of four of his probable successors. Unlike the first film, this one speeds along at a merry old clip, but loses much textural flesh along the way. Nonetheless, the Vatican makes a handsome villain and much of the ritual is really quite enthralling. JC-W

▶ Tom Hanks, Ewan McGregor, Ayelet Zurer, Stellan Skarsgård, Armin Mueller-Stahl, Pierfrancesco Favino.
▶ *Dir* Ron Howard, *Pro* Howard, John Calley and Brian Grazer, *Screenplay* David Koepp and Akiva Goldsman from the novel by Dan Brown, *Ph* Salvatore Totino, *Pro Des* Allan Cameron, *Ed* Daniel P Hanley and Mike Hill, *M* Hans Zimmer, *Cos* Daniel Orlandi.

Columbia Pictures/Imagine Entertainment/Sony Pictures Entertainment-Columbia Pictures
138 mins. USA. 2009. Rel: 14 May 2009. Cert 12A.

Angus Thongs and Perfect Snogging ★★★½

Lightweight and sometimes silly, this is nevertheless a characteristically warm-hearted work from Gurinder Chadha set on England's south coast. Adapting a female perspective it homes in on the problems of being fourteen years old and in its humour and occasional drama it is splendidly anchored by its central performance – that's from Georgia Groome so impressive previously in the very different *London to Brighton*. Imperfect but engaging. MS.

▶ Georgia Groome, Alan Davies, Karen Taylor, Aaron Johnson, Eleanor Tomlinson.
▶ *Dir* Gurinder Chadha, *Pro* Chadha and Lynda Obst, *Screenplay* Chadha, Paul Mayeda Berges, Will McRobb and Chris Viscardi from books by Louise Rennison, *Ph* Richard Pope, *Pro Des* Nick Ellis, *Ed* Martin Walsh and Justin Krish, *M* Joby Talbot, *Cos* Jill Taylor.

Paramount Pictures/Nickleodeon Movies/Goldcrest Pictures Limited etc.-Paramount Pictures.
100 mins. UK/USA/Germany. 2008.
Rel: 25 July 2008.
Cert 12A.

Georgia Groome (right) as a teenager with problems in *Angus Thongs and Perfect Snogging.*

Año uña ★ ★ ★ ★

A full feature consisting only of still shots sounds off-putting (the famous *La Jetée* by Chris Marker was but a short). However, writer-director Jonás Cuarón has supplied a first-class screenplay (dialogue, narration and thoughts all feature on the soundtrack) and this is a wholly persuasive portrait of a fourteen year old Mexican boy's infatuation with a visiting American of twenty one. Honest, sensitive, unforced, the film may make demands but it is genuinely rewarding. MS

‣ Diego Cataño, Eireann Harper, Salvador Elizondo, Katie Hegarty.
‣ *Dir* and *Written by* Jonás Cuarón, *Pro* Cuarón, Eireann Harper and Frida Torresblanco, *Ph* Cuarón and Alexis Zabé, *Ed* Cuarón and Harper, *M Supervisor* Annette Fradera.

An Esperanto Filmoj production-Halcyon Releasing. 79 mins. Mexico. 2007. Rel: 28 Nov 2008. Cert 15.

Anvil! The Story of Anvil
★ ★ ★ ½

Sacha Gervaski's affectionate tribute to Anvil, the Canadian heavy metal band, highlights the relationship between Steve 'Lips' Kudlow and Rob Reiner. They first decided to rock on together at the age of 14 in a Toronto school and now in their 50s they are trying to make a comeback and hit the big time. They reached their peak in 1982 when they released *Metal on Metal* but after that their careers fell into obscurity. Their dedication and commitment to reach their goal is admirable and funny as well as touching. GS

‣ Tiziana Arrigoni, Kevin Goocher, Glenn Gyorffy, William Howell, Steve 'Lips' Kudlow, Rob Reiner, Slash, Charles Tsangarides, Lars Ulrich.
‣ *Dir* Sacha Gervaski, *Pro* Rebecca Yeldham, *Ph* Christopher Soos, *Ed* Andrew Dickler and Jeff Renfroe, *M* David Norland.

Ahimsa Films/Little Dean's Yard/Metal on Metal Productions-The Works UK Distribution.
90 mins. USA. 2008. Rel: 2 Feb 2009. Cert. 15.

Anything for Her ★ ★ ★ ½

Fred Cavayé does well as director of this French drama about a husband (Vincent Lindon on good form) risking everything to get his unjustly accused wife (Diane Kruger) out of prison since she's there serving a long-term sentence for murder. As writer he's not

quite so adroit since the film hovers between being a well-characterised believable tale and a less likely thriller – but it's pretty good all the same. (Original title: *Pour elle*). MS

‣ Vincent Lindon, Diane Kruger, Lancelot Roch, Olivier Marchal. Liliane Rovère, Olivier Perrier.
‣ *Dir* Fred Cavayé, *Pro* Olivier Delbosc, Eric Jehelmann and Marc Missonnier, *Screenplay* Cavayé and Guillaume Lemans from Lemans' idea, *Ph* Alain Duplantier, *Art Dir* Philippe Chiffre, *Ed* Benjamin Weill, *M* Klaus Badelt, *Cos* Fabienne Katany.

Fidélité/Wild Bunch/TF1 Films Production Jerico etc.-Metrodome Distribution.
96 mins. France. 2008. Rel: 5 June 2009. Cert 15.

Appaloosa ★ ★ ★ ★

Old friends Virgin Cole (Ed Harris) and Everett Hitch (Viggo Mortensen) become Appaloosa's new marshal and deputy and are determined to bring to justice ruthless Randall Bragg (Jeremy Irons) and his gang who are terrorising the territory. Ed Harris does a terrific job as both actor and director and uses the picturesque landscape magnificently. His subtle performance is beautifully complemented by Mortensen's but it is Irons who steals the film as the calculated and snake like villain. GS

‣ Ed Harris, Viggo Mortensen, Jeremy Irons, Renée Zellweger, Timothy Spall, Timothy V Murphy.
‣ *Dir* Ed Harris, *Pro* Harris, Robert Knott and Ginger Sledge, *Screenplay* Knott and Harris, from the novel by Robert Parker, *Ph* Dean Semler, *Pro Des* Waldemar Kalinowski, *Ed* Kathryn Himoff, *M* Jeff Beal, *Cos* David S Robinson.

Axon Films/Eight Gauge Productions/New Line Cinema/Ground Swell Productions-Entertainment Film Distributors.
115 mins. USA. 2008. Rel: 3 Oct 2008. Cert 15.

Ashes of Time Redux
★ ★ ★ ★

This restored and enhanced version of Wong Kar Wai's *Ashes of Time* handles a martial arts plot involving swordsmen and the women who love them. Consequently it sounds like an uncharacteristic work. However, that's not the case at all since this saga in which men must fight and women must weep proves to be strongly romantic and visually stylish. Despite its intricate plotting this is emphatically a film not to be missed by Wong's admirers. (Original title: *Dongxie Xidu*). MS

‣ Leslie Cheung, Brigitte Lin, Tony Leung Chiu Wai, Carina Lau, Tony Leung Ka Fai.
‣ *Dir* and *Screenplay* (based on characters from *The Eagle-Shooting Hero* by Jin Yong) Wong Kar-Wai, *Pro* Tsai Mu Ho and Cheng Zhigu etc., *Ph* Christopher Doyle and Kwan Pun Leung, *Art Dir* William Chang Suk Ping, *Ed* Patrick Tam and others, *M* Franky Chan, Roel A. Garcia, Wu Tong and others, *Wardrobe* Luk Ha Fong, Kong Zhanjing and Zhao Wenxiu.

Scholar Films Co Ltd/ a Jet Tone Production Ltd etc.-Artificial Eye Film Company.
93 mins. Hong Kong/China/Japan.
1994/2008. Rel: 12 Sept 2008.
Cert 15.

Australia ★ ★ ★

Baz Luhrmann's saga is set against the background of World War II. English aristo Lady Sarah Ashley (Nicole Kidman) travels to Oz to meet her husband at their remote cattle ranch. On arrival she finds her husband has been murdered and a local cattle baron, King Carney (Bryan Brown), is stealing her stock. A cattleman, one Drover by name and drover by nature (Hugh Jackman), heads an expedition herding Lady Sarah's cattle to Darwin which the Japanese then bomb as they did Pearl Harbour .The inevitable romance between the lady and Hugh the drover raises its head... With lush views of the Australian landscape, bombastic music including Elgar and 'Over

the Rainbow', and the making of political points about the treatment of the 'Stolen Generations' of Aborigines, it adds up to a visually stunning but sprawling epic (c.f. late David Lean) that's all too much for one film alone. MHD

▶ Hugh Jackman, Nicole Kidman, Bryan Brown, Tony Barry, Eddie Baroo, David Gulpilil.
▶ *Dir* Baz Luhrmann, *Pro* Luhrmann, G Mac Brown and Catherine Knapman, *Screenplay* Luhrman and Stuart Beattie, *Ph* Mandy Walker, *Pro Des & Cos* Catherine Martin, *Ed* Dody Dorn and Michael McCusker, *M* David Hirschfelder.

**Bazmark Films/Spirit Horse Productions-Twentieth Century Fox Film Corporation 165 mins. Australia/USA. 2008.
Rel: 26 Dec 2008.
Cert 12A.**

Awaydays ★ ½

Liverpool; 1979. The 'grim up North' platitude is given a stale airing in this tale of football hooliganism, based on the novel by Kevin Sampson. Bad boy Paul Carty (Nicky Bell) longs to be a member of The Pack and ingratiates himself with the stylish bad boy Elvis (Liam Boyle). The subsequent narrative arc groans with inevitability as sex, drugs and the old ultra-violence take their turn to shock, nauseate and depress. The grey varnish of the photography just adds another defect. JCW

▶ Stephen Graham, Nicky Bell, Liam Boyle, Oliver Lee, Lee Battle, Sean Ward, Ian Puleston-Davies.
▶ *Dir* Pat Holden, *Pro* David A Hughes, *Screenplay* Kevin Sampson from his novel, *Ph* Curtis Lee Mitchell, *Pro Des* Mark Tanner, *Ed* Mark Elliot, *M* David A Hughes, *Cos* Gini Lewis.

Nicole Kidman gets the hell out of it in *Australia*.

Red Union Films/Away Days Films-
Optimum Releasing.
105 mins. UK. 2009. Rel: 22 May 2009.
Cert 18.

Baby Mama ★ ★ ★

Taking a break from Channel Five's *30 Rock*,
Tina Fey gives a sparklingly hard-edged
comedy turn as a pushing-40 career woman
who finds her chances of getting pregnant
are a million to one and decides to pay a
surrogate mother to have her baby. In an
obvious nod to the 'Odd Couple' idea with a
female switch, Fey finds herself sharing her
smart home with chain-smoking, junk-food-
eating, working-class surrogate mum Amy
Poehler. Fey's funny, though she isn't quite
as funny as she thinks she is, and Poehler's
a good laugh too. Sigourney Weaver's a hoot
as the steely head of the surrogacy centre Fey
consults and Greg Kinnear and Steve Martin
fill in some more gaps. DW

❯ Steve Martin, Amy Poehler, Tina Fey, Greg
Kinnear, Sigourney Weaver, Dax Shepard
❯ *Dir and Screenplay* Michael McCullen,
Pro John Goldwyn and Lorne Michaels, *Ph*
Daryn Okada, *Pro Des* Jess Gonchor, *Ed* Bruce

Green and Debra Neil-Fisher, *M* Jeff Richards,
Cos Renee Ehrlich Kalfus.

Broadway Video/Relativity Media-
Universal Pictures.
99 mins. USA. 2008. Rel: 25 July 2008. Cert 12A.

Babylon AD ★ ★ ½

A pretentious thriller packed full of
preposterous notions about society and
religion, this post-apocalyptic actioner takes
itself incredibly seriously and should be a
lot more fun than it is. A straight-faced,
monotoned Vin Diesel plays a mercenary
hired to shepherd a mystery girl from Russia
to America, jumping, chasing, fighting and
shooting every step of the way. A reasonable
spectacle, with some interesting production
design, but entirely unnecessary.
MJ

❯ Vin Diesel, Gérard Depardieu, Michele
Yeoh, Charlotte Rampling, Mélanie Thierry,
Lambert Wilson
❯ *Dir* Mathieu Kassovitz, *Pro* Alain Goldman
and Kassovitz, *Screenplay* Eric Besnard and
Kassovtz, *Ph* Thierry Arbogast, *Pro Des* Paul
Cross and Sonja Klaus, *Ed* Benjamin Weill,
M Atli Orvarsson, *Cos* Chattoune and Fab.

Vin Diesel loses
his appetite for
any more films
like *Babylon AD*.

The Baader-Meinhoff Complex: Uli Edel's film about the 1960s German terrorists.

Canal +/Legende FilmsEnterprise/Okko-Twentieth Century Fox Film Corporation. 90 mins. USA/France/UK. 2008. Rel: 29 Aug 2008. Cert 12A.

A Constantin Film production/Nouvelles Éditions de Films etc.-Momentum Pictures. 150 mins. Germany/France/Czech Republic. 2008. Rel: 14 Nov 2008. Cert 18.

The Baader Meinhof Complex ★★★

In 1986 Reinhard Hauff made a first-class film entitled *Stammheim* about the famed German terrorists of the 1960s, the Baader Meinhof group. It was a virtue then that the audience were invited to draw their own conclusions. This new film by Uli Edel simply covers the same material in a more violent manner without shaping the complex history into any statement relevant in this age of terrorism. That surely is what is required today irrespective of whether we choose to endorse or criticise any particular line taken. MS

❯ Martina Gedeck, Moritz Bleibtreu, Johanna Wokalek, Bruno Ganz, Alexandra Maria Lara.
❯ *Dir* Uli Edel, *Pro* Bernd Eichinger, *Written by* Eichinger and Edel in consultation with Stefan Aust and based on his book, *Ph* Rainer Klausmann, *Pro Des* Bernd Lepel, *Ed* Alexander Berner, *M* Peter Hinderthür and Florian Tessloff, *Cos* Birgit Missal and Hassan Taghriti.

Bangkok Dangerous ★★

Twin Thai directors Oxide Pang Chun and Danny Pang remake their own 1999 cult thriller for Hollywood, smoothing its edges, cheesing up the dialogue and, fatally, casting cadaverous Nic Cage who, judging by his mediocre output of late, appears to have given up trying. As a crack assassin on the job in Bangkok, Cage falls for an innocent deaf girl and begins to question the ethics of his occupation. The action is OK but, like the movie, wholly unremarkable.
MJ

❯ Nicolas Cage, Shahkrit Yamnarm, Charlie Young, Panward Hemmanee, Dom Hetrakul, Steve Baldocchi
❯ *Dir* Oxide Pang Chun and Danny Pang, *Pro* Cage, Norman Golightly, William Sherak and Jason Shuman, *Screenplay* Jason Richman based on the 1999 film by Chun and Pang, *Ph* Decha Srimantra, *Pro Des* James William Newport, *Ed* Mike Jackson and Curran Pang, *M* Brian Tyler, *Cos* Kristin M Burke.

Nicolas Cage wonders if it was worth getting a new hat for the remake of *Bangkok Dangerous*.

Bangkok Dangerous/Blue Star Pictures/Initial Entertainment Group/Living Films/Saturn Films/ Virtual Studios-Entertainment Film Distributors. 99 mins. USA. 2008. Rel: 5 Sep 2008. Cert 18.

A Renfilm and Intercinema production- Artificial Eye Film Company. 157 mins. Russia (Republic). 2007. Rel: 15 Aug 2008. Cert 12A.

The Banishment ★ ★ ★ ½

From the Russian director of *The Return* comes this brilliantly cinematic piece about a man with a criminal brother who, taking his wife and children, returns to his country roots. The husband dominates his family but his world is upturned when the wife admits to being pregnant and declares that the child is not his. Unfortunately the drama is not well constructed to sustain such a long film but, if it is sometimes obscure and unsatisfactory, *The Banishment* is also a film containing much of exceptional quality. (Original Title: *Izgnanie*). MS

▶ Konstantin Lavronenko, Maria Bonnevie, Alexander Baluev, Dmitry Ulianov. ▶ *Dir* Andrey Zvyagintsev, *Pro* Dmitry Lesnevsky, *Screenplay* Oleg Negin and Zvyagintsev based on William Saroyan's story *The Laughing Matter*, *Ph* Mikhail Krichman, *Art Dir* Andrey Ponkratov, *Ed* Anna Mass, *M* Andrey Dergatchev and Arvo Pärt, *Cos* Anna Barthuly.

El baño del Papa (The Pope's Toilet) ★ ★ ★ ½

Set in a small town in Uruguay this is a rather old-fashioned piece telling how a father takes advantage of a forthcoming visit from the Pope (this is 1988) by building a toilet for use by the record crowds anticipated. It's predictable fare and not always well-judged, but it is confidently played, especially by Virginia Méndez as the man's wife. The film's comic elements are not allowed to override its concern for the plight of the country's have-nots. MS

▶ César Troncoso, Virginia Méndez, Virginia Ruiz, Mario Silva, Nelson Lence. ▶ *Dir* and *Screenplay* Enrique Fernández and César Charlone, *Pro* Elena Roux, *Ph* Charlone, *Art Dir* Inés Olmedo, *Ed* Gustavo Giani, *M* Luciano Supervielle and Gabriel Casacuberta, *Cos* Alejandra Rosasco.

Laroux Cine/O2 Filmes/Chaya Films/ Tele Image etc.-Soda Pictures.

Adam Sandler goes to ridiculous lengths to make the kids get to sleep in *Bedtime Stories*.

98 mins. Uruguay/Brazil/France/Spain. 2007. Rel: 1 Aug 2008. Cert 15.

Entertainment-Walt Disney Pictures. 99 mins. USA. 2008. Rel: 26 Dec 2008. Cert PG.

Bedtime Stories ★ ★ ★

Adam Sandler is thankfully restrained and well used in this likeable family film. He plays Skeeter Bronson, a hotel handyman who dreams of running the hotel that his father once owned. His life changes when he starts telling bedtime stories to his niece and nephew which mysteriously come true. It is a fun idea well executed by Adam Shankman, who delivers the goods like he did in *Hairspray* and he is now almost forgiven for such turkeys as *Cheaper by the Dozen 2* and *The Pacifier*. GS

‣ Adam Sandler, Keri Russell, Guy Pearce, Lucy Lawless, Russell Brand, Richard Griffiths, Courteney Cox, Jonathan Pryce, Carmen Electra.
‣ *Dir* Adam Shankman, *Pro* Jack Giarraputo, *Screenplay* Matt Lopez and Tim Herlihy, *Ph* Michael Barrett, *Pro Des* Linda DeScenna, *Ed* Tom Costain and Michael Tronick, *M* Rupert Gregson-Williams, *Cos* Rita Ryack.

Walt Disney Pictures/Gunn Films/ Happy Madison Productions/Offspring

Before I Forget ★ ★ ★ ★

Proust wanted to portray the whole of Parisian high society whereas Jacques Nolot essays a film portrayal of the lives of elderly gay men in the city. Sexual explicitness at the start suggests something more sensational but, with Nulot playing the lead in his own film, the movie becomes instead an honest documentation of a certain area of life. Certainly it's not a film for everybody, but it achieves its aim without ever succumbing to sentimentality.
(Original title: *Avant que j'oublie*).
MS

‣ Jacques Nolot, Jean-Pol Dubois, Marc Rioufol, Jean Pommier, Bastien d'Asnières.
‣ *Dir* and *Written by* Jacques Nolot, *Pro* Pauline Duhault, *Ph* Josée Deshaies, *Art Dir* Gaëlle Guitard, *Ed* Sophie Reine, *Cos* Eléonore O'Byrne and Sophie Lifshitz.

Elia Films/CNC –Centre national de la cinématographie etc.-Peccadillo Pictures. 108 mins. France. 2007. Rel: 17 April 2009. No Cert.

Before the Rains ★ ★ ★ ★

It may be less memorable than John Curran's 2006 remake of *The Painted Veil* but this drama, set in India when the movement for independence was building, is effective. It utilises personal dramas (a tragic love story; the fate of an Indian loyal to his colonialist master) to create a good piece of story-telling that also amounts to a valid comment on the history of the British in India. MS

▶ Linus Roache, Rahul Bose, Nandita Das, Jennifer Ehle, John Standing.
▶ *Dir* and *Ph* Santosh Sivan, *Pro* Doug Mankoff, Andrew Spaulding and others, *Screenplay* Cathy Rabin based on the film *Red Roofs*, part of *The Desert Trilogy: Yellow Asphalt* by Dany Verete, *Pro Des* Sunil Babu, *Ed* Steven Cohen and A Sreekar Prasad, *M* Mark Kilian, *Cos* S B Satheesan.

Merchant Ivory presents an Echo Lake Entertainment production in association with Adirondack Pictures, Excalibur Pictures and Santosh Sivan Productions-Metrodome Distribution.
98 mins. USA/India/UK. 2007.
Rel: 25 July 2008. Cert 12A.

Belle toujours ★ ★ ★ ★

On its own minimalistic terms this sequel to Buñuel's *Belle du Jour* from the world's oldest practising filmmaker, Portugal's Manoel de Oliveira born in 1908, is a success. Little happens beyond a fresh encounter almost forty years on between two of Buñuel's characters but it's fitting that this unique homage should remain enigmatic to the end. It is played with absolute precision by Michel Piccoli (reprising his role), Bulle Ogier (replacing Catherine Deneuve) and Ricardo Trêpa. MS

▶ Michel Piccoli, Bulle Ogier, Ricardo Trêpa, Leonor Baldaque, Júlia Buisel.
▶ *Dir* and *Screenplay* Manoel de Oliveira, *Pro* Miguel Cadihe, *Ph* Sabine Lancelin, *Art Dir* Christian Marti, *Ed* Valérie Loiseleux, *M* Dvořák, *Cos* Milena Canonero.

A Filbox Produções (Portugal), Films d'Ici (France) co-production presented by Miguel Cadihe and Serge Lalou etc.-ICA Films.
69 mins. Portugal/France. 2006.
Rel: 21 Nov 2008. Cert 15.

Ben X ★ ★ ★

It's sad when this film ceases to convince in its last scenes because until then Nic Balthazar's work here is thoroughly invigorating. It shows real individuality and flair as it invites the audience to identify with the young hero and his fantasies, the latter being an escape from reality for a boy who is autistic and suffers from being bullied. He represents too the rebel who does not fit in. Despite the eventual disappointment it's a work of unusual interest. MS

▶ Greg Timmermans, Marijke Pinoy, Laura Verlinden, Titus de Voogdt, Maarten Claeyssens.
▶ *Dir* and *Written by* Nic Balthazar based on his own play and novel, *Pro* Peter Bouckaert and Erwin Provoost, *Ph* Lou Berghmans, *Art Dir* Kurt Loyens, *Ed* Philippe Ravoet, *M* Praga Khan, *Cos* Heleen Heintjes.

MMG presents a co-production with BosBros. Film-TV Productions etc.-Momentum Pictures.
93 mins. Belgium/Netherlands/Romania. 2007. Rel: 29 Aug 2008. Cert 15.

Better Things ★ ★ ★ ½

Duane Hopkins, writer and director here, is a name to note for he has all the exceptional filmmaking skills of a Terence Davies while his sombre pessimism, his use of non-professional players and this film's rural setting all suggest that he is Britain's answer to France's Bruno Dumont. This Cotswolds tale is one featuring young drug-takers but also one that shows relationships breaking down through a wider age range. The story-telling could be clearer and most will find it excessively downbeat but the talent blazes. MS

▶ Liam McIlfatrick, Che Corr, Tara Ballard, Megan Palmer, Kurt Taylor, Rachel McIntyre.
▶ *Dir* and *Written by* Duane Hopkins, *Pro* Samm Haillay and Rachel Robey, *Ph* Lol Crawley, *Pro Des* Jamie Leonard, *Ed* Chris Barwell, *M* Dan Berridge, *Cos* Mel O'Connor.

UK Film Council/Film4/EM Media/a Third Films production etc.-Soda Pictures. 93 mins. UK/Germany. 2007. Rel: 23 Jan 2009. Cert 15.

Beverly Hills Chihuahua ★★

When Chloe (Drew Barrymore), a pampered Beverly Hills Chihuahua, goes on vacation to Mexico she is dognapped, befriends a German Shepherd (Andy Garcia) and finally encounters a pack of feral Chihuahuas. The movie is firmly aimed at a very young audience and, while the CGI manipulation of the dogs' mouths and expressions is seamless, viewers may take exception to dogs forced to wear bootees and jewellery, have their hair washed and set and even have their nails painted. DP

▶ Jamie Lee Curtis plus the voices of Drew Barrymore, Andy Garcia, George Lopez, Cheech Marin, Paul Rodriguez, Plácido Domingo, Edward James Olmas.
▶ *Dir* Raja Gosnell, *Pro* Todd Lieberman, David Huberman and John Jacobs, *Screenplay* Analisa LaBianco and Jeff Bushell from his story, *Ph* Phil Meheux, *Pro Des* Bill Boes, *Ed* Sabrina Plisco, *M* Heitor Pereira, *Cos* Maria Estela Fernández.

Walt Disney Pictures/Art in Motion/ Mandeville Films/Walt Disney Pictures. 91 mins. USA. 2008. Rel: 16 Jan 2009. Cert U.

It's a dog's life for any pooch in Beverly Hills Chihuhua.

Beyond the Fire ★ ★ ★ ½

The priest in Maeve Murphy's story may be a paedophile but this is a fully-fledged religious drama about faith and redemption. It's told with a concern for the characters (the central fugure is a young ex-priest) which makes it compelling, and Murphy's direction is geared to the impressive editing. Thematically (add rape, trauma and abortion to the sexual abuse) it is overloaded, but it's a brave venture and one to be welcomed. MS

▶ Scot Williams. Cara Seymour, Hugh Sachs, Chris O'Neill. Alison Cain.
▶ *Dir* and *Written by* Maeve Murphy, *Pro* Helen L Alexander. Murphy and Colin McKeown, *Ph* Mattias Nyberg, *Pro Des* Duncan Howell, *Ed* Agnieszka Liggett, *M* Neel Dhorajiwala, Chris O'Neill and Kila, *Cos* Mahab Kizmi and others.

Swipe Films/MetFilm etc.-Met Film Distribution. 77 mins. UK/Ireland. 2008. Rel: 19 June 2009. Cert 15.

Bigga Than Ben ★ ★ ★ ½

Ben Barnes stars as a Russian who comes to London with a mate (Andrei Chadov) to try to make a (mostly illegal) fortune and succeed in business, but London comes as a bad shock all round. There's food for thought as well as entertainment value in this commendable, low-budget, documentary-style film in two parts, both of them clever and well observed. The first half is funny, and seems to owe a lot to *Borat* in its humour. In the second half, things turn serious but repay close attention. London has rarely seemed so alien yet so real and both stars give very likeable, expert performances. Barnes, suddenly everywhere in films, is a new Brit star. DW

▶ Ben Barnes, Andrei Chadov, Ovidiu Matesan, Hero Fiennes-Tiffin, Jeff Mirza, Sean O'Callaghan
▶ *Dir* and *Screenplay* Suzie Halewood, *Pro* Halewood, Liz Holwood and Melissa Simmonds, *Ph* Ben Moulden, *Pro Des* Damien Creagh, *Ed* James Smith-Rewse and Jamie Trevill, *M* Paul E Francis, *Cos* Liv Murton.

Bigga Than Ben-Swipe Films. 82 mins. UK. 2008. Rel: 10 Oct 2008. Cert 15.

Black White + Gray: A Portrait of Sam Wagstaff and Robert Mapplethorpe ★ ★ ★ ★

Sam Wagstaff, Robert Mapplethorpe and the 1970s and '80s New York art scene are the subjects of James Crump's enlightening documentary. Wagstaff was a groundbreaking museum curator who took his young lover Mapplethorpe under his wing and encouraged him to become a leading figure in art photography, celebrating the naked black male body. Patti Smith, a close friend, makes a strong contribution to this exciting document of a time when anything was possible before AIDS destroyed it all. GS

▶ Patti Smith, Dominick Dunne, Gordon Baldwin, Clark Worswick, Eugenia Parry
▶ *Dir, Pro* and *Screenplay* James Crump, *Ph* Christopher Felver, Harry Geller, David Koh, Eric Koziol and Paul Lundahl, *Ed* Dave Giles, *M* J Ralph.

Arthouse Films/L M Media-Revolver Entertainment. 77 mins. USA/Germany. 2007. Rel: 15 Aug 2008. No Cert.

Tell the press we're just good friends: Sam Wagstaff and Robert Mapplethorpe in *Black White + Gray*.

Blind Loves ★★★

Juraj Lehotsky in describing this first feature of his chooses to raise the issue of the blind possibly being richer in spirituality and better able to understand the true essence of happiness. Unfortunately his four-part film, poorly structured in that it rounds off each segment but only at its close and this without warning, never goes as deep as this despite its sincerity and its effective use of many blind or partially blind people. It has been categorised as a documentary but its style often suggests fiction. (Original title: *Slepe Lásky*). MS

❯ With Peter Kolesár, Iveta Koprdová, Miro Daniel, Monika Brabcová, Jolana Danielová.
❯ *Dir* Juraj Lehotsky, *Pro* Marko Skop, Ján Melis, Lehotsky and others, *Script* Lehotsky and Marek Lescák, *Ph* Juraj Chlpík, *Ed* Frantisek Krähenbiel, *Animation* Michal Struss and others.

Artileria/Atelier.doc etc.-ICA Films.
77 mins. Slovakia/Czech Republic. 2008.
Rel: 22 May 2009. No Cert.

Blindness ★★★½

On screen this allegorical drama in which blindness starts to overtake the world's population never settles into being a consistent work with a clear statement to make. That is frustrating, but the direction by Fernando Meirelles of *City of God* is brilliantly cinematic in the way it finds images to express a world thrown off kilter. Puzzlement eventually sets in, but until then this is a truly exciting piece of cinema. MS

❯ Julianne Moore, Mark Ruffalo, Alice Braga, Gael Garcia Bernal, Danny Glover.
❯ *Dir* Fernando Meirelles, *Pro* Niv Fichman, Andréa Barata Ribeiro and Sonoko Sakai, *Screenplay* Don McKellar based on José Saramago's novel *Ensaio sobre a cegueira*, *Ph* César Charlone, *Pro Des* Tulé Peake, *Ed* Daniel Rezende, *M* Marco Antônio Guimarães and Uakti, *Cos* Renée April.

Focus features International/Alliance Films/ Fox Film/GaGa Communications/Asmik Ace Entertainment/Potboiler Productions etc.- Pathé Distribution.
121 mins. Canada/Brazil/Japan/UK/Italy.
2008. Rel: 21 Nov 2008. Cert 18.

Blindsight ★★★½

Six blind Tibetan teenagers set out to climb Lhakpa Ri, 23,000 feet high on the north side of Everest. This inspirational documentary records their endeavours under the guidance of the mountaineer Erik Weihenmayer who himself lost his sight aged twelve. Not all aspects are confronted (what about the psychological effects of failure in the attempt?) and the film could be tidier and tauter. Even so, it's a fascinating document. MS

❯ With Erik Weihenmayer, Tashi Pasang, Sabriye Tenberken, Sonam Bhumtso, Kyila.
❯ *Dir* Lucy Walker, *Pro* Sybil Robson Orr, *Ph* Petr Cikhart and others, *Ed* Sebastian Duthy, *M* Nitin Sawhney.

A Robson Entertainment production- Spark Entertainment.
104 mins. UK. 2006. Rel: 8 Aug 2008. No Cert.

Blood: The Last Vampire ★★½

Saya (Gianna Jun) is the Buffy of her day. She may look sixteen but, born centuries ago, she has down the years ridden the world of all surviving vampires for her head office, The Council. However, there is still one to go, namely Onigen (Koyuki), the mother and father of all vampires. It's now the 1970s and Saya fetches up at a US army base in Japan where the bloodsuckers seem to be particularly prevalent. There's a twist when she meets Alice (Allison Miller), daughter of General McKee (*EastEnders*' Larry Lamb) who does nothing except remind Saya she was once human. Lots of wire work and slashing samurai swords can't disguise the poor script, a remake of an anime short from 2001. CB

> Gianna Jun, Allison Miller, Liam Cunningham, Koyuki, Masiela Lusha, J J Field, Michael Byrne, Colin Salmon, Larry Lamb.
> *Dir* Chris Nahon, *Pro* William Kong and Abel Nahmias, *Screenplay* Chris Chow, based on characters by Kenji Kamiyama and Katsuya Terada, *Ph* Hang-Sang Poon, *Pro Des* Nathan Amondson, *Ed* Marco Cavé, *M* Clint Mansell, *Cos* Connie Balduzzi, Shandy Fung Shan Lui.

East Wing Holdings/SAJ-Pathé Distribution. 91 mins. Hong Kong/Japan/France/ Argentina. 2009. Rel: 26 June 2009. Cert 18.

A Bloody Aria ★ ★ ★ ★ ★

South Korea's brilliant but bleak psychological thriller has a middle-aged, college lecturer with less than honourable intentions drive a girl student into the middle of nowhere in his Mercedes only to encounter a gang of youthful thugs. Employing minimal production resources, this exercise in alienated character dynamics recalls nothing so much as early Polanski (*Cul-de-Sac*). Gripping, lovingly lensed and impressive. (Original title: *Guta-Yubalja-Deul*). JC

> Cha Ye-ryeon, Han Suk-kyu, Jeong Kyeong-ho, Kim Shi-hoo.
> *Dir and Screenplay* Won Shin-yeon, *Pro* Lee Seo-yul, *Ph* Kim Byeong-jeong and Kim Dong-eun, *Ed* Choi Jae-geun and Eom Jin-hwa, *M* Kim Jun-seung,

Prime Entertainment-ICA Projects. 115 mins. South Korea. 2006. Rel: 24 Oct 2008. Cert 15.

Blue Eyelids ★ ★ ★

Here we have a Mexican take on the not unfamiliar theme of two loners meeting in a way that suggests that they may eventually come together. The players, Cecilia Suárez and Enrique Arreola, are good, but the film is rather too knowing despite or because of its stylishness. It lacks both the unassertiveness of *Marty* (1955) and the depth, insight and subtlety of *Whisky* (2004) (Original title: *Párpados azules*). MS

> Cecilia Suárez, Enrique Arreola, Anna Ofelia Murguía, Tiaré Scanda, Luisa Huertas.
> *Dir* Ernesto Contreras, *Pro* Luís Albores, Érika Ávila, Contreras and Sandra Paredes, *Written by* Carlos Contreras, *Ph* Tonatiuh Martínez, *Pro Des* Ávila, *Ed* Ernesto Contreras and José Manuel Cravioto, *M* Iñaki, *Cos* Gabriela Fernández.

An Agencia Sha production/Foprocine – Fondo para la produccíon cinematográfica de calidad, IMCINE etc.-Axiom Films. 98 mins. Mexico/USA,. 2007. Rel: 8 May 2009. Cert 15.

The Blue Tower ★ ★ ★

Set in Southall, this ambitious study of Pakistanis settled in England and of one young man's attempt to escape his sense of inferiority promises much. But events that follow on from an extra-marital affair and a series of misfortunes and which should end up as tragedy provoke instead a sense of overcooked melodrama. Furthermore, the added symbolism involving a red and a blue tower seems strained. Being a British film, the sex scenes are franker than one finds in Indian cinema. MS

> Abhin Galeya, Alice O'Connell, Indira Joshi, Manjinder Virk, Kayvan Novak.
> *Dir* and *Written by* Smita Bhide, *Pro* Jamie Nuttgens, *Ph* Annemarie Lean-Vercoe, *Pro Des* Sabina Sattar, *Ed* Nuttgens, Brian Hovmand and Nick Follows, *M* Sandy Nuttgens and Mike Scott, *Cos* Paneet Lally.

A Monkey in Heaven film-ICA Cinema. 85 mins. UK. 2008. Rel: 26 June 2009. No Cert.

The Boat That Rocked ★ ★ ½

Back in 1966 the BBC broadcast just two hours of pop music every week. However, more than half the population of Britain

Rhys Ifans
and Bill Nighy
join the radio
pirates in
Richard Curtis's
*The Boat That
Rocked.*

listened to pop and rock'n'roll every day on the radio. The music – highly disapproved of by the government – was being aired by pirate stations anchored offshore. Here, pop partisan Richard Curtis adds his own knockabout spin to the phenomenon with a lot of energy and a few dodgy jokes. It's a busy, sometimes unwieldy film, but the music carries all before it and if you're not expecting something as polished as *Love Actually* (which Curtis also wrote and directed), there is a good time to be had.
JC-W

▶ Rhys Ifans, Bill Nighy, Kenneth Branagh, Tom Brooke, Catherine Ashton, Gemma Arterton, Nick Frost, Philip Seymour Hoffman, Will Adamsdale
▶ *Dir and Screenplay* Richard Curtis, *Pro* Curtis, Tim Bevan and Eric Fellner, *Ph* Danny Cohen, *Pro Des* Mark Tildesley, *Ed* Emil E Hickox, *M* Various, *Cos* Joanna Johnston.

Working Title/Portobello Studios/Tightrope Pictures/Medienproduktion Prometheus Filmgesellschaft-Universal Pictures.
129 mins. UK/Germany. 2009.
Rel: 1 Apr 2009. Cert 15.

Body of Lies ★★★★

Undervalued generally (perhaps because its contemporary terrorist references led critics and public to expect a political drama on the lines of *Syriana*), this is a Ridley Scott action thriller about CIA agents and their Jordanian opposite numbers. As such, it is thoroughly professional in its staging and well acted, not just by Leonardo DiCaprio, Russell Crowe and Mark Strong but also by the Iranian actress Golshifteh Farahani whose presence enhances a romantic sub-plot.
MS

▶ Leonardo DiCaprio, Russell Crowe, Mark Strong, Golshifteh Farahani, Alon Aboutboul.
▶ *Dir* Ridley Scott, *Pro* Scott and Donald De Line, *Screenplay* William Monahan from the novel by David Ignatius, *Ph* Alexander Witt, *Pro Des* Arthur Max, *Ed* Petro Scalia, *M* Marc Streitenfeld, *Cos* Janty Yates.

Warner Bros. Pictures present a Scott Free/De Line Pictures production-Warner Bros Distributors.
128 mins. USA. 2008. Rel: 21 Nov 2008.
Cert 15.

B— La bohème

Leonardo DiCaprio and Russell Crowe get round the table in Ridley Scott's CIA action thriller *Body of Lies*.

La bohème ★★★

High marks for operatic performance go to Rolando Villazón (Rodolfo), Anna Netrebko (Mimi) and Nicole Cabell (Musetta) so this film version of Puccini's famed opera with its powerful tragic love story will appeal to many. Nevertheless, judged as filmed opera it's badly let down by director Robert Dornhelm's stylised approach which adds to the sense of artificiality and thus misses the emotional impact memorably attained in Frédéric Mitterand's 1995 film of Puccini's *Madame Butterfly*. MS

▸ Rolando Villazón, Anna Netrebko, Nicole Cabell, George von Bergen, Vitalij Kowaljow.
▸ *Dir* and *Screenplay* Robert Dornhelm (from the libretto by Giuseppe Giacosa and Luigi Illica based on the novel by Henry Murger), *Pro* Jan Mojto, Kurt J. Mrkwicka and Jeffrey D. Vanderveen, *Ph* Walter Kindler, *Pro Des* Florian Reichmann, *Ed* Ingrid Koller and Klaus Hundsbichler, *M* Giacomo Puccini, *Cos* Uli Fressler.

An UNITEL & MR-Film production/ZDF etc.-Axiom Films.

114 mins. Germany/Austria. 2008. Rel: 19 Dec 2008. Cert PG.

Bolt ★★★

The Truman Show meets *The Incredible Journey*. Canine superhero Bolt battles dastardly villains and their high tech gadgetry unaware his whole life is a fake: he's actually a prime time serial fixture on network television. This falls between the animation department having lost its way and the monumentally successful Pixar being incorporated into Disney to get things back on track. JC

▸ Voices of John Travolta, Miley Cyrus, Susie Essman, Mark Walton, Malcolm McDowell, James Lipton.
▸ *Dir* Byron Howard and Chris Williams, *Pro* Clark Spencer, *Screenplay* Williams and Dan Fogelman, *Pro Des* Paul A Felix, *Ed* Tim Mertens, *M* John Powell.

Walt Disney Animation Studio-Buena Vista International. 96 mins. USA. 2008. Rel: 6 Feb 2009. Cert PG.

Boogie ★★★★

This excellent Romanian film tells the story of 30-year-old Boogie (Bogdan Ciocazanu) who, while having a quiet seaside holiday with his wife (Anamaria Marinca) and four-year-old son, unexpectedly meets some old friends from high school. The idea of spending a night with them reminiscing about their youth, boozing and whoring is far too tempting. There is superb acting in Radu Muntean's seemingly simple film particularly in the scenes with Boogie and his wife (Anamaria Marinca) which are effectively shot in long takes. GS

▶ Bogdan Ciocazanu, Ananmaria Marinca, Mimi Branescu, Adrian Vancica, Vlad Muntean.
▶ *Dir* Radu Muntean, *Pro* Dragos Vilcu, *Screenplay* Muntean, Alexandru Baciu and Razvan Radulescu, *Ph* Tudor Lucaciu, *Pro Des* Sorin Dima, *Ed* Alexandru Radu, *M* Electric Brother, *Cos* Georgiana Bostan.

Multimedia Entertainment-Drunk Robot/ Films Sans Frontieres-Dogwood Pictures. 102 mins. Romania. 2008. 16 Jan 2009. Cert PG.

Bottle Shock ★★★½

Paris/Napa Valley; 1976. A self-proclaimed 'shepherd of the grape,' wine snob Steven Spurrier (Alan Rickman) decides to check out some Napa valley produce as a publicity stunt for his ailing shop in Paris. With a story inspired by fact, the glorious countryside of California and the effortless disdain of Alan Rickman, what is there not to like? True, the story is a tad predictable, the plotting occasionally banal, but overall this is fun, affectionate and quite fascinating, like *Sideways* with sex appeal. JC-W

▶ Chris Pine, Alan Rickman, Bill Pullman, Rachael Taylor, Dennis Farina.
▶ *Dir* Randall Miller, *Pro* Judy Savin, Marc Toberoff, J Todd Harris, Brenda Lhormer and Marc Lhormer, *Screenplay* Miller, Jody Savin and Ross Schwartz, *Ph* Mike Ozier, *Pro Des* Craig Stearns, *Ed* Miller and Dan O'Brien, *M* Mark Adler, *Cos* Jillian Kreiner.

Intellectual Properties Worldwide/Unclaimed Freight Productions/Zin Haze Productions-Paramount Pictures. 110 mins. USA. 2008. Rel: 20 Mar 2009. Cert 12A.

In *Bolt* a canine superhero has trouble with his fellow animated characters.

The Boy in the Striped Pyjamas ★★★½

On screen the sheer unlikelihood of the story's contrived finale weakens the impact. Nevertheless, this is a brave adaptation of John Boyne's novel which, with young readers in mind, told a tale of the Holocaust in which two children, a German and a Jew, were the central characters. In a good cast Vera Farmiga and David Thewlis stand out and the film deserves to be widely seen. MS

❯ Asa Butterfield, Jack Scanlon, Vera Farmiga, David Thewlis, Rupert Friend, David Hayman, Sheila Hancock, Richard Johnson.
❯ *Dir* and *Written by* Mark Herman based on John Boyne's novel, *Pro* David Heyman, *Ph* Benoit Delhomme, *Pro Des* Martin Childs, *Ed* Michael Ellis, *M* James Horner, *Cos* Natalie Ward.

Miramax Films/BBC Films/a Heyday Films production-Buena Vista International.
94 mins. USA/UK. 2008. Rel: 12 Sept 2008. Cert 12A.

Bride Wars ★

Best friends Liv (Kate Hudson) and Emma (Anne Hathaway) have always shared everything and after a mistake by their wedding planner they end up sharing the same venue and date for their weddings. This leads to bride rivalry and a fury of tit for tat pettiness as they try to spoil each other's big day. It is supposed to be a comedy but, instead, it's an embarrassing farce, portraying women as mean-spirited *Bride Wars* harpies with two supposedly sane, intelligent friends descending into *Stepford Wives* caricatures. DP

❯ Kate Hudson, Anne Hathaway, Bryan Greenberg, Chris Pratt, Candice Bergen, Kristen Johnson, Michael Arden.
❯ *Dir* Gary Winick, *Pro* Kate Hudson, Alan Riche, Peter Riche, Julie Yorn, *Screenplay* Greg De Paul, Casey Wilson and Julie Diane Raphael from a story by De Paul, *Ph* Frederick Elmes, *Pro Des* Dan Leigh, *Ed* Susan Littenberg, *M* Edward Shearmuir, *Cos* Karen Patch.

Firm Films/New Regency Pictures/Regency Enterprises/Sunrise Entertainment-20th Century Fox.
89 mins. USA. 2009. Rel: 9 Jan 2009. Cert PG.

Brideshead Revisited ★★★½

Those looking for a well mounted period drama will probably enjoy this far more

Kate Hudson and Anne Hathaway share a toast as well as a wedding venue in *Bride Wars*.

than they were led to expect by the critics. Evelyn Waugh's classic tale looks back to the period before the Second World War to portray a Catholic upper-class family, their live and loves. The screenplay prevents Matthew Goode from fully filling out the role of the outsider Charles Ryder but Emma Thompson's Lady Marchmain is a success and Ben Whishaw as the gay son Sebastian is superb. MS

▶ Matthew Goode, Ben Whishaw, Hayley Atwell, Emma Thompson, Michael Gambon, Greta Scacchi, Patrick Malahide, Jonathan Cake.
▶ *Dir* Julian Jarrold, *Pro* Robert Bernstein, Douglas Rae and Kevin Loader, *Screenplay* Andrew Davies and Jeremy Brock from the novel by Evelyn Waugh, *Ph* Jess Hall, *Pro Des* Alice Normington, *Ed* Chris Gill, *M* Adrian Johnston, *Cos* Eimer Ní Mhaoldomhnaigh.

Miramax Films/UK Film Council/BBC Films/ an Ecosse Films production etc.-Buena Vista International.
133 mins. UK/USA/Italy/Morocco. 2008. Rel: 3 Oct 2008. Cert 12A.

The Brøken ★★½

A beautiful radiologist (Lena Headey) sees herself drive past in the street and follows her double to her flat. Moments later, she drives her jeep into a taxi and finds herself in hospital. After this and last year's *Cashback*, Sean Ellis is shaping up to be one of Britain's most promising filmmakers. With its gorgeous aerial shots of London and Lena Headey's linear perfections, his new film builds up its atmosphere with fine grace. However, it's not really scary and by the conclusion only feels like half a movie. JC-W

▶ Lena Headey, Richard Jenkins, Asier Newman, Michelle Duncan, Melvil Poupaud, Howard Ward.
▶ *Dir* and *Screenplay* Sean Ellis, *Pro* Lene Bausager , *Ph* Angus Hudson, *Pro Des* Morgan Kennedy, *Ed* Scott Thomas, *M* Guy Farley, *Cos* Vicki Russell and Victoria Russell.

Ugly Duckling Films/Gaumont International/ Left Turn Films etc- The Works.
88 mins. France/UK. 2008. Rel: 30 Jan 2009. Cert 15.

Bronson ★★★★

Tom Hardy's superb performance as Britain's most violent prisoner who took the name of Charles Bronson would steal the limelight

Three's company for Matthew Goode, Hayley Atwell and Ben Whishaw in *Brideshead Revisited*.

here but for the brilliant stylised direction by Denmark's Nicolas Winding Refn. Making his first British feature he understandably claims to have been influenced by Stanley Kubrick's *A Clockwork Orange* and by Lindsay Anderson. The film's middle section is weaker but this is a tremendous piece offering not so much biography as a state of the nation comment featuring an individual who resists being controlled. It's also a stunning indictment of the prison system's inability to handle those psychologically disturbed. MS

‣ Tom Hardy, Matt King, James Lance, Kelly Adams, Amanda Burton, Hugh Ross.
‣ *Dir* Nicolas Winding Refn, *Pro* Rupert Preston and Danny Hansford, *Screenplay* Brock Norman Brock and Refn, *Ph* Larry Smith, *Pro Des* Adrian Smith, *Ed* Mat Newman, *M Supervisor* Lol Hammond, *Cos* Sian Jenkins.

Vertigo Films/Aramid Entertainment/ Str8jacket Creations/EM Media etc.- Vertigo Films.
92 mins. UK/Cayman Islands. 2008.
Rel: 13 March 2009.
Cert 18.

Buddha Collapsed Out of Shame ★ ★ ★ ½

The Taliban blew up huge statues of Buddha in Afghanistan and it's there that Hana, the younger daughter of Iran's filmmaking family the Makhmalbafs, sets this simple tale. It concerns life in this troubled land where children play at war games and a six year old girl (the wonderfully natural Bakhtay Noroozali) endeavours to be accepted as a school pupil. Short as it is, the film's last section is at times unnecessary and unpersuasive, but the piece is unquestionably heart-felt. MS

‣ Bakhtay Noroozali, Abdolai Hosseinali, Abbas Alijomeh.
‣ *Dir* Hana Makhmalbaf, *Screenplay* Marziyeh Meshkini, *Ph* Ostad Ali, *Ed* Mastaneh Mohajer, *M* Tolibhon Shakhidi.

Makhmalbaf Film House/Wild Bunch-Slingshot.
77 mins. Iran/France. 2007.
Rel: 25 July 2008. Cert PG.

A Bunch of Amateurs ★

An amateur theatre company in the middle of the Suffolk countryside is facing closure and can't believe their luck when a faded Hollywood star (Burt Reynolds) – who's never acted on stage let alone Shakespeare – agrees to play King Lear in their forthcoming production. The distinguished British cast is totally wasted in this naive and utterly unfunny comedy and the less said about Reynolds' performance the better. GS

‣ Burt Reynolds, Samantha Bond, Charles Durning, Derek Jacobi, Imelda Staunton, Ty Davies.
‣ *Dir* Andy Cadiff, *Pro* David Parfitt, *Screenplay* Nick Newman, Ian Hislop, John Ross and Jonathan Gershfield, *Ph* Ashley Rowe, *Pro Des* Melanie Allen, *Ed* Mark Thornton, *M* Christian Henson, *Cos* Amy Roberts.

Trademark Films/CinemaNX/Limelight/ Lipsync Productions-Entertainment Film Distributors.
96 mins. UK. 2008.Rel: 19 Dec 2008. Cert 15.

Burn after Reading ★ ★ ★

What talent! This film has the Coens as directors and a cast that includes Clooney, McDormand, Pitt, Swinton and a scene-stealing John Malkovich. However, as a Pinterish comedy satirising the CIA, it is not consistently comic enough (or indeed dramatic enough when its tone changes) to seem worthy of those involved. You admire the playing of it but it feels disappointingly slight. MS

‣ George Clooney, Frances McDormand, John Malkovich, Tilda Swinton, Brad Pitt, Richard Jenkins, J K Simmons, David Rasche.
‣ *Dir*, *Pro* and *Written by* Joel and Ethan Coen, *Ph* Emmanuel Lubezki, *Pro Des* Jess Gonchor, *Ed* Roderick Jaynes i.e. Joel and Ethan Coen, *M* Carter Burwell, *Cos* Mary Zophres.

Focus Features/StudioCanal/Relativity Media/a Working Title production-Universal Pictures International.
96 mins. USA/UK/France 2008.
Rel: 17 Oct 2008. Cert 15.

The Burning Plain ★ ★ ★ ½

This film by Guillermo Arriaga who wrote *Amores Perros* and *Babel* would gain from being more succinct towards the close but it has been underestimated nevertheless. As before he gives us story threads that gradually come together to reveal a single drama, this one telling of death, love and ultimate redemption. Without being exceptional material, it works well and shows Arriaga to be a born filmmaker albeit one indebted here to his photographer Robert Elswit. MS

▶ Charlize Theron, Kim Basinger, Jennifer Lawrence, Danny Pino, Joaquim de Almeida.
▶ *Dir* and *Written by* Guillermo Arriaga, *Pro* Walter Parkes and Laurie MacDonald, *Ph* Robert Elswit, *Pro Des* Dan Leigh, *Ed* Craig Wood, *M* Ornar Rodriguez Lopez and Hans Zimmer, *Cos* Cindy Evans.

2929 Productions/Costa Films/a Parkes + MacDonald production-Paramount Pictures.
106 mins. USA/Argentina. 2008.
Rel: 13 March 2009.
Cert 15.

Cadillac Records ★ ★ ★

The lives of producer Leonard Chess (Adrien Brody) and guitarist Muddy Waters (Jeffrey Wright) take an unexpected turn after a chance meeting in a Chicago shabby bar in 1947. Waters' early blues recordings with the free spirited harmonica player Little Walter (Columbus Short) are hugely successful and as the years go by more promising artists are given a break including Chuck Berry (Mos Def) and Etta James (Beyoncé Knowles). It is all good stuff in Darnell Martin's fascinating film which finally tries to cover far too much material better suited to a television miniseries. GS

▶ Adrien Brody, Jeffrey Wright, Gabrielle Union, Columbus Short, Cedric the Entertainer, Eamonn Walker, Mos Def, Beyoncé Knowles, Eric Bogosian
▶ *Dir* and *Screenplay* Darnell Martin, *Pro* Andrew Lack and Sofia Sondervan, *Ph* Anastas Michos, *Pro Des* Linda Burton, *Ed* Peter C Frank, *M* Terence Blanchard, *Cos* Johnetta Boone.

Sony Music Film/Parkwood Pictures-Sony Pictures Releasing.
109 mins. USA. 2008. Rel: 20 Feb 2009.
Cert 15.

El Cantante ★ ★ ½

Biopic about Puerto Rican singer Héctor Devoe who, with Willie Colón, invented the salsa dance craze. He arrives in New York in the 1970s and sets about bringing a new and exciting style of music to the city. Unfortunately, as with many musicians, his success grows, but personal life disintegrates as drugs and alcohol take over. Marc Anthony as Héctor and Jennifer Lopez as his wife Puchi offer only a superficial portrait of this phenomenal couple. CB

▶ Alfredo Suarez, Vianca Mercedes, Michael Caputo, Marc Anthony, Federico Castellucio.
▶ *Dir* Leon Ichaso, *Pro* Julio Caro, Simon Fields, David Maldonado and Jennifer Lopez, *Screenplay* Ichaso, David Darmstaedter and Todd Antony Bello, from a story by Darmstaedter and Bello, *Ph* Claudio Chea, *Pro Des* Sharon Lomofsky, *Ed* David Tedeschi, *M* Willie Colón and Andrés Levin, *Cos* Sandra Hernandez.

Nuyorican Productions/R-Caro Productions-Revelation Films.
116 mins. USA. 2006. Rel: 5 Sep 2008. Cert 15.

Cass ★ ★ ★ ½

Suggested by the autobiography of Cass Pennant, ex-football hooligan turned author, this is the story of a Jamaican boy adopted by an elderly white couple and brought up in London. The film sometimes betrays

Angelina Jolie in Clint Eastwood's drama about a missing child in *Changeling*.

the relative inexperience of those involved (by comparison Saul Dibb's *Bullet Boy* of 2004 was a far more finished product). Nevertheless, despite the emphasis on the hooliganism, this moral tale is presented with unquestionable sincerity. MS

▶ Nonzo Anozie, Natalie Press, Leo Gregory, Linda Bassett, Peter Wight, Lorraine Stanley.
▶ *Dir* and *Written by* Jon S. Baird based on the book by Cass Pennant and Mike Ridley, *Pro* Stefan Haller, *Ph* Christopher Ross, *Pro*

Des Daniel Taylor, *Ed* David Moyes, *M* Matteo Scumaci, *Cos* Guy Speranza.

**Cass Films-Optimum Releasing.
108 mins. UK. 2008. Rel: 1 Aug 2008. Cert 18.**

Changeling ★ ★ ★ ½

Clint Eastwood's film tells a true story of corruption in L A as linked to a 1928 case in which a mother was persecuted when she challenged the notion that the child returned to her by the police was her own missing son. There's another fine performance from Angelina Jolie but the film seems headed for a conclusion long before it ends and the structuring could definitely be improved. Furthermore, some touches seem fictionalized, but it's worthwhile viewing nevertheless. MS

▶ Angelina Jolie, Jeffrey Donovan, John Malkovich, Jason Butler Harner, Amy Ryan.
▶ *Dir* and *M* Clint Eastwood, *Pro* Brian Grazer, Ron Howard, Robert Lorenz and Eastwood, *Written by* J. Michael Straczynski, *Ph* Tom Stern, *Pro Des* James J. Murakami, *Ed* Joel Cox and Gary D. Roach, *Cos* Deborah Hopper.

Universal Pictures/Imagine Entertainment/ Relativity Media/a Malpaso production- Universal Pictures International.
142 mins. USA. 2008. Rel: 28 Nov 2008. Cert 15.

The Chaser ★★★½

This dark thriller, a debut by Korean writer/ director Na Hong-jin, is technically dazzling with a brilliant use of location footage shot in Seoul. The story concerning an ex-detective's involvement in the tracking down of a serial killer may not be highly original, but it's good enough until the film's last quarter when gross contrivances destroy the suspension of disbelief. Up to that point it's a genre movie but a very telling one. (Original title: *Chu-gyuck-ja*).
MS

▶ Kim Yoon-suk, Ha Jung-woo, Seo Young-hee, Jeong In-gi.
▶ *Dir* Na Hong-jin, *Pro* Kim Su-jin and Yun In-beom, *Screenplay* Na, Hong Won-chan and Lee Shin-ho, *Ph* Lee Sung-je, *Pro Des* Lee Min-bog, *Ed* Kim Sun-min, *M* Kim Jun-seok and Choi Yonh-rak, *Cos* Lee Eun-ju.

A Big House and Vantage Holdings presentation/A Bidangil Pictures production etc.-Metrodome Distribution.
125 mins. Republic of Korea. 2008. Rel: 19 Sept 2008. Cert 18.

Che, Part 1 ★★★½

Just to confuse things, the real *Che, Part 1* was *The Motorcycle Diaries* (2004) which had wide appeal in showing a youth growing up to find his way in life. Soderbergh's solid professional piece takes up Guevara's story when he joined Castro's guerrilla movement in Cuba in the second half of the 1950s. You need to have a special interest in Che to find this two hour plus film engrossing, but it's done without false heroics and Benicio del Toro is fully in tune with this approach. MS

▶ Benicio del Toro, Demián Bichir, Santiago Cabrera, Julia Ormond, Catalina Sandino Moreno.
▶ *Dir* Steven Soderbergh, *Pro* Laura Bickford and del Toro, *Screenplay* Peter Buchman based on Guevara's *Reminiscences of the Cuban Revolutionary War*, *Ph* Peter Andrews, *Pro Des* Antxón Gómez, *Ed* Pablo Zumárraga, *M* Alberto Iglesias, *Cos* Bina Daigeler and Louise Frogley.

Wild Bunch/Telecinco/Morena Films etc.- Optimum Releasing.
126 mins. USA/Spain/France. 2008. Rel: 2 Jan 2009. Cert 15.

Che, Part 2 ★★★★

The virtues of Part 1 remain and are here part of a stronger drama that comes to a powerful conclusion as it tells of Che Guevara's ill-fated attempt to help those being exploited in Bolivia in the mid-1960s to rebel. The location shooting by director Soderbergh under his usual pseudonym of Peter Andrews is particularly fine. His committed approach supplies Che with a credo: "I believe in humankind". MS

▶ Benicio del Toro, Carlos Bardem, Joaquim de Almeida, Lou Diamond Phillips, Matt Damon.
▶ *Screenplay* Peter Buchman and Benjamin A. Vander Veen based on Guevara's *The Bolivian Diary*, *Cos* Bina Daigeler. Other credits as per *Che, Part 1* above.

Wild Bunch/Telecinco/Morena Films etc.- Optimum Releasing. 127 mins. USA/Spain/ France. 2008. Rel: 20 Feb 2009. Cert 15.

Why, you're even prettier than me: Michelle Pfeiffer and Rupert Friend in *Chéri*.

Chéri ★ ★ ★

Well acted and well directed though it is, this adaptation of Colette's two novels about Chéri and the courtesans in this young man's life is all over the place stylistically. The early 20th century French atmosphere is crucial but we have Kathy Bates with a strong American accent, a pushy modern narrator and a tone that, sometimes echoing Coward and Wilde, is at odds with the tragic ending. Nevertheless admirers of Michelle Pfeiffer will want to see this film.
MS

▶ Michelle Pfeiffer, Rupert Friend, Felicity Jones, Kathy Bates, Bette Bourne, Iben Hjejle.
▶ *Dir* Stephen Frears, *Pro* Bill Kenwright, András Hámori and others, *Written by* Christopher Hampton based on Colette's novels *Chéri* and *The Last of Chéri*, *Ph* Darius Khondji, *Pro Des* Alan MacDonald, *Ed* Lucia Zucchetti, *M* Alexandre Desplat, *Cos* Consolata Boyle.

BK Films/a Tiggy Films, Pathé, MMC Studios production etc.-Pathé Distribution.
92 mins. UK/France/Germany/Cayman Islands. 2009. Rel: 8 May 2009.
Cert 15.

Cherry Blossoms ★ ★ ★

Although set in Germany until the scene shifts to Japan, Doris Dörrie's film devotes its first half to echoing Ozu's masterpiece *Tokyo Story* but without any overt acknowledgment. This is interesting if inevitably inferior to the original, but the second half of this tale of elderly parents visiting their children when death is imminent is fresh. Unfortunately, it's also less persuasive and comes closer to kitsch than to subliminity at the close. (Original title: *Kirschblüten Hanami*).
MS

▶ Elmar Wepper, Hannelore Elsner, Aya Irizuki, Nadja Uhl, Felix Eitner.
▶ *Dir* and *Screenplay* Doris Dörrie, *Pro* Molly von Fürstenberg and Harald Kügler, *Ph* Hanno Lentz, *Art Dir* Bele Schneider, *Ed* Inez Regnier and Frank Müller, *M* Claus Bantzer, *Cos* Sabine Greunig,

An Olga Film production/BR – Bayerischer Rundfunk/ARD/Degeto and Arte etc.-Dogwoof Pictures.
127 mins. Germany. 2007.
Rel: 3 April 2009. No Cert.

The Children ★ ★ ½

Two families congregate for Christmas at an isolated house in the woods. But what starts as a festive affair soon turns sour when the children start acting up. Actually, the children start acting up way too soon for the audience to care for them or their hedonistic, preening parents. The woods sigh menacingly and telephone reception is predictably poor but when the scares come they are indubitably well executed.
JC-W

‣ Eva Birthistle, Jake Hathaway, Raffiella Brooks, Stephen Campbell Moore, William Howes, Eva Sayer.
‣ *Dir* Tom Shankland, *Pro* Allan Niblo and James Richardson, *Screenplay* Shankland and Paul Andrew Williams, *Ph* Nanu Segal, *Pro Des* Suzie Davies, *Ed* Tim Murrell, *M* Stephen Hilton, *Cos* Andrew Cox.

Vertigo Films/Screen West Midlands-Vertigo Films.
84 mins. UK. 2008. Rel: 5 Dec 2008. Cert 15.

Chocolate ★ ★ ★

Martial arts director Prachya Pinkaew likes to shoot his high-kicking combat sequences without stunt doubles or special effects and the results are wincingly visceral. Here, the storyline is staccato with an autistic, self-taught female martial arts expert (JeeJa Yanin) and a bullied, overweight boy teaming up to make some money. However, the fight scenes are truly breathtaking, with the best being the climax shot as the actors grapple with each other on window ledges and neon signs above the city streets. DP

‣ JeeJa Yanin , Ammara Sripong, Hiroshi Abe, Pongpat Wachirabunjong.
‣ *Dir* and *Pro* Prachya Pinkaew, *Screenplay* Chukiat Sakveerakul and Napalee, *Ph* Decha Srimantra, *Pro Des* Rachata Panpayak, *Ed* Rashane Limstrakul and Pop Surasakuwat, *M* Nimit Jitranon and Rochan Madicar and Korrakot Sittivash *Cos* Ekasit Meepraseartsagool.

Baa/Ram/Ewe Film-ShowboxMedia Group
110 mins. Thailand. 2008. Rel: 24 Oct 2008. Cert 18.

Choke ★ ★ ★

Bizarre is the word for this tale but then it is an adaptation of a novel by Chuck Palahniuk, author of *Fight Club*. A mother/son relationship is central but so are sex addicts and a theme about cloning linked to Jesus, no less. Words with a tone of their own dominate and amid the outrageousness there's an unexpected sensitivity creating an underlying pathos. The piece may not satisfy but there's excellent work from Angelica Huston and from Kelly Macdonald in another convincing portrayal of an American. MS

‣ Sam Rockwell, Angelica Huston, Kelly Macdonald, Brad William Henke.
‣ *Dir* and *Written by* Clark Gregg based on Chuck Palahniuk's novel, *Pro* Beau Flynn, Tripp Vinson and others, *Ph* Tim Orr, *Pro Des* Roshelle Berliner, *Ed* Joe Klotz, *M* Nathan Larson, *Cos* Catherine George.

Fox Searchlight Pictures/a Contrafilm/ATO Pictures production etc.-20th Century Fox.
92 mins. USA/Cayman Islands. 2008. Rel: 21 Nov 2008. Cert 18.

Choking Man ★ ★ ★ ½

A tale about immigrants in the area of New York known as Jamaica, Steve Barron's appealing feature is also more than that. Minimalistic in approach but full of atmosphere and detail, it centres on a study of a youth from Ecuador suffering from painful shyness. Touches of surrealism and animation add to the oddity. Not all of it works but more than you might expect: it's very individual and decidedly sympathetic. MS

‣ Octavio Gómez Berrios, Eugenia Yuan, Aaron Paul, Mandy Patinkin, Kate Buddeke.
‣ *Dir* and *Written by* Steve Barron, *Pro* Joshua Zeman, Zachary Mortensen and Barron, *Ph* Antoine Vivas-Denisov, *Pro Des* Ethan

Tobman, *Ed* Todd Holmes and Jon Griggs, *M* Nico Muhly, *Cos* Rebecca Hofherr, *Title Des/Animation* Marina Zurkow.

Riley Films/a Ghost Robot production-Soda Pictures. 78 mins. USA/UK. 2006. Rel: 14 Nov. 2008. No Cert.

A Christmas Tale ★★

Pretentious is the word for Arnaud Desplechin's family drama featuring Catherine Deneuve as a matriarch in need of a bone marrow transplant. The tone of the dialogue keeps us at a distance as does the visual stylisation when it conflicts with naturalism. The kind of references to films and books that were fun in Godard's work here suggests cleverness for its own sake and, coming complete with an erratic use of music on the soundtrack, this is an irritating and very long film. (Original Title: *Un conte de Noël Roubaix!*). MS

‣ Catherine Deneuve, Jean-Paul Roussillon, Anne Consigny, Mathieu Amalric, Chiara Mastroianni, Melvil Poupaud, Emmanuelle Devos, Hippolyte Girardot, Laurent Capelluto, Emile Berling.
‣ *Dir* Arnaud Desplechin, *Executive Pro* Martine Cassinelli, *Screenplay* Desplechin and Emmanuel Bourdieu, inspired by the book *La Greffe* by J Asher and J P Jouet, *Ph* Éric Gautier, *Art Dir* Dan Bevan, *Ed* Laurence Briaud, *M* Grégoire Hetzel, *Cos* Nathalie Raoul.

Why Not Productions/Canal+/CinéCinéma etc.-New Wave Films. 153 mins. France. 2008. Rel: 16 Jan 2009. Cert 15.

City of Ember ★★

Teens Harry Treadaway (from *Control*) and Saoirse Ronan (from *Atonement*) must search the City of Ember for clues that will unlock the ancient mystery of the city's existence, and help the citizens escape before their lights go out forever – well, after all, their big fat generator's failing! With a marvellous, all-star cast and the most gorgeous-looking sets, it looks like money has been splashed everywhere over this lavish family fantasy adventure – everywhere except on the exceedingly dull script. Tim Robbins, as Treadaway's dad, and Bill Murray, as the mayor, look bored. Today's kids, used to dazzling special effects, funny comedy and fast-paced action, all of which are missing here, will be as bemused as the grown-ups. DW

‣ Tim Robbins, Bill Murray, Harry Treadaway, Saoirse Ronan, Toby Jones, David Ryall, Ian McElhinney, B J Hogg, Liz Smith, Martin Landau, Mackenzie Crook.
‣ *Dir* Gil Kenan, *Pro* Gary Goetzman, Tom Hanks, Steve Shareshian, *Screenplay* Caroline Thompson, from the book by Jeanne Duprau, *Ph* Xavier Pérez Grobet, *Pro Des* Martin Laing, *Ed* Adam P Scott and Zach Staenberg, *M* Andrew Lockington, *Cos* Ruth Myers.

Playtone/Walden Media-Entertainment Film Distributors. 95 mins. USA. 2008. Rel: 10 Oct 2008. Cert PG.

City of Men ★★★★

In the *favelas* of Rio de Janeiro Acerola (Douglas Silva), an 18-year-old with a small child, is trapped in a world of extreme violence. He wants to be a good parent and also help his friend Laranjinha (Darlan Cunha) find his father whom he never knew. The acting in Paul Morelli's raw film is outstanding, particularly from Silva as the young man running out of time in order to find his missing child. Not as operatic as *City of God* but equally powerful (Original title: *Cidade dos Homens*) GS

‣ Douglas Silva, Darlan Cunha, Camila Monteiro, Jonathan Haagensen, Rodrigo Dossantos.
‣ *Dir* Paulo Morelli, *Pro* Andrea Barata Ribeiro, Paulo Morelli, Bel Berlinck and Fernando Meirelles, *Screenplay* Elena Soarez, from a story by Soarez and Morelli, *Ph* Adriano Goldman, *Pro Des* Rafael Ronconi, *Ed* Daniel Rezende, *M* Antonio Pinto, *Cos* Inês Salgado.

Fox Filme do Brasil/Globo Filmes/O2 Filmes/ Petrobrás-Buena Vista International. 106 mins. Brazil. 2007. Rel: 18 July 2008. Cert 15.

City Rats ★ ★ ½

Steve M Kelly's rather bleak film follows the stories of eight lonely and desperate souls in modern day London from a recovering alcoholic to two people with suicidal tendencies. Most of these stories are far too gloomy and depressing but Kelly demonstrates enough originality to make this project interesting. This is particularly so in the story of the drug addict (Kenny Doughty) who desperately tries to find a sexual partner for his gay, deaf and autistic brother (James Lance). GS

❥ Tamer Hassan, Danny Dyer, Ray Panthaki, Susan Lynch, Kenny Doughty, James Lance.
❥ *Dir* Steve Kelly, *Pro* William Borthwick and Dean Fisher, *Screenplay* Simon Fantauzzo, *Ph* Adam Levins, *Pro Des* Amy Spicer, *Ed* Ben King, *M* Julia Johnson and Mark Maclaine, *Cos* Alice Walkling.

Face Films/Scanner-Rhodes Productions/ Urban Way Productions-Revolver Entertainment. 100 mins. UK. 2009. Rel: 24 Apr 2009. Cert 15.

CJ7 ★ ★ ★

Actor/director Stephen Chow, famous for his stylish *Kung Fu Hustle*, changes gear for this charming children's film written in the spirit of *ET*. He plays the penniless father of a nine-year-old boy who is being bullied at school. But the boy's situation changes dramatically when he finds a little toy dog left behind by a spaceship. It is well made and fun but occasionally sinks into sentimentality. (Original title: *Cheung Gong 7 hou*). GS

❥ Stephen Chow, Lei Huang, Kitty Zhang, Tze Chung Lam, Sheung Ching Lee
❥ *Dir* Stephen Chow, *Pro* Chow, Chui Po Chu and Han San Ping, *Screenplay* Chow and Vincent Kok, *Ph* Poon Hang Sang, *Pro Des*

Oliver Wong, *Ed* Angie Lam, *M* Raymond Wong, *Cos* Dora Ng.

Columbia Pictures Film Production Asia/ Star Overseas/Beijing Film Studio/China Film Group-Sony Pictures Releasing. 86 mins. Hong Kong. 2008. Rel: 8 Aug 2008. Cert PG.

The Class ★ ★ ★ ½

Highly praised at Cannes, this portrait of school life is a quite remarkable blend in which the acting by non-professionals yields a film that has every appearance of being an authentic documentary. One is reminded of that real documentary triumph *Etre et Avoir* (2002), but the teenage pupils here are inevitably far less engaging than the younger children in the earlier film and at 128 minutes *The Class* seems much too long. (Original title: *Entre Les Murs*). MS

❥ François Bégaudeau, Agame Malembo-Emene, Franck Keïta, Rachel Regulier, Wei Huang.
❥ *Dir* Laurent Cantet, *Pro* Carole Scotta, Caroline Benjo, Simon Arnal and Barbara Letellier, *Screenplay* Cantet, Robin Campillo and François Bégaudeau, freely inspired by Bégaudeau's book *Entre les murs*, *Ph* Pierre Milon and Catherine Pujol, *Art Dir* Sabine Barthélémy and Hélène Bellanger, *Ed* Campillo and Stéphanie Leger, *Cos* Babeth Joinet and others.

Haut et Court/France 2 Cinéma/Canal+/ CinéCinéma etc.-Artificial Eye Film Company. 130 mins. France. 2008. Rel: 27 Feb 2009. Cert 15.

Clubbed ★ ½

Neil Thompson's uneven film is set in the violent world of 1980s clubland and tells the story of Danny (Mel Raido), a lonely factory worker whose bleak existence changes when he meets a group of nightclub doormen. The film which is based on Geoff Thompson's memoirs *Watch My Back* lacks focus and purpose and it is difficult to care about its unlikeable characters. Raido's dispirited performance makes things even worse. GS

▶ Mel Raido, Shaun Parkes, Scot Williams, Maxine Peake, Ronnie Fox, Colin Salmon, Neil Morrssey, Nick Holder.
▶ *Dir* Neil Thompson, *Pro* Martin Carr, *Screenplay* Geoff Thompson, *Ph* Kate Stark, *Pro Des* Simon Godfrey, *Ed* David Kew, *M* Paul Heard, *Cos* Sam Dightam.

Formosa Films/Screen West Midlands-Route One Releasing
95 mins. UK. 2008. Rel: 16 Jan 2009. Cert 18.

College Road Trip ★★

In this ploddingly dreary Disney family comedy, Raven-Symoné gives a strident, motor-mouth turn as a brainy American high schooler who plans a girls-only road trip to check out prospective colleges. Martin Lawrence is hardly any more appealing as her charisma-challenged bossy police chief dad who insists on escorting her to Washington's Georgetown University. Donny Osmond's amateurish support act as an over-cheery, singing dad is way overconfident. With its simple-minded script and total lack of surprise or sense of good-natured, easy-going fun, adults will find it pretty much a laugh-free zone, but maybe some girls between seven and fourteen could be mildly pleased. DW

▶ Martin Lawrence, Raven-Symoné, Brenda Song, Kym E Whitley, Eugene Jones, Margo Harshman
▶ *Dir* Roger Kumble, *Pro* Louanne Brickhouse, Kristin Burr and Andrew Gunn, *Screenplay* Emi Mochizuki and Carrie Evans, Cinco Paul and Ken Daurio, *Ph* Theo van de Sande, *Pro Des* Ben Barraud, *Ed* Roger Bondelli, *M* Edward Shearmur, *Cos* Francine Jamison-Tanchuck.

Walt Disney Pictures/Gunn Films-Buena Vista International.
83 mins. USA. 2008.
Rel: 22 Aug 2008. Cert U.

Confessions of a Shopaholic ★ ½

Rebecca (Isla Fisher) lives in New York and is deeply in debt because of her shopping addiction. To her surprise she lands a job as a columnist for a financial magazine run by the handsome Luke (Hugh Dancy). There are some good ideas but the plot becomes more preposterous as it progresses. Isla Fisher is a likeable performer but she is encouraged to overact and it is sad to see the likes of Kristin Scott Thomas, Joan Cusack and John Goodman sink as low as this. GS

▶ Isla Fisher, Hugh Dancy, Krysten Ritter, Joan Cusack, John Goodman, John Lithgow, Kristin Scott Thomas, Lynn Redgrave.
▶ *Dir* P J Hogan, *Pro* Jerry Bruckheimer, *Screenplay* Tracey Jackson, Kayla Alpert and Tim Firth, from the books *Confessions of a Shopaholic* and *Shopaholic Takes Manhattan* by Sophie Kinsella, *Ph* Jo Willems, *Pro Des* Kristi Zea, *Ed* William Goldenberg, *M* James Newton Howard, *Cos* Patricia Field.

Jerry Bruckheimer Films/Touchstone Pictures-Walt Disney Studios Motion Pictures-Buena Vista International.
104 mins. USA. 2009. Rel: 20 Feb 2009. Cert PG.

Conversations With My Gardener ★★★

The beautifully controlled underplaying by both Daniel Auteuil (a successful painter now divorced and living in the country) and Jean-Pierre Darrousin (a local man working as gardener to the artist with whom he had once been at school) makes for an amiable, relaxed first-half. Sadly, the film comes to seem over-extended and then, when it turns to weepie territory, it seems clichéd. (Original title: *Dialogue avec mon jardinier*). MS

▶ Daniel Auteuil, Jean-Pierre Darroussin, Fanny Cottençon, Alexia Barlier, Hiam Abbass.
▶ *Dir* Jean Becker, *Pro* Louis Becker, *Screenplay* Jean Cosmos, Jacques Monnet and Jean Becker, based on the novel by Henri Cueco, *Ph* Jean-Marie Dreujou, *Art Dir* Thérèse Ripaud, *Ed* Jacques Witta, *Cos* Annie Périer Bertaux.

Isla Fisher bags all she can in *Confessions of a Shopaholic.*

Ice 3, KJB Production, StudioCanal, France 2 Cinéma, Rhône-Alpes Cinéma co-production etc.- Cinefile World.
109 mins. France. 2006. Rel: 21 Nov 2008. Cert 12A.

The Cool School ★★★

Morgan Neville's articulate documentary focuses on the Ferus Art Gallery, the famous LA institution which in the late 1950s and early '60s nourished the work of beatnik artists like Ed Kienholz, Ed Ruscha, Craig Kauffman, Wallace Berman, Ed Moses and Robert Irwin. Interesting interviews with Dennis Hopper and Dean Stockwell as well as Jeff Bridges' distinct narration make a strong contribution to this illuminating experience which benefits from Neville's undoubted passion for the artists' work. GS

▶ Frank O Geary, Robert Irwin, Edward Ruscha, Dean Stockwell
▶ *Dir* Morgan Neville, *Pro* Kristine McKenna, *Screenplay* Neville and McKenna, *Ed* Chris Perkel and Dylan Robertson, *M* Dan Crane.

Tremolo Productions-Arthouse Films. 86 mins. USA. 2008. Rel: 16 Aug 2008. No Cert.

Coraline ★★★★★

Neil Gaiman's children's book gets Henry Selick's stop-frame treatment. Coraline explores her family's new house to find an identical other house in which her parents have time for her. But there's a catch: buttons sewn over their eyes... A work of art, this is both thoroughly captivating and incredibly creepy. A milestone, one of the year's best. Shown in 3D in selected cinemas. JC

▶ Voices of Dakota Fanning, Teri Hatcher, Jennifer Saunders, Dawn French, Keith David, John Hodgman.
▶ *Dir* and *Pro Des* Henry Selick, *Pro* Mary Sandell, *Screenplay* Selick, from the book by Neil Gaiman, *Ph* Pete Kozachik, *Ed* Christopher Murrie and Ronald Sanders, *M* Bruno Coulais and They Might Be Giants.

Laika Entertainment/Pandemonium-United Pictures International. 100 mins. USA. 2009. Rel: 8 May 2009. Cert PG.

Crank 2: High Voltage ★★★

Despite the fact that Chev Chelios (Jason Statham) falls from an aeroplane without a parachute at the end of the first film, he

Jason Statham lives again to crank up the action for *Crank 2: High Voltage.*

is miraculously still alive in this energetic sequel. But when a group of Chinese gangsters cut out his heart, he provisionally replaces it with a battery-powered machine and begins a race against time in order to find them. The plot is preposterous and utterly implausible but the action races at such speed that it doesn't give time for thought and who cares when it is such fun? GS

▶ Jason Statham, Amy Smart, Dwight Yoakam, Efren Ramirez, Julanne Chidi Hill, Reno Wilson.
▶ *Dir* and *Screenplay* Mark Neveldine and Brian Taylor, *Pro* Gary Lucches, Tom Rosenberg, Skip Williamson, Richard Wright etc, *Ph* Brandon Trost, *Pro Des* Jerry Fleming, *Ed* Marc Jakubowicz and Fernando Villena, *M* Mike Patton, *Cos* Dayna Pink.

Lakeshore Entertainment-Lionsgate.
96 mins. USA. 2009. Rel: 16 Apr 2009. Cert 18.

CSNY/Déjà Vu ★ ★ ★ ½

Pop singers often get together again but it was no typical example of that when in 2006 Neil Young (directing here as Bernard Shakey) reunited with Crosby, Stills and Nash to tour. Far from reprising old hits,

they aimed to confront audiences with new songs by Young composed to question the attitudes of President Bush and America's involvement in Iraq. Unfortunately the film is over-long but much of it is great stuff, an honest investigation of song used to confront serious issues. MS

▶ With David Crosby, Stephen Stills, Graham Nash, Neil Young.
▶ *Dir* Bernard Shakey, *Pro* L.A. Johnson and Mike Cerre, *Written by* Neil Young and Cerre, *Ph* Mike Elwell, *Ed* Mark Faulkner, *M* Neil Young.

Shangri-La Entertainment/a Shakey Pictures production-Metrodome Distribution.
96 mins. USA. 2008. Rel: 18 July 2008. Cert 15.

The Curious Case of Benjamin Button ★ ★ ½

Curious, indeed, but also a folly. Adapting F Scott Fitzgerald's short story about a man born old and aging backwards so that at the end of his life he reaches childhood and then turning it into a film lasting 166 minutes is not a good idea. There are some good performances and effective make-up but the plot's novelty yields surprisingly little of interest and it all goes on and on. David

Michael Sheen gives an outstanding performance as Brian Clough in *The Damned United*.

Fincher would seem to be the wrong director, for this is surely the Tim Burton film that Burton, probably wisely, didn't make. MS

▶ Brad Pitt, Cate Blanchett, Taraji P. Henson, Tilda Swinton, Julia Ormond, Jason Flemyng, Jared Harris, Elias Koteas.
▶ *Dir* David Fincher, *Pro* Kathleen Kennedy, Frank Marshall and Ceán Chaffin, *Screenplay* Eric Roth from the short story by F Scott Fitzgerald, *Ph* Claudio Miranda, *Pro Des* Donald Graham Burt, *Ed* Kirk Baxter and Angus Wall, *M* Alexandre Desplat, *Cos* Jacqueline West.

Paramount Pictures/Warner Bros. Pictures-Warner Bros Distributors.
166 mins. USA 2008. Rel: 6 Feb 2009. Cert 12A.

The Damned United
★★★½

Playing football manager Brian Clough, Michael Sheen is at his brilliant best here. However, Peter Morgan's screenplay depicting Clough's rise and fall, a story of interest even to those who are not sports fans, leaves the impression that he has not quite nailed the man. The constant back and forth between Clough's time at Derby and his ultimate fiasco with Leeds United is not helpful to the film's forward momentum. Nevertheless the acting makes it well worth seeing – and that includes the contributions by a very fine supporting cast. MS

▶ Michael Sheen, Timothy Spall, Colm Meaney, Jim Broadbent, Henry Goodman, Martin Compston.
▶ *Dir* Tom Hooper, *Pro* Andy Harries, *Screenplay* Peter Morgan based on David Peace's novel, *Ph* Ben Smithard, *Pro Des* Eve Stewart, *Ed* Melanie Oliver, *M* Rob Lane, *Cos* Mike O'Neill.

Columbia Pictures/BBC Films/a Left Bank Pictures production etc.-Sony Pictures Releasing.
97 mins. UK/USA. 2009. Rel: 27 March 2009. Cert 15.

Dance Party, USA ★★★½

Filming in Portland, Oregon in 2004, Aaron Katz emulated Andrew Bujalsksi and echoed John Cassavetes by using simple and direct means to present a true-to-life portrayal of teenagers. The Fourth of July setting fits the bill, but not everything is persuasive and the later *Quiet City* (q.v) contains the better work.

However, Katz keeps this short film moving and it is not without telling scenes. MS

▷ Anna Kavan, Cole Pensinger, Ryan White, Sarah Bing, Natalie Buller.
▷ *Dir* and *Written by* Aaron Katz, *Pro* Marc Ripper and Brendan McFadden, *Ph* Sean McElwee, *Ed* Zach Clark, *M* Keegan DeWitt.

Distributed by ICA Films.
67 mins. USA. 2006. Rel: 25 July 2008. No Cert.

The Dark Knight ★ ★ ★ ★ ½

De-emphasising the more fantastic elements of Batman mythology in favour of a more realistic approach, Christopher Nolan's Batsequel focuses more closely on the emotional life of the characters and their relationships with one another, rather than the plot or the action, making for a fascinating, rather than fun, viewing experience. Posthumous Best Supporting Actor Oscar winner Heath Ledger steals the show as the psychotic, chaotic Joker, far more thrilling than Christian Bale's one-note caped Crusader. MJ

▷ Christian Bale, Heath Ledger, Aaron Eckhart, Michael Caine, Maggie Gyllenhaal, Gary Oldman, Morgan Freeman, Cillian Murphy.
▷ *Dir* Christopher Nolan, *Pro* Nolan, Charles Roven and Emma Thomas, *Screenplay* Christopher and Jonathan Nolan, *Ph* Wally Pfister, *Pro Des* Nathan Crowley, *Ed* Lee Smith, *M* James Newton Howard and Hans Zimmer, *Cos* Lindy Hemming.

Warner Bros Pictures/Legendary Pictures/DC Comics/Syncopy-Warner Bros Film Distributors. 152 mins. USA. 2008. Rel: 24 July 2008. Cert 12A.

It's all a joke for Heath Ledger in *The Dark Knight*.

The Day the Earth Stood Still ★ ★ ★

Ill-advised remake of Robert Wise's classic 1951 science fiction tale about an alien who comes to Earth to see how well we are managing to save the planet for its future occupants. None too well, it seems, so Klaatu (Keanu Reeves, for it is he, as po-faced as ever) sets about destroying Earth before we do, even though way back in 1951 Michael Rennie's Klaatu only issued a warning against what might happen. In order to get in some reasonably spectacular acts of destruction the remake goes to town on the sci-fi FX. It's OK but you would get more out of a re-run of Wise's seminal 1950s classic. MHD

▷ Keanu Reeves, Jennifer Connelly, Kathy Bates, Jaden Smith, John Cleese, Jon Hamm, Kyle Chandler.
▷ *Dir* Scott Derrickson, *Pro* Paul Harris Boardman, Gregory Goodman and Erwin Stoff. *Screenplay* David Scarpa, based on the 1951 screenplay by Edmund H North, *Ph* David Tattersall, *Pro Des* David Brisbin, *Ed* Wayne Wahrman, *M* Tyler Bates, *Cos* Tish Monaghan.

Twentieth Century Fox Film Corporation/3 Arts Entertainment/Earth Productions-20th Century Fox.
104 mins. USA. 2008. Rel: 12 Dec 2008. Cert 12A.

Daylight Robbery ★ ★ ★

A heist with a twist, this is a bank job with the World Cup in Germany allegedly providing a team of bank robbers with the perfect alibi. Having gone to the airport to check in their soccer alibi, the five villains head for the City and the London Exchange Bank where millions of used notes are just waiting to be snatched. All goes well until the inevitable glitch happens... Paris Leonti in his first feature film captures well the tried and tested British robbery genre (cf. *The League of Gentlemen*, *The Day They Robbed the Bank of England* and q.v. *Tuesday*) although some of his characters at times veer into stereotype. MHD

▷ Geoff Bell, Vas Blackwood, Robert Boulter, Max Brown, Antonio Gil, Leo Gregory, Paul Nicholls, Shaun Williamson.
▷ *Dir* and *Screenplay* Paris Leonti, *Pro* Nick O'Hagan, *Ph* Milton Kam, *Pro Des* Will Field, *Ed* Hasse Billing, *M* Richard Chester, *Cos* Alice Wolfbauer.

Daylight Productions/Giant Films-Liberation Entertainment.
99 mins. UK. 2008. Rel: 29 Aug 2008. Cert 15.

Dean Spanley ★ ★ ★ ★

Don't be put off! Being the Edwardian tale of a man who believes that he had lived a previous life as a dog, this can only be described in terms that suggest a tiresome piece of whimsy. Instead Alan Sharp's literate script has wittily transformed it into a wholly individual work that centres touchingly on a troubled father-son relationship and it is played by a perfect cast which includes Peter O'Toole still at the top of his form. MS

▷ Jeremy Northam, Sam Neill, Bryan Brown, Peter O'Toole, Judy Parfitt, Art Malik.
▷ *Dir* Toa Fraser, *Pro* Matthew Metcalfe and Alan Harris, *Written by* Alan Sharp from Baron Dunsany's novel *My Talks with Dean Spanley*, *Ph* Len Narbey, *Pro Des* Andrew McAlpine, *Ed* Chris Plummer, *M* Don McGlashan, *Cos* Odile Dicks-Mireaux.

New Zealand Film Commission/Screen East Content Investment Fund/a Matthew Metcalfe, Atlantic Film Group production etc.-Icon Film Distribution.
100 mins. UK/New Zealand/Cayman Islands 2008. Rel: 12 Dec 2008. Cert U.

Death Defying Acts ★ ★ ½

Featuring the escapologist Harry Houdini and set in Edinburgh in 1926, this film hopes to convince its audience that its highly fictional tale involving a bogus psychic and her daughter is factual. Given this script, that hope is doomed despite the presence of a strong cast including young Saoirse Ronan from *Atonement* and the ever

reliable Timothy Spall. The trickery both on stage and off as the psychic tries to persuade Houdini of her powers is far less convincing than in that other recent tale of on-stage fakery *The Prestige*.
MS

> Guy Pearce, Catherine Zeta-Jones, Saoirse Ronan, Timothy Spall.
> *Dir* Gillian Armstrong, *Pro* Chris Curling and Marian Macgowan, *Written by* Tony Grisoni and Brian Ward, *Ph* Haris Zambarloukos, *Pro Des* Gemma Jackson, *Ed* Nicholas Beauman, *M* Cezary Skubiszewski, *Cos* Susannah Buxton.

Film Finance Corporation Australia/BBC Films/UK Film Council/Myriad Pictures/a Macgowan Lupovitz Nasatir Films and Zephyr Films production etc.-Lionsgate. 96 mins. Australia/UK/USA. 2007. Rel: 8 Aug 2008. Cert PG.

Death Note: the Last Name ★★★★

Kaneko's second instalment to this successful Japanese franchise is more of a continuation rather than a sequel. The police and the mysterious 'L' are still trying to track down Kira, the young man who eliminates the city's criminals by simply writing down their name in his 'Death Note'. But now another book drops from the sky and a new Kira enters the scene. It is as thrilling and exciting as the original with another unexpected twist. (Original title: *Desu Nôto*).
GS

> Tatsuya Fujiwara, Takeshi Kaga, Shido Nakamura, Erika Toda, Shigeki Hosokawa.
> *Dir* Shusuke Kaneka, *Pro* Takahiro Sato, *Screenplay* Tetsuya Oishi, from the comic by Tsgumi Oba and Takeshi Obata, *Ph* Kenji Takama, *Pro Des* Oikawa Hajime, *Ed* Yousuke Yafune, *M* Kenji Kawai.

Death Note Film Partners/Nippon TV Network Corporation/Shueisha-Warner Bros. 141 mins. Japan/USA. 2006. Rel: 4 July 2008. Cert 12A.

Death Race ★★★½

Death Race 2000, shot on a shoestring budget in 1975 by director Paul Bartel, is an exploitation classic, shocking, satirical and subversive. This loose remake, written and directed by British B-movie marvel Paul W S Anderson, is none of those things, yet remains a reasonable laugh. Jason Statham plays a wrongly imprisoned tough guy, forced to take part in a pay-per-view race to the death. Dumb, crude, bloody, loud and explosive, but in a good way. MJ

> Jason Statham, Joan Allen, Ian McShane, Tyrese Gibson, Natalie Martinez, Max Ryan.
> *Dir* Paul W S Anderson, *Pro* Anderson, Jeremy Bolt, Roger Corman and Paula Wagner, *Screenplay* Anderson, from his own screen story based on the 1975 screenplay *Death Race 2000* by Robert Thom and Charles Griffith, and the story by Ib Melchior, *Ph* Scott Kevan, *Pro Des* Paul Denham Austerberry, *Ed* Niven Howie, *M* Paul Haslinger, *Cos* Gregory Mah.

Universal Pictures/Relativity Media/ Impact Pictures/C/W etc-Universal Pictures International. 105 mins. USA/Germany/UK. 2008. Rel: 26 Sep 2008. Cert 15.

Defiance ★★½

A good cast is here defeated by a screenplay which seems to remould historical events into the shape of popular melodrama. The story of the Bielski brothers, Jews who in 1941 and 1942 led a group in Belorussia to a place where they could survive the German onslaught, deserves a better telling. Factual it may be, but this comes across as closer to fiction given the clichés it so readily embraces. MS

> Daniel Craig, Liev Schreiber, Jamie Bell, Alexa Davalos, Jodhi May, Allan Corduner, Iben Hjejle.
> *Dir* Edward Zwick, *Pro* Zwick and Pieter Jan Brugge, *Screenplay* Clayton Frohman and Zwick from Nechama Tec's book *Defiance: The Bielski Partisans*, *Ph* Eduardo Serra, *Pro*

Daniel Craig on the run from the Germans in the Second World War drama *Defiance*.

Des Dan Weil, *Ed* Steven Rosenblum, *M* James Newton Howard, *Cos* Jenny Beavan.

Paramount Vantage/a Grosvenor Park/ Bedford Falls production etc.-Momentum Pictures.
137 mins. USA. 2008. Rel: 9 Jan 2009. Cert 15.

Delta ★ ★ ★ ½

If you won't accept a slow-paced film, stay well away. On its own terms, however, this latest work from Hungary's Kornél Mundruczó contains much of distinction. That applies to the visuals, to the use of sound and to the unsensational treatment of a story about country folks reacting violently to the genuine love that grows up between a brother and sister. But that the couple should not be on their guard is unlikely and results in a conclusion that feels not so much tragic as set up. MS

❧ Félix Lajkó, Orsi Tóth, Lili Monori, Sándor Gáspár.
❧ *Dir* Kornél Mundruczó, *Pro* Viktória Petrányi, Susanne Marian and Philippe Bober, *Written by* Yvette Biró and Mundruczó, *Ph* Mátyás Erdély, *Pro Des* Márton Ágh, *Ed* Dávid Jancsó, *M* Félix Lajkó, *Cos* János Breckl.

Coproduction Office/a Proton Cinema, Essential Filmproduktion, Filmpartners production etc.-ICA Films.
96 mins. Hungary/Germany/France. 2008. Rel: 8 May 2009. Cert 18.

Diminished Capacity ★ ½

Cooper (Matthew Broderick), a Chicago journalist returns home in order to help his mother move his uncle Rollie (Alan Alda) into a nursing home. Rollie's memory is deteriorating because of Alzheimer's but so is Cooper's due to a recent concussion. Cooper also comes across his old love Charlotte (Virginia Madsen) and together they take Rollie to a Chicago memorabilia market so he can sell his precious baseball card. The premise is not bad but the strong cast is wasted in this uneven and rather dull comedy. GS

❧ Matthew Broderick, Alan Alda, Virginia Madsen, Dylan Baker, Bobby Cannavale, Louis C K, Tom Aldredge.
❧ *Dir* Terry Kinney, *Pro* Tim Evans, Galt Niederhoffer and Celine Rattray, *Screenplay* Sherwood Kiraly and Doug Bost, *Ph* Vanja Cernjul, *Pro Des* Matthew Munn, *Ed* Tim Streeto, *M* Robert Burger, *Cos* Sarah J Holden.

Benedek Films/Plum Pictures/Hanson Allen Films/Hart-Lunsford Pictures/Steppenwolf Pictures-Paramount Pictures.
92 mins. USA. 2008. Rel: 20 Mar 2009.
Cert 15.

The Disappeared ★★

Matthew (Harry Treadaway) feels responsible for his younger brother's disappearance and finds it hard to cope. And things get even worse when he starts hearing his brother's ghostly voice calling for help. Johnny Kevorkian's atmospheric chiller begins well with a nod to *White Noise* and a strong central performance from Treadaway but the plot becomes more improbable as it moves along, leading to a preposterous and laughable climax. GS

▶ Harry Treadaway, Greg Wise, Alex Jennings, Tom Felton, Finlay Robertson, Nikki Amuka-Bird.
▶ *Dir* Johnny Kevorkian, *Pro* Kevorkian and Neil Murphy, *Screenplay* Kevorkian and Murphy, *Ph* Diego Rodriguez, *Pro Des* Malin Lindholm, *Ed* Celia Haining, *M* Ilan Eshkeri, *Cos* Rebecca Gore

Mindseye Films/Lost Tribe Productions-Jinga Films.
96 mins. UK. 2008. Rel: 16 June 2009. Cert 18.

Disaster Movie ★

Funnily enough - and maybe this is this film's one actual joke - not a single disaster movie is spoofed in this predictably awful movie send-up that mainly allows for rancid fun at the expense of Amy Winehouse, Michael Jackson and other troubled celebrities, plus useless digs at *Enchanted* (a fairy tale), *Alvin and the Chipmunks* (a family comedy), *The Happening* (a mystery drama), *Cloverfield* (a monster movie). *10,000BC* (an adventure), *Kung Fu Panda* (a cartoon), *Sex and the City* (a chick flick), *Step Up* (a dance musical), *Beowulf* (a fantasy), *Speed Racer* (a race car actioner) and *High School Musical* (a teen movie). Matt Lanter shows signs of talent as the hero and so does Nicole Parker

as the drugged-out Winehouse, the wide-eyed Princess from *Enchanted* and the well-endowed Jessica Simpson, but both stars are utterly sunk by the dreadful, no-laughs script. Yep, it's a disaster, all right: you have been warned!
DW

▶ Matt Lanter, Vanessa Minnillo, Gary 'G Thang' Johnson, Nicole Parker, Crista Flanagan, Kimberly Kardashian, Carmen Electra.
▶ *Dir* and *Screenplay* Jason Friedberg and Aaron Seltzer, *Pro* Friedberg, Seltzer and Peter Safran, *Ph* Shawn Maurer, *Pro Des* William A Elliott, *Ed* Peck Prior, *M* Christopher Lennertz, *Cos* Frank Helmer.

Lionsgate/Grosvenor Park/3 in the Box-Momentum Pictures.
88 mins. USA. 2008. Rel: 5 Sep 2008.
Cert 12A.

Il Divo ★★★★★

An astonishing performance by Toni Servillo - one of the year's best - lies at the heart of this film from the director of *The Consequences of Love*. In building a movie around the politician Giulio Andreotti, Sorrentino attempts not a naturalistic bio-pic but something more stylised and original. That he succeeds triumphantly is confirmed by the fact that certain aspects of the Italian character, epitomised by the links between politicians, men of the cloth, hit men and the Mafia, have never been so tellingly portrayed on film. MS

▶ Toni Servillo, Anna Bonaiuto, Giulio Bosetti, Flavio Bucci, Carlo Buccirosso, Fanny Ardant.
▶ *Dir* and *Written by* Paolo Sorrentino, *Pro* Nicola Giuliano, Francesca Cima and Andrea Occhipinti, *Ph* Luca Bigazzi, *Art Dir* Lino Fiorito, *Ed* Cristiano Travaglioli, *M* Teho Teardo, *Cos* Daniela Ciancio.

An Indigo Film, Lucky Red, Parco Film production/Babe Films/StudioCanal/Arte France Cinéma etc.-Artificial Eye Film Company.
118 mins. Italy/France. 2008.
Rel: 20 March 2009. Cert 15.

Doghouse ★★★½

Seven guys determine to treat Vince (Stephen Graham) – who's undergoing a painful divorce – to a weekend he'll never forget. So they decide to visit Moodley, a secluded village where the women outnumber the men three to one. It's time to find their 'inner bloke' – except all the women have turned into zombies. At one point Danny Dyer's Neil notes, "bloody hell, Vince, it's not very PC…" This film – which objectifies women to a frightening degree – is one for the boys, of either gender. The effects may be sickening and over-the-top, but the humour is nicely throwaway and the entertainment value red in tooth and claw. JC-W

▷ Danny Dyer, Stephen Graham, Noel Clarke, Terry Stone, Christina Cole, Lee Ingleby, Mary Tamm.
▷ *Dir* Jake West, *Pro* Mike Loveday, *Screenplay* Dan Schaffer, *Ph* Ali Asad, *Pro Des* Matthew Button, *Ed* Julian Gilbey, Will Gilbey and Jake West, *M* Richard Wells, *Cos* Hayley Nebauer.

Hanover Films/Carnaby International/Molinaire Studio-Sony Pictures or Vertigo Films.
89 mins. UK. 2009. Rel: 12 June 2009. Cert 15.

Donkey Punch ★½

A donkey punch is a rather misogynistic move in the bedroom, which can prove fatal for the female partner. When such an action is carried out on a luxury yacht off the coast of Mallorca, three girls from Leeds find themselves at the mercy of their male hosts… As *Dead Calm* turns into dead meat, all the old clichés come tumbling out of the closet. Devoid of momentum or suspense, the film plods from one implausibility to the next as the girls prove exasperatingly clueless and the guys come off as sinister as Take That wannabes. JC-W

▷ Robert Boulter, Sian Breckin, Tom Burke, Nichola Burley, Julian Morris, Jay Taylor, Jaime Winstone.
▷ *Dir* Oliver Blackburn, *Pro* Robin Gutch, Angus Lamont and Mark Herbert, *Screenplay* Blackburn and David Bloom, *Ph* Nanu Segal,

Pro Des Delarey Wagener, *Ed* Kate Evans, *M* François-Eudes Chanfrault, *Costumes* Sarah Ryan.

E M Media/Film 4/Madman Entertainment/ Screen Yorkshire/UK Film Council/ Warp X-Optimum Releasing.
99 mins. UK. 2008. Rel: 18 July 2008. Cert 18.

Doubt ★★★★

For a film that deals with a Catholic Church school in the Bronx where the head sister (Meryl Streep) suspects that a priest (Philip Seymour Hoffman) of paedophilia, this is a surprisingly traditional work rather than anything cutting edge. But on its own terms it is very well done and splendidly played by all (supporting actress Viola Davis was Oscar nominated). It satisfyingly leaves it to the audience to come to their own conclusions regarding the truth about the Father accused. MS.

▷ Meryl Streep, Philip Seymour Hoffman, Amy Adams, Viola Davis.
▷ *Dir* and *Written by* John Patrick Shanley from his own play, *Pro* Scott Rudin and Mark Roybal, *Ph* Roger Deakins, *Pro Des* David Gropman, *Ed* Dylan Tichenor, *M* Howard Shore, *Cos* Ann Roth.

Miramax Films/a Scott Rudin production-Buena Vista International.
104 mins. USA. 2008. Rel: 6 Feb 2009. Cert 15.

Drag Me to Hell ★★

Pasadena, California; today. Setting the tone with a diabolic prologue, Sam Raimi introduces a cheesy scenario in which a peaches 'n' cream loan officer refuses an old hag an extension on her mortgage. A somewhat predictable chain of events ensues, in which Raimi exploits the old building blocks of horror, from creaks, loud knocks and ambiguous shadows to orally fixated insects. It's all wildly OTT and silly, with the accent more on the gross-out and belly laughs (many unintentional) than on anything remotely scary. As the forgettable heroine, Alison Lohman exposes her limitations as an actress and is upstaged by a goat. JC-W

‣ Alison Lohman, Justin Long, Lorna Raver, Dileep Rao, David Raymer.
‣ *Dir* Sam Raimi, *Pro* Raimi, Robert G Tapert and Grant Curtis, *Screenplay* Sam and Ivan Raimi, *Ph* Peter Deming, *Pro Des* Steve Saklad, *Ed* Bob Murawski, *M* Christopher Young, *Cos* Isis Mussenden.

Ghost House Pictures/Mandate Pictures/ Buckaroo Entertainment-Lionsgate. 99 mins. USA. 2009. Rel: 27 May 2009. Cert 15.

Dragonball Evolution ★ ★

This Hollywood adaptation of a hugely popular Japanese manga epic blands out in its frenzied bid to appeal to everybody. Justin Chatwin is appealing as callow high-school warrior Goku, who sets out on a quest with Chi Chi (Jamie Chung), battling time and the vengeful, green-skinned Lord Piccolo (James Marsters) to collect seven magical orbs offering unlimited power. Director James Wong certainly turns in a fast paced, flashy and never boring entertainment, though it's never very coherent, logical, distinctive or satisfying. Those coming to marvel at the martial arts fight sequences, special effects and production values will find they are fine, rather than brilliant. The notably short running time indicates cuts: indeed there's a version 15 minutes longer than the cinema release print. Chow Yun-Fat simply collects the pay cheque as Master Roshi. DW

‣ Justin Chatwin, Chow Yun-Fat, Emily Rossum, Jamie Chung, James Marsters, Joon Park, Texas Battle.
‣ *Dir* James Wong, *Pro* Stephen Chow, *Screenplay* Ben Ramsey, from the *Dragonball* novel series, *Ph* Robert McLachlan, *Pro Des* Bruton Jones, *Ed* Matt Friedman and Chris G Willingham, *M* Brian Tyler, *Cos* Mayes C Rubeo.

Dune Entertainment/Star Overseas- 20th Century Fox. 85 mins. USA/Hong Kong. 2009. Rel: 8 Apr 2009. Cert PG.

The Duchess ★ ★ ★ ½

With this period piece about the sad life of Georgiana, Duchess of Devonshire, Saul Dibb as director is notably successful in switching from the gritty modern reality of his *Bullet Boy* (2004) to a tale that reflects on the lot of women in the late 18th century. The film has certain weaknesses and even Ralph Fiennes's properly unsympathetic portrayal of the Duke just misses the underlying pathos. Nevertheless *The Duchess* is a much more appealing film than many critics suggested. MS

‣ Keira Knightley. Ralph Fiennes, Charlotte Rampling, Dominic Cooper, Hayley Atwell.
‣ *Dir* Saul Dibb, *Pro* Gabrielle Tana and Michael Kuhn, *Screenplay* Jeffrey Hatcher, Anders Thomas Jensen and Dibb from the book by Amanda Foreman, *Ph* Gyula Pados, *Pro Des* Michael Carlin, *Ed* Masahiro Hirakubo, *M* Rachel Portman, *Cos* Michael O'Connor.

Pathé/BBC Films etc.-Pathé Distribution. 110 mins. UK/France/Italy/USA. 2008. Rel: 5 Sept 2008. Cert 12A.

Dummy ★ ★ ★

Despite promising elements in Matthew Thompson's direction and good efforts by the cast, this Sussex based drama falls short since the ambitious screenplay lacks the necessary depth and conviction. Nevertheless, as a study of brothers trying to cope after the loss of their mother – an 18 year old proving to be too immature to looks after his younger sibling on his own – the piece is never less than interesting. The dummy of the title is the mannequin figure which the younger boy substitutes for his dead mother. MS

‣ Aaron Johnson, Thomas Grant, Therese Bradley, Emma Catherwood, Moira Brooker.
‣ *Dir* Matthew Thompson, *Pro* David Langan, Thompson and Miranda Robinson, *Screenplay* Michael Mueller from story by Paula Barnes and Thompson, *Ph* Langan, *Pro Des* Philip Barber, *Ed* Kant Pan, *M* Nick Smith and Phil Hartnoll, *Cos* Juila Patkos.

Keira Knightley
suffers to
good effect
as Georgiana
in the period
drama *The
Duchess.*

A Format Films production/Highwire Films
etc.-Shoreline Entertainment (ICA Cinema).
89 mins. UK. 2008. Rel: 26 June 2009. No Cert.

Duplicity ★ ★ ★ ½

Former CIA agent Julia Roberts and ex-MI6
spy Clive Owen, with a romantic history
between them, now work for rival firms
investigating industrial espionage. They
meet up and get to work trying to outwit
their own employers. Writer-director Tony
Gilroy plots his script so that we, along with
his characters, do not know who to trust.
Unfortunately the plot gets out of hand as it
jumps backwards and forwards in time. It all
looks cool and the locations are pretty (Italy,
New York, the Bahamas and – er, Cleveland)
but there seems little real chemistry between
the two stars which seems to negate virtually
everything in the script. MHD

▶ Clive Owen, Julia Roberts, Tom Wilkinson,
Paul Giamatti, Lisa Roberts Gillan.
▶ *Dir* and *Screenplay* Tony Gilroy, *Pro* Laura
Bickford, Jennifer Fox and Kerry Orent,
Ph Robert Elswit, *Pro Des* Kevin Thompson,
Ed John Gilroy, *M* James Newton Howard,
Cos Albert Wolsky.

Universal Pictures/Laura Bickford
Productions/Relativity Media/Medien
Produktion Poseidon Filmgesellschaft-
Universal Pictures International.
125 mins. USA/Germany. 2009.
Rel: 20 Mar 2009. Cert 12A.

Eagle Eye ★ ★ ½

A routine techno-thriller as slick as it is
derivative, *Eagle Eye* stars the increasingly
unappealing Shia LaBeouf as an everyman
targeted by a mysterious organisation to do
increasingly hazardous things, all the while
observed and controlled via such everyday
technology as mobile phones and security
cameras. *Big Brother* meets *Wargames* in a
bland and unengaging entertainment that
will mostly remind you of other, better films
you should watch instead. MJ

▶ Shia LaBeouf, Michelle Monaghan, Rosario
Dawson, Billy Bob Thornton, Ethan Embrey.
▶ *Dir* D J Caruso, *Pro* Patrick Crowley, Robert
Orci and Alex Kurtzman, *Screenplay* John
Glenn, Travis Adam Wright, l Seitz and Dan
McDermot, from a story by McDermott, *Ph*
Dariusz Wolski, *Pro Des* Tom Sanders, *Ed* Jim
Page, *M* Brian Tyler, *Cos* Marie-Sylvie Deveau.

Shia LaBeouf wouldn't go anywhere without his mobile, he tells Michelle Monaghan in the rather routine actioner *Eagle Eye*.

DreamWorks SKG/KMP Film Investment/ Goldcrest Pictures-Paramount Pictures. 118 mins. USA/Germany. 2008. Rel: 17 Oct 2008. Cert 12A.

Easy Virtue ★ ★ ★ ½

This adaptation of an early Noël Coward play previously filmed by Hitchcock is as much a drama as a comedy in its critical portrayal of English upper class society in the late 1920s. Blending a modern tone with the period setting and farce with post-war traumas leads to an uneasy mix. Even so, it is often enjoyable, especially when it comes to Colin Firth who is on his best form for years. MS

▶ Jessica Biel, Colin Firth, Kristin Scott Thomas, Ben Barnes, Kris Marshall.
▶ *Dir* Stephan Elliott, *Pro* Barnaby Thompson, Joe Abrams and James D. Stern, *Written by* Elliott and Sheridan Jobbins, based on the play by Noël Coward, *Ph* Martin Kenzie, *Pro Des* John Beard, *Ed* Sue Blainey, *M* Marius de Vries, *Cos* Charlotte Walter.

Ealing Studios/Endgame Entertainment/ Odyssey Entertainment/BBC Films/a Fragile film etc.-Pathé Distribution.

97 mins. UK/USA. 2008. Rel: 7 Nov 2008. Cert PG.

Eden Lake ★ ★ ★ ★ ★

This powerful British film may have strayed into the horror category but its brutal picture of how human behaviour can get out of control is all too relevant. A young couple, Steve and Jenny, find an idyllic spot in the countryside for a romantic weekend. Their idyll is ruined by a gang of louts who taunt them and steal their belongings. Stranded, the couple try to fight their way out of a *Deliverance* style situation which only gets worse as the couple, the gang and their families become involved in the most appalling nightmare situations, from which there appears to be no escape. Writer-director James Watkins handles his screenplay and his actors with great determination. Kelly Reilly and Michael Fassbender as the couple are outstanding and among the gang Jack O'Connell, Thomas Turgoose and Shaun Dooley are particularly strong. Highly recommended. MHD

▶ Kelly Reilly, Michael Fassbender, Tara Ellis, Thomas Turgoose, Shaun Dooley, Jack

Jessica Biel and Ben Barnes are whiter than white in *Easy Virtue*, Stephan Elliott's adaptation of Noël Coward's classic play.

O'Connell, Finn Atkins.
▶ *Dir* and *Screenplay* James Watkins, *Pro* Christian Colson and Richard Holmes, *Ph* Christopher Ross, *Pro Des* Simon Bowles, *Ed* Jon Harris, *M* David Julyan, *Cos* Keith Madden.

Rollercoaster Films-Optimum Releasing.
91 mins. UK. 2008. Rel: 12 Sep 2008. Cert 18.

Elegy ★★★½

Don't pass by this one. It's true that this adaptation of a Philip Roth novella may disappoint in its last stages when it drags in extra drama linked to cancer but until then it's brilliant. That the film was written by a man but directed by a woman creates a balance invaluable to this study of an aging professor and his compulsive need to pursue much younger women. In this role Sir Ben Kingsley is at his finest, but Patricia Clarkson, Peter Sarsgaard and Dennis Hopper are superb too while Penélope Cruz is a convincing object of desire. MS

▶ Ben Kingsley, Penélope Cruz, Peter Sarsgaard, Patricia Clarkson, Dennis Hopper.
▶ *Dir* Isabel Coixet, *Pro* Tom Rosenberg, Gary Lucchesi and Andre Lamal, *Screenplay*

Nicholas Meyer from Philip Roth's novel *The Dying Animal*, *Ph* Jean-Claude Larrieu, *Pro Des* Claude Paré, *Ed* Amy Duddleston, *Cos* Katia Stano.

A Lakeshore Entertainment production-Entertainment Film Distributors.
112 mins. USA. 2007. Rel: 8 Aug 2008. Cert 15.

Elite Squad ★★½

José Padilla's documentary feature *Bus 174* (2002) was an outstanding work and this drama – fiction intended to reflect fact – won for Brazil the Golden Bear at the 2008 Berlin Film Festival. But storytelling does not appear to be Padilla's forte and contrary to expectation I was disappointed by this portrayal of life in the *favelas* of Rio de Janeiro where military police and drug lords are constantly at war. The characters lack depth while the echoes of so many tough action movies only serve to make the viewing of this film a thoroughly depressing experience. (Original title: *Tropa de elite*). MS

▶ Wagner Moura, André Ramiro, Caio Junqueira, Milhem Cortaz, Fernanda Machado.
▶ *Dir* José Padilha, *Pro* Marcos Prado and Padilha, *Screenplay* Padilha, Rodrigo Pimental and Bráulio Mantovani based on the book by

André Batista and Luiz Eduardo Soares, *Ph* Lula Carvalho, *Art Dir* Tulé Peake, *Ed* Daniel Rezende, *M* Pedro Bromfman, *Cos* Cláudia Kopke.

The Weinstein Company/Costa Films/ Zazen Produções/a Universal Pictures, Estudiosmega co-production etc.- Optimum Releasing. 115 mins. Brazil/Netherlands/USA. 2007. Rel: 8 Aug 2008. Cert 18.

Encounters at the End of the World ★ ★ ★ ½

Like *Grizzly Man* (2005) this is an engagingly idiosyncratic documentary from Werner Herzog who explores Antarctica and the people who choose to reside there. The film's shapelessness becomes a problem towards the close but it's visually commanding and varied as it portrays a part of the world unfamiliar to most of us. Herzog's delivery of his own commentary is part of the delight. MS

‣ With David Ainley, William Jirsa, Ashrita Furman, William McIntosh, Werner Herzog (narrator).
‣ *Dir* and *Written by* Werner Herzog, *Pro* Henry Kaiser, *Ph* Peter Zeitlinger, *Ed* Joe Bini, *M* Kaiser and David Lindley.

Discovery Films/Creative Differences Productions for the Discovery Channel- Revolver Entertainment. 101 mins. USA/Canada. 2007. Rel: 24 April 2009. Cert U.

The End ★ ★ ★

The title refers to London's East End home of a breed who whether or not they define themselves as criminals have spent time in jail. One such is the father of the film's director Nicola Collins and her documentary gives them a platform and captures some memorable faces. This is fine as far as it goes, but there's none of the in-depth probing that made Donal MacIntyre's *A Very British Gangster* (2007) so fascinating. MS

‣ With Les Falco, Bobby Reading, Mickey

Goldtooth, Victor Dark, Roy Shaw.
‣ *Dir* and *Written by* and *filmed by* Nicola Collins, *Pro* Teena Collins, *Ed* Noah Rosenstein, *M* Nick Page.

Instinctive Films/a Duckin & Divin production/IM Global-Kaleidoscope Home Entertainment. 81 mins. USA/Germany. 2008. Rel: 1 May 2009. Cert 15.

The End of the Line ★ ★ ★ ★

Here's a stark warning. This documentary sets out lucidly the threat to the fish in our oceans due to capitalist greed. It may be a touch overdramatised at times (listen to the music track) but that hardly matters when the dangers from excessive fishing are so well set out. It should be regarded as compulsory viewing, especially for school-children everywhere. MS

‣ With Charles Clover, Professor Jeffrey Hutchings, Professor Callum Roberts, Ben Bradshaw.
‣ *Dir* and *filmed by* Rupert Murray, *Pro* Claire Lewis and George Duffield, *Based on the book by* Charles Clover, *Ed* Claire Ferguson, *M* Srdjan Kurpjel and Marios Takoushis.

Arcane Pictures/Calm Productions/ Dartmouth Films etc.-Dogwoof Pictures. 86 mins. UK/USA/Costas Rica. 2009. Rel: 12 June 2009. Cert PG.

Everlasting Moments ★ ★ ★ ½

Sweden's Jan Troell – he of *The Emigrants* (1971) and *The New Land* (1972) – resurfaces with an early 20th century tale of a wife whose passion for photography compensates in part for being married to a husband who beats her when drunk. This shortened version of a longer original isn't badly done and it looks good. But inspiration seems to be lacking and there's none of the impact of that Spanish study of a put-upon wife, Icíar Bollaín's *Take My Eyes* (2003). (Original title:

Maria Larssons eviga ögonblick).MS

❯ Maria Heiskanen. Mikael Persbrandt, Jesper Christensen, Callin Öhrvall. Ghita Nørby.
❯ *Dir* Jan Troell, *Pro* Thomas Stenderup, *Screenplay* Niklas Rådström with Troell and Agneta Ulfsäter Troell based on her story, *Ph* Jan Troell and Mischa Garjusjov, *Art Dir* Peter Bävman, *Ed* Niels Pagh Andersen and Jan Troell, *M* Matti Bye, *Cos* Katja Watkins and Karen Gram.

**Final Cut Productions/Göta Film/Motlys/Blind Spot Pictures etc.-Icon Film Distribution.
111 mins. Sweden/Denmark/Norway/Finland/Germany. 2008. Rel: 17 April 2009. Cert 15.**

The Express ★★★

This tells the true story of college football hero Ernie Davis (Rob Brown), the first African-American to win the Heisman Trophy. Davis, who was known as 'The Elmira Express', fought poverty and racial prejudice as a child and became a national hero surpassing even Jim Brown's achievements during the 1960s. His story is fascinating with particularly powerful scenes when Ernie was still a young boy but this overlong film loses some of its impact towards the end. GS

❯ Rob Brown, Dennis Quaid, Nelsan Ellis, Darrin Dewitt Henson, Omar Benson Miller.
❯ *Dir* Gary Fleder, *Pro* John Davis, *Screenplay* Charles Leavitt, based on Robert Gallagher's book *Ernie Davis: The Elmira Express*, *Ph* Kramer Morgenthau, *Pro Des* Nelson Coates, *Ed* Padraic McKinley and William Steinkamp, *M* Mark Isham, *Costumes* Abigail Murray.

**Davis Entertainment/IDEA Film Produktions/Relativity Media-Universal Studios.
130 mins. USA/Germany. 2008. Rel: 5 Dec 2008. Cert PG.**

Face Addict ★★½

In this rather precious and humourless documentary photographer Edo Bertoglio reminiscences about the New York artistic community between the late 1970s and early '80s, known as the 'Downtown Scene'. He covers some interesting material especially when he talks with honesty about his drug addiction and the loss of his many friends from AIDS but as a friend of his suitably comments: "Your photographs are like a graveyard." GS

❯ Edo Bertoglio, Deborah Harry, Maripol, John Lurie, Glenn O'Brien, Walter Steding.
❯ *Dir* Edo Bertoglio, *Pro* Marco Mueller and Tiziana Soudani, *Screenplay* Bertoglio and Gaia Guasti, *Ph* Bertoglio, Vito Robbiani, Gianfranco Rosi and Adriano Schrade, *Pro Des* Andrea Crisanti, *Ed* Gilles Dinnematin and Jacopo Quadri, *M* Evan Lurie, John Lurie and Franco Piersanti.

**Downtown Pictures/Amka Film Productions/Televisione Svizzera ItalianaCompany-Bue Dolphin Film Distribution.
102 mins. Italy/Switzerland/USA. 2005. Rel: 22 Aug 2008. Cert 15.**

Faintheart ★★★

Vitto Rocco's likeable film follows the story of Richard (Eddie Marsan) a passionate man who spends most of his time re-enacting Viking battles with his friends known as the Bloody Broadswords. His neglected wife Cath (Jessica Hynes) kicks him out of the house when he fails to come to her father's funeral and soon after begins an affair with her son's PE teacher Gary (Paul Nicholls). The story is very predictable and occasionally very silly but the commitment and energy of the cast makes it rather fun. GS

❯ Eddie Marsan, Ewen Bremner, Jessica Hynes, Tim Healy, Anne Reid, Paul Nicholls, Bronagh Gallagher, Edward Tudor-Pole.
❯ *Dir* Vito Rocco, *Pro* Rachel Connors, Judy Counihan, Arvind Ethan David, James Fabricant etc, *Screenplay* Rocco and David Lemon from a story by Lemon, *Ph* David Katznelson, *Pro Des* Morgan Kennedy, *Ed* Neil Smith, *M* Mike Batt, *Cos* Andrew Cox.

Ancient meets modern in the comedy about reacting Viking battles, *Faintheart*, sponsored by My Space and starring Eddie Marsan.

My Space/Screen West Midlands/Slingshot Productions-Vertigo Films.
88 mins. UK. 2008. Rel: 23 Jan 2008. Cert 12A.

The Fall ★★★★

An astounding, wildly imaginative art movie, with Lee Pace as an injured stuntman in a 1920s Los Angeles hospital, who tells another patient, a little girl with a broken arm, a story about five mythical heroes. Rarely has a film looked so much like a majestic artwork – it's filmed across the world on the most incredible-looking locations – and it works on the mind, too, as a reflection on the theme of falling. Be amazed, be very, very amazed. Inspired director Tarsem Singh (atoning for his previous film, the 2000 J-Lo vehicle *The Cell*) won the Best Film award at the Sitges Film Festival and the Crystal Bear from Best Feature at the Berlin Film Festival, while Colin Watkinson won the Best Cinematography award from the Austin Film Critics. These are shamefully minor awards for such a masterpiece. DW

▶ Cantinca Untaru, Justine Waddell, Lee Pace, Ronald France.
▶ *Dir* Tarsem Singh, *Pro* Singh and Lionel

Kop, *Screenplay* Singh, Dan Gilroy, Nico Soultanakis, *Ph* Colin Watknson, *Pro Des* Ged Clarke, *Ed* Robert Duffy, *M* Krishna Levy, *Cos* Eiko Ishioka.

Deep Films/Googly Films/Absolute Entertainments-Momentum Pictures.
117 mins. India/UK/USA. 2006.
Rel: 3 Oct 2008. Cert 15.

Fast and Furious ★★

The fourth in the series is more or less a repetition of the previous films with Vin Diesel back as Dominic Toretto. He is now a fugitive with Letty (Michelle Rodriguez) in the Dominican Republic but after a tragic death he is forced to return to LA. Surprisingly he soon joins forces with agent Brian O'Conner (Paul Walker) in order to capture a drug baron. It opens with a stunningly choreographed action sequence on a mountainous road but it is downhill from then on and runs out of fuel long before the final credits. GS

▶ Vin Diesel, Paul Walker, Jordana Brewster, Michelle Rodriguez, John Ortiz, Laz Alonso.
▶ *Dir* Justin Lin, *Pro* Diesel, Neal H Moritz

and Michael Fotrell, *Screenplay* Chris Morgan based on characters by Gary Scott Thompson, *Ph* Amir M Mokri, *Pro Des* Ida Random, *Ed* Fred Raskin and Christian Wagner, *M* Brian Tyler, *Cos* Sanja Milkovic Hayes.

Universal Pictures/Original Film/Relativity Media/One Race Productions-Universal Pictures International.
107 mins. USA. 2009. Rel: 10 Apr 2009. Cert 15.

FAQ About Time Travel
★ ★ ★

Ray (Chris O'Dowd) spends most of his time in the pub with his friends Toby (Marc Wootton) and Pete (Dean Lennox Kelly) .He is obsessed with time travel and can't believe his luck when Cassie (Anna Faris), an attractive and mysterious young woman claims that she is from the future. The three actors work well together but it is Faris whose unconventional presence provides the exact amount of eccentricity. Director Gareth Carrivick injects enough energy and gusto to make the silly but fun story very watchable. GS

▶ Chris O'Dowd, Marc Wootton, Dean Lennox Kelly, Anna Faris, Dario Attanasio, John Snowden, John Warman.
▶ *Dir* Gareth Carrivick, *Pro* Neil Peplow and Justin Anderson Smith, *Screenplay* Jamie Mathieson, *Ph* John Pardue, *Pro Des* Kane Quinn, *Ed* Chris Blunden and Stuart Gazzard, *M* James L Venable, *Cos* Stephanie Collie.

BBC Films/Dog Lamp Films/HBO Films-Lionsgate
83 mins. UK. 2009. Rel: 24 Apr 2009. Cert 15.

Far North ★ ★ ★

Director Asif Kapadia who so impressed with his debut feature *The Warrior* in 2001 here reunites with photographer Roman Osin but the Arctic regions replace India as the setting. The landscapes are great but despite good performances the storytelling power of the earlier film goes missing in this awkwardly oblique and underpowered tale involving two women and a man. The extreme drama of

the conclusion comes as a surprise but seems to belong to another film altogether. MS

▶ Michelle Yeoh, Michelle Krusiec, Sean Bean, Gary Pillai, Bjarne Østerud.
▶ *Dir* Asif Kapadia, *Pro* Bertrand Faivre, *Screenplay* Kapadia and Tim Miller based on Sara Maitland's story *True North*, *Ph* Roman Osin, *Pro Des* and *Cos* Ben Scott, *Ed* Ewa J. Lind, *M* Dario Marianelli.

Ingenious Film Partners/Film4/Celluloid Dreams/The Bureau etc.-Soda Pictures.
89 mins. UK/France/Norway. 2007.
Rel: 26 Dec 2008. Cert 15.

Fear(s) of the Dark ★ ★ ★ ★

This underestimated and fascinating animated feature blends material by ten graphic artists working largely in black and white to create a dream-like world. Inevitably, it's not all equally effective but its nightmare quality, stopping short of out-and-out horror, is atmospheric and intriguing and indeed the material, whether consisting of complete tales or of fragments, casts its own spell. Guillermo Del Toro of *Pan's Labyrinth* liked it, and why not? (Original title: *Peur(s) du noir*). MS

▶ With the voices of Aure Atika, Guillaume Depardieu, Arthur H, Nicole Garcia, Louisa Pili.
▶ *Dir* Blutch, Charles Burns, Marie Caillou, Pierre Di Sciullo, Lorenzo Mattotti and Richard McGuire, *Pro* Valérie Schermann and Christophe Jankovic, *Screenplay* Blutch, Burns, Romain Slocombe, Di Sciullo, Jerry Kramsky, McGuire and Michel Pirus, *Art Dir* Céline Puthier and Jean-Michel Ponzio, *Ed* Céline Kelepikis, *M* René Aubry, Boris Gronemberger and others, *Animation* Vincent Carré, Haojun Zhou and many others.

A Prima Linea Productions, La Parti Production, Def2shoot , Denis Friedman Productions production etc.- Metrodome Distribution.
83 mins. France/Belgium. 2007.
Rel: 3 Oct 2008. Cert 12A.

Fermat's Room ★★★½

Assembled by invitation to solve a mathematical enigma, a group of distinguished mathematicians find themselves trapped in a room with the walls closing in on them. It's not a horror film but the novel emphasis on mathematical problems doesn't conceal the fact that at heart this is a less exciting reworking of Agatha Christie's classic *And Then There Were None*. It's ably done but not so engaging as René Clair's 1945 film of the Christie piece. (Original title: *La habitación de Fermat*). MS

‣ Lluís Homar, Alejo Sauras, Elena Ballesteros, Federico Luppi, Santi Millán.
‣ *Dir* and *Written by* Luis Piedrahita and Rodrigo Sopeña, *Pro* José Maria Irisarri. Adolfo Blanco and César Benítez, *Ph* Migue Amoedo, *Art Dir* Nestor Medeira, *Ed* Jorge Macaya, *M* Federico Jusid and Ale Martí, *Cos* Santos Sánchez.

Notro Films/Bocaboca Producciones S.A. production etc.-Revolver Entertainment. 88 mins. Spain. 2007. Rel: 29 May 2009. Cert 12A.

Fifty Dead Men Walking ★★★

Belfast in the 1980s is the setting for this tale of Martin McGartland, recruited by the British to inform on the IRA who were grooming him as one of their own. Suggested by the real-life McGartland's book, it is not actually based on it and where McQueen's *Hunger* was manifestly serious this plays like a popular action movie trading on tragic events. The accents are authentic enough to be troublesome but the role of the recruiter finds Sir Ben Kingsley on top form yet again. MS

‣ Ben Kingsley, Jim Sturgess, Kevin Zegers, Natalie Press, Rose McGowan, Tom Collins.
‣ *Dir* and *Written by* Kari Skogland, inspired by the book by Martin McGartland and Nicholas Davies, *Pro* Peter La Terriere,Skogland, Steve Hegyesand Shawn Williamson, *Ph* Jonathan Freeman, *Pro Des*

Eve Stewart, *Ed* Jim Munro, *M* Ben Mink, *Cos* Stephanie Collie.

HandMade Films International/a Future Films amd Brightlight Pictures production etc.-Metrodome Distribution. 117 mins. UK/Canada/USA. 2008. Rel: 10 April 2009. Cert 15.

Fighting ★★★½

Dito Montiel's hard-hitting drama tells the story of Shawn MacArthur (Channing Tatum). He is new in New York and finds it hard to make a living until he meets con artist Harvey Boarden (Terrence Howard) who promotes his talent for street fighting. The violent scenes, which bring to mind *Fight Club* and last year's stinker *Never Back Down*, are well balanced with the tender love scenes. Despite the fact that Tatum mumbles his way through the film, he is still one of the most exciting young actors of recent years. GS

‣ Channing Tatum, Terrence Howard, Zulay Henao, Flaco Navaja, Peter Tambakis.
‣ *Dir* Dito Montiel, *Pro* Kevin Misher, *Screenplay* Montiel and Robert Munic, *Ph* Stefan Czapsky, *Pro Des* Thérèse DePrez, *Ed* Saar Klein and Jake Pushinsky, *M* Jonathan Elias and David Wittman, *Cos* Kurt and Bart.

Misher Films/Relativity Media/Rogue Pictures-Universal Pictures International. 105 mins. USA. 2009. Rel: 15 May 2009. Cert 15.

Fine, Totally Fine ★★★½

"Life is more fun if you are an idiot," claims Teruo (YosiYosi Arakawa) in this eccentric Japanese comedy. He works part time as a manual worker and spends most of his time dreaming of building a haunted theme park or playing spooky pranks on his friends and family. Meanwhile, oversensitive hospital manager Hisanobu (Yoshinori Okada) finds his match when he meets accident-prone she-nerd Akari (Yoshino Kimura) . Fujita's unpredictable comedy is enjoyable thanks to

Channing Tatum packs punch as a street fighter in *Fighting*.

its colourful characters but it overstays its welcome towards the end. (Original title: *Zenzen Daijobu*). GS

▶ YosiYosi Arakawa, Yoshino Kimura, Yoshinori Okada, Noriko Eguchi, Shima Ise, Kitaro.
▶ *Dir* and *Screenplay* Yosuke Fujita, *Ph* Yoshihiro Ikeuchi, *Pro Des* China Hayashi, *M* E Komo Mai.

Third World Films-Third Window Films. 110 mins. Japan. 2008. Rel: 14 Nov 2008. Cert 15.

Fireflies in the Garden
★ ★ ★

For much of its length this first feature, a family drama from writer/director Dennis Lee, works well even if it lacks the impact of *You Can Count On Me* (2000), a film which he admires. A cast of largely familiar names (Julia Roberts appears in a key supporting role) do their best. Ultimately, however, it's a story about a son's relationship with his horrendous father and the film's attempt to soften our responses to this man drives it way off track. MS

▶ Ryan Reynolds, Willem Dafoe, Emily Watson, Julia Roberts, Carie-Anne Moss, Ioan Gruffudd.
▶ *Dir* and *Written by* Dennis Lee, *Pro* Marco Weber, Vanessa Coifman and Sukee Chew, *Ph* Danny Moder, *Pro Des* Rob Pearson, *Ed* Dede Allen and Robert Brakey, *M* Javier Navarrete, *Cos* Kelle Kutsugeras.

Senator Entertainment/Kulture Machine/a Marco Weber production-The Works UK Distribution.
99 mins. USA/Germany. 2007. Rel: 29 May 2009. Cert 15.

Flame & Citron ★ ★ ★ ½

The title refers to the nicknames of two members of a resistance group in Copenhagen in 1944. Their true story comes across as embellished although not so excessively as happened with *Black Book* and *Female Agents*. It has exaggerated moments but in general it's a well made and well acted picture which will appeal to those who like their Second World War dramas to be given a somewhat heightened treatment. MS

▶ Thure Lindhardt, Mads Mikkelsen. Stine Stengade, Hanns Zischler, Christian Berkel, Peter Mygind.
▶ *Dir* Ole Christian Madsen, *Pro* Lars Bredo

Michael Caine and Demi Moore plot a diamond heist in Michael Radford's *Flawless.*

Rahbek, *Screenplay* Lars K. Anderson and Madsen, *Ph* Jørgen Johansson, *Pro Des* Jette Lehmann, *Ed* Søren B. Ebbe, *M* Karsten Fundal, *Cos* Manon Rasmussen.

Nimbus Film/Wüste Filmproduktion etc.-Metrodome Distribution.
136 mins. Denmark/Germany/Norway/France/Sweden/Finland/Czech Republic. 2008. Rel: 6 March 2009. Cert 15.

Flash of Genius ★★★½

This tells the real life story of what it cost Robert Kearns and his family when they took on the motor giant Ford claiming that the company had appropriated Kearns's invention, an intermittent windscreen wiper which came into universal use. This engagingly individual film echoes Hitchcock's *The Wrong Man* and other small-scale movies of the 1950s. The script could be tighter yet more detailed, but this is an attractive, well acted film. MS

▶ Greg Kinnear, Lauren Graham, Dermot Mulroney, Alan Alda, Jake Abel.
▶ *Dir* Marc Abraham, *Pro* Gary Barber, Roger Birnbaum and Michael Lieber, *Written by* Philip Railsback based on the *New Yorker*

article by John Seabrook, *Ph* Dante Spinotti, *Pro Des* Hugo Luczyc-Wyhowski, *Ed* Jill Savitt, *M* Aaron Zigman, *Cos* Luis Sequeira.

Universal Pictures and Spyglass Entertainment/a Strike Entertainment production etc.-Optmum Releasing.
119 mins. USA. 2008. Rel: 20 March 2009. Cert 12A.

Flawless ★★

London; the early 1960s. Having been passed over for promotion, diamond executive Laura Quinn (Demi Moore) teams up with a janitor to steal a hefty haul of her company's priceless rock candy. After a promising start, this middle-aged caper settles for misty-eyed nostalgia in lieu of suspense. Unfortunately, the machinations of the couple prove more audacious than ingenious, while Michael Caine's wily, engaging presence provides the only real reason to catch this piece of old-fashioned fluff. JC-W

▶ Demi Moore, Michael Caine, Lambert Wilson, Nathaniel Parker, Joss Ackland, Shaughan Seymour, Nicholas Jones, David Barras.
▶ *Dir* Michael Radford, *Pro* Michael A Pierce and Mark Williams, *Screenplay* Edward

Anderson, *Ph* Richard Greatrex, *Pro Des* Sophie Becher, *Ed* Peter Boyle, *M* Stephen Warbeck, *Cos* Ul Simon.

Pierce-Williams Entertainment/Blue Rider Entertainment/Delux Productions etc-Metrodome Distribution.
108 mins. UK/Luxembourg. 2007.
Rel: 28 Nov 2007. Cert PG.

Fly Me to the Moon ★★★

Ben Stassen's likeable and entertaining animated feature looks good in 3-D and IMAX. It tells the story of housefly Nat who, inspired by his Grandpa's heroic stories, sneaks into Apollo 11 with his friends Scooter and IQ for a spaceship mission to the moon. It is all great fun but the message is overly patriotic with far too much American flag waving. Also the Russian subplot is totally redundant despite Tim Curry's effective voicing of villain Yegor. GS

▶ Voices of Tim Curry, Robert Patrick, Trevor Gagnon, Philip Bolden, Nicollette Sheridan, Christopher Lloyd, Adrienne Barbeau, Kelly Ripa
▶ *Dir* Ben Stasen, *Pro* Gina Gallo, Charlotte Huggins, Mimi Maynard, Caroline Van Iseghem, *Screenplay* Domonic Paris, *Pro Des* Jeremy Degruson, *M* Ramin Djawadi.

nWave Pictures/Illuminata Pictures-Momentum Pictures.
84 mins. Belgium. 2008.
Rel: 3 Oct 2008. Cert PG.

The Foot Fist Way ★

A no-budget mockumentary about a bungling martial arts instructor (Danny McBride), this shoots for the same awkward, real-life vibe as *The Office*, but misses by a mile. Every joke is so clearly signposted in advance, there are no surprises at all. Half the time, the filmmakers don't even appear to be trying to make us laugh. It's a fun idea done really poorly. MJ

▶ Danny McBride, Ben Best, Mary Jane Bostic, Jody Hill, Sean Baxter, Deborah Loates.

▶ *Dir* Jody Hill, *Pro* Jennifer Chikes, Erin Coates, Jody Hill and Robbie Hill, *Screenplay* McBride, Best and Jody Hill, *Ph* Brian Mandle, *Pro Des* Randy Gambill, *Ed* Zene Baker and Jeff Seibenick, *M* The Dynamite Brothers and Pyramid, *Cos* Johnna Lynn Gross.

MTV Films/Gary Sanchez Productions etc-Momentum Pictures.
85 mins. USA. 2006. Rel: 26 Sep 2008. Cert 15.

The Forbidden Kingdom ★★★

A child-friendly martial arts epic with *Karate Kid* stylings, this sees *Sky High*'s Michael Angarano magically transported back to ancient China, hooking up with several hero types in a bid to rescue a righteous king from an evil warlord. Notable as the first movie in which Kung Fu legends Jackie Chan and Jet Li have crossed paths; though it's woefully underwritten, visually it ticks all the right boxes, and action-wise there's much to enjoy. MJ

▶ Jet Li, Michael Angarano, Jackie Chan, Yifei Liu, Collin Chou, Bing Bing Li.
▶ *Dir* Rob Minkoff, *Pro* Casey Silver, *Screenplay* John Fusco, *Ph* Peter Pau, *Pro Des* Bill Brzeski, *Ed* Eric Strand, *M* David Buckley, *Cos* Shirley Chan.

Casey Silver Productions/China Film Production Corporation/Huyai Brothers/Relativity Media-Lionsgate.
113 mins. USA/China. 2008.
Rel: 9 July 2008. Cert 12A.

Four Christmases ★

When their flight to 'the island of Burma' is delayed by fog, Brad and Kate end up having to spend Christmas day with their four respective (and dysfunctional) families... In spite of its Scroogian agenda, this grim farce ploughs painfully towards its cloying, pro-festive climax. And along the way we're treated to a gallimaufry of obvious, crude and heavy-handed slapstick. But then the film might just be plying a political agenda to elucidate why foreigners so despise America. JC-W

Vince Vaughn, Reese Witherspoon, Robert Duvall, Sissy Spacek, Jon Voight, Jon Favreau, Mary Steenburgen, Kristen Chenoweth, Dwight Yoakam.

Dir Seth Gordon, Pro Gary Barber, Roger Birnbaum, Jonathan Glickman, Vaughn and Witherspoon, Screenplay Matthew R Allen, Caleb Wilson, Jon Lucas and Scott Moore, from a story by Allen and Wilson, Ph Jeffrey L Kimball, Pro Des Shepherd Frankel, Ed Mark Helfrich, M Alex Wurman, Cos Sophie Carbonell.

Birnbaum/Barber/New Line Cinema/ Ott Medien/Spyglass Entertainment etc-Warner Bros Pictures. 88 mins. USA/Germany. 2008. Rel: 26 Nov 2008. Cert 12A.

The Fox and the Child
★ ★ ★ ★

Luc Jacquet, who made the splendid documentary *March of the Penguins,* enters dangerous territory here: the film, although featuring a girl rather than a boy, nevertheless reflects his own childhood experience when in the mountains of Ain he established a life-enhancing rapport with a fox. Part documentary and part fable, the film works well against the odds avoiding whimsy and having in eleven year old Bertille Noël-Bruneau a child with the right gravitas. And it looks beautiful too. (Original title: *Le renard et l'enfant*). MS

Bertille Noël-Bruneau, Thomas Laliberté and with the voice of Kate Winslet (narrator in English language version).

Dir Luc Jacquet, Pro Yves Darondeau, Christophe Lioud and Emmanuel Priou, Screenplay Jacquet and Eric Rognard from Jacquet's story, Ph Gérard Simon, Eric Dumage and François Royet, Art Dir Marc Thiebault, Ed Sabine Emiliani, M Evgueni Galperine, Alice Lewis and David Reyes, Cos Pascale Arrou.

A Bonne Pioche Productions/France 3 Cinema production/Wild Bunch etc.-Pathé Distribution.

94 mins. France. 2007. Rel: 8 Aug 2008. Cert U.

Franklyn ★ ★ ½

Ambitious, yes; successful, no. Gerald McMorrow conceived this first feature by envisaging a climax involving a struggle during an assassination attempt and then went back to find various narrative threads that would converge at this point. They emerge thinly and limply however and a good cast can't save this from being a disappointing viewing experience even if it is different enough to earn a mark for trying. MS

Ryan Phillippe, Eva Green, Sam Riley, Bernard Hill, Susannah York, Kika Markham, Art Malik.

Dir and Written by Gerald McMorrow, Pro Jeremy Thomas, Ph Ben Davis, Pro Des Laurence Dorman, Ed Peter Christelis, M Joby Talbot, Cos Léonie Hartard.

Recorded Picture Company/UK Film Council/ Film4/HanWay Films etc.-Contender Entertainment Group. 98 mins. UK/Cayman Islands. 2008. Rel: 27 Feb 2009. Cert 15.

Free Jimmy ★ ★ ★

Cartoon and might even bewilder some non-Scandinavian audiences, but it's a lot of quirky fun with big laughs, while the eccentrically chosen English language voices – Woody Harrelson, Phil Daniels, Kyle MacLachlan, Samantha Morton, Jim Broadbent and Simon Pegg among them – add a useful layer of oddball entertainment. DW

Voices of Woody Harrelson, Jeremy Price, Simon Pegg, Emilia Fox, David Tennant, Jay Simpson, Kyle MacLachlan, Samantha Morton, Jim Broadbent, Kris Marshall.

Dir Christopher Nielsen, Pro Lars Andreas Hellebust, Screenplay Nielsen and Pegg (English screenplay), Pro Des Mikael Holmberg, Ed Alastair Reid, M Simon Boswell.

AnimagicNet A/S/Free Jimmy Productions/
Modelink/Storm Studio-Break Thru Films.
86 mins. Norway/UK. 2006. Rel: 17 Oct 2008.
Cert 15.

French Film ★ ★ ★ ★

Hack journalist and aspiring novelist
Jed Winter is researching the *oeuvre* of
the romantic French filmmaker Thierry
Grimandi. And the more Jed probes the
director's work, the more he finds in
common with his own unravelling love
life... Hugh Bonneville has come to embody
a certain dishevelled, uncertain, embarrassed
Englishness, like a quotidian Colin Firth.
Here, he and his marvellous co-stars are
given some rich comic material which first-
time director Jackie Oudney streamlines to
perfection. Strong silences are punctuated
by sublime comic moments, while London
is transformed into France before our
eyes. A romantic comedy delicately fine-
tuned. Favourite line: 'Racism is borne out
of ignorance, xenophobia is borne out of
knowledge.' JC-W

▶ Adrian Annis, Hugh Bonneville, Eric
Cantona, Jean Dell, Anne-Marie Duff,
Victoria Hamilton, Douglas Henshall.
▶ *Dir* Jackie Oudney, *Pro* Rachel Connors,
Judy Counihan, Arvind Ethan David, Stewart
Le Marechal and Jonny Persey, *Screenplay*
Aschlin Ditta, *Ph* Sean Van Hales, *Pro Des*
Rachel Payne, *Ed* Sylvie Landra, *M* Don Ellis,
Cos Angela Billows.

Slingshot Productions/APT Films/IWC
Media/Met Film Production-Slingshot
87 mins. UK. 2008. Rel: 15 May 2009. Cert 15.

Friday the Thirteenth ★ ★

Depending on taste you'll either be cheering
or booing at the return of hockey-masked,
machete-wielding Jason Voorhees (Derek
Mears), 29 years since his first appearance.
Marcus Nispel directs this extremely gory
and chilling horror movie with plenty of
confidence, moving swiftly and slickly from
one appallingly gruesome death to another,
as college kids once again get too close
for comfort to the secrets of Camp Crystal
Lake. Jared Padalecki makes a decent hero
as the earnest young guy who arrives in the
eerie woods around the lake searching for
his missing sister (Amanda Righetti) with
the help of a nice young woman (Danielle
Panabaker), who's there with a group of
obnoxious college kids. If *Freddy vs Jason* was
part 11 of the series in 2003, this is number
12. DW

▶ Jared Papalecki, Danielle Panabaker,
Amanda Righetti, Travis Van Winkle, Aaron
Yoo, Derek Mears.
▶ *Dir* Marcus Nispel, *Pro* Michael Bay, Brad
Fuller, Andrew Form, *Screenplay* Damian
Shannon and Mark Swift from a story by
Shannon, Swift and Mark Wheaton, based on
characters by Victor Miller, *Ph* Daniel C Pearl,
Pro Des Jeremy Conway, *Ed* Ken Blackwell, *M*
Steve Jablonsky, *Cos* Mari-An Ceo.

MTV Films/Paramount Pictures/New Line
Cinema/Crystal Lake Entertainment/
Platinum Dunes-Paramount Pictures.
97 mins. USA. 2009. Rel: 17 Feb 2009.
Cert 18.

Frost/Nixon ★ ★ ★ ½

Peter Morgan's fascinating piece about the
television interviews in 1977 in which David
Frost was initially out-manoeuvred by his
interviewee President Nixon but which led to
the latter's post-Watergate admissions worked
splendidly in the theatre. Here in close-up
Michael Sheen is less successful in making
us accept him as Frost, but Frank Langella is
brilliant, adjusting his performance to the
screen and living the role. Well worth seeing
despite its limitations. MS

▶ Michael Sheen, Frank Langella, Kevin
Bacon, Toby Jones, Rebecca Hall, Sam Rockwell.
▶ *Dir* Ron Howard, *Pro* Tim Bevan, Eric
Fellner, Brian Glazer and Howard, *Screenplay*
Peter Morgan from his play, *Ph* Salvatore
Totino, *Pro Des* Michael Corenblith, *Ed* Mike
Hill and Dan Hanley, *M* Hans Zimmer, *Cos*
Daniel Orlandi.

Hello, good evening and goodbye: Frank Langella as tricky Dicky Nixon waves farewell while Michael Sheen as Frosty looks on in *Frost/Nixon*.

Universal Pictures/Working Title Films/
Imagine Entertainment etc.-Universal
Pictures International.
122 mins.USA/UK/France. 2008.
Rel: 23 Jan 2009. Cert 15.

F★★k ★★★½

In studying the most common of swear
words this deliberately lightweight film
nevertheless becomes a document reflecting
changes in social attitudes over the last
fifty years or so. It's clear that director Steve
Anderson favours the freedom to use strong
language in public but he provides space for
those who disagree (Pat Boone among them).
It's very much American based and like
Religulous (q.v.) designed to entertain but it
does provide food for thought. MS

▶ With Billy Connolly, Pat Boone, Kevin
Smith. Alanis Morissette, Hunter S. Thompson.
▶ *Dir* and *Pro* Steve Anderson, *Ph* Andre
Fontanelle, *Ed* Jayne Rodericks, *M* Carvin
Knowles, *Animation* Bill Plympton.

Rainstorm Entertainment/Bad Apple Films/a
Mudflap Films production-ICA Films.
93 mins. USA. 2006. Rel: 13 Feb 2009. No Cert.

Fugitive Pieces ★★★

This heartfelt film based on Anne Michaels'
novel deals sympathetically with the long-
lasting traumas affecting Jewish survivors
of the Second World War. Apparently
it's a free adaptation by director Jeremy
Podeswa and on film the attempt to suggest
memories by frequent cuts between past
and present is arbitrary enough to impede
flow. Furthermore a decidedly fictional tone
colours those scenes concerning the central
character's love life so the work achieves less
than one had hoped.
MS

▶ Stephan Dillane, Rade Sherbedgia,
Rosamund Pike, Aylet Zurer, Ed Stoppard,
Robbie Kay.
▶ *Dir* and *Written by* Jeremy Podeswa from
the novel by Anne Michaels, *Pro* Robert
Lantos, *Ph* Gregory Middleton, *Pro Des*
Matthew Davies, *Ed* Wiebke Von Carolsfeld,
M Nikos Kypourgos, *Cos* Anne Dixon.

Serendipity Point Films/Strada Films/
Cinegram S.A. etc.-Soda Pictures.
106 mins. Canada/Greece. 2007.
Rel: 29 May 2009.
Cert 15.

Funuke: Show Me Some Love, You Losers! ★★

This may be a film that doesn't travel since this tale of a dysfunctional Japanese family in the wake of a car crash which has killed the parents is half way between drama and black comedy in a way that for me prevents either from working. Some really nasty behaviour freezes our smiles while sympathy is not sufficiently kindled to involve us on the serious level. Japanese audiences may respond differently. MS

‣ Sato Eriko, Satsukawa Aimi, Nagase Masatoshi, Nagasaku Hiromi, Yamamoto Horoshi.
‣ *Dir* and *Screenplay* Yoshida Daihachi, *Pro* Kakimoto Shuji, Konishi Keisuke and Suzuki Yutaka, *Ph* Ato Masakazu, *Art Dir* Harada Yasuaki, *Ed* Okada Kumi, *M* Suzuki Soichiro.

Monster Films-Third Window Films. 113 mins. Japan. 2007. Rel: 1 May 2009. No Cert.

Gardens in Autumn ★★½

The films of Russian-born, French-based Otar Iosseliani are an acquired taste and he's a true auteur whose world is not mine. Here an initially promising satire on ministerial office yields to an over-extended and ineffective if Renoiresque tale about an ex-minister finding happiness when he becomes unemployed. There's the unexpected sight of Michel Piccoli in drag inviting comparison with Alastair Sim as headmistress of St Trinian's, but this slow-moving, uncompromising piece is strictly for Iosseliani's admirers. MS

‣ Séverin Blanchet, Michel Piccoli, Muriel Motte, Otar Iosseliani, Lily Lavina
‣ *Dir* and *Screenplay* Otar Iosseliani, *Pro* Martine Marignac, *Ph* William Lubtchansky, *Art Dir* Manu de Chauvigny with Yves Brover, *Ed* Iosseliani and Ewa Lenkiewicz, *M* Nicolas Zourabichvili, *Cos* Maira Ramedhan-Levi.

Pierre Grise Productions/Cinemaundici/ Cinema Without Frontiers LLC etc.-Artificial Eye Film Company.

121 mins. France/Italy/Russia. 2006. Rel: 26 Dec 2008. Cert PG.

Genova ★★½

This disappointingly unengaging work suggests *Don't Look Now* without the horror and *The Son's Room* without the involving characterisation as it shows a father and his two daughters moving to Genoa as they try to adjust to the mother's death in a car crash. As an admirer of director Michael Winterbottom and not least of his *Wonderland*, also written with Laurence Coriat, it saddens me to have to regard this as a complete misfire despite the talented cast. MS

‣ Colin Firth, Catherine Keener, Willa Holland, Perla Haney-Jardine, Hope Davis.
‣ *Dir* Michael Winterbottom, *Pro* Andrew Eaton, *Screenplay* Laurence Coriat and Winterbottom, *Ph* Marcel Zyskind, *Pro Des* Mark Digby, *Ed* Paul Monaghan and Winterbottom, *M* Melissa Parmenter, *Cos* Celia Yau.

Film4/UK Film Council/Aramid Entertainment/HanWay Films/a Revolution Films production etc.-Metrodome Distribution. 94 mins. UK/Cayman Islands. 2008. Rel: 27 March 2009. Cert 15.

Get Smart ★★★

Maxwell Smart is a secret agent who's smart if not very adroit. He's a whole level above Inspector Clouseau, but can he save Los Angeles from the evil clutches of a ruthless Chechnyan egomaniac? The first film based on the eponymous 1965-1970 TV series – *The Nude Bomb* (1980) – was a flop. This one, in the capable hands of Steve Carell, has a suitably discombobulated hero (who loves ABBA) and a surprisingly gripping storyline. Good support, too, from Johnson and Arkin. JC-W

‣ Steve Carell, Anne Hathaway, Dwayne Johnson, Alan Arkin, Terence Stamp, James Caan, Bill Murray.

▶ *Dir* Peter Segal, *Pro* Alex Gartner and
Michael Ewing, *Screenplay* Tom J Astle and
Matt Ember, based on characters created by
Mel Brooks and Buck Henry, *Ph* Dean Semler,
Pro Des Wynn Thomas, *Ed* Richard Pearson,
M Trevor Rabin, *Cos* Deborah Lynn Scott.

**Warner Bros Pictures/Village Roadshow
Pictures/Mosaic Media Group etc-Warner
Bros. Pictures.
110 mins. USA. 2008. Rel: 22 Aug 2008. Cert 12A.**

Ghost Town ★★★★

Bertram Pincus (Gervais) is a dentist whose
people skills leave a lot to be desired.
Then, when he dies unexpectedly, Pincus is
miraculously revived after seven minutes,
waking up to discover that he now has
the annoying habit of seeing ghosts...
Here comes Mr Gervais in his first starring
role and proves more than up to the task.

Open wide,
please. Ricky
Gervais, in his
feature debut,
as a dentist
who returns
from the dead
in *Ghost Town*,
with Aasif
Mandvi and
Kristen Wiig.

Resurrecting the spectre of *Heaven Can Wait*
– with dollops of *The Sixth Sense* – this is a
surprisingly sweet, underplayed, unexpected
and very funny confection. It is perhaps the
most underrated rom-com of the year. JC-W

▶ Ricky Gervais, Greg Kinnear, Jordan Carlos,
Dequina Moore, Claire Lautier, Aasif Mandvi.
▶ *Dir* David Koepp, *Pro* Gavin Polone,
Screenplay Koepp and John Kamps, *Ph* Fred
Murphy, *Pro Des* Howard Cummings, *Ed* Sam
Seig, *M* Geoff Zanelli, *Cos* Sarah Edwards.

**DreamWorks SKG/Paramount Pictures/Pariah/
Spyglass Entertainment-Paramount Pictures.
102 mins. USA. 2008. Rel: 24 Oct 2008.
Cert 12A.**

Ghosts of Girlfriends Past ★

Poor Charles Dickens must be turning in
his grave. His *Christmas Carol* is the premise

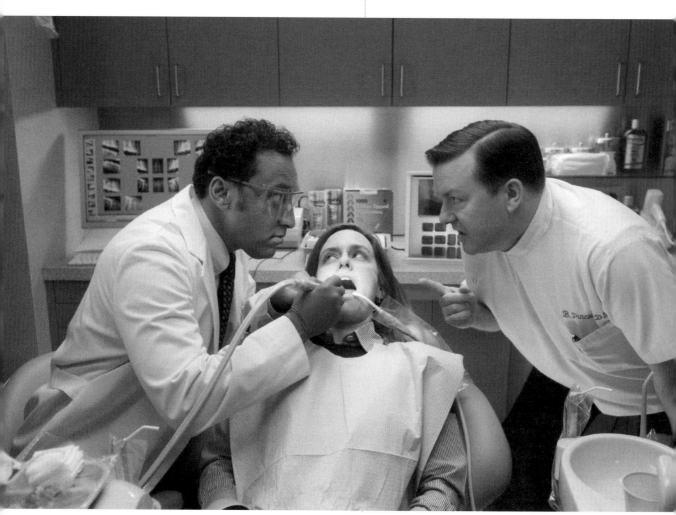

of yet another film, and in this indulgent and dull, romantic comedy Matthew McConaughey is the Scrooge-like and utterly unlikable philanderer who learns a lesson or two from his girlfriends' ghosts during his brother's wedding. The smug McConaughey is perfectly cast:"You are really as bad as they say", all the characters keep on reminding him. GS

▶ Matthew McConaughey, Jennifer Garner, Michael Douglas, Emma Stone, Robert Forster, Anne Archer.
▶ *Dir* Mark Waters, *Pro* Brad Epstein and Jonathan Shestack, *Screenplay* Jon Lucas and Scott Moore, *Ph* Daryn Okada, *Pro Des* Cary White, *Ed* Bruce Green, *M* Rolfe Kent, *Cos* Denise Wingate.

New Line Cinema/Panther-Entertainment Film Distributors.
100 mins. USA. 2009. Rel: 1 May 2009.
Cert 12A.

Gigantic ★ ★ ★

The title must be a joke since this is a quirky, small-scale American independent movie. Debutant director and co-writer Matt Aselton makes claims for his work by listing filmmakers he admires ranging from Buñuel to Lynch, but this is no more than an off-beat romantic comedy that desperately wants to be taken for a cult movie. In fact it's totally forgettable but kept afloat – just – by its leading players, Paul Dano and Zooey Deschanel. MS

▶ Paul Dano, Zooey Deschanel, John Goodman, Ed Asner, Jane Alexander.

▶ *Dir* Matt Aselton, *Pro* Mindy Goldberg and Christine Vachon, *Written by* Adam Nagata and Aselton, *Ph* Peter Donahue, *Pro Des* Rick Butler, *Ed* Beatrice Sisul, *M* Roddy Bottum, *Cos* Paola Ruby Weintraub, *Animation* Trevor Smith.

Epoch Films/Killer Films/John Wells Productions-The Works UK Distribution.
98 mins. USA. 2008. Rel: 19 June 2009.
Cert 15.

The Girl Cut in Two
★ ★ ★ ★

Like *A Comedy of Power* this is another Claude Chabrol work made with great efficiency that nevertheless obstinately refuses to lodge in the memory. This time around it's a tale about a TV weather forecaster played by Ludivine Sagnier who is pursued by two very different men, an older author ready to betray his wife and a younger man who belongs to the idle rich. What will be the outcome and who will die (there's a musical pointer to a death at the start)? We are curious enough to enjoy the tale but never become emotionally involved with the characters. MS

▶ Ludivine Sagnier, Benoît Magimel, François Berléand, Mathilda May, Caroline Silol.
▶ *Dir* Claude Chabrol, *Pro* Patrick Godeau, *Screenplay* Cécile Maistre and Chabrol, *Ph* Eduardo Serra, *Art Dir* Françoise Benoît-Fresco, *Ed* Monique Fardoulis, *M* Matthieu Chabrol, *Cos* Mic Cheminal.

Alicéleo Cinéma/Alicéleo/France2 Cinéma/ Rhône-Alpes Cinéma/Integral Film GmbH co-production etc.-Artificial Eye Film Company.
115 Mins. France/Germany. 2006.
Rel: 22 May 2009. Cert 15.

The Girl in the Park ★ ★ ½

There's a good cast here and a potentially interesting idea for a drama: a mother traumatised by the disappearance of her infant daughter who, fifteen years on, comes to believe that a young stranger is in fact the missing child. Unfortunately David Auburn, making an unpromising debut as director, has written a screenplay so lacking in likelihood and so built on coincidence that belief soon fritters away. MS

▶ Sigourney Weaver, Kate Bosworth, Alessandro Nivola, Keri Russell, Elias Koteas.
▶ *Dir* and *Written by* David Auburn, *Pro* Sean Furst, Bryan Furst and Dale Rosenbloom, *Ph* Stuart Dryburgh, *Pro Des* Kelly McGehee, *Ed* Kristina Boden, *M* Theodore Shapiro, *Cos* Michelle Matland.

Open Pictures/a Furst Films production/a Witox Film Produktions GmbH & Co KG production-Unanimous Pictures.
110 mins. USA/Germany/Singapore. 2007. Rel: 5 Dec 2008. Cert 15.

The Girl Who Leapt Through Time ★★★

Following an accident, teenage girl Makoto acquires the ability to travel back in time and change events in her life. Based on a novel by Japanese science fiction author Yasutaka Tsutsui, Mamoru Hosoda's irritatingly convoluted anime feature runs into one time travel loop too many somewhere beyond its first reel. *Neon Genesis Evangelion* veteran Yoshiyuki Sadamoto contributes visually arresting character designs.
(Original title: *Toki o Kakeru Shojo*). JC

➤ Voices of Riisa Naka, Takuya Ishida, Mitsutaka Itakura, Ayami Kakiuchi.
➤ *Dir* Mamoru Hosoda, *Pro* Shinichiro Inoue and Jungo Maruta, *Screenplay* Satoko Okudera, from the story by Yasutaka Tsutsui, *Ph* Tomita Yoshihiro, *Ed* Shigeru Nishiyama, *M* Kiyoshi Yoshida.

House/Happinet Pictures/Kado Kawa Pictures etc-Manga Entertainment.
98 mins. Japan. 2008. Rel: 19 Sep 2008. Cert 12A.

Gomorrah ★★★½

Although arguably lucky to have carried off the Grand Prix at Cannes, this Italian drama by Matteo Garrone is a powerful work that cleverly combines five tales to illustrate the power of the Camorra, the Naples equivalent of the Mafia. Given the length of 137 minutes, it's a pity that the last section features one of the less engaging plot lines since the preceding episode would have provided a far stronger climax.
(Original title: *Gomorra*). MS

➤ Toni Servillo, Gianfelice Imparato, Maria Nazionale, Salvatore Abruzzese, Carmine Paternoster, Salvatore Cantalupo, Marco Macor, Ciro Petrone, Simone Sacchettino.

➤ *Dir* Matteo Garrone, *Pro* Domenico Procacci, *Screenplay* Maurizio Braucci, Roberto Saviano, Garrone and others from Saviano's book *Gomorra*, *Ph* Marco Onorato, *Art Dir* Paolo Bonfini, *Ed* Marco Spoletini, *Cos* Alessandra Cardini.

A Fandango production/Rai Cinema etc.-Optimum Releasing.
137 mins. Italy. 2008. Rel: 10 Oct 2008. Cert 15.

Gonzo: The Life and Work of Dr Hunter S Thompson ★★★½

The iconic writer who killed himself in 2005 is now the subject of this often intriguing documentary portrait. It's a warts and all picture but one that despite its arguably excessive length never quite nails its complex subject. However, those who admire the author of *Fear and Loathing in Las Vegas* and his so-called gonzo style of journalism will find much of interest here. MS

➤ With Ralph Steadman, Sondi Wright, Tom Wolfe, Jimmy Carter, George McGovern, Charles Perry, Pat Buchanan and narration by Johnny Depp.
➤ *Dir* and *Screenplay* (from the words of Hunter S Thompson) Alex Gibney, *Pro* Gibney, Graydon Carter, Jason Kliot and others, *Ph* Maryse Alberti, *Pro Des*(*NY Studio Shoots*) Amanda Ford, *Ed* Alison Ellwood, *M* David Schwartz.

HDNet Films/Jigsaw Productions/ Consolidated Documentaries, Inc. etc.-Optimum Releasing.
120 mins. USA/UK/Japan. 2008. Rel: 19 Dec 2008. Cert 15.

Good ★★★

For producer Miriam Segal, bringing the late C P Taylor's play to the screen has been a labour of love and Viggo Mortensen is superb in it. Consequently it's sad to have to say that the film as a whole, set in Germany in the 1930s, is frustratingly inadequate. Where *Mephisto* (1981) succeeded brilliantly,

I love the smell of hot pants in the morning: Marco Macor and Ciro Petrone in Matteo Garrone's Cannes Grand Prix winning *Gomorrah*.

this film tracing how a well-meaning writer becomes a puppet of the Nazi propaganda machine lacks conviction. There are too many misjudgments in the plotting and a disastrous use of English by supposedly German characters who sound unreal. MS

▶ Viggo Mortensen, Jason Isaacs, Jodie Whittaker, Steven Mackintosh, Mark Strong, Gemma Jones.
▶ *Dir* Vicente Amorim, *Pro* Miriam Segal and others, *Screenplay* John Wrathall from C P Taylor's stage play, *Ph* Andrew Dunn, *Pro Des* Andrew Laws, *Ed* John Wilson, *M* Simon Lacey, *Cos* Györgyi Szakács.

Aramid Entertainment/a Good Films production/ Miromar Entertainment etc.-Lionsgate. 96 mins. UK/Germany/USA/Hungary/ Cayman Islands. 2007. Rel: 17 April 2009. Cert 15.

Good Dick ★ ★

What fifty years ago would have been an innocuous title now suggests either an outrageous sex comedy or a porn movie but Marianna Palka's film is neither. She plays a purchaser of porn videos who causes the young salesman to fall in love with her at first sight, although she shows little sign of reciprocating his feelings. Any potential interest is destroyed by the coincidences, contrivances and sheer improbabilities that feature in Palka's screenplay. MS

▶ Marianna Palka, Jason Ritter, Eric Edelstein, Martin Starr, Mark Webber, Tom Arnold.
▶ *Dir* and *Written by* Marianna Palka, *Pro* Jennifer Dubin, Cora Olson, Palka and Jason Ritter, *Ph* Andre Lascaris, *Pro Des* Andrew Trosmans, *Ed* Christopher Kroll, *M* Jared Nelson Smith, *Cos* Daphne Javitch.

Morning Knight and Present Pictures etc.- The Works UK Distribution. 86 mins. USA. 2008. Rel: 3 Oct 2008. Cert 15.

The Good, the Bad, the Weird ★ ★ ★ ★

The plot and characters of *The Good, the Bad and the Ugly* are gleefully ripped off for this incredibly full-on, all-guns-blazing South Korean story that's now set in 1930s Manchuria and about three Korean outlaws who try to survive in the face of the Japanese army and both Chinese and Russian bandits. Brilliantly done and hugely thrilling for action fans, this exciting and constantly

All dressed up and nowhere to go in *The Good, the Bad, the Weird*, a South Korean remake of you know what.

surprising movie is a non-stop rollercoaster of (often sick) laughs and violent thrills. Woo-sung Jung is The Good, Byung-hun Lee The Bad and Kang-ho Song The Weird: all three are good, but Song steals the movie in the showiest role. In the snazziest looking of films, the photography and visual effects are state of the art. DW

‣ Kang-ho Song, Byung-hun Lee, Woo-sung Jung, Kyeong-hun Jo, Kwang-il Jim.
‣ *Dir* Ji-woon Kim, *Pro* Jae-won Choi, *Screenplay* Ji-woon Kim, Min-suk Kim, *Ph* Mo-gae Lee and Seung-chui Oh, *Pro Des* Hwa Na-young, *Ed* Nam Na-young, *M* Dalparan and Yeong-gyu Jang, *Costumes* Choi Eui-yeong and Yu-jin Gweon.

Grimm Pictures/Cineclick Asia/Barunson/ CJ Entertainment-Tartan Films. 120 mins. South Korea. 2008. Rel: 6 Feb 2009. Cert 15.

Gran Torino ★★★★

If, as he has declared, Clint Eastwood's performance in this film is his last, he goes out on a high. The film set in Michigan shows a Korean War veteran (Eastwood) at odds with modern life and with neighbours

from Laos. It's a drama about this man's ultimate redemption told with a fair amount of humour but it's essentially serious, not least when it comes to the unexpected and compelling climax. MS

‣ Clint Eastwood, Bee Vang, Ahney Her, Christopher Carley, John Carroll Lynch.

‣ *Dir* Clint Eastwood, *Pro* Eastwood, Robert Lorenz and Bill Gerber, *Screenplay* Nick Schenk from a story by David Johannson and Schenk, *Ph* Tom Stern, *Pro Des* James J. Murakami, *Ed* Joel Cox and Gary D Roach, *M* Kyle Eastwood and Michael Stevens, *Cos* Deborah Hopper.

Warner Bros. Pictures/Village Roadshow Pictures/ a Double Nickel entertainment/a Malpaso production etc.-Warner Bros. Distributors. 116 mins. Germany/USA/Australia. 2008. Rel: 20 Feb 2009. Cert 15.

The Grocer's Son ★★★½

Set in Provence, this family drama from French debutant Eric Guirardo begins confusingly but then settles down as the story of a son who, having renounced country life, returns to help his mother by

Clint Eastwood's acting swan song as a Korean War veteran who just can't get on with his neighbours in *Gran Torino*.

running a mobile grocery business after his father is hospitalised. Nicolas Cazalé, so good in *Le Grand Voyage*, fails to arouse any sympathy as the dour son but the locations are well used and appealing. Consequently, this is a pleasant enough piece but one that could easily have been better.
(Original title: *Le fils de l'épicier*). MS

▶ Nicolas Cazalé, Clotilde Hesme, Daniel Duval, Liliane Rovère, Stéphan Guerin-Tillié.
▶ *Dir* Eric Guirado, *Pro* Miléna Poylo and Gilles Sacuto, *Screenplay* Guirado and Florence Vignon from Guirado's idea, *Ph* Lurent Brunet, *Art Dir* Valérie Faynot, *Ed* Pierer Haberer, *M* Christophe Boutin, *Cos* Ann Dunsford.

TS Productions/Rhône-Alpes Cinéma/Canal+ etc.-ICA Films.
99 mins. France. 2007. Rel: 24 April 2009. Cert 12A.

Gunnin' for that No. 1 Spot ★★★

Beastie Boy Adam Yauch directs this documentary about how talented young basketball players in the US get together in Harlem's Rucker Park for the Boost Mobile Elite 24 Hoops Classic, an amateur version of the National Basketball Association's All-Star Game. The film details the journey of these young players to New York and the varying backgrounds from which they emerge to join their likeminded buddies who have just one thing in common – they're all crazy for basketball. CB

▶ Jerryd Bayless, Michael Beasley, Tyreke Evans, Robert Garcia, Donte Greene, Brandon Jennings, Jason Kidd, Kevin Love, Kyle Singler, Lance Stephenson.
▶ *Dir* Adam Yauch, *Pro* Yauch and Jon Doran, *Ph* Chris Ekstein, *Ed* Neal Usatin, Remi Gletsos and Julian Ong.

Oscilloscope Pictures-Diffusion Pictures.
90 mins. USA. 2008. Rel: 10 Oct 2008. Cert 12A.

Hancock ★★★

As a disaffected super type with no particular love of the general public, Will Smith's Hancock is taken in hand by loveable PR guru Jason Bateman in this admirable but flawed attempt at a grown-up superhero comedy. Taking an emotionally intelligent swipe at the conventions of the genre, it's watchable enough, but totally illogical,

Is this where you lost your contact lens? Will Smith does his superhero best for Jason Bateman in *Hancock*.

riddled with plot holes and not nearly as clever, insightful, fresh or dramatic as it thinks it is. MJ

▶ Will Smith, Charlize Theron, Jason Bateman, Jae Head, Eddie Marsan, David Mattey.
▶ *Dir* Peter Berg, *Pro* Smith, Akiva Goldsman, James Lassiter and Michael Mann, *Screenplay* Vy Vincent Ngo and Vince Gilligan, *Ph* Tobias Schliessler, *Pro Des* Neil Spisak, *Ed* Colby Parker Jr and Paul Rubell, *M* John Powell, *Cos* Louise Mingenbach.

Columbia Pictures/Relativity Media/Blue Light etc-Sony Pictures Entertainment. 92 mins. USA. 2008. Rel: 2 July 2008. Cert 12A

The Hangover ★ ½

A groom and his three best friends 'enjoy' a stag night in Las Vegas. Not only did this witless shambles make a fortune at the box-office but it also reaped some ecstatic reviews. Why? The film's big gags can be seen a mile off, the protagonists are implausible and repellent and the presentation of male nudity for laughs (of the fat and the decrepit) is both desperate and humiliating. The truth is that director Todd Phillips (*Road Trip*, *Starsky & Hutch*) is no Judd Apatow, let alone Buster Keaton or

Oscar Wilde. JC-W

▶ Bradley Cooper, Ed Helms, Zach Galifianakis, Justin Bartha, Heather Graham, Jeffrey Tambor, Mike Tyson.
▶ *Dir* Todd Phillips, *Pro* Phillips and Daniel Goldberg, *Screenplay* Jon Lucas and Scott Moore, *Ph* Lawrence Sher, *Pro Des* Bill Brzeski, *Ed* Debra Neil-Fisher, *M* Christophe Beck, *Cos* Louise Mingenbach.

Warner Bros Pictures/Legendary Pictures/ Green Hat Films etc-Warner Bros Pictures. 100 mins. USA. 2009. Rel: 12 June 2009. Cert 15.

Hannah Montana: The Movie ★ ★ ★

Miley Stewart (Miley Cyrus) is a hugely popular pop phenomenon whose real identity is hidden behind her secret stage persona, that of Hannah Montana. But, when the pressure of her success threatens to take over her life, her father (Billy Ray Cyrus) takes her home to Crowley Corners, Tennessee for an injection of reality and home comfort. The film is fun and it works thanks to Miley's abundance of charm and talent but more time could have been invested in the rather lazy script and direction. GS

After all her singing success Miley Cyrus flies back home to rest awhile in *Hannah Montana: The Movie*.

▶ Miley Cyrus, Billy May Cyrus, Emily Osment, Jason Earles, Mitchel Musso, Vanessa Williams, Barry Bostwick.
▶ *Dir* Peter Chelsom, *Pro* Billy Ray Cyrus, Alfred Gough and Miles Millar, *Screenplay* Dan Berendsen, based on characters by Michael Poryes, Rich Connell and Barry O'Brien, *Ph* David Hennings, *Pro Des* Caroline Hanania *Ed* Virginia Katz, *M* John Debney, *Cos* Christopher Lawrence..

Walt Disney Pictures/ It's a Laugh Productions/Millar Gough Ink/ Buena Vista International.
102 mins. USA. 2009. Rel: 1 May 2009. Cert U.

Hannah Takes the Stairs
★ ★ ★

Apparently 'mumblecore' is the word for these cheaply made independent American movies improvised by their young casts and in which words outweigh action. This one is about Hannah and her involvment with three men in turn but it's uneven and despite some good scenes it already seems rather déjà vu. It does, however, end with a quirkily original nude sequence of a couple in a bath. MS

▶ Greta Gerwig, Kent Osborne, Andrew Bujalski, Mark Duplass, Ry Russo-Young.
▶ *Dir*, *Ph* and *Ed* Joe Swanberg, *Pro* Swanberg and Anish Savjani, *Written by* Swanberg, Greta·Gerwig and Kent Osborne.

Film Science-ICA Films.
83 mins. USA. 2006. Rel: 9 Jan 2009. No Cert.

Hansel and Gretel ★ ★ ★ ★

A little girl rescues Eun-Soo (Cheon Jeong-myeong) after he crashes his car in a remote country road. Her parents and two siblings take good care of him in their 'House of Happy Children' but when he tries to go back to his car the next day he finds himself trapped in this strange place. And the behaviour of these angelic children who seem to be eating nothing but cake grows odder by the minute. This stylish chiller is atmospherically directed by Pil-sung Yim who gives the familiar fairytale a welcome twist. GS

▶ Cheon Jeong-myeong, Sim Eun-kyung, Yeong-nam Jang, Ji-hee Jin, Kyeong-ik Kim.
▶ *Dir* Pil-sung Yim, *Pro* Jae-Won Choi and Woo-sik Seo, *Screenplay* Pil sung Yim, from the story by Min-sook Kim, *Ph* Ji-yong Kim, *Pro Des* Seong-hie Ryu, *Ed* Sun-min Kim, *M* Byung-woo Lee.

Barunson Film Division/Cineclick Asia/
C J Entertainment-Terracotta Media
117 mins. South Korea. 2007.
Rel: 16 Jan 2009. Cert 15.

The Haunting in Connecticut ★ ★ ½

Allegedly based on a true story about a
haunted house, Peter Cornwell's film is a
horror by numbers job, full of gratuitous
shocks designed to scare you witless. Martin
Donovan and Virginia Madsen play Peter
and Sara Campbell, a married couple who
hightail it to Connecticut to be nearer the
hospital where their cancer-stricken son Matt
(Kyle Gallner) has his radiation treatment.
Bad move... as all kinds of things in their
new home start going bump in the night.
This is formula stuff for addicts of the genre
only. CB

▷ Virginia Madsen, Martin Donovan, Kyle
Gallner, Elias Koteas, Amanda Crew, Ty Wood.
▷ *Dir* Peter Cornwell, *Pro* Wendy Rhoads,
Andrew Trapani, Paul Brooks, Daniel
Farrands, *Screenplay* Adam Simon and Tim
Metcalfe, *Ph* Adam Swica, *Pro Des* Alicia
Keywan, *Ed* Tom Elkins, *M* Robert J Kral,
Cos Meg McMillan.

**Good Circle Films/Integrated Films and
Management-Entertainment Film Distributors.
92 mins. USA. 2009. Rel: 27 Mar 2009. Cert 15.**

Heavy Load ★ ★ ★

Documentary about metal band Heavy Load
who comprise care home residents and
support workers – and are the instigators of
the Stay Up Late campaign to allow residents
to go to such places as pubs without having
to go home before 'normal' punters owing
to support worker job demands. Compelling,
but it pales beside *Heavy Metal in Baghdad*
(qv.). JC

▷ Paul Richards, Mick Williams, Michael
White, Simon Barker, Jim Nicholls, Jerry Rothwell.
▷ *Dir* Jerry Rothwell, *Pro* Rothwell, Alison
Morrow and Jonny Persey, *Ph* Stephanie

Hardt, *Ed* Alan Mackay, *M* Max De Wardener.

**Met Films/Art Films/HiBus-Met Film.
91 mins. UK. 2008. Rel: 31 Oct 2008. Cert 12A.**

Heavy Metal in Baghdad ★ ★ ★ ★

This compelling documentary follows
Acrassicauda (which means scorpion) – the
only heavy metal band in Iraq – from 2003
when Saddam fell from power up to the
present day in Syria where the band are now
forced to live as refugees. The success of the
film lies in not only creating an accurate
portrait of these young men's determination
to perform against all odds accompanied by
falling bombs, but also in painting a clear
picture of how impossible life in Iraq is at
present. GS

▷ *Dir* Syroosh Alvi and Eddy Moretti, *Pro*
Alvi, Moretti and Monica Hampton, *Ph*
Moretti, *Ed* Bernardo Loyola, *M* Acrassicauda.

**VBS TV/Vice Films-Slingshot
84 mins. USA/Canada. 2007.
Rel: 23 May 2008. Cert 15.**

Helen ★ ★ ★

Annie Townsend triumphs in the title role
of this British debut feature from Christine
Molloy and Joe Lawler which is admirably
photographed by Ole Birkeland. Helen
is a loner who starts to identify with a
missing school girl whose role she takes
in a police re-enactment. This may sound
potentially dramatic but the tone adopted
is largely meditative. This would be fine but
unfortunately the film leaves us uncertain
as to what the aims of the filmmakers really
were. MS

▷ Annie Townsend, Sandie Malia, Denis
Jobling, Sonia Saville, Danny Groenland.
▷ *Dir*, *Pro* and *Written by* Christine Molloy
and Joe Lawler, *Ph* Ole Birkeland, *Ed* Molloy,
M Dennis McNulty.

Arts Council England/Newcastle Gateshead

Initiative/ Irish Film Board/a Desperate Optimists production etc.-New Wave Films. 79 mins. UK/Ireland. 2008. Rel: 1 May 2009. Cert PG.

Hellboy 2: The Golden Army ★★★

The epitome of style over content, with overcooked visuals and a half-baked screenplay, Guillermo del Toro's superhero sequel is a flawless, live-action representation of the world created by Mike Mignola, an artist first and writer second. Much like Big Red's printed tales, though it's beautiful to behold with atmosphere to spare, the plot and the characters never truly engage. The action's suitably slam-bang though, and Ron Perlman's blue collar demon is certainly amusing. MJ

‣ Ron Perlman, Selma Blair, Doug Jones, James Dodd, Jeffrey Tambor, Luke Goss, John Hurt, Brian Steele.
‣ *Dir* and *Screenplay* Guillermo Del Toro based on a story by Del Toro and Mike Mignola, from the comic book by Mignola, *Pro* Lawrence Gordon, Lloyd Levin, Mike Richardson and Joe Roth *Ph* Guillermo Navarro, *Pro Des* Stephen Scott, *Ed* Bernat Vilaplana, *M* Danny Elfman, *Cos* Sammy Sheldon.

Universal Pictures/Dark Horse Entertainment/ Relativity Media etc-Universal Pictures International. 120 mins. USA/Germany 2008. Rel: 20 Aug 2008. Cert 12A.

He's Just Not That Into You ★★

Baltimore; today. Nine good-looking individuals grapple with the vicissitudes of love and rejection in a merry-go-round of superficial courtship. A slick adaptation of the eponymous self-help bestseller (by Greg Behrendt and Liz Tuccillo), this provides some laughs, some insights, but very little dramatic tension. P.S. This must be the first film inspired by a line of dialogue from a TV show (*Sex and the City*). JC-W

‣ Morgan Lily, Michelle Carmichael, Trenton Rogers, Kristen Faye Hunter, Kris Kristofferson, Sabrina Revelle.
‣ *Dir* Ken Kwapis, *Pro* Nancy Juvonen, *Screenplay* Abby Kohn and Marc Silverstein, from the book by Greg Behrendt and Liz Tuccillo, *Ph* John Bailey, *Pro Des* Gae S Buckley, *Ed* Cara Silverman, *M* Cliff Eidelman, *Cos* Shay Cunliffe.

Flower Films/Internationale Filmproduktion Black Swan/Sessions Payroll Management-Entertainment Film Distributors. 129 mins. USA/Germany/Netherlands. 2009. Rel: 6 Feb 2009. Cert 12A.

The Hide ★★★

This film from Joseph Losey's grandson Marek features a screenplay by Tim Whitnall which, essentially a two-hander, suggests the early work of Harold Pinter written for radio. Two strangers, an ornithologist and an intruder, meet in the former's hide in rural Suffolk. The dramatic resolution is more conventional than the drawn-out talk balancing humour and tension which precedes it. Neither the playing nor the writing come up to best quality Pinter, but if it's less than satisfying (the music is tiresome) it's certainly an interesting oddity. MS

‣ Alex Macqueen, Philip Campbell.
‣ *Dir* Marek Losey, *Pro* Christopher Granier-Deferre and John Schwab, *Screenplay* Tim Whitnall from his play *The Sociable Plover*, *Ph* George Richmond, *Pro Des* Nick Palmer, *Ed* Colin Sumsion, *M* Debbie Wiseman, *Cos* Alison Forbes-Meyler.

Poisson Rouge Pictures/Solution Films-ICA Cinema. 82 mins. UK. 2008. Rel: 5 June 2009. Cert 15.

High School Musical 3: Senior Year ★★

Troy (Zac Efron) and Gabriella (Vanessa Hudgens) are now high school seniors and fear separation as college time approaches. He hopes for a basketball scholarship whereas she wants to become an artist in New York. Efron has star quality but the zero chemistry with Hudgens fails to ignite the story. There are a couple of well crafted numbers but Kenny Ortega's dull direction makes this a very ordinary event – a highlight was when the little girl sitting behind me asked her mother: "What's a prom, mum?" GS

▶ Zac Efron, Vanessa Hudgens, Ashley Tisdale, Lucas Grabeel, Corbin Bleu, Monique Coleman.
▶ *Dir* Kenny Ortega, *Pro* Bill Borden and Barry Rosenbush, *Screenplay* Peter Barsocchini, *Ph* Daniel Aranyo, *Pro Des* Mark Mofeling, *Ed* Don Brochu, *M* David Lawrence, *Cos* Caroline Marx.

Borden and Rosenbush Entertainment/Walt Disney Pictures-Buena Vista International. 112 mins. USA. 2008. Rel: 22 Oct 2008. Cert U.

Hotel for Dogs ★ ★ ★

Two orphan siblings (Emma Roberts and Jake T Austin) turn an abandoned hotel into a dog sanctuary when their new guardians (Lisa Kudrow and Kevin Dillon) forbid them to have pets. They can't afford to lose their beloved dog Friday and this hotel also becomes the perfect place for all the stray dogs of the city. The two young protagonists along with their canine friends carry the film effortlessly and it is of no consequence if the adult roles are underwritten or if the plot occasionally becomes unbelievable. GS

▶ Emma Roberts, Jake T Austin, Don Cheadle, Johnny Simmons, Kyla Pratt, Troy Gentile, Lisa Kudrow, Kevin Dillon.
▶ *Dir* Thor Freundenthal, *Pro* Lauren Shuler Donner, Ewan Leslie and Jonathan Gordon, *Screenplay* Jeff Lowell, Mark McCorkle and Bob Schooley, from the book by Lois Duncan, *Ph* Michael Grady, *Pro Des* William Sandell, *Ed* Sheldon Kahn, *M* John Debney, *Cos* Beth Pasternak.

DreamWorks Pictures/Montecito Picture Company/Nickelodeon Movies/Coldspring Pictures/Donners' Company-Paramount Pictures. 100 mins. USA/Germany. 2009. Rel: 13 Feb 2009. Cert U.

The House Bunny ★ ★ ★

Shelley Darlington (Anna Faris) is a Playboy Bunny who lives a carefree lifestyle in the Playboy Mansion until a rival arranges for her dismissal. She has no experience of the

Orphans Emma Roberts and Jake T Austin go walkies in *Hotel for Dogs*.

outside world whatsoever, but luckily she ends up with the sorority girls from Zeta Alpha Zeta who are even more clueless than her. The preposterous plot is too silly to take seriously but Faris is highly watchable and manages the near impossible – to make her utterly implausible character credible and funny. GS

▶ Anna Faris, Colin Hanks, Emma Stone, Kat Dennings, Christopher McDonald, Beverly D'Angelo, Katharine McFee, Hugh Hefner.
▶ *Dir* Fred Wolf, *Pro* Allen Covert, Adam Sandler, Jack Garraputo and Heather Parry, *Screenplay* Karen McCullum Lutz and Kirsten Smith, *Ph* Shelly Johnson, *Pro Des* Missy Stewart, *Ed* Debra Chiate, *M* Waddy Wachtel, *Cos* Mona May.

Columbia Pictures/Relativity Media/ Happy Madison Productions/Alta Loma Entertainment-Columbia Pictures 97 mins. USA. 2008. Rel: 10 Oct 2008. Cert 12A.

How Ohio Pulled It Off ★★★

Fascinating and provocative documentary by students of Ohio University who investigated the irregularities of the US election in 2004. In interviews with state and federal officials it was discovered that thousands of voters were disenfranchised – some even saw their votes changing from John Kerry to George W Bush as they touched the voting screens, thereby showing the blatant theft of the presidency by fraudulent means. Only in America…? Or perhaps Zimbabwe too… CB

▶ J Kenneth Blackwell, John Kerry, Ted Strickland, Michael Vu, Stephanie Tubb Jones
▶ *Dir, Pro* and *Screenplay* Charla Barker, Matthew Kraus and Mariana Quiroga, *Ph* Mariana Quiroga, *Ed* Barker and Quiroga, *M* DJ Cal Boz (Wolfgang Amadeus) and Mike Sawitzke.

Ohio Film Makers-MercuryMedia International. 55 mins. USA. 2007. Rel: 4 Oct 2008. Cert 12A.

How to Lose Friends & Alienate People ★★★

It's a tribute to Simon Pegg's engaging screen persona that this adaptation of Toby Young's bestseller is quite enjoyable. What he is battling against is the fact that this comedy about an Englishman working in New York for a big magazine is a hopelessly inept blend of slapstick and satire always under the shadow of that immensely superior movie *The Devil Wears Prada*. Nice work too by Miriam Margolyes, Gillian Anderson and Bill Paterson, but it's really several films in one. MS

▶ Simon Pegg, Kirsten Dunst, Danny Huston, Gillian Anderson, Miriam Margolyes, Bill Paterson, Megan Fox, Jeff Bridges, Max Minghella.
▶ *Dir* Robert Weide, *Pro* Stephen Woolley and Elizabeth Karlsen, *Screenplay* Peter Straughan based on Toby Young's book, *Ph* Oliver Stapleton, *Pro Des* John Beard, *Ed* David Freeman, *M* David Arnold, *Cos* Annie Hardinge.

Intandem Films/Film4/UK Film Council/ Number 9 Films etc.-Paramount Pictures. 110 mins. UK/Cayman Islands/Ireland/USA. 2008. Rel: 3 Oct 2008. Cert 15.

Hunger ★★★★

Turner prize winner Steve McQueen proves his filmmaking skills with this feature debut written by playwright Enda Walsh and himself. In telling the story of Bobby Sands' hunger strike in Northern Ireland's Maze Prison in 1981, the filmmakers comment also on inhuman treatment of prisoners generally (Guantanamo Bay *et al*). It's too grim to be entertainment and may be preaching to the converted but it is splendidly realised and acted and without political bias. MS

▶ Michael Fassbender, Liam Cunningham, Stuart Graham, Brian Milligan, Liam McMahon.
▶ *Dir* Steve McQueen, *Pro* Laura Hastings-Smith and Robin Gutch, *Written by* Enda Walsh and McQueen, *Ph* Sean Bobbitt, *Pro Des* Tom McCullagh, *Ed* Joe Walker, *M* David Holmes with Leo Abrahams, *Cos* Anushia Nieradzik.

Film4/Northern Ireland Screen/a Blast! Films production etc.-Pathé Distribution.
96 mins. UK/Ireland. 2008. Rel: 31 Oct 2008. Cert 15.

Hush ★ ★ ★ ½

It's a dark and stormy night and Zakes and Beth are driving up the M1. As Beth dozes off, Zakes spots a woman in the back of an overtaking truck. It's only a split second, but Zakes is convinced that the woman is naked and screaming for help. For his directorial debut, former radio presenter Mark Tonderai has fashioned a lean, heart-pounding scenario. Eschewing the traditional obstacles that litter these kinds of films, Tonderai has created a very modern nightmare that hinges on the function of mobile phones, CCTV and internal-combustion engines. While the acting is a little rough, the trip is a genuinely scary one. JC-W

‣ William Ash, Robbie Gee, Sheila Reid, Christine Bottomley, Andreas Wisniewski, Claire Keelan, Stuart McQuarrie.
‣ *Dir* and *Screenplay* Mark Tonderai, *Pro* Robin Gutch, Mark Herbert, Colin Pons and Zoe Stewart, *Ph* Philipp Blaubach, *Pro Des* Matt Gant and Sabine Hviid, *Ed* Victoria Boydell, *M* Theo Green, *Cos* Lance Milligan.

Warp X/Shona Productions/Fear Factory/ Em Media/Film 4/Screen Yorkshire/UK Film Council-Optimum Releasing
91 mins. UK. 2008. Rel: 13 Mar 2009. Cert 15.

I Can't Think Straight
★ ★ ★ ★

Shamim Sarif's debut feature, a lesbian romantic comedy with dramatic elements, has much in common with the work of Gurinder Chadha: warmth and humanity, a desire to entertain and an underlying concern with social issues. The film would benefit from a more succinct close, but it's a pleasing work with Lisa Ray and Sheetal Sheth well cast as the leads. MS

‣ Lisa Ray, Sheetal Sheth, Antonia Frering,

Dalip Tahil, Nina Wadia, Ernest Ignatius.
‣ *Dir* Shamim Sarif, *Pro* Hanan Kattan, *Screenplay* Sarif and Kelly Moss, *Ph* Aseem Bajaj, *Pro Des* Katie Lee Carter, *Ed* David Martin, *M* Raiomond Mirza, *Wardrobe Des* Charlie Knight.

Enlightenment Productions/Shamim Sarif Indian Production Service etc.-Enlightenment Films.
82 mins. UK. 2008. Rel: 3 April 2009. Cert 12A.

I Love You Man ★ ★ ½

Peter Klaven (Paul Rudd), a successful estate agent, is over the moon when his beloved girlfriend Zooey (Rashida Jones) agrees to marry him. But he has no male friends so he begins to search for a Best Man. He surprisingly bonds with Sydney Fife (Jason Segel) -a free spirited and vulgar man -the total opposite of Peter. The premise and acting are not bad but the script is neither as funny nor as sharp as it should be. GS

‣ Paul Rudd, Rashida Jones, Sarah Burns, Jason Segel, Jaime Pressly, Jon Favreau, Jane Curtin.
‣ *Dir* John Hamburg, *Pro* Hamburg and Donald De Line, *Screenplay* Hamburg and Larry Levin, *Ph* Lawrence Sher, *Pro Des* Andrew Laws, *Ed* William Kerr, *M* Theodore Shapiro, *Cos* Leesa Evans.

DreamWorks SKG/Bernard Gayle Productions/De Line Pictures/The Montecito Picture Company-Paramount Pictures.
105 mins. USA. 2009. Rel: 17 Apr 2009. Cert 15.

Igor ★ ★ ★ ★

In the rainy city of Malaria the evil scientists are fiercely competing with each other for the ultimate invention but are outsmarted by the talented hunchback servant Igor. This imaginative animated feature is a cross between *Bride of Frankenstein* and *Metropolis* and its colourful designs and characters, which are very much influenced by Tim Burton, will certainly delight the children and as for the adults the amusing film references will do very nicely. You won't be able to hear 'Tomorrow' from *Annie* in the same way again. GS

▶ Voices of John Cusack, Myleene Klass, Robin Howard, Matt McKenna, John Cleese, Steve Buscemi, Eddie Izzard, Jay Leno.
▶ *Dir* Anthony Leondis, *Pro* Max Howard and John D Eraklis, *Screenplay* Leondis, Chris McKenna, John Hoffman and Dimitri Toscas, *Pro Des* Loic Rastout, *Ed* Hervé Schneid, *M* Patrick Doyle.

Exodus Films Group/Exodus Productions-Momentum Pictures.
87 mins. USA/France. 2008. Rel: 17 Oct 2008. Cert PG.

Import Export ★★★★
Confrontational but remarkable, Ulrich Seidl's latest film is cinematic, atmospheric and largely downbeat. It sets side by side the experiences of a nurse from the Ukraine seeking a better life in Vienna and of an unemployed youth from that city on a sales trip to the Ukraine by way of Slovakia. Unsparing in its portrayal of senility and gross sexual activity, this is not for the faint-hearted, but this bleak view of life (only the humanity of the heroine is truly positive) is

the work of an artist. MS

▶ Ekateryna Rak, Paul Hofmann, Michael Thomas, Natalija Baranova, Erich Finsches.
▶ *Dir* and *Pro* Ulrich Seidl, *Screenplay* Seidl and Veronika Franz, *Ph* Ed Lachman and Wolfgang Thaler, *Art Dir* Andreas Donhauser and Renate Martin, *Ed* Christof Schertenleib, *M* Marcus Davy, *Cos* Silvia Pernegger.

Conwert/an Ulrich Seidl Film production etc.-Trinity Filmed Entertainment.
141 mins. Austria/France. 2007. Rel: 3 Oct 2008. Cert 18.

In Prison My Whole Life
★★★
Curious but fairly engrossing documentary about the 1981 murder in Philadelphia of Daniel Faulkner, a white policeman, and the phoney trial of Mumia Abu-Jamal who was arrested for the crime merely because he was passing the murder scene in his taxi at the time and went to the aid of the victim. He was jailed because of the actions of a racist judge and police coercion of witnesses and he is still on Death Row in Pennsylvania nearly thirty years later, awaiting what should be a proper retrial. The film is

The Bride of Frankenstein meets *Metropolis* in *Igor*, Anthony Leonidis's delightful animated feature which should appeal to mums and dads as well as the tinies.

narrated by William Francome who was born on the day of Abu-Jamal's arrest. CB

► Mumia Abu-Jamal, Boots (Riley), Noam Chomsky, Mos Def, Alice S Walker, Snoop Dogg, Howard Zinn, William Francome.
► *Dir* Marc Evans, *Pro* Livia Giuglioli and Nick Goodwin Self, *Screenplay* Evans and Francome, *Ph* Ari Issler, *Ed* Mags Arnold, *M* Neil Davidge.

Fandango/Nana-MercuryMedia.
90 mins. UK/USA. 2007. Rel: 23 Oct 2008.
Cert 15.

In Search of Beethoven
★ ★ ★ ★

Serious in the best sense is this study of Beethoven's life and music, Phil Grabsky's documentary with comments from musicians and musicologists and with many striking musical extracts is a work that is arguably more digestible viewed in sections (it lasts for two and a half hours approximately). Nevertheless, it's even more adept and lively than its predecessor, Grabsky's film about Mozart. Recommended. MS

► With Sir Roger Norrington, Ronald Brautigam, Gianandrea Noseda, Juliet Stevenson (narrator).
► *Dir, Written* and *Filmed by* Phil Grabsky, *Exec Pro* John Cassy, *Ed* Phil Reynolds, *M* Beethoven.

Seventh Art Productions/Sky Arts etc.-
Seventh Art Productions.
138 mins. UK/Netherlands/Finland. 2009.
Rel: 17 April 2009. Cert U.

In the City of Sylvia ★ ★ ½
The emphasis on faces gives a personal flavour to this minimalistic work that may appeal to admirers of Bela Tarr and Fred Keleman although it lacks the poetic atmosphere that marks their best films. Here, a man returns to Strasbourg to trace a lost love, Sylvia, and follows a woman who looks like her, and that's just about it. Audiences

who can identify strongly with his situation may well find this film, totally consistent in style as it is, much more rewarding than I did. MS

► Xavier Lafitte, Pilar López de Ayala.
► *Dir* and *Screenplay* José Luis Guerin, *Pro* Luis Miñarro and Gaëlle Jones, *Ph* Natasha Braier, *Art Dir* Maite Sánchez Balcells, *Ed* Núria Esquerra, *Cos* Valérie-Elder Fontaine, Miriam Compte and Mar Fraga.

An Eddie Saeta s.a./Château-Rouge Production co-production etc.-Axiom Films Limited.
85 mins. Spain/France. 2007.
Rel: 13 March 2009. Cert PG.

In the Loop ★ ★ ★ ½
Fans of politicial satire in general and of the TV series *The Thick of It* in particular will welcome this well played and energetic feature set both in Britain and the US and derived from a series noted for its stong language. Being an exposure of inept, bungling politicians up to no good, the timing of this release was spot on, but it's not really cinema. It's the words not the images that count and for me it starts to lose impact because its style is best suited to half hour episodes. Nevertheless some audiences will love it. MS

► Peter Capaldi, Tom Hollander, James Gandolfini, Gina McKee, Chris Addison, Anna Chlumsky.
► *Dir* Armando Iannucci, *Pro* Kevin Loader and Adam Tandy, *Screenplay* Jesse Armstrong, Simon Blackwell, Iannucci and Tony Roche, *Ph* Jamie Cairney, *Pro Des* Cristina Casali, *Ed* Billy Sneddon and Ant Boys, *M* Adem Ilhan, *Cos* Ros Little.

BBC Films/UK Film Council/Aramid Entertainment etc.-Optimum Releasing.
106 mins. UK/Cayman Islands. 2009.
Rel: 17 April 2009. Cert 15.

Incendiary ★
It adds insult to injury that this grossly sentimental, unconvincing and sometimes

ludicrous London-set drama should attempt to study bereavement in the context of a terrorist bomb incident that brings to mind the 7/7 attack. Michelle Williams from *Brokeback Mountain* succeeds in taking on an English character but sympathy for the actress recedes when you think of her signing on for this after reading the script. Sadly there is competition but this is a strong candidate for the worst film of the year. MS

▷ Michelle Williams, Ewan McGregor, Matthew Macfadyen, Usman Khokhar.
▷ *Dir* and *Written by* Sharon Maguire, based on Chris Cleave's novel, *Pro* Andy Paterson, Anand Tucker and Adrienne Maguire, *Ph* Ben Davis, *Pro Des* Kave Quinn, *Ed* Valerio Bonelli, *M* Shigeru Umebayashi and Barrington Pheloung, *Cos* Stephanie Collie.

Film4/Aramid Entertainment/an Archer Street, Sneak Preview production etc.- Optimum Releasing.
100 mins. UK/USA/Cayman Islands. 2008. Rel: 24 Oct 2008. Cert 15.

Inkheart ★ ★ ★

Book restorer Mortimer Folchart (Brendan Fraser) has the curious ability of being able to bring characters out of books when he reads aloud. He sets out with daughter Meggie (Eliza Bennett) on a journey to find the legendary Inkheart tome which will locate his long-lost wife Resa (Sienna Guillory). When he finds the book, a character called Dustfinger (Paul Bettany) appears, demanding to be read back into the ancient volume. Folchart refuses and heads for Italy with Meggie to see great aunt Elinor (Helen Mirren). More chases ensue but there is a fatal lack of spirit in an adventure whose aim seems to be to say that books are good for you. Now read on... MHD

▷ Brendan Fraser, Helen Mirren, Sienna Guillery, Eliza Bennett, Richard Strange, Paul Bettany, Jamie Foreman, Andy Serkis.
▷ *Dir* Ian Softley, *Pro* Softley, Diana Pokorny, Ileen Maisel and Cornelia Funke, *Screenplay* David Lindsay-Abaire, from the novel by Funke, *Ph* Roger Pratt, *Pro Des* John Beard, *Ed* Martin Walsh, *M* Javier Navarette, *Cos* Verity Hawkes.

Internationale Filmproduktion Blackbird Dritte/New Line Cinema-Entertainment Film Distributors.
106 mins. UK/Germany/USA. 2008. Rel: 12 Dec 2008. Cert PG

Ewan McGregor wonders how he got involved in such an unconvincing terrorist bomb drama like *Incendiary*.

The International ★★★½

The man from Interpol, Louis Salinger (Clive Owen) and New York District Attorney Eleanor Whitman (Naomi Watts) are investigating the International Bank of Business & Credit for money laundering, arms trading, murder etc in this reasonably active thriller. With more plots and sub-plots the script fights to stay afloat but every so often there's a satisfying set-piece such as the assassination of an Italian politician at an open air rally and a big shoot-up in an exact replica of New York's Guggenheim Museum during which you feel more for the exhibits and the building than you do for the assailants. Clive Owen makes an average hero, but again proves he's no 007. Naomi Watts is a good sidekick and director Tom Tykwer keeps things on the move. MHD

▶ Clive Owen, Naomi Watts, Armin Mueller-Stahl, Ulrich Thomsen, Brian F O'Byrne, Ben Wishaw.
▶ *Dir* Tom Tykwer, *Pro* Lloyd Phillips, Charles Roven and Richard Suckle, *Screenplay* Eric Warren Singer, *Ph* Frank Griebe, *Pro Des* Uli Hanisch, *Ed* Mathilde Bonnefoy, *M* Tykwer, Reinhold Heil anJohnny Klimek, *Cos* Ngila Dickson.

Relativity Media/Rose Line Productions/Atlas Entertainment/Mosaic Media Group/Papillon Productions etc-Sony Pictures Releasing. 118 mins. USA/Germany/UK. 2009. Rel: 27 Feb 2009. Cert 15.

I O U S A ★★★½

Patrick Creadon's rather bleak but well timed documentary examines the USA's deep financial crisis and its rapidly increasing federal debt to foreign countries. Many experts are interviewed about the 8.7 trillion dollars debt including former US Comptroller General David Walker who travels around the country explaining America's fiscal policies to its citizens. It is no surprise that Bush's government – with wars in Afghanistan and Iraq – has escalated the debt beyond comprehension. This is a strong document about America's fast economic decline but it is probably preaching to the converted. GS

▶ Archive footage of Dwight Eisenhower, George Bush, George W Bush, Jimmy Carter, John Kennedy, Ronald Reagan, Bill Clinton etc
▶ *Dir* Patrick Creadon, *Pro* Sarah Gibson and Christine O'Malley, *Screenplay* Creadon and O'Malley, based on the book *Empire of Debt*

Clive Owen is kept on the run in *The International*, a fairly lively thriller set in the crazy, murderous world of banks and banking.

by William Bonner and Addison Wiggin, *Ed* Douglas Blush, *M* Peter Golub.

O'Malley Creadon Productions/Agora Entertainment/Open Sky Entertainment etc-MercuryMedia.
85 mins. USA. 2008. Rel: 14 Nov 2008. Cert U.

Is Anybody There? ★★

Sir Michael Caine turns in an impressive performance here as an aged magician now a widower about to be overtaken by senility. His friendship in a retirement home with the young son of the owners (the boy is Bill Milner from *Son of Rambow*) is meant to be engaging but inept comedy and overt sentimentality linked to the depressing sight of inmates played by elderly actors render this a non-starter in the entertainment stakes. MS

▶ Michael Caine, David Morrissey, Anne-Marie Duff, Thelma Barlow, Rosemary Harris, Leslie Phillips, Elizabeth Spriggs, Sylvia Syms, Peter Vaughan, Bill Milner.
▶ *Dir* John Crowley, *Pro* David Heyman, Marc Turtletaub and Peter Saraf, *Written by* Peter Harness, *Ph* Rob Hardy, *Pro Des* Kave Quinn, *Ed* Trevor Waite, *M* Joby Talbot, *Cos* Jane Petrie.

BBC Films/Big Beach/Heyday Films/Odyssey Entertainment-Optimum Releasing.
95 mins. UK/USA. 2009. Rel: 1 May 2009. Cert 12A.

I've Loved You So Long ★★★★★

This, a debut for director Philippe Claudel, a French university professor, is one of the most moving films of the year, with Kristin Scott Thomas giving the performance of her career. She plays Juliette, a woman who hasn't seen her family for fifteen years, who goes to live with her married sister Léa (Elsa Zylberstein) and her family. She at first finds it difficult to assimilate because the cause of her absence was a prison sentence. Léa's husband Luc is cold towards her but gradually the rest of the family accept her and she finds a kind of peace and restores the faltering relationship between Léa and Luc. Claudel subtly delineates the many prisons we make for ourselves and, with beautifully modulated performances from his ensemble cast, has come up with a touching and all too human story. (Original title: *Il y a longtemps que je t'aime*).
MHD

▶ Kristin Scott Thomas, Elsa Zylberstein, Serge Hazanavicius, Laurent Grévil, Frédéric Pierrot.
▶ *Dir* and *Screenplay* Philippe Claudel, *Pro* Yves Marmion, *Ph* Jérôme Alméras, *Pro Des* Samuel Deshors, *Ed* Virginie Bruant, *M* Jean-Louis Aubert, *Cos* Laurence Esnault.

UGC YM/Canal +/Eurimages/France 3 Cinema/Integral Film etc-Lionsgate.
115 mins. France/Germany. 2008. Rel: 26 Sep 2008. Cert 12A.

Jar City ★★★½

This gritty police thriller from Iceland may not ingratiate itself with the Icelandic Tourist Board. The bleak story involves murder, rape, paedophilia and police corruption in a complex narrative which is, perhaps, slightly less significant than the filmmakers would have us believe. Nevertheless, if you buy into the story you will find it very competently handled in all respects. (Original title: *Myrin*).
MS

▶ Ingvar E. Sigurdsson, Ágústa Eva Erlendsdóttir, Atli Rafn Sigurdarson.
▶ *Dir* and *Written by* Baltasar Kormákur (from Arnaldur Indridason's novel *Myrin*), *Pro* Agnes Johansen, Lilja Pálmadóttir and Kormákur, *Ph* Bergsteinn Björgúlfsson, *Art Dir* Atli Geir Grétarsson, *Ed* Elísabet Ronaldsdóttir, *M* Mugison.

Blueeyes Productions/Bavaria Pictures/Trust Film Sales etc.-The Works UK Distribution.
95 mins. Iceland/Germany/Denmark. 2006. Rel: 12 Sept 2008. Cert 15.

JCVD ★ ★ ½

A surprisingly novel, low-budget drama starring Jean-Claude Van Damme as a world-weary version of himself, inexplicably caught up in a *Dog Day Afternoon*-style hostage situation. The Muscles always maintained he could act and, as he returns to Brussels to reflect on his life in his native language, his performance in this ambitious oddity is heartfelt and believable, even though the movie itself is kind of gimmicky. Fascinating viewing for old school action fans. MJ

▸ Jean-Claude Van Damme, François Damiens, Zinedine Soualem, Karim Belkhadra, Liliane Becker.
▸ *Dir* Mabrouk El Mechri, *Pro* Sidonie Dumas, *Screenplay* Mechri, Frédéric Benudis and Christophe Turpin, *Ph* Pierre-Yves Bastard, *Pro Des* André Fonsny, *Ed* Kako Kelber, *M* Gast Waltzing, *Cos* Uli Simon.

Sam Sa Film/Gaumont-Revolver Entertainment. 97 mins. Belgium/Luxembourg/France. 2008. Rel: 30 Jan 2009. Cert 15.

Jimmy Carter Man from Plains ★ ★ ★

This appealing documentary portrait of America's 39th President puts much emphasis on Carter's book *Palestine Peace Not Apartheid* which he was promoting amidst controversy when Jonathan Demme shot his film. This aspect is stressed to the detriment of a wider study of Carter's life and the running length (over two hours) comes to seem excessive in the circumstances. However, the octogenarian Carter emerges as one of that rarest of breeds, a sympathetic politician. MS

▸ With Jimmy Carter, Rosalynn Carter, Alan Dershowitz, Jay Leno.
▸ *Dir* and *Written by* Jonathan Demme, *Pro* Demme and Neda Armian, *Ph* Declan Quinn, *Ed* Kate Amend, *M* Djamel Ben Yelles and Alejandro Escovedo.

Sony Pictures Classics/Participant Productions /a Clinica Estetico production-BFI Southbank. 127 mins. USA, 2007. Rel: 15 Aug 2008. No Cert.

Jonas Brothers: The 3D Concert Experience ★ ★ ½

Bruce Hendricks, the director of *Hannah Montana/Miley Cyrus: Best of Both Worlds* tries to repeat the same formula for this rockumentary but not as successfully. The concert looks great in 3-D but that is only one third of the film. The rest feels padded out with some unnecessary scenes like those in the park with the Jonas Brothers lookalikes. The brothers are likeable and their concert is entertaining but that is not enough! GS

▸ Kevin, Joe and Nick Jonas, John Lloyd Taylor, John Cahill Lawless, Ryan Matthews Liestman, Gregory Robert Garbowsky.
▸ *Dir* Bruce Hendricks, *Pro* Kevin Jonas, Phil McIntyre, Johnny Wright, Arthur F Repola, Alan Sacks, *Ph* Mitchell Amundsen and Reed Smoot, *Ed* Michael Tronick, *M* The Jonas Brothers.

Walt Disney Pictures-
Walt Disney Studios Motion Pictures.
76 mins. USA. 2009. Rel: 29 May 2009. Cert U.

Journey to the Centre of the Earth 3D ★ ★

Blandly beefy Brendan Fraser plays a science type accompanied by nephew Josh Hutcherson on a perilous expedition to an impossible lost world in a film so loosely based on the classic Jules Verne novel that it hardly deserves the title. Though forgettable fun for kids with plenty of in-your-face effects, beyond the prehistoric monsters and whizzy action sequences, it's as routine and formulaic as you would expect, barely written nonsense that nobody really needs to see. MJ

▸ Brendan Fraser, Josh Hutcherson, Anita Briehm, Seth Myers, Jean Michel Paré.
▸ *Dir* Eric Brevig, *Pro* Beau Flynn, Cary Granat and Charlotte Huggins, *Screenplay* Michael D Weiss, Jennifer Flackett and Mark Levin from the Jules Verne novel, *Ph* Chuck Shuman, *Pro Des* David Sandefur, *Ed* Steven Rosenbloom, Paul Martin Smith and Mark Levin, *M* Andrew Lockington, *Cos* Mario Davignon.

Aging party girl Tilda Swinton gets involved in kidnapping Aidan Gould in Erick Zonca and Camille Natta's *Julia*.

New Line Cinema/Walden Media-Walt Disney Company.
93 mins. USA. 2008. Rel: 11 July 2008. Cert PG.

Julia ★ ★ ★

Erick Zonca's delayed follow-up to his brilliant debut film *The Dream Life of Angels* offers a great opportunity to Tilda Swinton who dominates the film as a rootless, aging American party girl who becomes involved in a kidnapping. In its second half this over-long film goes right off the rails of probability but it is still worth seeing for Swinton, superb in a role unlike any other she has taken.
MS

▶ Tilda Swinton, Kate Del Castillo, Aidan Gould, Saul Rubinek, Gastón Peterson.
▶ *Dir* Erick Zonca with Camille Natta, *Pro* François Marquis and Bertrand Faivre, *Written by* Aude Py, Zonca and others, *Ph* Yorick Le Saux, *Pro Des* François-Renaud Labarthe, *Ed* Philippe Kotlarski, *Cos* April Napier.

Les Productions Bagheera and Le Bureau/ France 3 Cinéma/StudioCanal etc.-Artificial Eye Film Company.
144 mins. France/Belgium/USA/Mexico. 2008. Rel: 5 Dec 2008. Cert 15.

Katy ★ ★ ★ ★ ★

Poland's greatest filmmaker, Andrzej Wajda, who has chronicled so much of his country's history on screen, is back on his best form in this deeply felt drama concerned with the wartime massacre of Polish officers in the forest of Katy and the subsequent postwar attempt by the Russians to shift the blame onto the Germans as perpetrators. It's a minor weakness that the characters can occasionally confuse one but this is splendid stuff, a requiem that makes an indelible impression aided by the music of Penderecki. MS

▶ Andrzej Chyra, Maja Ostaszewska, Artur Zmijewski, Maja Komorowska, Danuta Stenka.
▶ *Dir* Andrzej Wajda, *Pro* Michal Kwiecinski. *Screenplay* Wajda, Wladyslaw Pasikowski and Przemyslaw Nowakowski based on the novel *Post Mortem* by Andrzej Mularczyk and the diary of Major Adam Solski, *Ph* Pawel Edelman, *Art Dir* Magdalena Dipont, *Ed* Milenia Fiedler and Rafal Listopad, *M* Krzysztof Penderecki, *Cos* Magdalena Biedrzycka and Justyna Stolarz.

Akson Studio/Telewizja Polska S.A./ Telekomunikacja Polska S.A. etc.- Artificial Eye Film Company.
121 mins. Poland. 2007. Rel: 19 June 2009. Cert 15.

King of the Hill ★ ★ ★ ★

Quim (Leonardo Sbaraglia) is having a perfectly dreadful day: he has his wallet stolen during a sexual encounter at a petrol station, he gets lost driving through a remote forest and then he surprisingly joins forces with Bea (Maria Valverde), the woman who robbed him at the petrol station, when a sniper starts shooting at them for no reason at all. Gonzalo López-Gallego's masterly and sparse direction entirely focuses on his actors' faces and expressions and succeeds in creating terrific tension and suspense. (Original title: *El Rey de la Montaña*) GS

▶ Leonardo Sbaraglia, Maria Valverde, Thomas Riordan, Andres Juste, Pablo Menasanch, Francisco Olmi.
▶ *Dir* and *Ed* Gonzalo López-Gallego, *Pro* Juanma Arance, Alvaro Augustin, Juan Pita and Miguel Bardem, *Screenplay* López-Gallego and Javier Guillon, from his story, *Ph* José David Montero, *Pro Des* Juana Arance and Pello Villalba, *M* David Crespo, *Cos* Tatiana Hernández and Rocio Redondo.

Goodfellas/Decontrabando/Telecinco-Optimum Releasing.
90 mins. Spain. 2007. Rel: 13 Feb 2009. Cert 15.

Knowing ★ ★ ½

"Shit happens" notes astrophysics professor John Koestler (Nicolas Cage) during his MIT class on randomness vs. determinism. Then the waste matter really hits the fan when his son comes by a sheet of numbers scribbled by a child fifty years earlier. It turns out the figures detail a series of catastrophes over the last half century and that there's worse to come... There's plenty of fun with numbers in this gloomy piece of hokum that gives mathematics a more profound run for its money than in either *Proof* or *A Beautiful Mind*. Unfortunately, for sci-fi buffs it's all terribly, terribly familiar. JC-W

▶ Nicolas Cage, Chandler Canterbury, Rose Byrne, D G Maloney, Lara Robinson, Nadia Townsend
▶ *Dir* Alex Proyas, *Pro* Proyas, Todd Black, Jason Blumenthal and Steve Tisch, *Screenplay* Ryne Douglas Pearson, Juliet Snowden and Stiles White, from a story by Pearson, *Ph* Simon Duggan, *Pro Des* Steven Jones-Evans, *Ed* Richard Learoyd, *M* Marco Beltrani, *Cos* Terry Ryan.

Wintergreen Productions/Kaplan-Perrone Entertainment/Summit Entertainment/

Astrophysics professor Nicolas Cage (oh yeah?) investigates catastrophes predicted by a child fifty years earlier in the glorious and gloomy piece of hokum that is *Knowing*.

Comin' at ya: *Kung Fu Panda* flexes his muscles for some super animated martial arts action.

Escape Artists/Mystery Clock Cinema/
Goldcrest Pictures-Contender
Entertainment Group.
121 mins. USA/UK. 2009.
Rel: 25 Mar 2009. Cert 15.

Kung fu Panda ★★★★★

Ancient China. Frustrated martial arts hero wannabe noodle waiter panda (voice: Jack Black) trains alongside his unhappy-about-him idols as their Master awaits the return of an evil, renegade pupil. The film delivers the goods not only as an animated epic but also as a martial arts action movie. Appropriately the voice cast includes Jackie Chan. Prepare for awesomeness indeed. Also released in IMAX. JC

➤ Voices of Jack Black, Dustin Hoffman, Angelina Jolie, Ian McShane, Jackie Chan, Seth Rogen, Lucy Liu.
➤ *Dir* Mark Osborne and John Stevenson, *Pro* Melissa Cobb, *Screenplay* Jonathan Abel and Glenn Burger, from a story by Ethan Reiff and Cyrus Voris, *Ph* Yong duk jhun, *Pro Des* Raymond Zibach, *Ed* Clare Knight, *M* John Powell and Hans Zimmer.

DreamWorks Animation/Pacific Data Images-Paramount Pictures.
92 mins. USA. 2008. Rel: 4 July 2008. Cert PG.

Lake Tahoe ★★★★

Quietly humorous this minimalist work from the Mexican director who made *Duck Season* oddly contains passing echoes of Kelly Reinhardt's *Wendy and Lucy* (q.v.) as it shows a teenager seeking a replacement part for the car he has crashed. As formal and unsentimentally heartfelt as Ozu's work, it develops into a touching portrayal of grief for a dead father as life continues. Get on its wavelength if you can because repeated viewings might well reveal a masterpiece expressed through controlled understatement. MS

➤ Diego Cantaño, Daniela Valentine, Juan Carlos Lara, Héctor Herrera, Yemil Sefani.
➤ *Dir* Fernando Eimbcke, *Pro* Christian Valdelièvre, *Screenplay* Eimbcke and Paula Markovitch, *Ph* Alexis Zabé, *Art Dir* Diana Quiroz, *Ed* Mariana Rodriguez, *Cos* Mariana Watson.

Cinepantera/Grupo Bal/Cinépolis etc-Yume Pictures.
81 mins. Mexico/USA/Japan. 2008.
Rel: 26 June 2009. Cert 15.

Lakeview Terrace ★★★

Who hasn't at some time suffered a neighbour from hell? That's the trigger

Samuel L Jackson as a racist Los Angeles veteran cop in Neil LaBute's melodramatic *Lakeview Terrace*.

to identify here with a mixed race couple confronted by a racist living next door, the novelty being that the racist is black. You tend to be one step ahead as the conflict grows, but the real problem is that Neil LaBute (director but not writer this time) is lumbered with a screenplay which eventually goes way over-the-top into out-and-out melodrama. MS

▶ Samuel L. Jackson, Patrick Wilson, Kerry Washington, Jay Hernandez.

▶ *Dir* Neil LaBute, *Pro* James Lassiter and Will Smith, *Screenplay* David Loughery (from his story) and Howard Korder, *Ph* Rogier Stoffers, *Pro Des* Bruton Jones, *Ed* Joel Plotch, *M* Mychael and Jeff Danna, *Cos* Lynette Meyer.

Screen Gems/an Overbrook Entertainment production-Sony Pictures Releasing. 110 mins. USA. 2008. Rel: 5 Dec 2008. Cert 15.

Last Chance Harvey ★ ★ ★

Romantic fiction for female audiences (preferably of fifty plus), this film delivers on its own terms which are such that its tale of late love between single Emma Thompson and divorced Dustin Hoffman can shamelessly milk its conclusion (will they get together or not?). Hoffman, especially, refuses to give it less than his best, even as the London locations used defy geography. MS

▶ Dustin Hoffman, Emma Thompson, Eileen Atkins, Kathy Baker, Liane Balaban, James Brolin.
▶ *Dir* and *Written by* Joel Hopkins, *Pro* Tim Perell and Nicola Usborne, *Ph* John De Borman, *Pro Des* Jon Henson, *Ed* Robin Sales, *M* Dickon Hinchliffe, *Cos* Natalie Ward.

Overture Films/a Process production-Momentum Pictures. 93 mins. USA. 2008. Rel: 5 June 2009. Cert 12A.

The Last House on the Left
★ ★ ★ ★

Shortly after their arrival at their home on a lake, John and Emma Collingwood are left to their own devices as Mari, their 17-year-old daughter, takes the car to visit a friend. And, unbeknownst to them, Mari is kidnapped by three sadistic killers... A remake of Wes Craven's notorious 1972 debut – itself inspired by Bergman's *The Virgin Spring* – this is sick made slick in the best sense. While there's one cheesy shock effect and one really dumb character move, the film is surprisingly smart for this kind of fare. More importantly, director Iliadis manages to sustain the suspense for most of the film's running time. In short, this is a horror film that truly horrifies, like *Funny Games* with the violence left in. JC-W

▶ Tony Goldwyn, Monica Potter, Michael Bowen, Josh Cox, Riki Lindhome, Aaron Paul, Sara Paxton.
▶ *Dir* Dennis Iliadis, *Pro* Wes Craven, Sean S Cunningham and Marianne Maddalena, *Screenplay* Adam Alleca and Carl Ellsworth based on Wes Craven's 1972 film, *Ph* Sharone Meir, *Pro Des* Johnny Breedt, *Ed* Peter McNulty, *M* John Murphy, *Cos* Katherine Jane Bryant.

Rogue Pictures/Film Afrika Worldwide/ Midnight Entertainment-Universal Pictures International.

110 mins. USA. 2009. Rel: 12 June 2009. Cert 18.

83 mins. UK/Bangladesh/Switzerland. 2008. Rel: 26 June 2009. Cert 15.

The Last Thakur ★ ★ ★ ½

A first feature by Sadik Ahmed, this tale of tension is set in Bangladesh but has been described as a contemporary western. Certainly there's an armed stranger in town on a mission and a community possibly misled in supporting its chairman rather than Thakur his Hindu opponent. Stylishly shot by the director, the film creates its own world, one hermetically sealed in a way gives the piece its character, but the finale is unpersuasive. MS

▶ Tariq Anam, Ahmed Rubel, Tanveer Hassan, Tanju Miah, Anisur Rahman Milon, Gazi Rakayet.
▶ *Dir* and *Ph* Sadik Ahmed, *Pro* Atif Ghani and Tamsin Lyons, *Screenplay* Heather Taylor and Ahmed from Ahmed's story, *Pro Des* Byron Broadbent, *Ed* Hugh Williams, *M* Kishon Khan and Birger Clausen, *Cos* Anwar Hossain Chowdhury.

Curzon Artificial Eye/NFTS/Front Page Films/ Aimimage/Breakthru Films etc.-Artificial Eye Film Company

Lemon Tree ★ ★ ★ ★

This engaging and heart-felt drama is the story of a widow (the splendid Hiam Abbass) fighting for the right to continue cultivation of her lemon trees. The grove is on the border between Israel and the occupied West bank and the Israeli security forces seek to take it over on the grounds that it could provide cover for Palestinian terrorists targeting the Israeli Defence Minister who lives next door. The subsequent introduction of a love story too sketchily drawn is less successful, but it remains an impressive work beautifully photographed. MS

▶ Hiam Abbass, Rona Lipaz-Michael, Ali Suliman, Doron Tavory, Tarik Copti.
▶ *Dir* Eran Riklis, *Pro* Bettina Brokemper, Antoine de Clermont-Tonnerre, Michael Eckelt and Riklis, *Screenplay* Suha Arraf and Riklis, *Ph* Rainer Klausmann, *Pro Des* Miguel Markin, *Ed* Tova Ascher, *M* Habib Shehadeh Hanna, *Cos* Rona Doron.

Heimatfilm/Mact Productions/Eran Riklis Productions/Riva Film etc.-Unanimous Pictures.

Will they, won't they...? Late blossoming love between Dustin Hoffman and Emma Thompson in *Last Chance Harvey.*

106 mins. Israel/Germany/France, 2008.
Rel: 12 Dec 2008. Cert PG.

Lesbian Vampire Killers ★

Fletch (James Corden) and Jimmy (Mathew Horne) are two nerdy types who can't get a girlfriend even between them. When they decide to holiday in Cragwich, home of a coven of lesbian vampires, it turns out that Jimmy is a descendant of the man who did for Carmilla, the vampire queen. Will she regain her powers or can the sword of Dialdo (sic) destroy her forever… as if you cared? Horne and Corden once again prove they are basically not funny. *LVK* just puts the tin lid on their careers as it must be the worst British film of this or any year, plumbing new depths of direness hitherto never reached. They don't even deserve a single star. May they rest in peace. MHD

▶ James Corden, Mathew Horne, Paul McGann, MyAnna Buring, Silvia Colloca, Vera Filatova.
▶ *Dir* Phil Claydon, *Pro* Steve Clarke-Hall, *Screenplay* Paul Hupfield and Stewart Williams, *Ph* David Higgs, *Pro Des* Keith Maxwell, *Ed* James Herbert, *M* Debbie Wiseman, *Cos* Diana Moseley.

AV Pictures-Momentum Pictures.
88 mins. UK. 2009. Rel: 20 Mar 2009. Cert 15.

Let's Talk About the Rain ★★★

The best work of Agnès Jaoui and Jean-Pierre Bacri (*Le Gout des Autres*, 2000/*Look at Me*, 2004) presents believable characters in convincing situations that are fruitful ground for tragic-comedy. Here, however, there's an attempt to emphasise the comedy more in the tale of a family that includes a successful female politician (Jaoui) who is interviewed by an inept filmmaker (Bacri). It's well played and has its moments but several aspects lack conviction and by their own high standards this latest offering from Jaoui and Bacri is something of a disappointment. (Original title: *Parlez-moi de la pluie*). MS

▶ Jean-Pierre Bacri, Jamel Debbouze, Agnès Jaoui, Pascale Arbillot, Mimouna Hadji.
▶ *Dir* Agnès Jaoui, *Pro* Jean-Philippe Andraca and Christian Bérard, *Screenplay* Jaoui and Jean-Pierre Bacri, *Ph* David Quesemand, *Art Dir* Christian Marti, *Ed* François Gédigier and Sylvie Lager, *Cos* Ève-Marie Arnault.

Les Films A4/StudioCanal/France 2 Cinéma etc.-Artificial Eye Film Company.
99 mins. France. 2008. Rel: 7 Nov 2008. Cert 12A.

A Letter to True ★★★★

This oddball of a movie is presented by Bruce Weber as a letter, one read in the film's voice-over by the director himself but addressed to True who is one of his dogs. Against the background of 9/11, Weber seeks to re-establish a world of innocence by using film clips, old songs and interviews all woven into an essay that praises dogs. There's a clear gay sensibility to all this and it is a divertingly idiosyncratic film. MS

▶ With narration by Bruce Weber with Julie Christie and Marianne Faithfull.
▶ *Dir* and *Written by* Bruce Weber, *Pro* Nan Bush, *Ph* Pete Zuccarini, Evan Estern and others, *Art Dir* Dimitri Levas, *Ed* Chad Sipkin, *M* John Leftwich, *Animation* Postworks: Brian Benson.

Just Blue Films-Metrodome Distribution.
78 mins. USA. 2003. Rel: 1 Aug 2008. Cert PG.

Let The Right One In ★★★★

This Swedish movie from Tomas Alfredson is quality work. It may not break the bounds of its genre like *Pan's Labyrinth* but this vampire tale has lots going for it: excellent performances in well characterised roles, an adept music score, admirably atmospheric photography. Since the story features a twelve year old boy drawn to a girl who appears to be of the same age but is in reality a vampire, it could be thought of as a variation on *Twilight*. You probably need to like the genre to get the most out of it, but this is certainly outstanding of its kind. A British remake entered production at the end of 2009. MS

▶ Kåre Hedebrant, Lina Leandersson. Per Ragnar, Peter Carlberg, Henrik Dahl, Karin Bergquist.
▶ *Dir* Tomas Alfredson, *Pro* John Nordling and Carl Molinder, *Screenplay* John Ajvide Lindqvist from his novel *Låt den rätte komma in*, *Ph* Hoyte van Hoytema, *Art Dir* Eva Norén, *Ed* Dino Jonsäter and Alfredson, *M* Johan Söderqvist, *Cos* Maria Strid.

ETFI/SVT – Sveriges Television/Fido Film/The Chimney Pot/Canal+ etc.-Momentum Pictures. 114 mins. Sweden/Norway. 2008. Rel: 10 April 2009. Cert 15.

The Life Before Her Eyes ★★

Vadim Perelman's disappointing film tells the story of teenager Diana (Evan Rachel Wood) whose peaceful existence at high school is one day shattered when a classmate begins to shoot his fellow students and teachers. And then fifteen years later Diana (now Uma Thurman) reminisces about that

fateful day and the effects it had on their small community. It is superbly shot but the endless switching between past and present becomes irritating. This would have made a perfect half-hour film but as it stands it is overstretched and pointless GS

▶ Uma Thurman, Evan Rachel Wood, Eva Amurri, Gabrielle Brennan, Oscar Isaac, Brent Cullen, Jack Gilpin.
▶ *Dir* Vadim Perelman, *Pro* Perelman, Aimee Peyronnet, Marc Butan, Anthony Katagas, *Screenplay* Emil Stern, from the novel by Laura Kasischke, *Ph* Pawel Edelman, *Pro Des* Maia Javan, *Ed* David Baxter, *M* James Horner, *Cos* Hala Bahmet.

2929 Productions-Paramount Pictures. 90 mins. USA. 2007. Rel: 27 Mar 2009. Cert 15.

Linha de passe ★★★

Dissatisfied youngsters in São Paulo where unemployment is rife seek escape in soccer, crime or religion. So say the statistics and Walter Salles and Daniela Thomas have crafted a drama which seems rather too obviously to have been constructed around that by locating all three examples in one family. The film is well meant and

Lena Leandersson in *Let the Right One In*, Tomas Alfredson's superior Swedish tale of vampires, one of the best shockers of the year.

atmospherically shot, but the conclusion is somewhat muddled and the film is less persuasive than Salles's best work.
MS

‣ Sandra Corveloni, Vinícius de Oliveira, João Baldasserini, Kaique de Jesus Santos.
‣ *Dir* Walter Salles and Daniela Thomas, *Pro* Mauricio Andrade Ramos and Rebecca Yeldham, *Screenplay* George Moura and Thomas with Bráulio Mantovani, *Ph* Mauro Pinheiro Jr, *Art Dir* Valdy Lopes Jr, *Ed* Gustavo Giani and Livia Serpa, *M* Gustavo Santaolalla, *Cos* Cássio Brasil.

Pathé/a VideoFilmes production-Pathé Distribution. 113 mins. USA/UK/Brazil. 2008. Rel: 19 Sept 2008. Cert 15.

Little Ashes ★★

Although it concludes with the execution of the gay Spanish poet and playwright Lorca in 1936, the emphasis here is on the student friendship of Lorca, Salvador Dalí and Luis Buñuel in Madrid. Dalí's unwillingness to yield to his feelings for Lorca could be seen as tragic in its consequences, but here with a feeble script, English dialogue and banal music the story seems increasingly ludicrous and it doesn't even achieve pathos, only bathos. MS

‣ Javier Beltrán, Robert Pattison, Matthew McNulty, Marina Gatell, Arly Jover.
‣ *Dir* Paul Morrison, *Pro* Carlo Dusi, Johnny Persey and Jaume Vilalta, *Written by* Philippa Goslett, *Ph* Adam Suschitzky, *Pro Des* Pere Francesch, *Ed* Rachel Tunnard, *M* Miguel Mera, *Cos* Antonio Belart.

Factotum Barcelona/Aria Films/Met Film/APT Films etc.-Kaleidoscope Home Entertainment. 112 mins. Spain/UK/USA. 2008. Rel: 8 May 2009. Cert 15.

Little Box of Sweets ★★★

Finely photographed by Dusan Todorovic, Meneka Das's well-intentioned film shot on location around Allahabad looks at the changing face of India by featuring a love story across a class divide and by looking at such issues as the limited opportunities for women and the need for education. All of this would have engaged Das's hero, the late Satyajit Ray, but compared to his work there is a naivety here apparent through some indifferent acting and a screenplay that lacks real quality.
MS

‣ Joe Anderson, Meneka Das, Sheenu Das, Helena Michell, Rahul Vohra, Mohini Mathur.
‣ *Dir* and *Written by* Meneka Das, *Pro* Sheenu Das, *Ph* Dusan Todorovic, *Art Dir* Sharad Singh and Sujoy Ghoshal, *Ed* Huw Jenkens and David Charap, *M* Andrew T. Mackay with Meneka Das, *Wardrobe Supervisor* Pooja Chatervedi.

OceanSonic Pictures-OceanSonic Pictures. 89 mins. UK. 2006. Rel: 15 Aug 2008. No Cert.

Live! ★★★

Eva Mendes plays an unscrupulous television executive looking for the worst but most popular format for a reality game show and hits on the idea of Russian Roulette in which the winner is actually the ultimate loser. She then gets a documentary maker to film her progress, and thus the whole thing is presented by director and writer Bill Guttentag as a mockumentary. If it doesn't sound credible, that's probably because it could just happen. Wait and see!
CB

‣ Eva Mendes, David Krummholtz, Eric Lively, Katie Cassidy, Jeffrey Dean, Rob Brown, Jay Hernandez.
‣ *Dir* and *Screenplay* Bill Guttentag, *Pro* William Green and Charles Roven, *Ph* Stephen Kazmiersiu, *Pro Des* Robert De Vico, *Ed* Jim Stewart, *M* Phil Marshall, *Cos* Dayna Pink.

Atlas Entertainment-Mosaic Media Group-Lionsgate
97 mins. USA. 2008. Rel: 19 Sept 2008. Cert 15.

Looking For Eric ★★★½

Despite the humour Ken Loach's likable new film is about a man overcoming a sense of guilt and inferiority to rebuild his life aided by his hero, footballer Eric Cantona, present as an imaginary adviser. The real Eric will please his fans while the fictional Eric is splendidly played by Steve Evets. It's a warm-hearted movie that plays well both dramatically and comically until the last stretch when its near-farcical climax loses sight of the underlying truthfulness. A re-write might have saved the day and averted a last-minute own goal. MS

‣ Steve Evets, Eric Cantona. John Henshaw, Stephanie Bishop, Lucy-Jo Hudson.
‣ *Dir* Ken Loach, *Pro* Rebecca O'Brien, *Screenplay* Paul Laverty, *Ph* Barry Ackroyd, *Pro Des* Fergus Clegg, *Ed* Jonathan Morris, *M* George Fenton, *Cos* Sarah Ryan.

Canto Bros/Sixteen Films/Why Not Productions/Wild Bunch/Film4 etc.-Icon Film Distribution.
116 mins. France/UK/Italy/Belgium/Spain. 2009. Rel: 12 June 2009. Cert 15.

The Lost City ★½

There is no doubt that this is a labour of love for Cuban born Andy Garcia who not only plays the leading role but also directs and writes the music. The time is the late 1950s and the place is Havana just before Castro's revolution. Life is good for successful nightclub owner Fico Fellove until his beloved Cuba starts falling apart. There is no dramatic line here – it drifts from one scene to the next. Garcia gives it all he's got but his uneven and overlong project becomes an endurance test. GS

‣ Andy Garcia, Dustin Hoffman, Inés Sastre, Bill Murray, Tomas Milian, Steven Bauer, Richard Bradford.
‣ *Dir* and *Music* Andy Garcia, *Pro* Joe Drago and Lorenzo O'Brien, *Screenplay* G Cabrera Infante and D Daniel Vujic, *Pro Des* Waldemar Kalinowski, *Ed* Christopher Cibelli, *Cos* Deborah Lynn Scott.

Lionsgate Films/CineSon Entertainment/Platinum Equity/Crescent Drive Pictures-Lionsgate.
144 mins. USA. 2005. Rel: 5 Dec 2008. Cert 15.

Love and Honour ★★★½

Compare this with the samurai classics and it's clearly a journeyman work. Nevertheless, despite the sentimentality that mars its conclusion, it is a pleasing enough tale centred on a lowly samurai who loses his sight. It completes a trilogy by veteran filmmaker Yamada Yôji and again puts stress on domestic details and a woman's lot, even if action takes over at the climax. (Original title: *Bushi no ichibun*). MS

‣ Kimura Takuya, Sasano Takashi, Dan Rei, Ogata Ken, Bando Mitsugoro.
‣ *Dir* Yamada Yôji, *Pro* Hisamatsu Takeo and others, *Screenplay* Yamada, Hiramatsu Emiko and Yamamoto Ichiro from story by Fujisawa Shûhei, *Ph* Naganuma Mutsuo, *Pro Des* Degawa Mitsuo, *Ed* Ishii Iwao, *M* Tomita Isao, *Cos* Kurosawa Kazuko.

Shochiku/TV Asahi Corporation/Sumitomo Corporation etc.-ICA Films.
122 mins. Japan. 2006. Rel: 12 Dec 2008. Cert 12A.

Lou Reed's Berlin ★★★½

Julian Schnabel filmed Lou Reed's concert 'Berlin' over five nights in December 2006 at St Ann's Warehouse in Brooklyn. This was the first time that Reed performed the album live since its release in 1973 and he shared the stage with performers like Fernando Saunders and Sharon Jones. The film is more like a psychedelic dream, as is emphasised by the presence of Emmanuelle Seigner who acts as the narrator. It is a mesmerising experience and will be a treat for Reed's fans. GS

‣ Lou Reed, Fernando Saunders, Antony Hegarty, Sharon Jones, Emmanuelle Seigner.
‣ *Dir* Julian Schnabel, *Pro* Jon Kilik and Tom Sarig, *Ph* Ellen Kuras, *Ed* Benjamin Flaherty, *M* Lou Reed.

Waterboy Productions-
Artificial Eye Film Company.
85 mins. USA/UK. 2007.
Rel: 25 July 2008. Cert 12A.

The Love Guru ★ ½

Maurice Pitka (Mike Myers) is a self-styled love guru distraught that Deepak Chopra is still considered the number one self-help mentor in the US. Chopra's trick, apparently, is that he has appeared on *The Oprah Winfrey Show*. So Pitka sets his sights on Oprah by turning round the declining skills of hockey star Darren Roanoke (Romany Malco). It's complicated... A jumble of crude gags harnessed to a loose narrative, *The Love Guru* is a painful excuse for a comedy. There are three great jokes, but it's not enough to save a whole movie. JC-W

▸ Mike Myers, Jessica Alba, Justin Timberlake, Romany Malco, Meagan Good, Ben Kingsley, Omid Djalili, Kanye West.
▸ *Dir* Marco Schnabel, *Pro* Michael de Luca, Donald L Lee Jr and Myers. *Screenplay* Myers and Graham Gordy, *Ph* Peter Deming, *Pro Des* Charles Wood, *Ed* Lee Haxall, Gregory Perler and Billy Weber, *M* George S Clinton, *Cos* Karen Patch.

Paramount Pictures/Goldcrest Picures/
Spyglass Entertainment-United International
Pictures
87 mins. USA/Canada/Germany. 2008.
Rel: 1 Aug 2008. Cert 12A.

Mad Detective ★ ★ ★

This is director Johnnie To's blazing Hong Kong action thriller with a wacky twist. Lau Ching-wan gives a riveting, manic star turn as crazy Inspector Bun who solves crimes via his supposedly supernatural, intuitive gifts. Andy On gets a much less interesting role as Bun's young helper Ho who talks him out of retirement to hunt a serial killer. This is one of those convoluted, unsolvable cases known only to thrillers, in which a cop (Wong Kwok-chu) has gone inexplicably missing months ago, but his gun has since been used in a series of armed robberies. This complex and imaginative movie casts its strange spell as a satisfyingly disconcerting, weird and exciting experience. Expect strong bloody violence along with eye-catching visuals, snappy editing and many flashes of oddball humour. (Original title: *Sun taam*) DW

▸ Lau Ching-wan, Andy On, Lam Ka tung, Kelly Lin, Lee Kwok lun, Karen Lee, Lam suet.
▸ *Dir* and *Pro* Johnnie To and Wai ka fai, *Screenplay* Wai ka fai and Au kin yee, *Ph* Cheng siu keung, *Pro Des* Raymond Chan, *Ed* Tina Baz, *M* Xavier Jamaux, *Cos* Stanley Cheung.

China Star Entertainment/One Hundred
Years of Film Company/Milky Way Image
Company-Eureka Entertainment.
89 mins. USA. 2007. Rel: 18 July 2008. Cert 15.

Madagascar: Escape 2 Africa ★

Having escaped from the New York Zoo to Madagascar, that film's talking animals catapult a plane from that island into the wilds of mainland Africa. Like its predecessor, this has a really good premise but no idea how to develop it. That said, the mafioso penguins and Sacha Baron Cohen's partying lemur monarch provide light relief. JC

▸ Voices of Ben Stiller, Chris Rock, David Schwimmer, Jada Pinkett Smith, Sacha Baron Cohen, Cedric the Entertainer, Alec Baldwin.
▸ *Dir* Eric Darnell and Tom McGrath, *Pro* Mireille Soria and Mark Swift, *Screenplay* Darnell, McGrath and Etan Cohen, *Pro Des* Kendal Cronkhite, *Ed* Mark H Hester and H Lee Peterson, *M* Hans Zimmer.

DreamWorks Animation/Pacific Data Images-
Paramount Pictures.
89 mins. USA. 2008. Rel: 5 Dec 2008.
Cert PG.

Make It Happen ★ ★

Lauryn is a young woman from a small Indiana town who has ambitions of

becoming a world class dancer but after failing her audition for the Chicago School of Music and Dance she ends up as a club dancer. The premise of this average film is very familiar with a predictable climax but it benefits from Mary Elizabeth Winstead who makes the most of an underwritten role with a strong presence.
GS

▶ Mary Elizabeth Winstead, Tessa Thompson, John Reardon, Riley Smith, Ashley Roberts.
▶ *Dir* Darren Grant, *Pro* Brad Luff and Anthony Mosawi, *Screenplay* Duane Adler and Nicole Avril, from a story by Adler, *Ph* David Claessen, *Pro Des* Ray Kluga, *Ed* Scott Richter, *M* Paul Haslinger, *Cos* Karyn Wagner.

The Mayhem Project-Optimum Releasing. 90 mins. USA. 2008. Rel: 8 Aug 2008. Cert PG.

Mamma Mia! ★ ★ ★ ★

Stage director Phyllida Lloyd's film version of the ABBA musical is so cinematic that it's remarkable that critics largely failed to acclaim the movie that became the year's biggest hit with the public. The songs may be a matter of personal taste, but the energy of the piece memorably captured by Meryl Streep and her co-stars makes this into that rare commodity, a film that looks to have been fun to make and which conveys all of that to the audience.
MS

▶ Meryl Streep, Pierce Brosnan, Colin Firth, Stellan Skarsgård, Julie Walters, Dominic Cooper, Amanda Seyfried, Christine Baranski.
▶ *Dir* Phyllida Lloyd, *Pro* Judy Craymer and Gary Goetzman, *Screenplay* Catherine Johnson based on her original musical book and based on the songs of ABBA as conceived originally by Craymer, *Ph* Haris Zambarloukos, *Pro Des* Maria Djurkovic, *Ed* Lesley Walker, *M* Benny Andersson and Björn Ulvaeus with Stig Andersson, *Cos* Ann Roth.

Universal Pictures/Relativity Media/a Littlestar/Playtone production etc.-Universal Pictures International. 109 mins. USA/Germany/UK. 2008. Rel: 10 July 2008. Cert PG.

From New York to mainland Africa, those talking animals know how to put on a show in *Madagascar: Escape 2 Africa*.

The Man from London
★ ★ ★ ½

Derived from the same Simenon story that gave us *Temptation Harbour* in 1946, this is nevertheless every inch a Béla Tarr film: avant-garde, extremely slow-moving, atmospheric. The dockside drama dealing with robbery, murder and an unhappy father's concern for his daughter, yields pride of place to Tarr's stylistic and philosophical concerns. Highly demanding but supremely consistent, the film offers a play of light and shadow fully realised in Fred Kelemen's black and white photography. MS

▶ Miroslav Krobot, Erika Bók, János Derzsi, Tilda Swinton, Ági Szirtes.
▶ *Dir* Béla Tarr with Ágnes Hranitzky, *Pro* Gábor Téni, Paul Saadoun and others, *Screenplay* Lászlo Krasznahorkai and Tarr from Georges Simenon's novel *L'Homme de Londres*, *Ph* Fred Kelemen, *Art Dir* Lászlo Rajk, Hranitzky and Jean-Pascal Chalard, *Ed* Hranitzky, *M* Mihály Vig, *Cos* János Breckl.

Fortissimo Films/T.T. Filmmühely/
13 Production/Cinéma Soleil etc.-
Artificial Eye Film Company.
139 mins. Hungary/France/Germany/
Switzerland. 2007. Rel: 12 Dec 2008. Cert 12A.

Man on Wire ★ ★ ★ ★

Echoing the format of *Touching the Void*, James Marsh's impressive documentary features actors in dramatized re-enactments. It also uses an extremely varied music track that turns documentary into poetry as he tells the extraordinary story of Philippe Petit whose obsession with illegal high wire walks eventually led him to walk on one connecting the twin towers of New York's World Trade Centre. This is something out of the ordinary both in subject matter and in treatment. MS

▶ With Philippe Petit, Annie Allix and actors including Paul McGill and Ardis Campbell.
▶ *Dir* James Marsh, *Pro* Simon Chinn, Based on the book *To Reach the Clouds* by Philippe Petit, *Ph* Igor Martinovic with Rick Siegel, *Pro Des* Sharon Lomofsky, *Ed* Jinx Godfrey, *M* Michael Nyman, *Cos* Kathryn Nixon.

A Wall to Wall production/Red Box Films etc.-Icon Film Distribution.
94 mins. UK. 2007. Rel: 1 Aug 2008. Cert 12A.

The Mark of an Angel ★ ★ ★

Catherine Frot and Sandrine Bonnaire give fine performances as two women brought

Marley and Me is the film of the book of the newspaper column about married life with a dog. Owen Wilson and Jennifer Aniston play ball as the humans.

into conflict through a mother's obsessive belief that she has found again the child who had supposedly died within days of being born. The risk of melodrama is largely avoided but oddly the director and co-writer, Safy Nebbou, courts disbelief through a positive disregard for smooth, persuasive story-telling. (Original title: *L'Empreinte de l'ange*). MS

‣ Catherine Frot, Sandrine Bonnaire, Wladimir Yordanoff, Antoine Chappey, Héloise Cunin.
‣ *Dir* Safy Nebbou, *Pro* Michel Saint-Jean, *Screenplay* Nebbou and Cyril Gomez-Mathieu, *Ph* Éric Guichard, *Art Dir* Gomez-Mathieu, *Ed* Bernard Sasia, *M* Hugues Tabar-Nouval, *Cos* Corinne Jorry.

Diaphana Films/France 2 Cinéma/Canal+/ CinéCinéma etc.-Momentum Pictures. 95 mins. France. 2008. Rel: 22 May 2009. Cert 12A.

Marley and Me ★ ★ ★ ½

Based on the writings of John Grogan (Owen Wilson) this shaggy dog tale is full of homespun charm. It charts the chaotic life of John, his wife Jenny (Jennifer Aniston) and their dog Marley, whose antics give John all the material he needs for his newspaper column. Wilson and Aniston epitomise wholesomeness and the film has 'family appeal' written right across it. It's soppy, mildly amusing and so eager to be liked it almost sits up and begs. DP

‣ Owen Wilson, Jennifer Aniston, Eric Dane, Kathleen Turner, Alan Arkin, Clarke Peters, Joyce Van Patten.
‣ *Dir* David Frankel, *Pro* Gil Netter and Karen Rosenfeldt, *Screenplay* Scott Frank and Don Ross, from the book by John Grogan, *Ph* Florian Ballhaus, *Pro Des* Stuart Wurtzel, *Ed* Mark Livolsi, *M* Theodore Shapiro, *Cos* Cindy Evans.

Fox 2000 Pictures/Regency Enterprises/ Sunswept Entertainment-20th Century Fox. 120 mins. USA. 2008. Rel: 11 Mar 2008. Cert PG.

Married Life ★ ★ ★ ½

Inviting comparisons with the acclaimed *Far from Heaven* (2002), this 1949 period piece features Chris Cooper as an unfaithful husband whose concern for the feelings of his wife (Patricia Clarkson) leads ironically to his planning to murder her. Pierce Brosnan is less well cast as the husband's best friend but there is much to enjoy in this melodrama stronger on character and insights than on suspense despite clever twists. Cooper and Clarkson are great and while not wholly successful the movie nevertheless deserves to be much better known. MS

‣ Chris Cooper, Pierce Brosnan, Patricia Clarkson, Rachel McAdams, David Wenham.
‣ *Dir* Ira Sachs, *Pro* Steve Golin, Sachs, Sidney Kimmel and Jawal Nga, *Screenplay* Sachs and Oren Moverman from John Bingham's novel *Five Roundabouts to Heaven*, *Ph* Peter Deming, *Pro Des* Hugo Luczyc-Wyhowski, *Ed* Alfonso Gonçalves, *M* Dickon Hinchliffe, *Cos* Michael Dennison.

Metro-Goldwyn-Mayer Pictures/Sidney Kimmel Entertainment/an Anonymous Content/Firm Films production-Verve Pictures. 90 mins. USA. 2007. Rel: 1 Aug 2008. Cert PG.

Martyrs ★ ★

Ten-year-old Lucie (Mylène Jampanoï) manages to escape from violent kidnappers and fifteen years later she is still deeply scarred and disturbed by the experience. One day she takes a shotgun and heads for a family's country house convinced that she has traced her tormentors. Pascal Laugier's truly revolting and extremely violent film examines the roots of evil and successfully manages to shock with one of the nastiest endings ever, and that is not a recommendation. GS

‣ Morjana Alaoui, Mylène Jampanoï, Catherine Bégin, Robert Toupin, Patricia Laugier.
‣ *Dir* and *Screenplay* Pascal Laugier, *Pro* Richard Grandpierre and Simon Trottier, *Ph* Stephane Martin and Nathalie Moliavko-

Visotzky, *Pro Des* Jean-Andre Carriere, *Ed* Sébastien Pragère, *M* Alex Cortés and Willie Cortés, *Cos* Claire Nadon.

Canal Horizons/Canal +/TCB Film/Wild Bunch/ Cinecinema/Eskwad-Optimum Releasing. 99 mins. France/Canada. 2008. Rel: 27 Mar 2009. Cert 18.

Max Manus ★ ★ ★ ★

'Man of War' has been added to the British release title for those unaware that Manus was a real-life hero who played a significant role as a saboteur undermining German control of his country during the Second World War. That country was Norway where this film, straightforward and able but unexceptional, has had a sensational success. Its approach is decidedly traditional but it avoids the obvious exaggerations which have unfortunately marred many recent films about this period which have treated true facts with excessive licence. MS

▶ Aksel Hennie, Agnes Kittelsen, Nicolai Cleve Broch, Ken Duken, Christian Rubeck.
▶ *Dir* Espen Sandberg and Joachim Rønning, *Pro* John M. Jacobsen and Sveinung Golimo, *Screenplay* Thomas Nordseth-Tiller, *Ph* Geir Hartly Andreassen, *Pro Des* Karl Juliusson, *Ed* Anders Refn, *M* Trond Bjerknaes, *Cos* Manon Rasmussen.

A B&T Film GmbH, Miso Film Aps, Roenbergfilm AS co-production etc.- Revolver Entertainment. 118 mins. Norway/Germany/Denmark. 2008. Rel: 5 June 2009. No Cert.

Max Payne ★

A numbing experience for both mind and bottom, this soullessly stylish revenge thriller stars an emotionally comatose Mark Wahlberg as a cop on the warpath for the perps who blew away his wife and kid. Saddled with a ridiculous pun for a name and a DOA screenplay, he's a shallow videogame creation good for nothing but blowing people away. A tiring, increasingly

gruelling experience, it's simply no fun at all. MJ

▶ Mark Wahlberg, Mila Kunis, Beau Bridges, Chris O'Donnell, Chris 'Ludacris' Bridges, Kate Burton.
▶ *Dir* John Moore, *Pro* Moore, Scott Faye and Julie Yorn, *Screenplay* Beau Thomas based on the video game by Sam Lake, *Ph* Jonathan Sela, *Pro Des* Daniel T Dorrance, *Ed* Dan Zimmerman, *M* Marco Beltrami and Buck Sanders, *Cos* George L Little..

Abandon Entertainment/Collision Entertainment/Depth Entertainment/ Dune Entertainment etc-20th Century Fox. 100 mins. USA/Canada. 2008. Rel: 14 Nov 2008. Cert 15.

Meet Dave ★

Vaguely reminiscent of the final segment of Woody Allen's *Everything You Always Wanted to Know About Sex * *But Were Afraid to Ask*, this sci fi comedy from *Norbit* director Brian Robbins revolves around a crew of miniature, humanoid aliens, captained by Eddie Murphy, who travel to Earth in a man-shaped spaceship that also looks like Murphy. As lame and laughter-free as most Murphy vehicles, and extremely easy to stop watching. MJ

▶ Eddie Murphy, Elizabeth Banks, Scott Caan, Ed Helas, Kevin Hart, Mike O'Malley.
▶ *Dir* Brian Robbins, *Pro* Jon Berg, Todd Komarnicki and David T Friendly, *Screenplay* Rob Greenberg and Bill Corbett, *Ph* J Clark Mathis, *Pro Des* Clay A Griffith, *Ed* Ned Bastille, *M* John Debney, *Costumes* Ruth E Carter.

Twentieth Century Fox/Regency Enterprises/ Friendly Films etc-20th Century Fox. 90 mins. USA. 2008. Rel: 18 July 2008. Cert PG.

Mes Amis, Mes Amours ★ ★ ★ ½

Two Frenchmen, Matthias and Antoine, both old friends and both divorced, decide to live together in London, with their

Mark Wahlberg and Mila Kunis get out the hardware in John Moore's revenge thriller *Max Payne* – possibly the year's worst film title.

respective children. The relationship soon falls apart when a woman comes between them. Despite the oddity of the film's premise – it all takes place in London's French community in South Kensington in a kind of friendly ghetto where nobody speaks English – it offers stunning shots of London landmarks seen from odd viewpoints and the performances of Vincent London as Matthias and Pascal Elbé as Antoine assure Lorraine Levy's film, based on her brother's novel, more than enough charm. This is a Richard Curtis movie as directed by Jacques Demy. MHD

▶ Vincent Lindon, Pascal Elbé, Virginie Ledoyen, Florence Foresti, Bernadette Lafont, Richard Syms.
▶ *Dir* Lorraine Levy, *Pro* Dominique Farrugia, *Screenplay* Philippe Guez and Lorraine Levy, from the novels by Marc Levy, *Ph* Emmanuel Soyer, *Pro Des* Françoise Dupertuis, *Ed* Sophie Reine, *M* Sébastien Souchois, *Cos* Jacqueline Bouchard.

Evidence Films/Few/Pathé/Poisson Rouge Pictures-Pathé Distribution.
99 mins. France. 2008. Rel: 4 July 2008.
Cert 15.

The Midnight Meat Train
★ ★ ½

Struggling photographer Leon Kaufman wants to impress the owner of a prestigious art gallery with his dark, raw pictures that he takes late at night in the New York subway. But his life takes an unexpected turn when he comes across Mahogany, a ruthless serial killer who butchers late-night travellers. It is suitably atmospheric and gory but never really scary and luckily Vinnie Jones' speaking role is confined to only one word. GS

▶ Bradley Cooper, Leslie Bibb, Brooke Shields, Vinnie Jones, Roger Bart, Tony Curran.
▶ *Dir* Ryuhei Kitamura, *Pro* Clive Barker, Gary Lucchesi, Eric Reid etc, *Screenplay* Jeff Buhler, from the story by Barker, *Ph* Jonathan Sela, *Pro Des* Clark Hunter, *Ed* Toby Yates, *M* Johannes Kobilke and Robb Williamson, *Cos* Christopher Lawrence.

GreeneStreet Films/Lions Gate Films/ Midnight Picture Show/seraphim films/ Lakeshore Entertainment-Lionsgate.
98 mins. USA. 2008. Rel: 3 Oct 2008.
Cert 18.

Milk ★ ★ ★ ★ ★

Gay activist Harvey Milk was the first openly gay man to be elected to public office in the USA. The freedoms that many lesbian and gay men now enjoy can be traced back to the work of Harvey Milk. He may have started to ghettoise gays into action when he moved to San Francisco but it did work and he is recognised as a hero by all minorities, including blacks, the old, the unions, or anybody who was done down by authority. Tragically Milk died in the process. Sean Penn gives a remarkable performance as Harvey, with good support from James Franco as his partner Scott. Gus Van Sant's documentary-style approach is both highly creditable and revealing.
MHD

‣ Sean Penn, Emile Hirsch, Josh Brolin, Diego Luna, James Franco, Alison Pill, Victor Garber, Denis O'Hare.
‣ *Dir* Gus Van Sant, *Pro* Bruce Cohen, Dan Jinks and Michael London, *Screenplay* Dustin Lance Black, *Ph* Harris Savides, *Pro Des* Bill Groom, *Ed* Elliot Graham, *M* Danny Elfman, *Cos* Danny Glicker.

Focus Features/Axon Films/Groundswell Productions/Jinks-Cohen Company/Sessions Payroll Management-Momentum Pictures. 128 mins. USA. 2008. Rel: 23 Jan 2009. Cert 15.

Mirrors ★ ★

Kiefer Sutherland does his usual briskly competent job as a troubled ex-cop who takes a job as a nightwatch security guard at an abandoned department store devastated by a fire years ago. There, he's apparently targeted by some sort of ghostly killer evil force using reflections in mirrors and other shiny objects as – er, um – 'gateways' into his estranged family's home. French horror director Alexandre Aja, who remade *The Hills Have Eyes* in 2006, does a slick, polished-looking job again but has less success with this rejig of the 2003 Korean film *Into the Mirror*. Some of this is admirably atmospheric, suspenseful and creepy, but some of it is also pretentious and bewildering, so while it's watchable and acceptable it is finally unsatisfying and underwhelming. DW

‣ Kiefer Sutherland, Paula Patton, Cameron Boyce, Erica Gluck, Amy Smart, John Shrapnel, Jason Flemyng, Julian Glover.
‣ *Dir* Alexandre Aja, *Pro* Gregory Levasseur, Marc Sternberg and Alexandra Milchan, *Screenplay* Aja and Levasseur, based on the Korean film *Into the Mirror, Ph* Maxine Alexandre, *Pro Des* Joseph C Nemec III, *Ed* Baxter, *M* Javier Navarette, *Cos* Michael Dennison and Ellen Mirojnick.

Regency Enterprises/New Regency Pictures/ Luna Pictures/ASAF-20th Century Fox. 110 mins. USA/Romania. 2008. Rel: 10 Oct 2008. Cert 15.

Miss Pettigrew Lives for a Day ★ ★ ★ ★

A big hit in America but not seen very widely here, this is an admirably judged feelgood movie set in London in the 1930s. The eponymous figure is a vicar's daughter splendidly played by Frances McDormand who, when employed by an American actress, becomes a positive influence on the lives of others but also triumphs herself. Lightweight but spot on, the film is not only good fun but unexpectedly reveals Ciarán Hinds to be the Rossano Brazzi of the 21st century. MS

‣ Frances McDormand, Amy Adams, Ciarán Hinds, Shirley Henderson, Lee Pace, Mark Strong.
‣ *Dir* Bharat Nalluri, *Pro* Nellie Bellflower and Stephen Garrett, *Screenplay* David Magee and Simon Beaufoy from the novel by Winifred Watson, *Ph* John de Borman, *Pro Des* Sarah Greenwood, *Ed* Barney Pilling, *M* Paul Englishby, *Cos* Michael O'Connor.

Focus Features/a Kudos Pictures and Keylight Entertainment production etc.- Momentum Pictures. 92 mins. USA/UK. 2007. Rel: 15 Aug 2008. Cert PG.

Paula Patten and Kiefer Sutherland go through the looking glass in search of an evil force in Alexandre Aja's *Mirrors*.

The Mist ★ ★ ★ ★

This Stephen King-penned horror very efficiently ratchets up the suspense. A group of Maine residents, led by a local artist (Thomas Jane), find themselves trapped within a supermarket when fearsome creatures start emerging from an all-enveloping mist. With no help at hand, they have to keep the monsters at bay themselves. Director Frank Darabont frames the film beautifully and Marcia Gay Harden stands out as a religious fanatic, while the 'horrors' will make your flesh crawl. This is a knuckle-biter with a truly shocking ending.
DP

▶ Thomas Jane, Marcia Gay Harden, Laurie Holden, Andre Braugher, Toby Jones, Frances Sternhagen.
▶ *Dir* Frank Darabont, *Pro* Darrabont and Liz Glotzer, *Screenplay* Darabont from the novella by Stephen King, *Ph* Rohn Schmidt, *Pro Des* Gregory Melton, *Ed* Hunter M Via, *M* Mark Isham, *Cos* Giovanna Ottobre-Melton.

Dimension Films/Dark Woods Productions-Momentum Pictures.
126 mins. USA. 2007. Rel: 4 July 2008.
Cert 15.

Modern Life ★ ★ ★ ★ ★

Its concern may be with France's rural farmers rather than with country children but this wonderful documentary feature by Raymond Depardon is the true successor to the acclaimed *Etre et Avoir* (2002). Both films portray with sensitivity a way of life that may soon vanish and in each case you come to feel by the close that you really know the people on screen. The 'Scope format ensures that the numerous interviews by Depardon never smack of TV footage but provide an experience that is truly cinematic. It's also a work of real significance for the social historian. (Original Title: *La vie moderne*).
MS

▶ With Marcel Privat, Raymond Privat, Abel Jean Roy, Marcel Challaye, Amandine Valla.
▶ *Dir* and *Ph* Raymond Depardon, *Pro* Claudine Nougaret, *Ed* Simon Jacquet, *M* Gabriel Fauré.

Palmeraie et désert/France 2 Cinéma etc.-Soda Pictures.
87 mins. France. 2008. Rel: 3 April 2009.
Cert PG.

Momma's Man ★★★

Mikey (Matt Boren) after a visit to see his parents in New York begins to have doubts about his life in LA so he cancels his flight back home and refuses to answer his wife's frequent telephone calls. Azazel Jacobs' careful study of a lonely man on the brink of a nervous breakdown takes its time to unfold but its measured pace soon grasps attention. It is not as bleak as it sounds and it's also quite funny especially in the scenes with Mikey's overcaring parents (acted with great enthusiasm by Jacobs' real parents).GS

❯ Matt Boren, Ken Jacobs, Richard Edson, Piero Arcilesi, Eleanor Hutchins, Flo Jacobs, Dana Varon.
❯ *Dir* and *Screenplay* Azazel Jacobs, *Pro* Hunter Gray and Alex Orlovsky, *Ph* Tobias Datum, *Ed* Darrin Navarro, *M* Mandy Hoffman.

Artists Public Domain-Diffusion Pictures. 94 mins. USA. 2008. Rel: 8 May 2009. Cert 15.

Monsters vs Aliens ★★★½

An enjoyable sci fi 'toon with lots of fun retro stylings, this efficient but unremarkable computer-generated adventure sees a squad of well-meaning monsters facing off against an egotistical alien invader. Best seen in the original 3D, though well worth a watch no matter the format, it's a parent-friendly kiddie-pleaser, a gag-fuelled primer for little ones to get acquainted with classic fantasy flicks from *The Blob* to *Close Encounters*. MJ

❯ Voices of Reese Witherspoon, Seth Rogen, Hugh Laurie, Will Arnett, Kiefer Sutherland, Rainn Wilson, Renée Zellweger, Paul Rudd.
❯ *Dir* Rob Letterman and Conrad Vernon, *Pro* Lisa Stewart, *Screenplay* Letterman, Maya Forbes, Wallace Wolodarsky, Jonathan Aibel and Glenn Berge, from a story by Letterman and Vernon, *Pro Des* Scott Wills, *Ed* Joyce Arrastia and Eric Dapkewicz, *M* Henry Jackman..

DreamWorks Animation-Paramount Pictures. 94 mins. USA. 2009. Rel: 3 Apr 2009. Cert PG.

Mum and Dad ★★

Well-made and resourceful but really unpleasant, low-budget British horror film that starts with a foreign Heathrow airport cleaner accompanying an apparently friendly workmate home only to find herself imprisoned by Mum and Dad – her workmate's insane parents. Frighteningly realistic, this is vile stuff – but Perry Benson and Dido Miles give very good performances indeed in their sick roles. DW

❯ Perry Benson, Dido Miles, Olga Fedori, Ainsley Howard, Toby Alexander, Mark Devenport.
❯ *Dir* and *Screenplay* Steven Sheil, *Pro* Lisa Trnovski, *Ph* Jonathan Bloom, *Pro Des* Jess Alexander, *Ed* Leo Scott, *Music Supervisor* Dan Rose, *Cos* Claire Finlay.

2am Films/EM Media-Film London. 84 mins. UK. 2008. Rel: 26 Dec 2008. Cert 18.

The Mummy: Tomb of the Dragon Emperor ★

Indiana Jones wannabe Rick O'Connell (Brendan Fraser) faces an onslaught of flashy special effects in the worst film ever made by Rob (*Dragon, Dragonheart*) Cohen with the word Dragon in the title. This Asian-themed instalment of the decreasingly interesting Mummy franchise sees Rick and the family face off against evil shape shifter Jet Li. The results, though noisy, colourful and explosive, are also painfully dull, with a duff plot, cardboard characters and idiotic dialogue. MJ

❯ Brendan Fraser, Jet Li, Maria Bello, John Hannah, Michelle Yeoh, Luke Ford, David Calder.
❯ *Dir* Rob Cohen, *Pro* Sean Daniel, James Jacks, Stephen Sommers and Bob Ducsay, *Screenplay* Alfred Gough and Miles Millar, *Ph* Simon Duggan, *Pro Des* Nigel Phelps, *Ed* Kelly Matsumoto and Joel Hegron, *M* Randy Edelman, *Cos* Sanja Milkovic Hays

Universal Pictures/Relativity Media/The Sommers Company/Alphaville Films etc-Universal Pictures International.

112 mins. Germany/USA. 2008.
Rel: 6 Aug 2008. Cert 12A.

The Mutant Chronicles ★

Set on a post-apocalyptic Earth ravaged by mutants and stuff, this execrable screen adaptation of a geeky role-playing game follows the desperate, final efforts of a dirty half-dozen (Thomas Jane, Ron Perlman…) to save mankind. Taking itself far too seriously for its own good, it's a B-movie at best, with wooden acting, leaden dialogue and poorly directed action sequences. Though it has some of the qualities of a good/bad movie, it's mostly just unengaging tosh. MJ

▶ Thomas Jane, Ron Perlman, Devon Aoki, Sean Pertwee, John Malkovich, Nicholas Ball.
▶ *Dir* Simon Hunter, *Pro* Stephen Belafonte, Edward R Pressman, Tim Dennison, Peter La Terriere and Pras Michel, *Screenplay* Philip Eisner, *Ph* Geoff Boyle, *Pro Des* Caroline Greville-Morris, *Ed* Sean Barton and Alison Lewis, *M* Richard Wells, *Cos* Yves Barre.

Entertainment-Entertainment Film Distributors.
111 mins. USA. 2008. Rel: 10 Oct 2008. Cert 18.

My Best Friend's Girl ★ ★

'Tank' (Dane Cook) is a professional bastard. He's a guy who takes women out on traumatic dates so that they'll crawl back sobbing to their jilted ex-boyfriends. It's a fail-proof plan until Tank's modus operandi backfires when he dates his best friend's would-be girlfriend (Kate Hudson). Most films are calculating, however hard they try to hide the fact. The problem with this predictable, male chauvinistic stuff is that we're not sure *how* we're meant to be manipulated. There's nobody to root for and only Neanderthal thugs and Dane Cook adherents are likely to be engrossed. JC-W

▶ Dane Cook, Kate Hudson, Alec Baldwin, Jason Biggs, Lizzy Caplan, Riki Lindhorne.
▶ *Dir* Howard Deutsch, *Pro* Cook, Adam Herz, Doug Johnson, Barry Katz etc *Screenplay* Jordan Cahan, *Ph* Jack N Green, *Pro Des* Jane

Ann Stewart, *Ed* Seth Flaum, *M* John Debney, *Cos* Marilyn Vance.

Management 360/Terra Firma Films/
New Wave Entertainment/Superfinger
Entertainment-Lionsgate.
101 mins. USA. 2008. Rel: 21 Nov 2008. Cert 15.

My Bloody Valentine 3D ★ ★ ★ ½

In the small town of Harmony the only survivor of a coalmining accident wakes up from a coma and starts brutally murdering people until the police track him down and kill him. Exactly ten years later Tom Hanniger (Jensen Ackles), the young man who managed to escape from the hands of the killer on that fateful Valentine's Day, returns to Harmony in order to sell his father's mine. But the man with the miner's mask and the pickaxe is also back slashing his way through town. The film is very gory with well used 3-D effects. GS

▶ Jensen Ackles, Jaime King, Kerr Smith, Betsy Rue, Ed Gathegi, Tom Atkins.
▶ *Dir* Patrick Lussier, *Pro* Jack L Murray, *Screenplay* Todd Farmer and Zane Smith, from the 1981 screenplay by John Beaird and the story by Stephen Miller, *Ph* Brian Pearson, *Pro Des* Zack Grobler, *Ed* Lussier and Cynthia Ludwig, *M* Michael Wandmacher, *Cos* Leeann Radeka.

Lionsgate-Lionsgate.
101 mins. USA. 2009. Rel: 16 Jan 2009. Cert 18.

My Sister's Keeper ★ ★ ★ ½

The subject matter of this film may keep potential patrons away, although readers of the original novel may wish to see Nick Cassavetes' film about a family with a terminally ill daughter Kate (Sofia Vassilieva) who has suffered from leukaemia for most of her life. Now a teenager she has been kept alive through organ and blood donations by her sister Anna (Abigail Breslin). The parents played by Cameron Diaz and Jason Patric, have an older son whom they virtually

ignore. When Anna decides to go to law to release herself from the onus of keeping her sister alive, the family is torn apart and Kate's life is threatened. It is fine if you can stomach the subject and the situation, while the performances are good and far from sentimental, but all the same it's not a fun film. CB

▶ Abigail Breslin, Walter Raney, Sofia Vassilieva, Cameron Diaz, Heather Wahlquist, Jason Patric, Alec Baldwin, Nicole Lenz.
▶ *Dir* Nick Cassavetes, *Pro* Mendel Tropper, Stephen Furst, Mark Johnson, Scott Goldman and Chuck Pacheco, *Screenplay* Cassavetes and Jeremy Leven, *Ph* Caleb Deschanel, *Pro Des* Jon Hutman, *Ed* Jim Flynn and Alan Heim, *M* Aaron Zigman, *Cos* Shay Cunliffe.

Curmudgeon Films/Gran Via Productions/ Mark Johnson Productions-Entertainment Film Distributors.106 mins. USA. 2009. Rel: 26 June 2008. Cert 12A.

My Winnipeg ★★★★

This is a film poem about Guy Maddin's home town and wholly idiosyncratic in its blend of old documentary footage, re-enactments (here the late Ann Savage makes a last appearance) and stylisation that even extends to some animation. It's about memory, about change, and about our reactions to our birthplace and as such invites comparisons with Terence Davies's *Of Time and the City* (q.v.). Maddin's style will not suit all but this is probably his most completely realised film. MS

▶ Ann Savage, Louis Negin, Amy Stewart, Darcy Fehr. Narrated by Guy Maddin.
▶ *Dir, Written and conceived by* Guy Maddin, *Pro* Jody Shapiro and Phyllis Laing, *Ph* Shapiro, Maddin and others, *Pro Des* Réjean Labrie, *Ed* John Gurdebeke, *Cos* Meg McMillan.

A Documentary Channel Original production etc.-Soda Pictures.
80 mins. Canada/USA. 2007.
Rel: 4 July 2008. Cert 12A.

New in Town ★

Renée Zellweger is less irritating than usual in this bland and totally unfunny rom-com. She plays Lucy Hill, a Miami consultant who is sent to a small Minnesota town in order to oversee the reconstruction of a factory. She is like a fish out of water but she soon warms up to the community's easygoing ways. To say that it's predictable and sentimental is a total understatement. GS

▶ Renée Zellweger, Harry Connick Jr, Siobhan Falllon Hogan, J K Simmons, Mike O'Brien, Frances Conroy.
▶ *Dir* Jonas Elmer, *Pro* Darryl Taja, Paul Brooks, Andrew Paquin, Phyllis Laing and Tracey E Edmonds, *Screenplay* Ken Rance and C Jay Cox, *Ph* Chris Seager, *Pro Des* Dan Davis, *Ed* Troy Takaki, *M* John Swihart, *Cos* Lee Harper and Darena Snowe.

Edmonds Entertainment Group/Epidemic Pictures/Gold Circle Films/The SafranCompany-Entertainment Film Distributors. 97 mins. USA/ Canada. 2009. Rel: 27 Feb 2009. Cert 12A.

New Town Killers ★★★

As director Richard Jobson plays a winning hand but as writer he serves up a preposterous thriller in which a teenage nobody (the promising James Anthony Pearson) is tricked into a deadly game by a mad banker (Dougray Scott, suitably nasty). It's the rich playing with the poor but less an allegory than an over-violent action piece that will be better suited to the video game to which it is being linked. MS

▶ Alastair Mackenzie, Dougray Scott, Liz White, James Anthony Pearson.
▶ *Dir* and *Written by* Richard Jobson, *Pro* Luc Roeg and Jobson, *Ph* Simon Dennis, *Pro Des* James Lapsley, *Ed* Steven Sander, *M* Stephen Hilton, *Cos* Francesca Oddi.

Independent/Str8jacket Creations/Scottish Screen/Screen East Content Investment Fund/an Independent Film production etc.-High Fliers Distribution.
100 mins. UK. 2009. Rel: 12 June 2009. Cert 15.

New in Town but a hoary rom-com as old as the hills of Minnesota where Miami consultant Renée Zellweger goes to oversee a building project.

Nick & Norah's Infinite Playlist ★★★½

This lightweight rom-com set in New York during the course of one night makes the mistake of going on too long and some of its mainstream appeal may be limited to the young audiences who will readily identify with its characters. But if this is at heart formula stuff it's made unexpectedly engaging by the playing of Michael Cera (so good in *Juno*) and of Kit Dennings as the duo who are, we hope, headed for a happy ending. MS

▷ Michael Cera, Kat Dennings, Alexis Dziena, Ari Graynor, Aaron Yoo, Rafi Gavron.
▷ *Dir* Peter Sollett, *Pro* Kerry Kohansky, Chris Weitz, Paul Weitz and Andrew Miano, *Screenplay* Lorene Scafaria from the novel by Rachel Cohn and David Levithan, *Ph* Tom Richmond, *Pro Des* David Doernberg, *Ed* Myron Kerstein, *M* Mark Mothersbaugh, *Cos* Sandra Hernandez.

Columbia Pictures/Mandate Pictures/a Depth of Field production-Sony Pictures Entertainment.
89 mins. USA. 2008. Rel: 30 Jan 2009. Cert 12A.

Night at the Museum 2 ★★★½

Larry (Ben Stiller), the night guard from the first film, is now a prosperous inventor but he soon comes back to rescue his old friends – the Museum exhibits that come to life at night – when they are packed into crates and sent to the Smithsonian Institute in Washington DC. In this likeable sequel Hank Azaria effortlessly steals the film from Stiller as the outrageously over the top and lisping Pharaoh Kahmunrah who threatens to kill those that oppose his plans for world domination. Also Amy Adams is delightful as Amelia Earhart. (Original title: *Night at the Museum: Battle of the Smithsonian*). GS

▷ Ben Stiller, Amy Adams, Owen Wilson, Hank Azaria, Robin Williams, Christopher Guest, Alain Chabat, Steve Coogan, Ricky Gervais.
▷ *Dir* Shawn Levy, *Pro* Levy, Michael Barnahan, Chris Columbus and Mark Radcliffe, *Screenplay* Robert Ben Garant and Thomas Lennon, *Ph* John Schwartzman, *Pro Des* Claude Paré, *Ed* Dean Zimmerman and Don Zimmerman, *M* Alan Silvestri, *Cos* Marlene Stewart.

Tissues ready as Richard Gere and Diane Lane share a prelude to romance in George C Wolfe's watchable weepie *Nights in Rodanthe*.

Twentieth Century Fox Film Company/ Museum Canada Productions/1492 Pictures/21 Laps Entertainment-20th Century Fox. 105 mins. USA/Canada. 2009. Rel: 20 May 2008. Cert PG.

Nights in Rodanthe ★★★

Adrienne Willis is a lonely woman trying to cope after her husband leaves her but is given a second chance when she meets Dr Paul Flanner in the tiny coastal town of Rodanthe. He has his own cross to bear but together they find love and affection. It is predictable to say the least but Diane Lane and Richard Gere, who repeat their successful *Unfaithful* chemistry, lift the thin material of this average weepie to another dimension and make it quite watchable. GS

▶ Diane Lane, Richard Gere, Christopher Meloni, Viola Davis, Becky Ann Baker, Scott Glenn.
▶ *Dir* George C Wolfe, *Pro* Denise Di Novi, *Screenplay* Ann Peacock and John Romano from the novel by Nicholas Sparks, *Ph* Affonso Beato, *Pro Des* Patrizia von Brandenstein, *Ed* Brian A Kates, *M* Jeanine Tesori, *Cos* Victoria Farrell.

Warner Bros Pictures/Village Roadshow Pictures/Di Novi Pictures-Warner Bros Pictures 97 mins. USA/Australia. 2008. Rel: 10 Oct 2008. Cert PG.

The North Face ★★★

This tale about rival climbers attempting to scale the Eiger in 1936 has a partly factual basis and may appeal strongly to those addicted to mountaineering dramas. However, the tense conclusion admirably unpredictable as to its outcome only serves to emphasise that there are no surprises earlier. The characters are scarcely more than cyphers and the film, well mounted though it is, follows a routine course until its finale. (Original title: *Nordwand*). MS

▶ Benno Fürmann, Johanna Wokalek, Florian Lukas, Simon Schwarz, Ulrich Tukur.
▶ *Dir* Philipp Stölzl, *Pro* Danny Krausz, Boris Schönfelder, Rudolf Santschi and Benjamin Herrmann, *Screenplay* Christoph Silber, Rupert Henning, Stölzl and others, *Ph* Kolja Brandt, *Pro Des* Udo Kramer, *Ed* Sven Budelmann, *M* Christian Kolonovits, *Cos* Birgit Hutter.

Majestic Filmverleih/a Dor Film-West production etc.-Metrodome Distribution. 127 mins. Germany/Austria/Switzerland. 2008. Rel: 12 Dec 2008. Cert 12A.

Not Easily Broken ★

It is difficult to understand why Dave Johnson (Morris Chestnut) tries so hard to save his marriage to Clarice (Taraji P Henson) who always nags him and unfairly suspects him of infidelity. Chestnut is a strong presence in this poorly written family melodrama which verges on the misogynistic. The acting is not bad, but Bill Duke's heavy-handed direction sends out the wrong signals especially in the way he uses the over-sentimental and manipulative music. GS

‣ Morris Chestnut, Taraji P Henson, Maeve Quinlan, Wood Harris, Kevin Hart, Eddie Cibrian, Jenifer Lewis.
‣ *Dir* Bill Duke, *Pro* Clint Culpeper, T D Jakes, Aaron Norris and Curtis Wallace, *Screenplay* Brian Bird, from the novel by T D Jakes, *Ph* Geary McLeod, *Pro Des* Cecil Gentry, *Ed* Josh Rifkin, *M* Kurt Farquhar, *Cos* Diane Charles.

Screen Gems/T D Jakes Ministries-Sony Pictures Entertainment. 99 mins. USA. 2009. Rel: 17 Apr 2009. Cert PG.

Not Quite Hollywood: The Wild Untold Story of Ozploitation! ★★★★

Mark Hartley's enjoyable documentary celebrates Australian exploitation cinema of the 1970s and '80s up to the present day. Apart from the emergence of the Australian New Wave with such classics as *Picnic at Hanging Rock* and *My Brilliant Career* Down Under became the centre of explicit sex comedies and gory horror as well as very violent action films that influenced a whole generation of filmmakers including Tarantino. It makes you want to check out these titles and is very entertaining. GS

‣ Jamie Lee Curtis, Phillip Adams, Ian Barry, Jeremy Thomas, Dennis Hopper, Barry Crocker, Barry Humphries.
‣ *Dir* and *Screenplay* Mark Hartley, *Pro* Michael Lynch and Craig Griffin, *Ph* Karl von Moller and Germain McMicking, *Ed* Hartley, Jamie Blanks and Sara Edwards, *M* Stephen Cummings and Billy Miller.

City Films Worldwide/ Film Finance-Optimum Releasing. 103 mins. Australia/USA. 2008. Rel: 13 Mar 2008. Cert 18.

Notorious ★★★½

This slick and stylish film tells the remarkable story of Christopher 'The Notorious BIG.' Wallace from a young age as a lonely Catholic child through his teenage years as a tough drug dealer, followed by his meteoric rise as one of America's leading hip-hop figures. But his success went hand in hand with corruption and rivalry with West Coast rapper Tupac Shakur (Anthony Mackie). Biggie's connections to the mafia were hinted at much more in Nick Broomfield's 2002 documentary *Biggie and Tupac*. Brooklyn rapper Jamal Woolard is a strong presence and delivers an excellent performance as the tortured anti- hero. GS

‣ Jamal Woolard, Mohammed Dione, Angela Bassett, Derek Luke, Dennis L A White, Marc John Jeffries, Ginger Kroll.
‣ *Dir* George Tillman Jr, *Pro* Voletta Wallace, Robert Teitel, Wayne Barrow, Trish Hofmann, Edward Bates and Mark Pitts, *Screenplay* Reggie Rock Blythewood and Cheo Hedari Coker, *Ph* Michael Grady, *Pro Des* Jane Musky, *Ed* Dirk Westervelt, *M* Danny Elfman, *Cos* Paul A Simmons.

Fox Searchlight Pictures/Voletta Wallace Films/By Storm Films/ Bad Boy Films/State Street Pictures-20th Century Fox 122 mins. USA. 2009. Rel: 13 Feb 2009. Cert 15.

Numb ★ ★ ★ ½

Centre screen here is Matthew Perry of *Friends* and writer/director Harris Goldberg's film is a comedy but one with engagingly unusual ingredients. It satirises doctors and psychiatrists but features the hero's disorder – one of depersonalisation stemming from stress and trauma in the modern world – as something that may put off his dream girl. Lynn Collins in this role makes a limited impression and the film is uneven, but much of it is enjoyable and it should appeal to those who liked the comedies of Elaine May. (Note: this review was omitted from *Film Review 2008-9*). MS

▶ Matthew Perry, Lynn Collins, Kevin Pollak, Bob Gunton, Helen Shaver, Mary Steenburgen.
▶ *Dir* and *Written by* Harris Goldberg, *Pro* Kirk Shaw, *Ph* Etric Steelberg, *Pro Des* Phil Schmidt, *Ed* Jeff Wishengrad, *M* Ryan Shore, *Cos* Sylvie Gendron.

**Fries Film Group/an Insight Film Studios production/Proud Mary Entertainment, etc.-Scanbox Entertainment.
93 mins. Canada/USA. 2007.
Rel: 14 June 2008. No Cert.**

Obscene ★ ★ ★ ★

Neil Ortenberg and Daniel O'Connell's fascinating documentary paints a clear picture of the life of Barney Rosset, the innovative publisher of Grove Press and the Evergreen Review. He was an impulsive character and as John Waters says, "We benefited from the wars he fought." Rosset changed the obscenity laws of his country and was the first American publisher of Samuel Beckett, Tom Stoppard, Che Guevara, Malcolm X and of controversial novels such as *Lady Chatterley's Lover*, *Tropic of Cancer* and *Naked Lunch*. Illuminating stuff! GS

▶ Amiri Baraka, Jim Carroll, Al Goldstein, Erica Jong, John Sayles, Gore Vidal, John Waters.
▶ *Dir* Daniel O'Connell and Neil Ortenberg, *Pro* Alex Meillier and Tanya Meillier, *Ph* Alex Meillier, *Ed* Tanya Meillier, *M* Askold Buk.

**Double O Film Productions-Arthouse Films.
97 mins. USA. 2007. Rel: 27 Feb 2009. No Cert.**

Observe and Report ★ ½

Comparisons are inevitable with the recent but much funnier *Paul Blart: Mall Cop* (qv.). This time Seth Rogen is the Mall Cop – he is the head of security at the Forest Ridge Mall and is determined to use any unorthodox methods necessary to bring order to his Mall. And things get even worse when a flasher arrives on the scene... Rogen made an impact last year with *Knocked Up* but here his performance is smug and unfunny and the less said about the morality of the whole thing the better. GS

▶ Seth Rogan, Ray Liotta, Michael Peña, Anna Faris, John Yuan, Matt Yuan.
▶ *Dir* and *Screenplay* Jody Hill, *Pro* Donald De Line, *Ph* Tim Orr, *Pro Des* Chris L Spellman, *Ed* Zene Baker, *M* Joseph Stephens, *Cos* Gary Jones.

**De Line Pictures/Legendary Pictures-Warner Bros Distributors.
86 mins. USA. 2009. Rel: 24 Apr 2009. Cert 15.**

Obsessed ★ ★ ★

Lisa (Ali Larter) is the temp secretary from hell who, after becoming obsessed with her new boss Derek (Idris Elba), tries hard to steal him from his wife Sharon (Beyoncé Knowles). Director Steve Shill's stylish and enjoyable psychological thriller, despite an ending that belongs to a different film, is blessed with the striking presence of Elba. He shares a strong chemistry with Knowles who comes into her own in the final scenes when she decides to put an end to her rival's psychotic behaviour. "I will show you crazy," she threatens Lisa on the phone. Larter is seductively believable in an otherwise one-dimensional role. GS

▶ Idris Elba, Beyoncé Knowles,.Ali Larter, Jerry O'Connell, Bonnie Perlman, Christine Lahti, Nathan Myers, Nicolas Myers.
▶ *Dir* Steve Shill, *Pro* William Packer,

Screenplay David Loughery, *Ph* Ken Seng, *Pro Des* Jon Gary Steele, *Ed* Paul Seydor, *M* James Dooley, *Cos* Maya Lieberman.

Screen Gems/Rainforest Films-Sony Pictures Releasing.
108 mins. USA. 2009. Rel: 29 May 2009.
Cert 12A.

Of Time and the City
★★★★½

Welcome back Terence Davies. His first film for some years is a poetic documentary about the changing face of Liverpool. It is nowhere more idiosyncratic than in its commentary delivered by Davies himself. Guy Maddin's comparable film *My Winnipeg* (q.v.) connects more strongly with universal emotions but on a second viewing this essay film is even more satisfying, an intensely personal meditation expressed through film poetry. The use of music of many kinds on the soundtrack is part of the film's very essence. MS

❧ Narrated by Terence Davies.
❧ *Dir* and *Written by* Terence Davies, *Pro* Solon Papadopoulos and Roy Boulter, *Ph* Tim Pollard, *Ed* Liza Ryan-Carter, *M Supervisor* Ian Neil.

Northwest Vision and Media & Digital Departures/Liverpool Culture Company/ BBC Films/a Hurricane Films production etc.- British Film Institute.
74 mins. UK. 2008. Rel: 31 Oct 2008. Cert 12A.

O'Horten ★★★½

Norway's Bent Hamer who made *Kitchen Stories* (2003) comes up with another offbeat tale, this one concerning an engineer and train driver on the eve of retirement. Like Sweden's Roy Andersson his highly personal vision – this is auteur cinema with a vengeance – blends Tatiesque comedy and pathos. If I find Andersson's work more precise and focused, that could be a matter of taste. Those who prefer Hamer won't be let down by *O'Horten* which has the bonus of a great visual coup early on. MS

❧ Bård Owe, Espen Skjønberg, Ghita Nørby, Henny Moan, Bjørn Floberg, Kai Remlov.
❧ *Dir, Pro* and *Written by* Bent Hamer, *Ph* John Christian Rosenlund, *Pro Des* Kalli Juliusson, *Ed* Pål Gengenbach, *M* Kaada, *Cos* Anne Pedersen.

BulBul Films/Pandora Filmproduktion/ZDF/ ARTE etc.-Artificial Eye Film Company.
90 mins. Norway/Germany/France/Denmark. 2007. Rel: 8 May 2009. Cert 12A.

Origin: Spirits of the Past
★★

An imaginatively designed anime movie with a confusing and over complicated futuristic plot about Agito a young boy who tries to bring back hope to what is left of mankind after many years of environmental destruction. He comes across a young girl called Toola who calls upon ancient technology in order to reshape the future. This is ultimately a frustrating experience despite the stunningly beautiful colours and the topical environmental message. (Original title: *Gin-iro no kami no agito*). GS

❧ Voices of Ryo Katsuji, Aoi Miyazaki, Greg Ayres, Laura Bailey, John Burgmeier, Luci Christian.
❧ *Dir* Keiichi Sugiyama, *Pro* Horiuchi Maki etc, *Screenplay* Naoko Kakimoto and Nana Shiina *Ph* Kuwa Yoshihito, *Ed* Hida Aya, *M* Taku Iwasaki.

Gin-iro no kami no agito Production Committee/Media Factory-Manga Entertainment.
95 mins. Japan. 2006. Rel: 12 July 2008. Cert 12.

OSS 117: Cairo, Nest of Spies ★★★

Based on books that pre-date the creation of James Bond, this French spy spoof certainly has Bond in its sights together with B-picture clichés. For a third of the time it's good humoured fun but well before the end it has come to be dangerously close to what it set out to parody. MS

Astronaut James Caviezel hits eighth century Norway looking for a dragon in *Outlander* but turns his thoughts to Sophia Myles instead.

❱ Jean Dujardin, Bérénice Béjo, Aure Atika, Philippe Lefebvre, Constantin Alexandrov.
❱ *Dir* Michel Hazanavicius, *Pro* Éric and Nicolas Altmayer, *Screenplay* Jean-Francois Halin with Hazanavicius from the OSS 117 novels by Jean Bruce, *Ph* Guillaume Schiffman, *Art Dir* Maamar Ech Cheikh, *Ed* Reynald Bertrand, *M* Ludovic Bource and Kamel Ech Cheikh, *Cos* Charlotte David.

A Mandarin Films, Gaumont, M6 Films co-production etc.-ICA Films.
99 mins. France/Belgium. 2006.
Rel: 7 Nov 2008. Cert 12A.

Outlander ★ ★

Jim Caviezel is Kainan, an astronaut who arrives, somewhat unceremoniously, in Norway 709 AD. Explaining to the barbaric locals that he is after a dragon, he is beaten up and shackled. Then the dragon – which has hitched a ride on Kainan's ship – turns up to create utter mayhem. A tricky idea, this. First-time director Howard McCain opts for a straight-faced approach but misses so many opportunities. Far from being entertained as a technologically advanced spaceman, Kainan is treated with all the awe of a nomadic Inuit. And the battle

scenes, beheadings and all, are edited out of existence. JC-W

❱ James Caviezel, Ron Perlman, Sophia Myles, Jack Huston, John Hurt, Cliff Saunders.
❱ *Dir* Howard McCain, *Pro* Chris Roberts, *Screenplay* McCain and Dirk Blackman, *Ph* Pierre Gill, *Pro Des* David Hackl, *Ed* David Dodson, *M* Geoff Zanelli, *Cos* Debra Hanson.

The Weinstein Company/Ascendant Pictures/ Outlander Productions-Momentum Pictures.
115 mins. USA/Germany. 2008.
Rel: 24 Apr 2009. Cert 15.

Outlanders ★ ★ ★ ½

Promisingly cinematic in its style, Dominic Lees' first feature made in 2006 looks at the exploitation of Polish workers in London, many of whom are illegal immigrants misused by their own countrymen. It's amoral drama reminiscent of but better than Woody Allen's recent *Cassandra's Dream* and with odd echoes of *The Third Man*, but it goes off track when it becomes a thriller with an unlikely conclusion. MS

❱ Jakub Tolak, Przemyslaw Sadowski, Alexis Raben, Shaun Dingwall, Joe Tucker.

▷ *Dir* Dominic Lees, *Pro* Michael Riley, *Written by* Jimmy Gardner and Lees, *Ph* Adam Jeppesen, *Pro Des* Natasha Van Kampen, *Ed* Agnieszka Liggett, *M* Peter Gosling, *Cos* Beata Frankowicz.

**A Sterling Pictures production/Storm Entertainment-Organic Marketing.
99 mins. UK/USA. 2006. Rel: 24 Oct 2008.
Cert 15.**

Paris ★★★
Better than some say but hardly special, Cédric Klapisch's latest is a tale of two pairs of siblings living in present day Paris, but it's a work filled out with numerous subsidiary characters, Even when serious (a central figure is a man awaiting a heart transplant), the film maintains a relatively light tone. All told, it's watchable, yet being relatively superficial it is never truly involving and soon forgotten. MS

▷ Juliette Binoche, Romain Duris, Fabrice Luchini, François Cluzet, Albert Dupontel.
▷ *Dir* and *Written by* Cédric Klapisch, *Pro* Bruno Levy, *Ph* Christophe Beaucarne, *Art Dir* Marie Cheminal, *Ed* Francine Sandberg, *M* Loïk Dury and Robert 'Chicken' Burke, *Cos* Anne Schotte.

**A Ce qui me meut/StudioCanal and StudioCanal Image/France 2 Cinéma co-production etc.-Optimum Releasing.
129 mins. France. 2008. Rel: 25 July 2008.
Cert 15.**

Paris 36 ★★½
Carrying many echoes of French films of the 1930s and set in that period, this is initially an engaging pastiche built around the fate of a music hall in the suburbs of Paris. Unfortunately it is much too long and in the second half the clichés pile up remorselessly in a way that would suit parody but is alien to pastiche. Consequently it's strictly a film for those with a strong camp sensibility. (Original title: *Faubourg 36*).
MS

▷ Gérard Jugnot, Clovis Cornillac, Kad Merad, Nora Arnezeder, Bernard-Pierre Donnadieu.
▷ *Dir* Christophe Barratier, *Pro* Jacques Perrin and Nicolas Mauvernay, *Written by* Barratier and others from an idea by Frank Thomas, Reinhardt Wagner and Jean-Michel Derenne, *Ph* Tom Stern, *Art Dir* Jean Rabasse, *Ed* Yves Deschamps, *M* Wagner and Thomas, *Cos* Carine Sarfati.

**Galatée Films/Pathé Production/
Constantin Film/France 2 Cinéma etc.-Pathé Distribution.
120 mins. France/Germany/Czech Republic. 2008 . Rel: 23 Jan 2009. Cert 15.**

Partition ★★½
Vic Sarin's sincerity in making a film about the partition of India and Pakistan in 1947 is not to be doubted. It's his abilities that are open to question as the conflicts of the time are routed through a Romeo and Juliet style love story and a drama of family intransigence that destroys the happiness of the couple. The storyline becomes contrived and manipulative while the screenplay embracing clichés reduces the proceedings to banality. MS

▷ Jimi Mistry, Kristin Kreuk, Neve Campbell, John Light. Irrfan Khan, Madhur Jaffrey.
▷ *Dir* and *Ph* Vic Sarin, *Pro* Tina Pehme and Kim Roberts, *Screenplay* Sarin and Patricia Finn, *Pro Des* Tony Devenyi, *Ed* Reginald Harkema, *M* Brian Tyler, *Cos* Dolly Ahluwalia.

**Seville Pictures/Myriad Pictures/a Sepia Films production etc.-Soda Pictures.
116 mins. UK/Canada/USA. 2006. Rel: 12 Sept 2008. Cert 12A.**

Patti Smith: Dream of Life ★★★★
This is an articulate portrait of this amazing artist known as the godmother of punk who first emerged on the music scene in the 1970s and quickly established herself as

a unique talent in the industry. As narrator Smith's honest storytelling, is injected with masses of humour and is fascinating from beginning to end. Strange but true whilst on a private plane sitting next to the pilot this incredible woman was capable of peeing in a plastic bottle without him knowing. GS

‣ Patti Smith, Sam Shepard, Flea, Bob Dylan, Lenny Kaye, Tom Verlaine, Jaydee Daugherty.
‣ *Dir* and *Screenplay* Steven Sebring, *Pro* Margaret Smilov and Scott Vogel, *Ph* Sebring and Philip Hunt, *Ed* Angelo Corrao and Lin Polito.

Clean Socks/Thirteen/WNET New York-Celluloid Dreams.
109 mins. USA. 2008. Rel: 5 Dec 2008. Cert 15.

Paul Blart: Mall Cop ★ ★ ★

This is a good vehicle for the likeable talent of Kevin James who also wrote the script. He carries the film effortlessly as an overweight diabetic who, after failing to become a policeman, ends up as a mall cop. But he is given the opportunity to prove his worth when the mall is overtaken by a gang of criminals. Despite a weak opening and some lazy plotting the film changes gear for a very funny climax. GS

‣ Kevin James, Keir O'Donnell, Jayma Mays, Rani Rodriguez, Shirley Knight, Stephen Rannazzisi.
‣ *Dir* Steve Carr, *Pro* Doug Belgrad, Barry Bernardi, Todd Garner, Jack Giarraputo, Kevin James, Adam Sandler and Matthew Tolmach, *Screenplay* Kevin James and Nick Bakay, *Ph* Russ T Alsobrook, *Pro Des* Perry Andelin Blake, *Ed* Jeff Freeman, *M* Waddy Wachtel, *Cos* Ellen Lutter.

Columbia Pictures/Relativity Media/Happy Madison Productions-Sony Pictures Releasing.
91 mins. USA. 2008. Rel: 20 Mar 2009. Cert PG.

Pineapple Express ★ ★ ★ ★

Seth Rogen and James Franco are hilarious as a roly-poly slacker pothead and his amiable, stoned-out dealer who have to go on the run from the law after Rogen witnesses cop Rosie Perez commit a murder. Taken at breathless speed, this is an awesome stoner comedy, as incredibly juvenile as it is hysterically funny. Odd couple Rogen and Franco are a brilliant comedy duo – the Laurel and Hardy of stoner comedy – and the script (co-written by Rogen) is jam-packed with big laughs and lots of daft action. If you liked *Anchorman* and *Knocked Up*, you'll love this. DW

‣ Seth Rogen, James Franco, Danny McBride, Kevin Corrigan, Craig Robinson, Gary Cole, Ed Begley Jr, Nora Dunn.
‣ *Dir* David Gordon Green, *Pro* Judd Apatow, Shauna Robertson and Nicholas Weinstock, *Screenplay* Rogen and Evan Goldberg from a story by Rogen, Apatow and Goldberg, *Ph* Tim Orr, *Pro Des* Chris Spellman, *Ed* Craig Alpert, *M* Graeme Revell, *Cos* John A Dunn.

Columbia Pictures/Relativity Media/Apatow Company-Sony Pictures Releasing.
111 mins. USA. 2008. Rel: 12 Sep 2008. Cert 15.

The Pink Panther 2 ★

Inspector Clouseau addresses the Pope as 'Mr Pope', falls over a lot and burns down a restaurant not once, but twice. Meanwhile, John Cleese – replacing Kevin Kline as Dreyfus – bangs his head against a wall for comic effect. This is pretty life-sapping stuff, particularly with such an all-star cast to bear witness to the desperation. This time Clouseau joins an international dream team to recover various stolen artefacts (including the Shroud of Turin!) in the tenth outing for the inept French detective. Dreadful. JC-W

‣ Steve Martin, Jean Reno, Emily Mortimer, Andy Garcia, Alfred Molina, John Cleese, Lily Tomlin, Jeremy Irons, Johnny Halliday, Geoffrey Palmer.
‣ *Dir* Harald Zwart, *Pro* Robert Simonds, *Screenplay* Martin, Scott Neustadter and Michael H Weber, based on a story by Neustadter and Weber, *Ph* Denis Crossan, *Pro Des* Rusty Smith, *Ed* Julia Wong, *M* Christophe Beck, *Cos* Joseph G Aulisi.

Metro-Goldwyn-Mayer/Columbia Pictures/ Robert Simonds Productions-Metro- Goldwyn-Mayer. 92 mins. USA. 2009. Rel: 13 Feb 2009. Cert PG.

New Line Cinema/Solaris Entertainment/ O'Connor Brothers/Avery Pix-Entertainment Film Distributors. 130 mins. USA/Germany. 2008. Rel: 7 Nov 2008. Cert 15.

Pride and Glory ★★½

Manhattan police chief Tierney assigns his son Detective Ray to lead the investigation when four of their colleagues are killed in an ambush on a drugs bust. Ray reluctantly agrees as these cops were working with his brother and his brother-in-law but as he digs deeper into the case he realizes that there must have been a tip-off from the inside... O'Connor creates a realistically grim and violent world in a ruthless city but unfortunately it is difficult to care about his immensely unsympathetic characters. GS

▶ Colin Farrell, Edward Norton, Jon Voight, Noah Emmerich, Jennifer Ehle, John Ortiz, Frank Grillo.
▶ *Dir* Gavin O'Connor, *Pro* Greg O'Connor, *Screenplay* Joe Carnahan and Gavin O'Connor, from a story by Gavin O'Connor, Gregory O'Connor and Robert Hopes, *Ph* Declan Quinn, *Pro Des* Dan Leigh, *Ed* Lisa Zeno Churgin and John Gilroy, *M* Mark Isham, *Cos* Abigail Murray.

Puffball ★★

Director Nicolas Roeg's return to the cinema after a decade's break is no cause for celebration. Fay Weldon's novel, here adapted by her son Dan, falls flat on its face with unintentionally hilarious results. A young architect (Kelly Reilly) is working on converting a ruined cottage in Ireland into a dream home when she's not rolling in the hay with her visiting boyfriend. She unwillingly gets pregnant and then falls foul of the nutty family next door, a witch (Miranda Richardson) who cannot conceive, and her batty old mother (Rita Tushingham) who longs for a baby to replace the one she lost. They take an unnatural interest in the girl's condition and start working their magic. Supernatural forces seem to be at work here, but they are all totally unbelievable. Some superfluous sexual anatomy scenes (penis penetrating vulva) and heavy symbolism (the puffball of the title is a pregnant-looking mushroom)

Look out Jensen Button, here comes *Paul Blart: Mall Cop*, the perfect comic vehicle for Kevin James.

clobbers any intentions Roeg had of making a credible film. Seriously bad nonsense. MHD

▶ Kelly Reilly, Miranda Richardson, Rita Tushingham, Donald Sutherland, Oscar Pearce, William Houston.
▶ *Dir* Nicolas Roeg, *Pro* Dan Weldon, Julie Baines, Michael Garland, Ben Woolford etc, *Screenplay* Dan Weldon from the novel by Fay Weldon, *Ph* Nigel Willoughby, *Pro Des* Anna Rackard, *Ed* Tony Palmer, *M* Chris Crilly, Thierry Gauthier and Delphine Measroch, *Cos* Lorna Marie Mugan.

Amérique Film/Dan Films/Grand Pictures/ Tall Stories-Yume Pictures.
120 mins. UK/Ireland/Canada. 2007.
Rel: 18 July 2008. Cert 18.

Punisher: The War Zone ★

Old school action fans convinced that movies don't get much worse than Dolph Lundgren's 1989 *Punisher* flick have a surprise in store: this latest instalment of the adventures of vengeful ex-cop Frank Castle is, in every way, even worse. A comic book dud that isn't fit to call itself a sequel to Tom Jane's underrated 2004 *Punisher* death-fest, it sees the *Rome* TV series' Ray Stevenson in the role, the awkward heart of an embarrassing fiasco. MJ

▶ Ray Stevenson, Dominic West, Doug Hutchison, Colin Salmon, Wayne Knight, Dash Mihok, Julie Benz.
▶ *Dir* Lexi Alexander, *Pro* Gale Ann Hurd, *Screenplay* Nick Santora, Art Marcum and Matt Holloway, *Ph* Steve Gainer, *Pro Des* Andrew Neskoromny, *Ed* William Yeh, *M* Michael Wandmacher, *Cos* Odette Gadoury.

Lionsgate Films/Media Magik Entertainment/ Valhalla Motion Pictures/Red Corner Productions/Marvel Enterprises/Marvel Knights/MHF Zweite Academy Film-Sony Pictures Entertainment.
103 mins. USA/Canada/Germany. 2008.
Rel: 6 Feb 2009.
Cert 18.

Push ★ ½

It is difficult to find anything positive to say about this muddled thriller about psychic espionage. The premise is similar to *Jumper* and here Chris Evans plays Nick, a unique individual who has inherited special psychic abilities. He lives a quiet life in Hong Kong but he soon finds himself on the run along with another psychic, Cassie (Dakota Fanning), trying to escape from Carver (Djimon Hounsou) and his evil henchmen. The story is incomprehensible, the special effects less than basic but the actors survive the lame dialogue. GS

▶ Chris Evans, Djimon Hounsou, Dakota Fanning, Robert Tsonos, Brandon Rhea.
▶ *Dir* Paul McGuigan, *Pro* Bruce Davey, Glenn Williamson and William Vince, *Screenplay* David Bourla, *Ph* Peter Sova, *Pro Des* François Séguin, *Ed* Nicolas Trembasiewicz, *M* Neil Davidge, *Cos* Laura Goldsmith and Nina Proctor.

Icon Productions/Summiet Entertainment/Infinity Features Entertainment-Icon Film Distribution.
111 mins. Canada/UK/USA. 2009.
Rel: 20 Feb 2009. Cert 12A.

Quantum of Solace ★ ★ ★ ½

The second in the new series of Bond movies seems to typify the way the franchise is heading. It's action all the way with scant regard for a tortuous plot about harnessing illegal water supplies. So it's just a case of what situation will James get out of next as he hares along in a mountain road car chase, speeds around in a boat, slurps about in a drain, jumps up and over rooftops or gets down on a fight in a lift. What plot there is seems only to be the step you take to go from one action scene to another. The witty humour of old has gone and Daniel Craig still seems less than comfortable as 007. Perhaps he's still smarting from the loss of Vesper, his girlfriend from *Casino Royale*, although, as we know, there will always be another beauty on the horizon: calling Olga Kurylenko as Camille. If you want bang bang all the way, this is it. MHD

▶ Daniel Craig, Olga Kurylenko, Mathieu Amalric, Judi Dench, Giancarlo Giannini, Gemma Arterton, Jeffrey Wright, Tim Pigott-Smith.
▶ *Dir* Marc Forster, *Pro* Barbara Broccoli and Michael G Wilson, *Screenplay* Paul Haggis, Neal Purvis and Robert Wade , *Ph* Roberto Schaefer, *Pro Des* Dennis Gassner, *Ed* Matt Chesse and Richard Pearson, *M* David Arnold, *Cos* Louise Frogley.

MGM/Columbia Pictures/United Artists/ Danjaq/Eon Productions-Sony Pictures Releasing. 106 mins. USA. 2008. Rel: 31 Oct 2008. Cert 12A.

Quarantine ★ ★ ½

Faithful American remake of the 2007 Spanish original, *[REC]*, about a TV reporter and her cameraman trapped inside a quarantined apartment building after the outbreak of a virus which turns humans into bloodthirsty killers. It's all seen from the point of view of the cameraman, as he shoots the action. Slightly glossier, slower to get going and more graphically violent with Jennifer Carpenter more of a professional reporter than her Spanish counterpart, and this time we get a glimpse of her cameraman (Steve Harris) too. Some good, scary moments but if you've seen the first one, the shock value is lessened. CA

▶ Jennifer Carpenter, Steve Harris, Jay Hernandez, Columbus Short, Jermaine Jackson.
▶ *Dir* John Eric Dowdle, *Pro* Sergio Aguero, Clint Culpepper, Doug Dawson, Carlos Fernandez, Julio Fernandez and Roy Lee, *Screenplay* John Eric Dowdle and Drew Dowdle, based on the film *[REC]* by Jaume Balagueró, Luis Berdejo and Paco Plaza, *Ph* Ken Seng, *Pro Des* Jon Gary Steele, *Ed* Elliot Greenberg, *M* Pilar McCurry, *Cos* Maya Lieberman.

Andale Pictures/Screen Gems/Vertigo Entertainment-Sony Pictures Releasing. 89 mins. USA. 2008. Rel: 21 Nov 2008. Cert 18.

Tell me what *Quantum of Solace* means – or I shoot! Daniel Craig as 007 in his latest all-action outing.

Quiet Chaos ★★★

Antonello Grimaldi who made the sympathetic but little known *Bits and Pieces* in 1996 returns with this drama of bereavement starring Nanni Moretti. The latter is excellent but has already appeared in his own film *The Son's Room* (2001) which was far more persuasive in its study of a drawn out adjustment to a sudden death. This film is continually under the shadow of its superior predecessor. (Original title: *Caos calmo*). MS

❧ Nanni Moretti, Valeria Golino, Isabella Ferrari, Alessandro Gassman, Blu Yoshimi, Hippolyte Girardot, Denis Podalydès, Charles Berling, Roman Polanski.
❧ *Dir* Antonello Grimaldi, *Pro* Domenico Procacci, *Screenplay* Nanni Moretti, Laura Paolucci and Francesco Piccolo from Sandro Veronesi's novel *Caos calmo*, *Ph* Alessandro Pesci, *Art Dir* Giada Calabria, *Ed* Angelo Nicolini, *M* Paolo Buonvino, *Cos* Alexandra Toesca.

A Fandango production/Rai Cinema/Portobello Pictures/Phoenix Film Investment etc.-New Wave Films.
112 mins. Italy/UK. 2008.
Rel: 24 Oct 2008.
Cert 15.

Quiet City ★★★½

At its best this is a vast improvement on Aaron Katz's earlier *Dance Party, USA* (q.v.). A Brooklyn tale, it studies quite beautifully the way in which two people come together. The images are poetic and the acting first class (Erin Fisher is to Katz what Anna Karina once was to Godard). Irritatingly, the film, which could have been a virtual two-hander, seeks feature length by becoming seriously over-extended as it introduces other characters. Seek it out all the same. MS

❧ Erin Fisher, Cris Lankenau, Joe Swanberg, Sarah Hellman, Tucker Stone.
❧ *Dir* and *Ed* Aaron Katz, *Pro* Brendan McFadden and Ben Stambler, *Written* by Katz, Erin Fisher and Cris Lankenau, *Ph* Andrew Reed, *M* Keegan DeWitt.

Distributed by ICA Films.
78 mins. USA. 2007. Rel: 25 July 2008. No Cert.

Race to Witch Mountain ★★★

This update of Disney's live action 'Witch Mountain' franchise sees Dwayne Johnson's cab driver running from the mob to pick up two child passengers (an underused

What do you mean, you can't map-read? Carla Gugino and Dwayne 'The Rock' Johnson in *Race to Witch Mountain*.

AnnaSophia Robb, formerly of *Bridge to Terabithia*, and Alexander Ludwig) unaware that they are aliens with telepathic powers on the run from a deadly assassin. The proceedings move along at a satisfying pace, yet the whole thing feels distinctly average. JC

‣ Dwayne Johnson, AnnaSophia Robb, Alexander Ludwig, Carla Gigino, Ciarán Hinds, Tom Everett Scott.
‣ *Dir* Andy Fickman, *Pro* Andrew Gunn, *Screenplay* Matt Lopez and Mark Bomback from the book *Escape to Witch Mountain* by Alexander Key, *Ph* Greg Gardiner, *Pro Des* David J Bomba, *Ed* David Rennie, *M* Trevor Rabin, *Cos* Genevieve Tyrrell.

Walt Disney Pictures/Gunn Films-Walt Disney Studios Motion Pictures.
98 mins. USA. 2009. Rel: 10 Apr 2009. Cert PG.

Rachel Getting Married
★ ★ ★ ★ ½

In this family drama that blends pathos and irony the sharp screenplay by Sidney Lumet's daughter Jenny provides a wholly convincing portrait of a certain stratum of contemporary American society. The last section is drawn out self-indulgently, but even so the film is a near masterpiece that recalls both Chekhov and Eugene O'Neill. The acting is superlative, the quasi-home movie style of shooting undercuts any risk of melodrama and it's the more moving for being quite without sentimentality in the way that it is observed. MS

‣ Anne Hathaway, Rosemarie DeWitt, Bill Irwin, Debra Winger, Tunde Adebimpe.
‣ *Dir* Jonathan Demme, *Pro* Neda Armian, Demme and Marc Platt, *Written by* Jenny Lumet, *Ph* Declan Quinn, *Pro Des* Ford Wheeler, *Ed* Tim Squyres, *M* Zafer Tawil and Donald Harrison Jr. *Cos* Susan Lyall

Sony Pictures Classics/a Clinica Estetico production/Marc Platt productions-Sony Pictures Releasing.
113 mins. USA. 2008. Rel: 23 Jan 2009. Cert 15.

The Reader ★ ★ ★ ★

There's great work not only from Kate Winslet but also from newcomer David Kross in this gripping drama about a woman's secret history in Nazi Germany that comes to light only after the war. Some have found the film controversial, but that depends on how one interprets its message and it's well enough done to justify everyone making up their own minds on this point. What initially seems to be a perceptive tale about a boy's sexual initiation by an older woman develops into the story of one woman's role during the Holocaust and the shame she feels. MS

‣ Kate Winslet, David Kross, Ralph Fiennes, Lena Olin, Bruno Ganz.
‣ *Dir* Stephen Daldry, *Pro* Anthony Minghella, Sydney Pollack, Donna Gigliotti and Redmond Morris, *Screenplay* David Hare based on the book by Bernhard Schlink, *Ph* Chris Menges and Roger Deakins, *Pro Des* Brigitte Broch, *Ed* Claire Simpson, *M* Nico Muhly, *Cos* Ann Roth and Donna Maloney.

The Weinstein Company/a Mirage Enterprises production/a Neunte Babelsberg Film GmbH production- Entertainment Film Distributors Ltd.
124 mins. USA/Germany, 2008. Rel: 2 Jan 2009. Cert 15.

Red Cliff ★ ★ ★ ★ ★

This is the story of the three Kingdoms in 208 AD China during the Han Dynasty. The corrupt Prime Minister Cao Cao is hungry for more power and has declared war against the emperor's uncle Liu Bei who in turn joins forces with Sun Quan. And thus the stage is set for some brutal battles on both land and sea. John Woo's terrific war epic is truly spectacular with breathtaking battle sequences. He wisely takes his time to establish his characters and makes the rather complex plot crystal clear. (Original title: *Chi Bi*) GS

‣ Tony Leung Chiu Wai, Takeshi Kaneshiro, Fengyi Zhang, Chen Chang, Wei Zhao, Jun Hu.
‣ *Dir* John Woo, *Pro* Woo, Han Sanping

and Terence Chang, *Screenplay* Woo, Chan Khan, Kuo Cheng and Sheng Heyu, based on the book *Romance of Three Kingdoms* by Guanzhong Luo, *Ph* Lu Yue and Zhang Li, *Pro Des* and *Cos* Tim Yip, *Ed* Robert A Ferretti, Angie Lam and Yang Hong Yu, *M* Tarô Iwashiro.

**Beijing Film Studio/China Film Group/Lion Rock Productions/Three Kingdoms etc-Contender Entertainment Group.
148 mins. China. 2008. Rel: 12 June 2009. Cert 15.**

Redbelt ★★★½

Chiwetel Ejiofor gets better and better. David Mamet's interest in jiujitsu explains why he should have created a drama linked to what he sees as an honourable art. Ejiofor is totally convincing as a good man at the mercy of fate but the tale, not without twists typical of Mamet's con game movies, seems at times contrived. The other actors are good, however, and Ejiofor is great. MS

➤ Chiwetel Ejiofor, Tim Allen, Alice Braga, Joe Mantegna, Emily Mortimer, Rebecca Pidgeon, Ricky Jay, David Paymer.

➤ *Dir* and *Written by* David Mamet, *Pro* Chrisann Verges, *Ph* Robert Elswit, *Pro Des* David Wasco, *Ed* Barbara Tulliver, *M* Stephen Endelman, *Cos* Debra McGuire.

Sony Pictures Classics-Sony Pictures Releasing. 99 mins. USA. 2007. Rel: 26 Sept 2008. Cert 15.

Religulous ★★★

This superficial but not unentertaining film features Bill Maher who goes around talking to people about religious belief. He claims that he himself has a 'don't know' attitude regarding the existence of God, but we can tell that in truth he's a total disbeliever (as, indeed, the title's play on words suggests). Those as committed to this view as Maher may love the movie, but it's all very glib. MS

➤ With Bill Maher, Kathy Maher, Julie Maher, Father Reginald Foster, Pastor John Westcott.

➤ *Dir* Larry Charles, *Pro* Jonah Smith, Palmer West and Bill Maher, *Ph* Anthony Hardwick, *Ed* Jeff Groth, Christian Kinnard and Jeffrey M. Werner, *M Consultant* Richard Henderson.

**Thousand Words/Bill Maher production-Momentum Pictures.
101 mins. USA. 2008. Rel: 3 April 2009. Cert 15.**

Reverb ★★

Aspiring rock'n'roll musician Alex (Leo Gregory) and his former keyboardist Maddy (Eva Birthistle) lock themselves overnight in a recording studio in one last attempt to resurrect his declining career. He wants to record a new CD but instead ends up in a nightmarish situation when a voice from an old recording begins to haunt them. Eitan Arrusi's stylish film is strong on atmosphere but the implausible plot becomes more preposterous as it develops. GS

➤ Leo Gregory, Eva Birthistle, Pamela Banks, Margo Stilley, Luke de Woolfson, Stephen Lord, Neil Newbon.
➤ *Dir* and *Screenplay* Eitan Arrusi, *Pro* Frank Mannion, *Ph* Simon Dennis, *Pro Des* Richard Campling, *Ed* Richard Elson and Joseph Pisano, *M* James Edward Barker and Tim Despic, *Cos* Ian Fulcher.

**Reverb Productions/Swipe Films-Guerilla Films.
88 mins. UK. 2008. Rel: 6 Mar 2009. Cert 15.**

Revolutionary Road ★★★★

The horrors of suburban life surface again for director Sam (*American Beauty*) Mendes in this adaptation of Richard Yates' novel about a family living in a rut in 1955 Connecticut. April Wheeler (Kate Winslet) is a failed actress stuck at home playing desperate housewife. Husband Frank (Leonardo DiCaprio), in a dull, corporate job, has an affair with his secretary to stave off boredom. April suggests they move to Paris to fulfil their dreams, but they row and fight and external events put paid to their search for happiness. Sympathetic performances by

Winslet and DiCaprio almost always ring true and there are fine contributions by Kathy Bates as a real estate agent, Richard Easton as her awful husband and Michael Shannon as their handicapped son who understands the Wheelers' problems only too well. Not a joyride but for most of the way an impressive journey. MHD

▷ Leonardo Di Caprio, Kate Winslet, Michael Shannon, Kathy Bates, Richard Easton, Ryan Simkins, Ty Simkins.
▷ *Dir* Sam Mendes, *Pro* Mendes, Bobby Cohen, Scott Rudin and John Hart, *Screenplay* Justin Haythe, *Ph* Roger Deakins, *Pro Des* Kristi Zea, *Ed* Tariq Anwar, *M* Thomas Newman, *Cos* Albert Wolsky.

Goldcrest Pictures/DreamWorks Pictures/ BBC Films/Movies/Evamere Entertainment/ Neal Street etc-Paramount Vantage.
119 mins. USA/UK. 2008. Rel: 30 Jan 2009. Cert 15.

Righteous Kill ★ ★ ★

Main attraction here is De Niro and Pacino sharing significant screen time as never before. They flesh out superficially written roles as veteran cops with a dark secret. A competent cop thriller with good supporting performances from John Leguizamo, Carla Gugino and Brian Dennehy, it has plenty of action, particularly of the gun variety, some intriguing twists and turns to the plot and an effective and startling resolution, though some of the detail of police procedures is a bit muzzy and the pace drops to dangerously slow in places. CA

▷ Robert De Niro, Al Pacino, Curtis (50 Cent) Jackson, Carla Gugino, John Leguizamo, Donnie Wahlberg, Brian Dennehy, Barry Primus.
▷ *Dir* Jon Avnet, *Pro* Avnet, Rob Cowan, Avi Lerner, Randall Emmett, George Furch etc, *Screenplay* Russell Gewitz, *Ph* Denis Lenoir, *Pro Des* Tracey Gallacher, *Ed* Paul Hirsch, *M* Ed Shearmuir, *Cos* Debra McGuire.

Millennium Films/Emmett-Furla Films/ Nu Image Films-Lionsgate.
101 mins. USA. 2008. Rel: 25 Sep 2008. Cert 15.

Rivals ★ ★ ★ ½

The French title *Les Liens du Sang* seems more apt for this family tale set in Lyon in the late 1970s. It revolves around two brothers, the one a criminal and the other a policeman, and the bonds between them that are never

It's no dance of joy for Leonardo DiCaprio and Kate Winslet in *Revolutionary Road*, a savage portrait of suburban life in 1950s Connecticut.

I've got a good hand here – I'll raise you again: Robert De Niro and Al Pacino in *Righteous Kill.*

broken. The storytelling could be clearer but the filmmaker Jacques Maillot aided by an excellent cast presents characters of some depth. Not all that it might have been, the piece is nevertheless absorbing when at its best. MS

❧ Guillaume Canet, François Cluzet, Marie Denarnaud, Clothilde Hesme, Mehdi Nebbou.
❧ *Dir* Jacques Maillot, *Pro* Cyrile Colbeau-Justin and Jean-Baptiste Dupont, *Screenplay* Maillot, Pierre Chosson and Eric Veniard based on the book *Deux frères: flic et truand* by Michel and Bruno Papet, *Ph* Luc Pagès, *Art Dir* Mathieu Menut, *Ed* Andréa Sedlacková, *M* Stéphan Oliva, *Cos* Bethsabée Dreyfus.

LGM Cinéma/StudioCanal/France 3 Cinéma/13ème Rue co-production etc.-Optimum Releasing.
107 mins. France/Belgium. 2007.
Rel: 5 Dec 2008. Cert 15.

The Rocker ★ ★ ★

Rainn Wilson (from the US version of *The Office*) stars as heavy metal drummer Fish, who's still bitter about being kicked out of his group Vesuvius in 1986 just before they hit the big time. But he gets a second chance when he starts playing with his nephew's high-school band. Though perhaps on the amusing side rather than laugh-out-loud and not as good as *School of Rock* – this is a likeable and funny, silly movie that moves swiftly along without any dull patches. Wilson may not quite be film star material but a lot of the time he's a hoot – and he can play the drums – while Christina Applegate is appealing as Wilson's love interest. DW

❧ Rainn Wilson, Christina Applegate, Teddy Geiger, Josh Gad, Emma Stone, Jeff Garlin, Jane Lynch.
❧ *Dir* Peter Cattaneo, *Pro* Shawn Levy and Tom McNulty, *Screenplay* Maya Forbes and Wally Wolodarsky, from a story by Ryan Jaffe, *Ph* Anthony B Richmond, *Pro Des* Brandt Gordon, *Ed* Brad E Wilhite, *M* Chad Fischer, *Cos* Christopher Hargadin.

Fox Atomic/21 Laps Entertainment-20th Century Fox.
102 mins. USA. 2008. Rel: 17 Oct 2008. Cert 12A.

RocknRolla ★

Guy Ritchie's obsession with the world of London gangsters continues with this tale

Toby Kebbell
lets rip in
RocknRolla,
another of Guy
Ritchie's London
gangsterland
action thrillers.

of guns, dodgy deals, drugs and diamond geezers. A fantastic cast including Tom Wilkinson, Mark Strong, Gerard Butler and Thandie Newton is wasted on material that lacks imagination and vision, mainly being a rehash of *Two Smoking Barrels*. *RocknRolla* is slick, expertly edited and shows off the substantial sum spent on it, but it is far too unoriginal to either rock or roll. DP

▷ Jimi Mistry, Nonso Anozie, Gerard Butler, Gemma Arterton, Tom Wilkinson, Mark Strong, Karel Roden, Thandie Newton
▷ *Dir* and *Screenplay* Guy Ritchie, *Pro* Ritchie, Joel Silver, Steve Clark-Hall and Susan Downey, *Ph* David Higgs, *Pro Des* Richard Bridgland, *Ed* James Herbert, *M* Steve Isles, *Cos* Suzie Harman.

Warner Bros Pictures/Toff Guy Films/Dark Castle Entertainment/Studio Canal-Warner Bros. Pictures.
114 mins. UK. 2008. Rel: 5 Sep 2008. Cert 15.

Role Models ★★

It is good to see the likeable Paul Rudd and Seann William Scott being promoted into leading roles after having supported many less capable performers. But they deserve

better material than this average gross-out comedy. They play two salesmen who, after smashing their company truck, are given a choice by the court – either jail or community service with children from the Sturdy Wings programme. It is not a bad idea but the script runs out of steam about half an hour in and the repetitive gags fail to raise even a smile. GS

▷ Seann William Scott, Paul Rudd, Christopher Mintz-Plasse, Bobb'e J Thompson, Elizabeth Banks, Jane Lynch.
▷ *Dir* David Wain, *Pro* Luke Greenfield, Scott Stuber and Matt Seigel, *Screenplay* Wain, Rudd, Ken Marino and Timothy Dowling, from a story by Dowling and William Blake Herron, *Ph* Russ T Alsobrook, *Pro Des* Stephen Lineweaver, *Ed* Eric Kissack, *M* Craig Wedren, *Cos* Molly Maginis.

Universal Pictures/Relativity Media/Stuber-Parent/ New Regency Pictures etc-Universal Studios
101 mins. USA/Germany. 2008.
Rel: 9 Jan 2009. Cert 15.

The Romance of Astrea and Celadon ★★★★

This piece by the veteran Eric Rohmer,

one which could well prove to be his last, is a quintessentially French work set in an ancient world of shepherds and shepherdesses. Whatever the links to legends and to classical French literature, its study of a troubled love evokes the late plays of Shakespeare and Rohmer's seemingly simplistic approach creates a sense of purity and timelessness. Not to everyone's taste I suspect, but in its first half especially it offers reflections on love that are perfectly expressed. (Original title: *Les Amours d'Astrée et Céladon*). MS

▶ Andy Gillet, Stéphanie Crayencour, Cécile Cassel, Véronique Reymond, Serge Renko.
▶ *Dir* and *Screenplay* Eric Rohmer (based on Honoré d'Urfé's novel *L'Astrée*), *Pro* Françoise Etchegaray, Jean-Michel Rey and Philippe Liégeois, *Ph* Diane Baratier, *Ed* Mary Stephen, *M* Jean-Louis Valéro, *Cos* Jean-Pierre Larroque and Pu-Laï.

A Rezo Productions/C.E.R./Bim Distribuzione /Alta Producción production etc-Artificial Eye Film Company. 109 mins. France/Italy/Spain. 2006. Rel: 12 Sept 2008. Cert 12A.

Rudo & Cursi ★ ★ ★ ★

Made with absolute assurance, this concerns the bonds and the rivalry between two brothers played out against a sporting background in Mexico City. The football element is less key than the invitation for a young male audience to identify with the bid for fame of both brothers (Gael García Bernal and Diego Luna) while the cynical conclusion strikes a different but effective note. The writer/director is Carlos Cuarón, the third member of this family to take to directing. MS

▶ Gael García Bernal, Diego Luna, Guillermo Francella, Adriana Paz, Jessica Mas.
▶ *Dir* and *Written by* Carlos Cuarón, *Pro* Alfonso Cuarón, Alejandro González Iñárritu, Guillermo del Toro and Frida Torresblanco, *Ph* Adam Kimmel, *Pro Des* Eugenio Caballer *Ed* Alex Rodríguez, *M* Felipe Pérez Santiago, *Cos* Annaí Ramos and Ana Terrazas.

Cha Cha Cha/Universal Pictures International/Focus Features International-Optimum Releasing. 101 mins. USA/Mexico/UK. 2008. Rel: 26 June 2009. Cert 15.

Sakuran ★ ★ ★ ★

Strange but sure-footed, this Japanese film may tell an 18th century tale about the life of a young woman growing up in a high-class Tokyo brothel but its tone is far from traditional. Its heroine is portrayed by the model and pop star Anna Tsuchiya, the music score is sometimes deliberately anachronistic, the tone recalls Douglas Sirk's movies and the bold colour design *The Umbrellas of Cherbourg*. In case you were wondering, it's a film made by a team of women and not by a gay man. MS

▶ Anna Tsuchiya, Shiina Kippei, Narimiya Hiroki, Kimura Yoshino, Ando Masanobu.
▶ *Dir* Ninagawa Mika, *Pro* Uda Mitsuru and Fujita Yoshinori, *Screenplay* Tanada Yuki from the manga story by Anno Moyoco, *Ph* Ishizaka Takuro, *Art Dir* Iwaki Namiko, *Ed* Morishita Hiroaki, *M* Shena Ringo.

Asmik Ace Entertainment, Inc./Parco Co, Ltd/TV Asahi Corporation etc.-ICA Films. 111 mins. Japan. 2007. Rel: 29 Aug 2008. Cert 15.

Sarah Silverman: Jesus is Magic ★ ★ ★ ½

This is controversial Sarah Silverman's stage show turned into a feature film with the addition of some sketches about her family and agent, padded out with amusing songs. Stand up comedy artist Silverman's success relies on her being politically incorrect and very provocative. She is very funny and manages to offend almost everybody including blacks and dwarfs (sorry little people) with her outrageous stories about the Holocaust, 9/11, rape, anal sex and old age. GS

▶ Sarah Silverman, Brian Posehn, Laura Silverman, Bob Odenkirk, Jim Bodma, Steve Agee.

Dir and *Ed* Liam Lynch, *Pro* Heidi Herzon, Mark Williams and Randy Sosin, *Screenplay* Sarah Silverman, *Ph* Rhet W Bear, *Pro Des* Henry Arce, *M* Lynch and Sarah Silverman, *Cos* Dayna Pink.

Roadshow Attractions/Black Gold Films-Warner Music Entertainment.
72 mins. USA. 2005. Rel: 1 Aug 2008. Cert 15.

Savage Grace ★★★½

Like *Swoon,* his 1992 debut, Tom Kalin's new film derives from a real-life murder case. Here the crime erupts out of the unhealthy closeness that had grown up between a mother and her bisexual son. Told in six Acts, an approach that disrupts the flow of the tale, it leaves one unclear what Kalin wished to say here and the screenplay's investigation of the son's sexuality is inadequate. Nevertheless, the material is unusual enough to be interesting and Julianne Moore as the mother is on fine form. MS

Julianne Moore, Stephen Dillane, Eddie Redmayne, Elena Anaya, Hugh Dancy, Anne Reid.

Dir Tom Kalin, *Pro* Iker Monfort, Katie Roumel, Pamela Koffler and Christine Vachon, *Screenplay* Howard A Rodman based on the book by Natalie Robins and Steven M L Aronson, *Ph* Juanmi Azpiroz, *Pro Des* Victor Molero, *Ed* Kalin, John F. Lyons and Enara Goicoetxea, *M* Fernando Velázquez, *Cos* Gabriela Salaverri.

A Celluloid Dreams presentation/a Montfort Producciones, Killer Films/John Wells production etc.-Revolver Entertainment.
94 mins. Spain/USA/France. 2007.
Rel: 11 July 2008. Cert 15.

Saw V ★★

Detective Costas Mandylor and special agent Scott Patterson clash as Tobin Bell's (deceased) Jigsaw killer apparently strikes again. This twisted, morbid, fourth sequel in the revoltingly sick horror thriller series is masterminded by the scenic designer of the previous three movies and you could say he does make a slick, professional job of it, especially with the ingenious and elaborate series of traps set up for the five victims. But this is mostly mediocre stuff by its own grisly standards, topped off with an overhasty, unsatisfying ending as *Saw VI* is set up. DW

Special agent Scott Patterson tries on a new disguise in the fifth outing in the sick thriller series, *Saw V.*

Tobin Bell, Costas Mandylor, Scott Patterson, Betsy Russell, Julie Benz, Meagan Good, Mark Rolston.
Dir David Hackl, Pro Mark Burg and Oren Koules, Screenplay Patrick Melton and Marcus Dunstan, Ph David A Armstrong, Pro Des Tony Ianni, Ed Kevin Greutert, M Charlie Clouser, Cos Alex Kavanagh.

A Burg/Koules/Hoffman production/ Twisted Pictures-Lionsgate. 92 mins. USA/Canada. 2008. Rel: 24 Oct 2008. Cert 18.

Scar 3D ★★

A bad time's guaranteed with this gory and gruesome horror thriller starring Angela Bettis as a troubled young woman who returns to her home town for her niece's graduation. It's her first visit since she was abducted as a teenager by a sick psycho who ran the local funeral home and forced her to kill her best friend. Naturally, again, a twisted killer is on the rampage – the very one she thought she'd killed back then – and she's soon one of his intended victims. Bettis is fine and the film's slickly handled, but it's as clichéd and predictable as it is nasty and, boy, is it nasty. DW

Angela Bettis, Brittney Wilson, Tefgan Moss, Ben Cotton, Christopher Titus, Kirby Bliss Blanton.
Dir Jed Weintrob, Pro Jamie Gordon, Norman Twain, Douglas Berquist and Courtney Potts, Screenplay Zack Ford, Ph Toshiaki Ozawa, Pro Des Trevor Smith, Ed Chris Figler, M Roger Neill, Costumes Christine Thomson.

DB Entertainment-The Works UK Distribution. 90 mins. USA. 2007. Rel: 9 Nov 2008. Cert 18.

The Secret Life of Bees
★★★½

In 1964, during the turbulent Civil Rights era in South Carolina, the home of the beekeeping Boatwright sisters is thrown into turmoil with the arrival of a 14-year-old white girl. The latter, Lily Owens (Dakota Fanning), has been adopted by a black woman (Jennifer Hudson), and they're on the run... Based on the critically acclaimed, best-selling novel by Sue Monk Kidd, this is a heartfelt and heart-warming – some may say saccharine – tale of loss, racial repair and redemption. It's also beautifully made and acted and often extremely moving. JC-W

Dakota Fanning, Queen Latifah, Jennifer Hudson, Alicia Keys, Sophie Okondedo, Paul Bettany, Hilaire Burton.
Dir and Screenplay Gina Prince-Bythewood, based on the novel by Sue Monk Kidd Pro Will Smith, James Lassiter, Joe Pichirallo, Ewan Leslie and Lauren Shuler Donner, Ph Rogier Stoffers, Pro Des Warren Alan Young, Ed Terilyn A Shropshire, M Mark Isham, Cos Sandra Hernandez.

Fox Searchlight Pictures/Overbrook Entertainment/Donners' Company-Twentieth Century Fox Film Corporation. 110 mins. USA. 2008. Rel: 5 Dec 2008. Cert 12A.

Secret of Moonacre
★★★★

Animation (Rugrats) turned live action director Gabor Csupo tackles an adaptation of Elizabeth Goudge's children's classic The Little White Horse. A young girl is sent away to a country manor in a locality bound by a curse. A meandering script augmented with special effects and surprises galore results in an uneven affair, but the tale's ending proves highly satisfying. JC

Ioan Gruffudd, Dakota Blue Richards, Tim Curry, Natascha McElhone, Juliet Stevenson, Augustus Prew.
Dir Gabor Csupo, Pro Michael Cowan, Jasn Piette, Monica Penders, Meredith Garlick and Samuel Hadida, Screenplay Graham Alborough and Lucy Shuttleworth from the book The Little White Horse by Elizabeth Goudge, Ph David Eggby, Pro Des Sophie Becher, Ed Julian Rodd, M Christian Henson, Cos Beatrix Aruna Pasztor.

Dakota Fanning and Queen Latifah check out the honey quota in *The Secret Life of Bees*.

Grand Allure Entertainment/Forgan-Smith Entertainment/Australian Film Commission/ UK Film Council/Eurofilm Stúdió etc-Warner Bros. 103 mins. Hungary/UK/France. 2008. Rel: 6 Feb 2009. Cert U.

Sex Drive ★ ★ ★

After *Road Trip* came *EuroTrip* and now there's *Sex Drive* with its familiar catalogue of carnal catastrophes, vehicular vicissitudes and loathsome low-lifes. The sweet-natured, 18-year-old virgin Ian Lafferty (Zuckerman) drives from Chicago to Knoxville in the hope of popping his cherry, dragging his two best friends along for the ride. On the way he meets a wisecracking Amish mechanic (who misses irony) and a tearful sales clerk with an unexpected sexual secret. It's very crude – and surprisingly sweet. And surprisingly funny. JC-W

▶ Josh Zuckerman, Amanda Crew, Clark Duke, James Marsden, Seth Green, Katrina Bowden.
▶ *Dir* Sean Anders, *Pro* Bob Levy, Leslie Morgenstein and John Morris, *Screenplay* Anders and Morris, *Ph* Tim Orr, *Pro Des* Aaron Osborne, *Ed* George Folsey Jr, *M* Stephen Trask, *Cos* Kristin M Burke.

Alloy Entertainment/Goldcrest Pictures/ Summit Entertainment-Contender Films. 109 mins. USA. 2008. Rel: 9 Jan 2009. Cert 15.

Shadows in the Sun
★ ★ ★ ½

A family tale set in Norfolk in the 1960s, David Rocksavage's film draws on his own youthful memories and in the role played by Jean Simmons now eighty, he commemorates his own grandmother. The story he has built around this is rather slight compared to *The Go-Between* which it distantly echoes but, despite being somewhat insubstantial, the film does feel intensely personal. MS

▶ Jean Simmons, James Wilby, Jamie Dornan, Ophelia Lovibond, Peter Eyre, Toby Marlow.
▶ *Dir* David Rocksavage, *Pro* Nick O'Hagan, *Screenplay* Margaret Glover and Rocksavage from his story, *Ph* Milton Kam, *Pro Des* Will Field, *Ed* Eduardo Vidal, *M* Richard Chester, *Cos* Alice Wolfbauer.

A Giant Films and Seashell production- Artificial Eye Film Company. 81 mins. UK, 2008. Rel: 5 June 2009. Cert 12A.

Shifty ★★★½
Misguidedly promoted as a thriller, Eran Crevy's promising debut feature may be a story of drug-dealing and violence (and, as such, slightly over-familiar), but the piece is character-driven. Filmed in Harrow and Borehamwood, it is at heart a story of the troubled friendship between two young men, one of them being a Muslim from Pakistan. Its impact is somewhat less than that of *Bullet Boy* (2004) but it's a promising calling card for a filmmaker with a definite visual sense. MS

‣ Riz Ahmed, Daniel Mays, Jason Flemyng, Jay Simpson, Francesca Annis, Nitin Ganatra.
‣ *Dir* and *Written by* Eran Creevy, *Pro* Rory Aitken and Ben Pugh, *Ph* Ed Wild, *Pro Des* Erik Rehl, *Ed* Kim Gaster, *M* Molly Nyman and Harry Escott, *Cos* Rebecca Duncan.

Film London/a Between the Eyes production/a Microwave Film etc.-Metrodome Distribution.
85 mins. UK. 2008. Rel: 24 April 2009. Cert 15.

Shirin (no star rating given)
Quality work though it is, this latest piece by Abbas Kiarostami cannot fairly be given a rating. He experiments by showing us an audience, mainly women, supposedly reacting to a film which is unseen by us although we hear its soundtrack. That imagined film is a version of a tragic love story about Shiran, a princess, and Khosrow, a prince, said to be as famous as *Romeo and Juliet* is in the west. But since we don't know it we have the extra work of trying to follow an unfamiliar tale from its dialogue while reading sub-titles that distract us from studying the faces on screen. Consequently, the film as I saw it was not truly the work as intended by this highly imaginative director. MS

‣ With Rana Azadivar, Juliette Binoche, Azita Hajian, Leila Rashidi, Sahar Valadbeigi.
‣ *Dir* and *Pro* Abbas Kiarostami, *Screenplay* Mohammad Rahmanian based on Farrideh Golbou's *Khosrow and Shirin* inspired by

Hakim Nezami Ganjavi's *The Story of Khosrow and Shirin*, *Ph* Mahmoud Kalari and Houman Behmanesh, *Ed* Kiarostami and Arash Sadeghi, *M* Heshmat Sanjari, Morteza Hananeh and others.

Distributed by British Film Institute.
91 mins. Iran. 2008. Rel: 26 June 2009. Cert PG.

The Silence of Lorna ★★★
The latest film by the Dardenne Brothers has more plot than usual but it's a weakness not a strength when the storyline is so unlikely (it concerns the setting up of a marriage for a Russian mafioso seeking Belgian citizenship, so why select an Albanian who must first be married off to a Belgian who is later eliminated?). We are kept guessing as to how it will all work out, but the Bressonian aspirations don't really deliver this time. MS

‣ Arta Dobroshi, Jérémie Renier, Fabrizio Rongione, Alban Ukaj, Olivier Gourmet.
‣ *Dir* and *Written by* Jean-Pierre and Luc Dardenne, *Pro* The Dardenne Brothers and Denis Freyd, *Ph* Alain Marcoen, *Art Dir* Igor Gabriel, *Ed* Marie-Hélène Dozo, *Cos* Monic Parelle.

Les Films du Fleuve, Archipel 35, Lucky Red, RTBF (Télévision Belge), Arte France Cinéma and ARTE/WDR co-production etc.-New Wave Films. 105 mins. France/Italy/Belgium/Germany. 2008. Rel: 28 Nov 2008. Cert 15.

Sisterhood ★★½
Two half sisters, one, Catherine, a sophisticated Chelsea-living Brit, the other, Shirley, a Kiwi sheep farmer, get together after both their mothers' deaths, in order to locate their recalcitrant father who is trying to make claims on their properties. The film details their efforts to find their con-man dad just as he has latched on to an elderly female lottery winner. This is an over the top British comedy with promise but it doesn't materialise in the screenplay or some of the acting. Emily Corcoran wrote the script and plays Shirley. Isabelle Defaut is Catherine

and Nicholas Ball is their wayward father, although comedy is not his forte. Maria Charles as Ethel the lottery winner provides good characterisation, but as a whole, it is unfunny stuff. Richard Curtis won't be losing any sleep. MHD

▶ Nicholas Ball, Isabelle Defaut, Emily Corcoran, Al Hunter Ashton, Maria Charles, Robert Faith, Paul Gregory.
▶ *Dir* Richard Wellings-Thomas, *Pro* Corcoran, Tim Hart and A Sirokh A, *Screenplay* Corcoran, *Ph* John Christoffels and Nathan Sheppard, *Pro Des* Nicola Dietmann, *Ed* Sean Barton and James Westcott, *M* Paul Lawler, *Cos* Tess Kurzeme.

Cork Films/Hart Films/Sirokh Films/Sisterhood Film etc-Blue Dolphin Film Distribution. 90 mins. UK. 2008. Rel: 17 Oct 2008. Cert 12A.

sleep furiously ★ ★ ½

Director Gideon Koppel composes pictures beautifully and in portraying the decline of a hill-farming community in Wales his commitment is beyond question. That said, this shapeless, meandering work never gets to the heart of the people to involve us in their situation. Coming out just after the French masterpiece *Modern Life* (q.v.) which achieved its comparable aims perfectly, the timing of this release is unfortunate to say the least. MS

▶ With inhabitants and friends of the Trefeurig community.
▶ *Dir* and *Ph* Gideon Koppel, *Pro* Margaret Matheson and Koppel, *Ed* Mario Battistel, *M* Aphex Twin.

Asiantaeth Ffilm Cymru/Film Agency for Wales/Bard Entertainments Ltd/Van Film Ltd etc.-New Wave Films. 94 mins. UK. 2007. Rel: 29 May 2009. Cert U.

Slumdog Millionaire
★ ★ ★ ★ ★

The title says it all: it's a fairytale about a boy from the slums of Mumbai who gets to enter the television quiz *Who Wants to Be a Millionaire?* As a boy Jamal (Dev Patel) was a petty thief, ducking and diving just to stay alive. Now he has the chance to get rich quick. But how come he, a slumdog, knows all the answers to the questions? He is suspected of cheating and tortured by the authorities, but truth will out and, despite the best or worst efforts of the appalling quizmaster (Anil Kapoor) Jamal wins through and is even reunited with his lost girlfriend Latika (Freida Pinto). Director Danny Boyle gets such winning performances from his leads that it is impossible not to take their side. Despite the scenes of torture the film is ultimately a feelgood experience, even more so than, say, the somewhat overrated *Mamma Mia!* MHD

▶ Dev Patel, Anil Kapoor, Saurabh Shukla, Raj Zutshi, Freida Pinto, Irrfan Khan, Sanchita Choudhary.
▶ *Dir* Danny Boyle and Loveleen Tandan, *Pro* Christian Colson, *Screenplay* Simon Beaufoy, from the novel *Q & A* by Vikas Swarup, *Ph* Mark Dod Mantle, *Pro Des* Mark Digby, *Ed* Chris Dickens, *M* A R Rahman, *Cos* Suttirat Anne Larlarb.

Celador Films/Pathé Pictures International-Pathé Pictures Distribution. 120 mins. UK. 2008. Rel: 9 Jan 2009. Cert 15.

Soi Cowboy ★ ★ ★

Thomas Clay's highly demanding follow-up to his undervalued *The Great Ecstasy of Robert Carmichael* is, like *Tropical Malady*, a film in two parts. The first offers a minimalistic western perspective on a young Thai girl's relationship with a fat European (the excellent Nicolas Bro), a situation accepted by her as preferable to prostitution. The shorter second piece, not entirely unrelated, switches from black and white to colour to reveal the desperate straits of poor Thais including one who for money is prepared to carry out an employer's vengeance by delivering the head of his own brother. It's an oddity that will bore some but which invites reflection. MS

➤ Nicolas Bro, Pimwalee Thampanyasan, Petch Mekoh, Natee Srimanta.
➤ *Dir* and *Written by* Thomas Clay, *Pro* Tom Waller and Joseph Lang, *Ph* Sayombhu Mukdeeprom, *Cos* Nick Kemp.

Pull Back Camera/a De Warrenne Pictures production-Network Releasing.
117 mins. UK. 2008. Rel: 12 June 2009. Cert 15.

Somers Town ★ ★ ★ ½

This minor but engaging piece brings to London a boy from the Midlands (the excellent Thomas Turgoose from Shane Meadows' earlier hit *This is England*) where he is befriended by a Polish teenager (Piotr Jagiello, equally good). The boys' rivalry over a pretty waitress is persuasively handled but the wish-fulfilment ending seems to belong to a different movie. MS

➤ Thomas Turgoose, Piotr Jagiello, Ireneusz Czop, Kate Dickie, Perry Benson.
➤ *Dir* Shane Meadows, *Pro* Barnaby Spurrier, *Written by* Paul Fraser based on an idea by Mother Vision, *Ph* Natasha Braier, *Pro Des* Lisa Marie Hall, *Ed* Richard Graham, *M* Gavin Clarke, *Cos* Jo Thompson.

Thomas Turgoose as Tomo, a runaway from Nottingham who hits the big city in Shane Meadows' *Somers Town.*

Tomboy Films/Mother Vision/a Big Arty production-Optimum Releasing.
71 mins. UK. 2008. Rel: 22 Aug 2008. Cert 12A.

Sounds Like Teen Spirit ★ ★ ★ ★ ½

What a surprise! This documentary about Europe's Junior Eurovision song competition may fit to a formula (the film follows four contestants in particular) but director Jamie J Johnson has selected all four with care and adopts an approach that is affectionate and devoid of kitsch. His subjects are engaging and sensible teenagers and this is a film which for older audiences is capable of restoring their faith in the young. Bravo! MS

➤ With Marina Baltadzi, Laurens Platteeuw, Mariam Romelashvili, Yiorgos Ioannides, Bab Buelens.
➤ *Dir* and *Ph* Jamie J Johnson, *Pro* Elizabeth Karlsen and Stephen Woolley, *Ed* Lucien Clayton, *M* Mat Davidson.

UK Film Council/Aramid Entertainment/the C4 British Documentary Film Foundation/a Number 9 Films (Junior) Limited/Number 9 Films production etc.-Warner Music Entertainment.
93 mins. UK/Cayman Islands. 2008. Rel: 8 May 2009. Cert 12A.

Space Chimps ★ ★

Ham III is a happy-go-lucky circus performer who is very proud of the fact that his grandfather was the first chimpanzee to go into space. Unsurprisingly Ham is chosen by the Space Agency to join Lieutenant Luna and Commander Titan on a dangerous space mission. They land on a distant planet and attempt to save its peaceful inhabitants from their evil dictator. This routine animation is likeable but predictable and seems to have been written and directed by numbers. GS

➤ Voices of Andy Samberg, Cheryl Hines, Jeff Daniels, Patrick Warburton, Kristin Chenoweth, Stanley Tucci.
➤ *Dir* Kirk DeMicco, *Pro* Barry Sonnenfeld and John H Williams, *Screenplay* DeMicco

and Rob Moreland from a story by DeMicco, *Ph* Jericca Cleland, *Pro Des* Bo Welch, *Ed* Debbie Berman, *M* Chris P Bacon.

**Vanguard Animation/Starz Animation/Starz Media/Studiopolis/Odyssey Entertainment-Entertainment Film Distributors.
81 mins. USA. 2008. Rel: 1 Aug 2008. Cert U.**

Special People ★ ★ ★

There's a welcome attempt here by Justin Edgar to tell a story about disabled people including four such teenagers taking a film course. The unintended condescension of the filmmaker who is teaching them provides comedy, but as the story develops it comes to lack conviction (a late twist in the plot is not at all persuasive). Uneven, then, but certainly heartfelt and pleasingly individual. MS

▶ Dominic Coleman, Robyn Frampton, Jason Maza, Sasha Hardway, David Proud.
▶ *Dir* Justin Edgar, *Pro* Alex Usborne and Edgar, *Written by* Dominic Coleman and Edgar, *Ph* Zac Nicholson, *Ed* Mark Burgess, *M* Kim Humphrey, *Cos Supervisor* Bart Cariss.

**A 104 films production in association with Screen West Midlands/IMISON/Tansoo Productions etc.-Guerilla Films.
81 mins. UK. 2007. Rel: 21 Nov 2008. Cert 12A.**

The Spirit ★

Artist, writer and fledgling filmmaker Frank Miller, the visionary creator of *Batman: The Dark Knight Returns*, *300* and *Sin City*, pays homage to his mentor, the great Will Eisner, with an adaptation of his seminal comic book creation. Sadly it's a dud: corny, cheesy, clumsy, dreary and uncomfortably over-stylised. This tale of a mysteriously reborn crime fighter should itself never have been brought to life. Eisner deserved better. Boo. Hiss. MJ

▶ Jaie King, Gabriel Macht, Dan Gerrity, Kimberley Cox, Eva Mendes, Samuel L Jackson, Scarlet Johansson.
▶ *Dir* and *Screenplay* Frank Miller, from the comic book series by Will Eisner, *Pro* Michael E Uslan, Gigi Pritzker and Deborah Del Prete, *Ph* Bill Pope, *Pro Des* Rosario Provenza, *Ed* Gregory Nussbaum, *M* David Newman, *Cos* Michael Dennison.

**Lionsgate/Odd Lot Entertainment/Continental Entertainment/Media Magik Entertainment-Lionsgate.
103 mins. USA. 2008. Rel: 1 Jan 2009. Cert 12A.**

Please don't call me the Lone Ranger! Gabriel Macht in *The Spirit*, allegedly a tribute to comic book master Will Eisner but one that misses on all counts.

Standard Operating Procedure ★ ★ ★ ★

Errol Morris' excellent documentary traces similar ground to *Taxi to the Darkside* but is as powerful in its depiction of the horrifying Abu Ghraib prison scandal. Morris interviews the American soldiers about the taking of the shocking photographs of the Iraqi prisoners and paints a clear picture of what had actually happened there and the subsequent military cover-up. It is a shameful story that needs to be told and Morris' urgent filmmaking accompanied by Danny Elfman's haunting score is essential viewing! GS

‣ Christopher Bradley, Sarah Denning, Robin Dill, Merry Grissom, Daniel Novy.
‣ *Dir* Errol Morris *Pro* Morris and Julie Ahlberg, *Ph* Robert Chappell and Robert Richardson *Pro Des* Steve Hardie, *Ed* Andy Grieve, Steven Hathaway and Dan Mooney, *M* Danny Elfman, *Cos* Marina Draghici.

Participant Productions/Sony Pictures Classics-Sony Pictures Releasing.
116 mins. USA. 2008. Rel: 18 July 2008. Cert 15.

Star Trek ★ ★ ★ ★

In the capable hands of J J Abrams, this eleventh edition in the *Star Trek* film franchise fires on all cylinders. Cutting back to the genesis of the original characters, the prequel chronicles the birth of James Tiberius Kirk, the childhood of Spock and the introduction of the cosmopolitan crew, while the merciless Romulan Nero (Eric Bana) threatens to destroy the entire Federation. Visually superior to the preceding episodes, the film is a little too complicated for its own good but is nonetheless thrilling, funny, pacy, wildly imaginative and replete with the awe factor. It should benefit nicely from repeated viewings. JC-W

‣ Chris Pine, Zachary Quinto, Leonard Nimoy, Eric Bana, Bruce Greenwood, Karl Urban, Zoe Saldana, Simon Pegg, Winona Ryder, Ben Cross, John Cho, Anton Yelchin.
‣ *Dir* J J Abrams, *Pro* Abrams and Damon Lindelof, *Screenplay* Roberto Orci and Alex Kurtzman, based on Gene Roddenberry's television series, *Ph* Dan Mindel, *Pro Des* Scott Chambers, *Ed* Maryann Brandon and Mary Jo Markey, *M* Michael Giacchino, *Cos* Michael Kaplan.

Paramount Pictures/Spyglass Entertainment/Bad Robot-Paramount Pictures.
127 mins. USA. 2009. Rel: 8 May 2009. Cert 12A.

Star Wars: The Clone Wars ★

George Lucas cranks out yet another humourless money-making endeavour. This time it's a computer generated 'toon, but akin to the live action prequels that killed our enthusiasm for *Star Wars*. Although it's a grand spectacle full of laser-blasting, sabre-swishing, Yoda-leaping action, it has no heart, and the only thing less interesting than the characters is the plot. The Force is not with this one. MJ

‣ Voices of Matt Lanter, Ashley Eckstein, James Arnold Taylor, Dee Bradley Baker, Anthony Daniels, Christopher Lee, Tom Kane, Nika Futterman.
‣ *Dir* Dave Filoni, *Pro* George Lucas and Catherine Winder, *Screenplay* Henry Gilroy, Scott Murphy and Steven Melching, based on characters and universe by Lucas and Darren Marshall, *Pro Des* Russell G Chong, *Ed* Jason Tucker, *M* Kevin Kiner.

CGCG/Lucasfilm Animation/Lucasfilm-Warner Bros Pictures.
98 mins. USA. 2008. Rel: 15 Aug 2008. Cert PG.

State of Play ★ ★ ★ ½

Condensing Paul Abbott's six-hour BBC TV series into a feature film meant losing characters and changing the sex of one of the leads, as well as moving the whole thing to the US. The three screenwriters have made a reasonable job of this lone-newspaper-reporter-uncovers-government-and-corporate-business-scandal script but it seems like a different entity altogether and it makes one yearn to see the original again with the likes of John Simm, David Morrissey, Kelly MacDonald, Bill Nighy and James McAvoy. Russell Crowe appeals as the Washington Globe's slobby reporter, Ben Affleck is effective as a dodgy Congressman playing cat and mouse, but turning editor Bill Nighy into Helen Mirren is just stepping too far over the mark. MHD

▶ Russell Crowe, Ben Affleck, Rachel McAdams, Helen Mirren, Robin Wright Penn, Jason Bateman, Jeff Daniels.
▶ *Dir* Kevin Macdonald, *Pro* Tim Bevan, Eric Fellner and Andrew Hauptman, *Screenplay* Matthew Michael Carnahan, Tony Gilroy and Billy Ray, based on Paul Abbott's television series, *Ph* Rodrigo Prieto, *Pro Des* Mark Friedberg, *Ed* Justine Wright, *M* Alex Heffes, *Cos* Jacqueline West.

Universal Pictures/Working Title Films/ Bevan-Fellner/Relativity Media/Studio Canal/ Andell Entertainment-Universal Pictures International.
127 mins. USA/UK/France. 2009. Rel: 24 Apr 2009. Cert 12A.

Steep ★★★★

Forget any television screenings since this stunningly photographed documentary about the sport of extreme skiing requires the biggest screen possible. Interviews with those drawn to the sport because of its danger (one of them, Doug Coombs, died in a mountain accident shortly after the filming) provide insights if not full understanding of what motivates them. The film offers a celebration and a caution and is expertly put together. MS

▶ With Doug Coombs, Bill Briggs, Ingrid Backstrom and narrated by Peter Krause.
▶ *Dir* and *Written by* Mark Obenhaus (based on a factual story by William A Kerig), Mark Obenhaus, *Pro* Jordan Kronick and Gabrielle Tenenbaum, *Ph* Erich Roland and others, *Ed* Peter R Livingston Jr, *M* Anton Sanko and Victor Magro.

High Ground Productions/The Documentary Group-Metrodome Distribution.
90 mins. USA. 2007. Rel: 26 Sept 2008. Cert PG.

Step Brothers ★★★½

Brennan (Will Ferrell) is 39 and still lives with his mother Nancy and 40-year-old Dale (John C Reilly) still lives with his father Robert. They are both totally immature, spoilt brats who have never worked in their lives and are forced to share a room when Nancy (Mary Steenburgen) and Robert (Richard Jenkins) get married. It is a good idea, well scripted with fun set-pieces and strong performances, particularly from Steenburgen and Jenkins whose loving relationship is put to the test by their idle sons. GS

▶ Will Ferrell, John C Reilly, Mary Steenburgen, Richard Jenkins, Adam Scott, Kathryn Hahn.
▶ *Dir* Adam McKay, *Pro* Judd Apatow and Jimmy Miller, *Screenplay* Ferrell and McKay, from a story by Ferrell, McKay and Reilly, *Ph* Oliver Wood, *Pro Des* Clayton Hartley, *Ed* Brent White, *M* Jon Brion, *Cos* Susan Matheson.

Columbia Pictures/Relativity Media/Apatow Company/Mosaic Media Group-Sony Pictures Releasing.
98 mins. USA. 2008. Rel: 29 Aug 2008. Cert 15.

Stone of Destiny ★★½

In 1950 a Scottish nationalist called Ian Hamilton (Charlie Cox) led a group of university students on a mission to steal the legendary, eponymous stone. This was the slab over which Scottish kings were traditionally crowned in Perthshire and, as legend has it, was used by Jacob to rest his head (Genesis 28:10-18). However, the stone was nicked by Edward I and installed under his throne at Westminster Abbey. And Hamilton, aged just 25, was having none of it... An inspirational story, this, but it does feel like a highly fictionalised version of true events. And the treatment is a little mundane and old-fashioned. JC-W

Hello and welcome to *Blind Date*. Three horrific visitors turn up unannounced in *The Strangers*.

▶ Charlie Cox, Robert Carlyle, Kate Mara, Billy Boyd, Brenda Fricker, Peter Mullan.
▶ *Dir* and *Screenplay* Charles Martin Smith based on the book *The Taking of the Stone of Destiny* by Ian Hamilton, *Pro* Rob Merrilees , *Ph* Glen Winter, *Pro Des* Tom Sayer, *Ed* Fredrik Thorsen, *M* Mychael Danna, *Cos* Trisha Biggar.

Infinity Features Entertainment/The Mob Film Company-Odeon Sky Filmworks. 96 mins. Canada/UK. 2008. Rel: 19 Dec 2008. Cert PG.

The Strangers ★ ½

Following a wedding party, James and Kristen (Scott Speedman and Liv Tyler) retire for a night of romance and deliberation. But at James's house in the woods there are strangers waiting in the dark... This is truly a horror film stripped to the bone. That is, there is no back-story, no motive and no twist. Furthermore, there is nothing new or clever here and without textured characters we have no reason to care. JC-W

▶ Liv Tyler, Scott Speedman, Glenn Howerton, Gemma Ward, Kip Weeks, Laura Margolis.

▶ *Dir* and *Screenplay* Bryan Bertino, *Pro* Doug Davison, Roy Lee and Nathan Kahane, *Ph* Peter Sova, *Pro Des* John D Kretschmer, *Ed* Kevin Greutert, *M* tomandandy, *Cos* Susan Kaufmann.

Rogue Pictures/Intrepid Pictures/Mandate Pictures/Vertigo Entertainment-Universal Pictures International. 85 mins. USA. 2008. Rel: 29 Aug 2008. Cert 15.

Stuck ★ ★ ½

In this psychological thriller Mena Suvari is almost unrecognisable as a compassionate retirement home worker whose life takes an unexpected turn when her car collides with Tom (Stephen Rea), an unemployed man who is having a truly bad day. As she has been driving under the influence, she is unwilling to give him medical help when his body gets stuck through her windscreen. Stuart Gordon makes the most of this bizarre and almost unbelievable story which surprisingly is inspired by true events. GS

▶ Mena Suvari, Stephen Rea, Russell Hornsby, Rukiya Bernard, Carolyn Purdy-Gordon.
▶ *Dir* Stuart Gordon, *Pro* Gordon, Robert

Katz, Jay Firestone and Ken Gord, *Screenplay* John Trysik from a story by Stuart Gordon, *Ph* Denis Maloney, *Pro Des* Craig Lathrop, *Ed* Andy Hornitch, *M* Bobby Johnson, *Cos* Carol Cutshall.

Prodigy Pictures/Amicus Entertainment/ Turnidor-Rigel Entertainment. 85 mins. Canada/UK/Germany/USA. 2007. Rel: 9 Jan 2009. Cert 15.

Sugar ★★★★

Following their success with *Half Nelson*, Anna Boden and Ryan Fleck offer contrasting material in a tale about a young baseball player from the Dominican Republic. This youth, known as 'Sugar', is relying on his sporting skills to achieve success in America and this is more a story about immigrants than about sport. The ending could be sharper but it's beautifully realised both by the actors and technically (slick editing, great photography). MS

▶ Algenis Pérez Soto, José Rijo, Walki Cuevas, Jaime Tirelli, Ellary Porterfield.
▶ *Dir* and *Written by* Anna Boden and Ryan Fleck, *Pro* Paul Mezey, Jamie Patricof and Jeremy Kipp Walker, *Ph* Andrij Parekh, *Pro Des* Elizabeth Mickle, *Ed* Boden, *M* Michael Brook, *Cos* Erin Benach.

HBO Films/a Journeyman Pictures/Hunting Lane Films production etc.-Axiom Films. 114 mins. USA. 2008. Rel: 5 June 2009. Cert 15.

Summer ★★

Judging by certain favourable reviews, this film must be regarded as a matter of taste. It is well played, but its miserable story of stunted lives and impending death linked to characters whom I found uniformly unsympathetic and unengaging left me cold. Touches of stylisation seem at odds with the naturalism of the Derbyshire locations. MS

▶ Robert Carlyle, Steve Evets, Rachael Blake, Michael Socha, Sean Kelly, Jo Doherty.
▶ *Dir* Kenny Glenaan, *Pro* Camilla Bray,

Screenplay Hugh Ellis, *Ph* Tony Slater-Ling, *Pro Des* Jane Levick, *Ed* Kristina Heatherington, *M* Stephen McKeon, *Cos* Sarah Ryan.

UK Film Council/EM Media/a Sixteen Films co-production with Mediopolis Film, Cinema Two etc.-Vertigo Films. 83 mins. UK/Germany. 2008. Rel: 5 Dec 2008. Cert 15.

Summer Hours ★★★½

In 2000 with *Les Destinées Sentimentales* Olivier Assayas offered a family saga in which a porcelain business featured. That film overshadows this new work of his about a family suffering bereavement and the division of an estate including paintings and other art objects. Juliette Binoche gets star billing although her part is comparatively small. The whole piece, watchable though it is, never attains the depth or emotional power that would make it memorable. (Original title: *L'Heure d'été*). MS

▶ Juliette Binoche, Charles Berling, Jérémie Renier, Edith Scob, Isabelle Sadoyan.
▶ *Dir* and *Written by* Olivier Assayas, *Pro* Marin and Nathanaël Karmitz and Charles Gillibert, *Ph* Éric Gautier, *Art Dir* François-Renaud Labarthe, *Ed* Luc Barnier, *Cos* Anaïs Romand and Jürgen Doering.

MK2/France 3 Cinéma/Canal+/TPS Star etc.-Artificial Eye Film Company. 103 mins. France. 2008. Rel: 18 July 2008. Cert 12A.

Summer Scars ★★★½

The story follows a group of teenagers who, after stealing a moped, skip school in order to spend a day in the woods. But they soon regret their decision when they come across Peter (Kevin Howarth), a seemingly friendly drifter. The young actors are perfectly cast and Howarth is terrifying in his transformation. The nightmarish story of Julian Richards' chilling film has echoes of *Eden Lake* (q.v.) but in my opinion this is a much more involving affair. GS

▷ Kevin Howarth, Ciaran Joyce, Amy Harvey, Jonathan Jones, Darren Evans, Christopher Conway, Ryan Conway.

▷ *Dir* Julian Richards, *Pro* Richards, Sabina Sattar and Mike Tims, *Screenplay* Al Wilson, from an idea by Richards, *Ph* Bob Williams, *Pro Des* Sue Harding, *Ed* Kant Pan, Mark Talbot-Butler and Ian Seymour, *M* Simon Lambros, *Cos* Gemima Coleman

Prolific Films/Forget About Films/Arts Council of Wales-Jinga Films.
73 mins. UK. 2007. Rel: 6 June 2009. Cert 15.

Sunshine Cleaning ★★★½

Albuquerque, New Mexico; today. Rose (Amy Adams) is up to her eyes coping with an unconventional son (he licks people), a wayward sister and long days cleaning other people's houses. It wasn't always like this: she was once captain of the cheerleading team and was going steady with Mac (Steve Zahn). Now she sleeps with Mac behind his wife's back. Then she starts a business cleaning up the mess left behind at crime scenes. Opening with a gloopy suicide, this eminently likeable dramedy brandishes its quirkiness on its sleeve. But there's real heart within its menagerie of eccentrics and, while the film loses momentum in its last third, it leaves enough telling moments dangling in the memory to be a charming achievement. JC-W

▷ Amy Adams, Emily Blunt, Alan Arkin, Jason Spevack, Steve Zahn, Mary Lynn Rajskub, Paul Dooley.

▷ *Dir* Christine Jeffs, *Pro* Glenn Williamson, Marc Turtletaub, Peter Saraf and Jeb Brody, *Screenplay* Megan Holley, *Ph* John Toon, *Pro Des* Joseph Garrity, *Ed* Heather Persons, *M* Michael Penn, *Cos* Alix Friedberg.

Big Beach Films/Clean Sweep Productions/ Back Lot Pictures-Anchor Bay Entertainment.
91 mins. USA. 2008. Rel: 26 June 2008. Cert 15.

Surveillance ★★★½

Arguably closer to Agatha Christie's play *The Mousetrap* than to *Rashomon*, this is nevertheless an American tale about carnage on a country road told largely in flashbacks from the varying viewpoints of those involved. Made by David Lynch's daughter Jennifer, it has an excellent first half making splendid use of the flat rural location. The later stages seem more exaggerated and confirm that any claims that this is more than an adroit thriller are unjustified. MS

Amy Adams and Emily Blunt get to clean up their act at crime scenes in Christine Jeffs' comedy-drama *Sunshine Cleaning.*

▶ Julia Ormond, Bill Pullman, Pell James, Ryan Simpkins, Cheri Oteri, Michael Ironside, Kent Harper, French Stewart.
▶ *Dir* Jennifer Lynch, *Pro* Marco Mehlitz, Kent Harper and David Michaels, *Written by* Lynch and Harper, *Ph* Peter Wunstorf, *Pro Des* Sara McCudden, *Ed* Daryl K. Davis, *M* Todd Bryanton, *Cos* Cathy McComb and Sonja Clifton-Remple.

**Arclight Films & Blue Rider Pictures/ Lago Film etc.-Odeon Sky Filmworks.
97 mins. Germany/USA/Canada/Australia. 2007. Rel: 6 March 2009. Cert 18.**

Swing Vote ★★★★

For the first time in the history of American elections, both the Republican and Democratic incumbents receive the identical number of votes. However, due to a technical hitch, one man's ballot was not counted. So both political parties pitch their election campaigns – their TV commercials, conventions and unalloyed attempts at bribery – at one man. Yet the latter couldn't really care less. This is a terrific idea for a political satire and is slickly executed and acutely observed. The mawkish ending is a shame, but the performances are ace, particularly from 12-year-old newcomer Madeline Carroll. JC-W

▶ Kevin Costner, Madeline Carroll, Paula Patton, Kelsey Grammer, Dennis Hopper, Nathan Lane, Stanley Tucci, Judge Reinhold.
▶ *Dir* Joshua Michael Stern, *Pro* Costner and Jim Wilson, *Screenplay* Stern and Jason Richman, *Ph* Shane Hurlbut, *Pro Des* Steve Saklad, *Ed* Jeff McEvoy, *M* John Debney, *Cos* Lisa Jensen.

**Touchstone Pictures/Radar Pictures/1821 Pictures etc-Delanic Films.
120 mins. USA. 2008. Rel: 26 Sep 2008. Cert 12A.**

Synecdoche New York ★★½

Choosing a title that few can pronounce is characteristic of Charlie Kaufman's approach to cinema. He has a great cast for this first film that finds him directing as well as writing but the highly stylised story of a New York theatre director and those surrounding him is irritatingly pretentious. It's about many things ranging from death to despair and from metaphysics to heartbreak but, while aiming at pathos as well as comedy, it never enables us to relate to the characters as real people. MS

▶ Philip Seymour Hoffman, Samantha Morton, Tom Noonan, Michelle Williams, Catherine Keener, Emily Watson, Dianne Wiest, Hope Davis, Jennifer Jason Leigh.

▶ *Dir* and *Written by* Charlie Kaufman, *Pro* Anthony Bregman, Kaufman, Spike Jonze and Sidney Kimmel, *Ph* Frederick Elmes, *Pro Des* Mark Friedberg, *Ed* Robert Frazen, *M* Jon Brion, *Cos* Melissa Toth.

**Sidney Kimmel Entertainment/a Likely Story, Projective Testing Service, Russia Inc. production-Revolver Entertainment.
124 mins. USA. 2008. Rel: 15 May 2009. Cert 15.**

Taken ★★★★

Luc Besson's screenplay for *Taken* is everything a Bond movie should be but these days isn't. It's a human story about ex-Secret Service man Bryan Mills (a retired 007?) who has to put his old skills to use again when his daughter and her friend are abducted by an Albanian prostitute ring in Paris. There's plenty of action but none of it too exaggerated to make it incredible. It has twists and turns, plenty of surprises and at least one genuinely heart-stopping moment on the streets of Paris. Liam Neeson is suitably stone-faced as Mills, at ease honing his skills as a former spy, showing strength of character and physique when it comes to the fisticuffs. Yes, Neeson could well be the best Bond we never had. The sequel will be worth anticipating especially if Neeson is in it. MHD

▶ Liam Neeson, Kate Cassidy, Maggie Grace, Jon Gries, Famke Janssen, Xander Berkeley.

It's good cheese but is it Leerdammer?: the little hero of *The Tale of Despereaux* actually prefers a good book to a lump of mouldy old mousetrap.

▶ *Dir* Pierre Morel, *Pro* Luc Besson, *Screenplay* Besson and Robert Mark Kamen, *Ph* Michel Abramowicz, *Pro Des* Hugues Tissandier, *Ed* Frédéric Thoraval, *M* Nathaniel Méchaly, *Cos* Olivier Beriot.

EuropaCorps/M6Films/Grive Productions/ Canal + etc-20th Century Fox.
93 mins. France. 2008. Rel: 26 Sep 2008. Cert 15.

The Tale of Despereaux
★ ★ ★ ★ ★

This animated adaptation of Kate DiCamillo's children's bestseller is a sheer delight, borrowing medieval visuals from Flemish artist Brueghel. The kingdom of Dor is in the doldrums owing to the king's decree following the death of his beloved queen, but then the sprightly mouse Despereaux is born with a preference for reading books rather than eating them... Unassuming, intelligent and compelling, this is a real treat. JC

▶ Voices of Matthew Broderick, Dustin Hoffman, Emma Watson, Tracey Ullman, Kevin Kline, William H Macy, Stanley Tucci, Ciarán Hinds, Robbie Coltrane.
▶ *Dir* Sam Fell and Robert Stevenhagen, *Pro* Gary Ross and Alison Thomas, *Screenplay* Ross and Kate DiCamillo, from a screen story by Will McRobb and Chris Viscardi, *Ph* Brad Blackbourn, *Pro Des* Evgeni Tomov, *Ed* Mark Solomon, *M* William Ross.

Universal Pictures/Relativity Media/ Larger Than Life Productions etc-United International Pictures.

90 mins. USA/UK. 2008. Rel: 19 Dec 2008. Cert U.

Teeth ★ ★ ½

Dawn is a poster girl for pre-marital chastity. In fact, she's so innocent that she has little knowledge of her own private anatomy. So, when she does get down and dirty, she's surprised that her condition of *vagina dentata* acts as an extreme case of birth control. Writer-director Lichtenstein deserves top marks for tackling something quite so outrageous. However, once we've cottoned on to Dawn's dilemma – or attribute – the film feels decidedly stretched. David Cronenberg was doing this sort of thing thirty years ago – and with more, er, bite. (Note: this review was omitted from *Film Review 2008-2009*). JC-W

▶ Jess Weixler, John Hensley, Josh Pais, Hale Appleman, Lenny von Dohlen.
▶ *Dir, Pro* and *Screenplay* Mitchell Lichtenstein, *Ph* Wolfgang Held, *Pro Des* Paul Avery, *Ed* Joe Landaller, *M* Robert Miller, *Cos* Rita Ryack.

Teeth-Momentum Pictures.
94 mins. USA. 2007. Rel: 20 June 2008. Cert 18.

Telstar ★ ★ ★

Actor Nick Moran turns director with this adaptation of his stage play about the gay record producer Joe Meek. Telling his story offers musical nostalgia for those who remember British pop of the 1960s, but in its second half the film becomes a vain attempt to turn Joe into an effective figure of tragedy. Joe Orton's story in contrast had a tragic stature; Meek's history, however, emerges here as merely pathetic and not emotionally engaging despite a strong lead performance from Con O'Neill. MS

▶ Con O'Neill, Pam Ferris, J J Feild, James Corden, Kevin Spacey, Tom Burke, Ralf Little.
▶ *Dir* Nick Moran, *Pro* Adam Bohling, Simon Jordan and David Reid, *Written by* James Hicks and Moran from their play, *Ph* Peter Wignall, *Pro Des* Russell De Rozario, *Ed* Alex Marsh, *M* Ilan Eshkeri, *Cos* Stephanie Collie.

Aspiration Films/a Simon Jordan production/ an Aspiration production etc.-Aspiration Films/Miracle.
119 mins. UK. 2008. Rel: 19 June 2009. Cert 15.

Tenderness ★★

Talented Sophie Traub has the ill luck to be playing opposite Jon Foster whose blank performance fatally drains away interest in this psychological drama about a troubled girl who seeks love and perhaps death with a young man who, although released from jail, could well be a serial killer. Much of the plotting is singularly unpersuasive which increases bemusement over the presence of Russell Crowe with star billing in what is really a supporting role as an obsessed detective. Echoes of several other films only remind you that they were better. MS

▶ Sophie Traub, Jon Foster, Russell Crowe, Alexis Dziena, Arija Bareikis, Laura Dern.
▶ *Dir* John Poulson, *Pro* John Penotti, Howard Meltzer and Charles Randolph, *Screenplay* Emil Stern from Robert Cormier's novel, *Ph* Tom Stern, *Pro Des* Mark Friedberg, *Ed* Lisa Zeno Churgin and Andrew Marcus, *M* Jonathan Goldsmith, *Cos* Eric Daman.

Lionsgate/iDeal Partners/Hanson Allen Films/a Greenestreet Films, TurtleBack production etc.-Lionsgate.
101 mins. USA 2007. Rel: 26 June 2009. Cert 15.

Terminator: Salvation ★

From *Charlie's Angels* director McG comes a supposed reboot of the *Terminator* series that is so poor it makes *T3* look like *T2*. Following mankind's post-apocalyptic struggle against the machines, the movie sees a typically grim, mono-emotional Christian Bale as the great John Connor, desperately trying to navigate an incomprehensible time-twister

A baleful Christian Bale walks his way through *Terminator: Salvation*, a poor action sequel going nowhere. No salvation here...

of a plot, building to a nonsensical dud of a climax. Ugly visuals, plasticky Terminators, lame dialogue, stilted performances, dreary action – and there's more to come. MJ

‣ Christian Bale, Sam Worthington, Moon Bloodgood, Helena Bonham Carter, Anton Yelchin, Bryce Dallas Howard, Jane Alexander.
‣ *Dir* McG (Joseph McGinty Nichol), *Pro* Jeffrey Silver, Victor Kubicek, Derek Anderson and Moritz Borman, *Screenplay* John Brancato and Michael Ferris, *Ph* Shane Hurlbut, *Pro Des* Martin Laing, *Ed* Conrad Buff, *M* Danny Elfman, *Cos* Michael Wilkinson.

The Halcyon Company/Wonderland Sound and Vision/Sony Pictures Releasing. 115 mins. USA/UK/Italy/Germany. 2009. Rel: 3 June 2009. Cert 12A.

Then She Found Me ★★
Sadly for Helen Hunt's many fans this venture by her – she is lead actress and a debutante as director – proves to be a dud. The first half comes across as a feeble rom-com for older audiences (a teacher nearing forty whose childless marriage is floundering meets a potential new love). But it is all so superficial that it makes no sense whatever to aim for drama later on. The acting of Hunt and Colin Firth disappoints too. MS

‣ Helen Hunt, Colin Firth, Matthew Broderick, Bette Midler, Salman Rushdie.
‣ *Dir* Helen Hunt, *Pro* Hunt, Connie Tavel, Christine Vachon and others, *Screenplay* Alice Arlen, Victor Levin and Hunt from a novel by Elinor Lipman, *Ph* Peter Donahue, *Pro Des* Stephen Beatrice, *Ed* Pam Wise, *M* David Mansfield, *Cos* Donna Zakowska.

Odyssey Entertainment/a Hunt/Tavel picture/a Killer Films/John Wells production etc.-Chelsea Films. 100 mins. USA 2007. Rel: 19 Sept 2008. Cert 15.

Three Monkeys ★★★
With *Climates* in particular the Turkish

director Nuri Bilge Ceylan justified his acclaim as a major director of arthouse cinema and here too sound and images show his qualities although the use of stylised colour just seems odd. As a study of a politician's employee paid to take the rap for his employer over a hit and run accident, it sounds like a strong drama, one that also involves the employee's son and his wife who becomes the politician's mistress. Yet the slow pace and oblique style water it down and, despite good acting and telling moments, you never really sense what Ceylan wants to say. MS

‣ Yavuz Bingöl, Hatice Aslan, Ahmet Rifat Sungar, Ercan Kesal, Cafer Köse.
‣ *Dir* Nuri Bilge Ceylan, *Pro* Zeynep Özbatur, *Screenplay* Ebru Ceylan, Ercan Kesal and Nuri Bilge Ceylan, *Ph* Gökhan Tiryaki, *Art Dir* Ebru Ceylan, *Ed* Ayhan Ergürsel, Bora Göksingöl and Nuri Bilge Ceylan.

Zeyno Film/NBC Film/Pyramide Productions/ BIM Distribuzione etc.-New Wave Films. 109 mins. Turkey/France/Italy. 2008. Rel: 13 Feb 2009. Cert 15.

Times and Winds ★★★
In arthouse terms this country drama from Turkey made by Reha Erdem is the real thing, but it's also an example of self-conscious artistry as it tells of children approaching their teenage years in an Anatolian village. The film is also concerned with the relationship between fathers and sons. Music is a part of the texture, but too often the piece suggests an absorption in art for art's sake. (Original title: *Bes vakit*). MS

‣ Özakan Özen, Ali Bey Kayali, Elit Isçan, Bülent Emin Yarar, Taner Birsel.
‣ *Dir, Screenplay* and *Ed* Reha Erdem, *Pro* and *Art Dir* Ömer Atay, *Ph* Florent Herry, *Cos* Mehtap Tunay.

A T.C. Kültür ve Turizm Bakanligi production-Artificial Eye Film Company. 112 mins. Turkey. 2006. Rel: 29 Aug 2008. Cert 15.

'Tis Autumn: The Search for Jackie Paris ★★★½

Jackie Paris was the star who might have been, a singer admired by Ella Fitzgerald and Nat 'King' Cole whose career went awry. Rediscovered in 2004 attempting a comeback shortly before his death, he features here in this slightly over-long but appealing documentary which investigates his life as well as his art. It's fascinating on more than one level. MS

▶ With Jackie Paris, Anne Marie Moss, Stacy 'Sissy' Paris, Michael Paris.
▶ *Dir* and *Written by* Raymond De Felitta, *Pro* David Zellerford, *Ph* Jeremy Saulnier, Chad Davidson, Zellerford and others, *Ed* John Wayland.

Hangover Lounge-Verve Pictures.
99 mins. USA. 2007. Rel: 21 Nov 2008. Cert 15.

To Get to Heaven First You Have to Die ★★★

This broken-backed film from Tajakistan provides a brilliant first half in which an impotent but married youth seeks to cure his condition and eventually becomes involved with a woman who is also married. This is pared-down filmmaking of the highest calibre but the second half sidetracks into a tale of enforced criminal activity before reaching a conclusion of questionable validity. MS

▶ Khurched Golibekov, Dinara Droukarova, Maruf Pulodzoda, Djonibek Mourodov.
▶ *Dir* and *Written by* Djamshed Usmonov, *Pro* Denis Carot, Marie Masmonteil and Robert Boner, *Ph* Pascal Lagriffoul, *Art Dir* Mavlodod Farosatshoev and Tim Pannen, *Ed* Jacques Comets, *M* Pierre Aviat, *Cos* Aksinia Pastukh.

Elzévir Films/Ciné Manufacture/Saga Production/Pandora Film Produktion etc-Trinity Filmed Entertainment.
96 mins. France/Germany/Switzerland/Russia. 2006. Rel: 28 Nov 2008.
Cert 15.

Tokyo Sonata ★★★

A Japanese family drama featuring a boy who proves gifted as a pianist and a father who conceals the fact that he has become unemployed, this piece could be called Ozu-like. However, in contrast to that master Kiyoshi Kurosawa favours long shots that make one feel distanced and the second half is in any case both more stylised and pretentious. An interesting oddity but not really satisfactory. MS

▶ Kagawa Teruyuki, Koizumi Kyoko, Koyanagi Yu, Inowaki Kai, Igawa Haruka, Yakusho Kôji.
▶ *Dir* Kurosawa Kiyoshi, *Pro* Kito Yukie and Wouter Barendrecht, *Screenplay* Max Mannix. Kurosawa and Tanaka Sachiko, *Ph* Ashizawa Akiko, *Art Dir* Maruo Tomoyuki and Matsumoto Tomoe, *Ed* Takahashi Koichi, *M* Hashimoto Kazumasa.

An Entertainment FARM/Fortissimo Films/Hakuhodo DY Media Partners, PiX presentation-Eureka Entertainment.
120 mins. Netherlands/Hong Kong/Japan. 2008. Rel: 30 Jan 2009. Cert 12A.

Tony Manero ★★★

A film about a murderous individual besotted on John Travolta in *Saturday Night Fever* and emulating him both on a dance floor and in a TV lookalike competition sounds intriguing, even commercial. But Pablo Larrain's movie from Chile is a slow-moving piece of arthouse cinema which suggests but never develops parallels between the man's unhealthy obsession and Chile's fixation on a modern American life-style. Alfredo Castro plays well but his character allows no room for development or understanding. MS

▶ Alfredo Castro, Amparo Noguera, Héctor Morales, Elsa Poblete, Paola Lattus.
▶ *Dir* Pablo Larraín, *Pro* Juan de Dios Larraín, *Screenplay* Pablo Larraín. Mateo Iribarren and Alfredo Castro, *Ph* Sergio Armstrong González, *Art Dir* Polin Garbisú, *Ed* Andrea Chignoli, *Cos* Muriel Parra.

A Fabula production/ProDigital, Universidad
UNIACC etc.-Network Releasing.
97 mins. Chile/Brazil/Netherlands. 2008. Rel:
10 April 2009. Cert 18.

Tormented ★ ★

Justine Fielding (Tuppence Middleton) is
delighted when she is asked for a date by the
popular Alexis (Dimitri Leonidas) and be part
of the in-crowd. But strange things begin
to happen at their school after the funeral
of Darren Mullett (Calvin Dean) who was
bullied to death. Jon Wright's high school
horror film doesn't add anything new to an
over-familiar genre. The acting in uneven
and the story after the first couple of killings
becomes very predictable. GS

▶ Alex Pettyfer, April Pearson, Dimitri
Leonidas, Calvin Dean, Tuppence Middleton,
Georgia King, Mary Nighy.
▶ *Dir* Jon Wright, *Pro* Kate Myers, Cavan
Ash, Tracy Brimm and Arvind Ethan David,
Screenplay Stephen Prentice, *Ph* Trevor
Forrest, *Pro Des* Julian Nagel, *Ed* Matt Platts-
Mills, *M* Paul Hartnoll, *Cos* Julian Day and
Alison McLaughlin.

BBC Films/Forward Films/Pathe/Screen West
Midlands/Slingshot Productions-
Warner Bros Pictures.
91 mins. UK. 2009 Rel: 22 May 2009. Cert 15.

Trade ★ ★ ★ ★

Veronika (Alicja Bachleda), a beautiful Polish
woman, and Adriana (Paulina Gaitan), a
13-year-old Mexican girl become human
cargo and are being taken to New Jersey
after they have been abducted in Mexico. In
the meantime Adriana's petty thief brother
Jorge (Cesar Ramos) and Ray (Kevin Kline), a
mysterious American, are determined to find
them. This powerful story is not dissimilar
to Channel 4's *Sex Traffic* but the intelligent
script here is crafted more like a thriller and is
driven by assured and energetic direction. GS

▶ Kevin Kline, Cesar Ramos, Alicja Bachleda,
Paulina Gaitan, Marco Pérez, Linda Emond.

▶ *Dir* Marco Kreuzpaintner, *Pro* Roland
Emmerich and Rosilyn Heller, *Screenplay*
Jose Rivera, from a story by Rivera and Peter
Landesman based on Landesman's article *The
Girls Next Door*, *Ph* Daniel Gottschalk, *Pro
Des* Bernt Capra, *Ed* Hansjorg Weissbrich, *M*
Leonardo Heiblum and Jacobo Lieberman,
Cos Carol Oditz.

Brass Hat Films/Centropolis Entertainment/
Reelmachine/VIP 4 Meridienfons-Lionsgate.
120 mins. Germany/USA. 2007.
Rel: 12 Dec 2008. Cert 15.

Traitor ★ ★ ★ ½

Developed from a story idea by Steve
Martin, this is much less adept than *Syriana*
(2005) in creating a thriller entertainment
that also manages to deal seriously with
issues concerning those caught up in
terrorism. Suspected by the FBI's Guy Pearce
of involvement in terrorist activities is
the American born Muslim played by the
talented Don Cheadle. As the plot develops it
holds us, but there's an uneasy feeling when
scenes that seem to belong to a Hollywood
action movie start to echo real life tragedies. MS

▶ Don Cheadle, Guy Pearce, Saïd Taghmaoui,
Neal McDonough, Archie Panjabi, Jeff Daniels.
▶ *Dir* and *Screenplay* Jeffrey Nachmanoff
from a story by himself and Steve Martin, *Pro*
David Hoberman, Todd Lieberman, Cheadle
and Jeffrey Silver, *Ph* J Michael Muro, *Pro
Des* Laurence Bennett, *Ed* Billy Fox, *M* Matrk
Kilian, *Cos* Gersha Phillips.

Overture Films/a Mandeville Films, Hyde
Park Entertainment, Crescendo production
etc.-Momentum Pictures.
114 mins. USA/Canada. 2008.
Rel: 27 March 2009. Cert 12A.

Transformers: Revenge of the Fallen ★ ½

A fans-only experience that zigzags
uncomfortably between stiff self-importance
and lame-brained jokiness, between puerile,
kiddy content and crass, adult stylings, this

monster sequel to a lousy movie is also much too long. Maybe if it was a Transformer itself, it could somehow transform from a hyperactive, headache-inducing blur of special effects and cheesy, barked dialogue into an enjoyable time-waster. MJ

‣ Shia LaBeouf, Josh Duhamel, Hugo Weaving, Megan Fox, Isabel Lucas, John Tuturro, Rainn Wilson.
‣ *Dir* Michael Bay, *Pro* Ian Bryce, Tom De Santo, Lorenzo Di Bonaventura and Don Murphy, *Screenplay* Ehren Kruger, Roberto Orci and Alex Kurtzman, *Ph* Ben Seresin, *Pro Des* Nigel Phelps, *Ed* Roger Barton, Paul Rubell, Joel Negron and Thomas A Muldoon, *M* Steve Jablonsky, *Cos* Deborah L Scott.

DreamWorks Pictures/Paramount Pictures/ Hasbro/Di Bonaventura Pictures-Paramount Pictures.
147 mins. USA. 2009. Rel: 19 June 2009. Cert 12A.

Transporter 3 ★ ½

Saddled with an explosive bracelet that will blow him to pieces if he wanders too far from his car, Jason Statham is forced by a sneering Robert Knepper to drive an annoying girl to a distant location. Even for a Statham movie, this Eurotrashy actioner falls way below acceptable standards. Lacking any kind of flair or originality, this tiresome actioner plods from mediocre fight scene to seen-it-before car chase without anything of interest in-between. MJ

‣ Jason Statham, Jeroen Krabbé Natalya Rudakova, François Berléand, Robert Knepper.
‣ *Dir* Olivier Megaton, *Pro* Luc Besson and Steve Chasman, *Screenplay* Besson and Robert Mark Kamen, *Ph* Giovanni Fiore Coltellacci, *Pro Des* Patrick Durand, *Ed* Camille Delamarre and Carlo Rizzo, *M* Alexandre Azaria, *Cos* Olivier Bériot.

Europa Corporation/Grive Productions/ TFI Films Production/Canal +/Current Entertainment-Icon Film Distribution.
104 mins. France. 2008. Rel: 5 Dec 2008. Cert 15.

Triangle ★ ★ ½

Three acclaimed Hong Hong directors join forces for this violent but stylish film which tells the story of three down-on-their-luck friends who agree to do a heist for some local gangsters. They change their minds when they hear about an ancient treasure but things get even worse when an alligator appears in the river and one of the wives is revealed to be having an affair with a corrupt cop. It is hard to know who to trust in this complex and rather confusing thriller and even harder to care. (Original title: *Tie saam gok*) GS

‣ Louis Koo, Simon Yam, Sun Hing Lei, Kelly Lin, Yao Yun, Lam Suet.
‣ *Dir* and *Pro* Ringo Lam, Tsui Hark and Johnnie To, *Screenplay* Sharon Chung, Yip Tin Shing, Kenny Kan, Yau Nai Hoi and Au Kin Yee, *Ph* Cheng Siu Keung, *Pro Des* Raymond Chan and Tony Yu, *Ed* David Richardson, *M* Dave Klotz and Guy Zerafa, *Cos* Stanley Cheung and William Fung.

Media Asia Films/Beijing Enlight Pictures/ Milky Way Image Company/Film Workshop etc-Manga Entertainment.
101 mins. China/Hong Kong. 2007. Rel: 29 Aug 2008. No Cert.

Tropic Thunder ★ ★ ★

A disjointed comedy from occasional filmmaker and star Ben Stiller, this follows a squad of hapless actors as they're mistaken for DEA agents in opium country and forced to fight for their lives. Less a cohesive film than a collection of comic sketches built around the themes of Hollywood and war, but still pretty funny, with a scene-stealing performance from Oscar-nominee Robert Downey Jr as a 'dude playin' the dude, disguised as another dude'. MJ

‣ Ben Stiller, Jack Black, Robert Downey Jr, Nick Nolte, Tom Cruise, Steve Coogan, Danny McBride, Reggie Lee, Matthew McConaughey.
‣ *Dir* Ben Stiller, *Pro* Stiller, Stuart Cornfeld and Eric McLeod, *Screenplay* Stiller, Justin

Action film
actors Ben
Stiller, Robert
Downey Jr and
Jack Black get
caught up in
a real battle
of wits in the
comedy *Tropic
Thunder*.

Theroux, Etan Cohen from a story by Stiller
and Theroux, *Ph* John Toll, *Pro Des* Jeff
Mann, *Ed* Greg Hayden, *M* Theodore Shapiro,
Cos Marlene Stewart.

**DreamWorks Pictures/Red Hour Films/
Goldcrest Pictures etc-Paramount Pictures.
107 mins. USA/Germany. 2008. Rel: 19 Sep
2008. Cert 15.**

Trouble the Water ★ ★ ★ ★
This brilliant documentary follows aspiring
rap artist Kimberley and her husband Scott

who used their home movie camera as a vital
witness to their experiences when they were
trapped during Hurricane Katrina in New
Orleans. They kept their unsteady camera
rolling as the waters were rising and dead
bodies were floating. Directors Tia Lessin
and Carl Deal use some of the brave couple's
riveting material to breathtaking and deeply
upsetting effect. GS

➤ *Dir* and *Pro* Carl Deal and Tia Lessin, *Ph* P
J Raval and Kimberley River Roberts, *Ed* Todd
Woody Richman, *M* Neil Davidge and Robert
Del Naja.

Elsewhere Films/Louverture Films-Maximum Film Distribution.
95 mins. USA. 2008. Rel: 5 Dec 2008. Cert 15.

Tuesday ★★★

Here we have three heists for the price of one. *Life on Mars* stars Philip Glenister and John Simm and their mates are trying to steal a priceless emerald being delivered to a bank. Meanwhile, two other bright sparks have the same idea. Told in flashback with Kevin McNally as a dour cop trying to figure out whether it was the bank robbers, or the bank teller or two female employees disaffected by their lack of promotion who did the job, *Tuesday* is a reasonable variation on the favourite British bank job movie, but its limited budget gives it a B-picture air. However, as the first feature from new company Japan Films it is worth encouragement. MHD

▷ Philip Glenister, Ashley Walters, Cristian Solimeno, Kevin McNally, John Simm, Kate Magowan, Kirsty Mitchell, Linal Haft.
▷ *Dir* and *Screenplay* Sacha Bennett, *Pro* Bennett and Jonathan Parsons, *Ph* Nic Lawson, *Pro Des* Richard Hudson and Ana Viana, *Ed* Jake Robertson, *M* Edwin Sykes, *Cos* Verity Cleary.

Hangman Film Company/Japan Films-Verve Pictures.
79 mins. UK. 2008. Rel: 10 Oct 2008. Cert 15.

Twentieth-Century Boys ★★★★

In the first part of an extraordinary Japanese trilogy of live-action, comic book adventures based on a manga series that's sold more than 20 million copies, it's 1969 and a group of Tokyo school kids put onto paper the *Book of Prophecy*, a comic book adventure in which they imagine themselves battling aliens. Then it's 1999, and the ex-school pals are drawn into a world-threatening conspiracy: a religious cult leader known as 'Friend', maybe someone from their youth, is replicating the disasters in the *Book of Prophecy* to exact revenge on them. Though it's slow to get going and, oh so darned long, this is an astounding-looking, thrilling movie made on a big budget that is all up there on screen. The title is explained by T-Rex's 1973 hit '20th Century Boy'. (Original title:*20-Seiki Shônen: Honakaku Kagaku Bôken Eiga*). DW

▷ Toshiaki Karasawa, Etsushi Toyokawa, Takako Tokiwa, Teruyuki Kagawa.
▷ *Dir* Yukihiko Tsutsumi *Pro* Morio Amagi, Nobuyuki Iinuma, Ryuuji Ichiyama, *Screenplay* Yashushi Fukuda, Yûsuke Watanabe, Takashi Nagasaki and Naoki Urasawa, from Urasawa's Manga series, *Ph* Satoru Karasawa, *Ed* Nobuyuki Ito, *M* Ryomei Shirai.

Cine Bazar/Dentsu/Nippon TV Network/Office Crescendo/Toho Company etc-4Digital Media.
142 mins. Japan. 2008. Rel: 20 Feb 2008. Cert 15.

Twilight ★★★★

A modern day love story with a twist, *Twilight* is a prime slice of wish fulfilment for teenage girls, the tale of a small-town sheriff's daughter (Kristen Stewart) who falls for a dreamy-eyed vampire (Robert Pattinson). Aside from the wussy mythology that paints too childlike a portrait of undead living, this is a stylish, atmospheric and surprisingly watchable adaptation of Stephanie Meyer's international best-seller. And if you were 12 and female in 2009, it was the best film ever made. MJ

▷ Kristen Stewart, Robert Pattinson, Billy Burke, Ashley Greene, Nikki Reed, Jackson Rathbone.
▷ *Dir* Catherine Hardwicke, *Pro* Wyck Godfrey, Karen Rosenfelt, Greg Mooradian and Mark Morgan, *Screenplay* Melissa Rosenberg, based on the novel by Stephanie Meyer, *Ph* Elliot Davis, *Pro Des* Christopher Brown, *Ed* Nancy Richardson, *M* Carter Burwell, *Cos* Wendy Chuck.

Maverick Films/Goldcrest Pictures/Imprint Entertainment/Summit Entertainment etc-Contender Films.
122 mins. USA. 2008. Rel: 19 Dec 2008. Cert 12A.

Robert Pattinson is the dreamy-eyed vampire in *Twilight*: strictly for teenage girls and their private fantasies.

Two Lovers ★ ★ ★ ★

The setting – Brooklyn – may remain the same but James Gray's latest film moves away from his usual stories of families and criminals to look at a romantic triangle. Leonard (Joaquin Phoenix) is set to marry the engaging and intelligent Sandra (Vinessa Shaw) when he falls in love with Michelle (Gwyneth Paltrow) who treats him as a friend able to advise her regarding her relationship with a married man (Elias Koteas). Insightful in its character drawing and well cast, this breaks free of the conventions that usually dominate such tales. MS

▶ Joaquin Phoenix, Gwyneth Paltrow, Vinessa Shaw, Isabella Rossellini, Elias Koteas.
▶ *Dir* James Gray, *Pro* Donna Gigliotti. Gray and Anthony Katagas, *Written* by Gray and Richard Menello, *Ph* Joaquin Baca-Asay, *Pro Des* Happy Massee, *Ed* John Axelrad, *Cos* Michael Clancy.

Magnolia Pictures/2929 Productions/Wild Bunch/a Tempesta Films production-Lionsgate.
110 mins. USA/France. 2008.
Rel: 27 March 2009.
Cert 15.

Tyson ★ ★ ★ ★

James Toback who featured the boxer Mike Tyson in his 1999 drama *Black and White* now offers the man again but this timer in a biopic featuring Tyson's own words and how they flow! This is what counts here and, despite a few stylised flourishes, this is virtually an autobiography on film. It provides audiences with a splendid opportunity to make their own assessment of a man who never guards his tongue. MS

▶ With Mike Tyson, Bill Cayton, Jim Jacobs, Desiree Washington, Lt Tim Horty.
▶ *Dir* James Toback, *Pro* Toback and Damon Bingham, *Ph* Larry McConkey, *Ed* Aaron Yanes, *M* Salaam Remi.

Fyodor Productions/Green Room Films/ Defiance Entertainment Production etc.- Revolver Entertainment.
88 mins. USA. 2008.
Rel: 27 March 2009. Cert 15.

The Unborn ★ ★

Odette Yustman (from *Cloverfield* and TV's *October Road*) lands a meaty meal of a part as a teen babysitter who's attacked by one of her charges and finds out she had a twin who died in the womb and is now terrorising her from beyond the grave! Probing her family's Holocaust past with the help of old Jane Alexander, Yustman finds her sibling has been possessed by an ancient Jewish demon, the Dybbuk, that will stop at nothing to be born. There's something sneakily enjoyable about this supernatural horror chiller, if you ignore the idea that it trivialises the untrivialisable. It's not a star-making moment for Yustman, but she goes to it with a will. Gary Oldman does the same with his role (as the Rabbi who agrees to perform an exorcism) by hysterically overacting. DW

▶ Odette Yustman, Gary Oldman, Meagan Good, Cam Gigandet, Idris Elba, Jane Alexander, James Remar.
▶ *Dir* and *Screenplay* David S Goyer, *Pro* Michael Bay, Bradley Fuller and Andrew Form, *Ph* James Hawkinson, *Pro Des* Craig Jackson, *Ed* Jeff Bethancourt, *M* Ramin Djawadi, *Cos* Christine Wada.

Rogue Pictures/Platinm Dunes/Phantom Four-Universal Pictures International. 87 mins. USA. 2009. Rel: 27 Feb 2009. Cert 15.

Under the Sea 3D ★ ★ ★

Filming underwater usually pays off because the aquatic depths are so photogenic, and you can't fail to impress an audience, especially in 3D and IMAX. Even a fairly mundane documentary such as this is transformed by the sight of giant whales, the scariest of great white sharks, the extraordinary stonefish and ancient turtles. The view is literally breathtaking in Howard Hall's latest undersea journey around the waters of Indonesia, Papua New Guinea, Southern Australia and the Great Barrier Reef. Jim Carrey narrates in almost serious mode. Learn about Australian sea lions, the leafy sea dragon and its amazing camouflage and the odd mating habits of the giant cuttlefish. At just forty minutes it's not too tough a lesson. MHD

▶ Narration by Jim Carrey.
▶ *Dir* and *Screenplay* Howard Hall, *Pro* Toni Myers, *Ph* Peter Kragh, *Ed* Christopher Holland, *M* Micky Erbe and Maribeth Solomon.

Howard Hall Productions/Warner Bros Pictures/IMAX-Warner Bros Pictures. 40 mins. USA/Canada. 2009. Rel: 13 Feb 2009. Cert U.

Boxer Mike tells his own story in *Tyson*, the film autobiography of a man who has more than enough to say for himself.

No one believed Bill Nighy when he said he was the king of the vampires, but here he is in *Underworld: Rise of the Lycans*, doing what comes naturally.

Underworld 3: Rise of the Lycans ★ ★ ½

You will probably have to have seen the first two films in the Underworld series to enjoy the third, which is actually a prequel telling of Viktor, king of the vampires (Bill Nighy, no less) and his war against the lycans, a species of werewolves who can change their shape. They are led by Lucan (Michael Sheen) and in the back story he is one of Viktor's slaves who's having a secret dalliance with Viktor's vampire daughter Sonja (Rhona Mitra, replacing the black leather clad Kate Beckinsale of the first two films). No doubt this script has gone about as far as it can go. Fanatics only need seek out this one. CB

▶ Michael Sheen, Bill Nighy, Rhona Mitra, Steven Mackintosh, Kevin Grevioux, David Ashton.
▶ *Dir* Patrick Tatopoulos, *Pro* Gary Lucchesi, Tom Rosenberg, Skip Williamson, Len Wiseman etc, *Screenplay* Danny McBride, *Ph* Ross Emery, *Pro Des* Dan Hennah, *Ed* Peter Amundson and Eric Potter, *M* Paul Haslinger, *Cos* Jane Holland.

Sketch Films/Intelligent Creatures/Lakeshore Entertainment/UW3 Film Productions/Screen Gems-Entertainment Film Distributors.

92 mins. USA/New Zealand. 2009. Rel: 23 Jan 2008. Cert 18.

The Uninvited ★ ★ ½

Kim Jee-Woon's 2003 Korean chiller *A Tale of Two Sisters* is transported to America in this unimaginative remake. Following her mother's tragic accident fragile teenager Anna (Emily Browning) returns home after a spell in a psychiatric hospital. She is reunited with her sister (Arielle Kebbel) but they are both deeply distressed when their father (David Strathairn) gets engaged to their mother's nurse Rachel (Elizabeth Banks) who they believe may be responsible for the accident. The intriguing story keeps one guessing until the final credits but doesn't come close to the far superior and much scarier original. GS

▶ Emily Browning, Arielle Kebbel, David Strathairn, Elizabeth Banks, Maya Massar.
▶ *Dir* Charles Guard and Thomas Guard, *Pro* Roy Lee, Walter F Parkes and Laurie Macdonald, *Screenplay* Craig Rosenberg, Carlo Bernard and Doug Miro based on Kim Jee-Woon's screenplay *Changhwa, Hongryon*, *Ph* Daniel Landin, *Pro Des* Andrew Menzies,

Ed Jim Page and Christian Wagner, *M* Christopher Young, *Cos* Trish Keating.

DreamWorks SKG/Cold Spring Pictures/ DWBC Productions/Macdonald-Parkes Productions etc-Paramount Pictures. 87 mins. USA/Canada/Germany. 2009. Rel: 24 Apr 2009. Cert 15.

Unrelated ★ ★ ★ ★

Joanna Hogg's impressive debut as writer/ director has a woman (the excellent Kathryn Worth) as the central figure. She visits a woman friend in Italy and there is drawn into a flirtation with an Englishman of the younger generation. Greater clarity in presenting the characters would improve the film, but as a portrayal of the British moneyed classes it recalls Losey's *Accident* and shows Mike Leigh how to do it. The film's essential subject matter becomes apparent quite late on and adds to the film's individuality. MS

▶ Kathryn Worth, Tom Hiddleston, Mary Roscoe, David Rintoul, Michael Hadley.
▶ *Dir* and *Written by* Joanna Hogg, *Pro* Barbara Stone, *Ph* Oliver Curtis, *Pro Des* and *Cos* Stephane Collonge, *Ed* Helle Le Fevre.

Distributed by New Wave Films. 100 mins. UK. 2007. Rel: 19 Sept 2008. Cert 15.

Valkyrie ★ ★ ★ ½

Bryan Singer rounds up the usual British suspects for his 'let's kill Hitler' real-life fantasy. David Bamber plays Adolf, with Kenneth Branagh and Bill Nighy as the German Generals heading the movement to assassinate the Führer, with the aid of Claus von Stauffenberg (Tom Cruise) and other parties played by Terence Stamp, Kevin R McNally and Eddie Izzard. Actually, despite the mixed collection of English and German accents (Cruise sticks to his American twang), it is quite a well-made

Tom Cruise plays Claus von Stauffenberg who tries to help the German Generals assassinate Hitler in Bryan Singer's tense wartime thriller *Valkyrie*.

and tense thriller that nearly approaches the excitement of those other assassination attempt movies, *The Day of the Jackal* and *The Eagle Has Landed*. MHD

‣ Tom Cruise, Kenneth Branagh, Bill Nighy, Tom Wilkinson, Terence Stamp, Carice van Houten, Eddie Izzard, Kevin R McNally, David Bamber, Kenneth Cranham.
‣ *Dir* Bryan Singer, *Pro* Singer, Christopher McQuarrie and Gilbert Adler, *Screenplay* McQuarrie and Nathan Alexander, *Ph* Newton Thomas Sigel, *Pro Des* Lilly Kilvert and Patrick Lumb, *Ed* and Music John Ottman, *Cos* Joanna Johnston.

United Artists/Achte Babelsberg Film/Bad Hat Harry Productions/Sessions Payroll Management-20th Century Fox.
121 mins. USA/Germany. 2008.
Rel: 23 Jan 2009. Cert 12A.

Vicky Cristina Barcelona
★ ★ ★ ½

Rebecca Hall shines in this agreeable yet overpraised lightweight romantic comedy from Woody Allen in which two young women visiting Spain become entangled with a stereotypically passionate and promiscuous artist. Humour is always there, but the tone darkens somewhat (there's no happy ending) and its themes about an artist's physical needs and the desirability of following your heart regardless of conventions suggest something akin to a statement by Allen about himself. MS

‣ Javier Bardem, Rebecca Hall, Scarlett Johansson, Penélope Cruz, Patricia Clarkson, Kevin Dunn.
‣ *Dir* and *Written by* Woody Allen, *Pro* Letty Aronson, Gareth Wiley and Stephen Tenenbaum, *Ph* Javier Aguirresarobe, *Pro Des* Alain Bainée, *Ed* Alisa Lepselter, *Cos* Sonia Grande.

A MediaPro & Gravier production/Antena 3 Films/Antena 3 TV/a Dumaine production-Optimum Releasing.
96 mins. USA/Spain. 2008. Rel: 6 Feb 2009. Cert 12A.

The Visitor ★ ★ ★ ★

Oscar contender Richard Jenkins is superb as a withdrawn widower in his sixties who re-engages with life consequent on the initially disturbing discovery that his New York apartment has been let by a conman to a couple of immigrants. Subtly handled, this is an engaging theme and the film builds further by touching on social issues. It may be middlebrow in tone (it chooses to incorporate a love story) but it is very well realised and splendidly acted by all. MS

‣ Richard Jenkins, Hiam Abbass, Haaz Sleiman, Danai Gurira. Marian Seldes.
‣ *Dir* and *Written by* Tom McCarthy, *Pro* Mary Jane Skalski and Michael London, *Ph* Oliver Bokelberg, *Pro Des* John Paino, *Ed* Tom McArdle, *M* Jan A P Kaczmarek, *Cos* Melissa Toth.

Groundswell Productions/Participant Productions/a Next Wednesday production-Halcyon Pictures.
106 mins. USA. 2007.
Rel: 4 July 2008. Cert 15.

Viva ★ ★

This may be eye-catching with its sets and bright colour photography but Anna Biller's take on soft porn films of the early 1970s is not sharp enough to become a good laugh or, one speech excepted, a smart social comment. The bad acting fits the concept, but the film stretches over two hours and quickly becomes a pointless piece of self-indulgence with a final tribute to Jacques Demy sinking in its own banality. MS

‣ Anna Biller, Bridget Brno, Jared Sanford, Chad England, John Klemantaski, Marcus DeAnda.
‣ *Dir, Ed, Sets, M, Animation, Cos* and *Written by* Anna Biller, *Pro* Biller and Jared Sanford, *Ph* C. Thomas Lewis and others.

Anna Biller Productions-Nouveaux Pictures.
123 mins. USA. 2006. Rel: 15 May 2009.
No Cert.

W ★ ★ ★

Oliver Stone's latest presidential portrait is not a soft view of George W Bush as some have suggested but a critical appraisal which, eschewing satire, seeks to present him as a tragic figure. Josh Brolin's playing of the role is excellent but the not unconvincing notion of Bush as a man desperately needing to impress his father is not so much fleshed out but reiterated in a manner that can only be called heavy-handed. MS

❧ Josh Brolin, Elizabeth Banks, Ellen Burstyn, James Cromwell, Richard Dreyfuss, Scott Glenn, Toby Jones, Stacy Keach, Thandie Newton, Bruce McGill, Jeffrey Wright.
❧ *Dir* Oliver Stone, *Pro* Bill Block, Eric Kopeloff, Paul Hanson and Moritz Borman, *Screenplay* Stanley Weiser, *Ph* Phedon Papamichael, *Pro Des* Derek Hill, *Ed* Julie Monroe, Joe Hutshing and Alexis Chavez, *M* Paul Cantelon, *Cos* Michael Dennison.

**Lionsgate/Omnilab Media/QED International and Block/Hanson present a Moritz Borman/ Ixtlan production etc.-Lionsgate.
129 mins. USA/Australia/Hong Kong/ Switzerland/China. 2008.
Rel: 7 Nov 2008. Cert 15.**

The Wackness ★ ★ ★ ½

This strange off-beat movie finds Sir Ben Kingsley triumphing in the most unlikely of roles as an eccentric therapist living in New York in 1994. He's a mentor sold on drugs and advocating sex to a young patient (Josh Peck) who falls for the doctor's more knowing daughter (Olivia Thirlby). The young players are great too, but the film shifts between the sensitive and the sentimental while failing to adopt a clear attitude to the subject of drug-taking. MS

❧ Ben Kingsley, Josh Peck, Olivia Thirlby, Famke Janssen, Jane Adams.
❧ *Dir* and *Written by* Jonathan Levine, *Pro* Keith Calder, Felipe Marino and Joe Neurauter, *Ph* Petra Korner, *Pro Des* Annie Spitz, *Ed* Josh Noyes, *M* David Tom, *Cos* Michael Clancy.

**Occupant Films/SBK Films-Revolver Entertainment.
99 mins. USA. 2007. Rel: 29 Aug 2008. Cert 15.**

A Walk Into the Sea: Danny Williams and the Warhol Factory ★ ★ ★ ★

In 1966 Danny Williams, a relatively unknown or simply forgotten filmmaker who worked with Andy Warhol at The Factory, took his parents' car, drove it to the coast and disappeared, leaving the car abandoned. His body was never found. His niece Esther Robinson's documentary about Williams goes some way towards explaining why he vanished. He was talented, perhaps even more so than Warhol, but obviously couldn't keep up with the pace or the personalities of the other Factory workers. The film is a fascinating human document about a forgotten artist whose talent was barely recognised. CB

❧ Gerard Malanca, Calle Anger, Albert Maysles, John Cale, Brigid Berlin, Nat Finkelstein, Paul Morrissey.
❧ *Dir* Esther B Robinson, *Pro* Robinson, Doug Block and Tamra Raven, *Screenplay* Robinson and Shannon Kennedy, *Ph* Adam Cohen, *Ed* Kennedy and James Lyons, *M* T Griffin.

**Chicken & Egg Pictures/
That Girl Media-Arthouse Films.
75 mins. USA. 2007. Rel: 15 Aug 2008. No Cert.**

Wall.E ★ ★ ★ ★ ★

On a future, deserted Earth, garbage-compacting droid Wall.E finds love with a newer model, the stalker Eve, before (in the second half) an adventure aboard a lost spaceship of obese, couch potato humans. A genre bending mix of science fiction, childlike character study and homage to musicals sees our hero watch and rewatch an old VHS copy of *Hello, Dolly!* Well up to Pixar par. JC

❧ Voices of Ben Burtt, Elissa Knight, Sigourney Weaver, Jeff Garvin, Fred Willard, John Ratzenberger, Kathy Najimy, Kim Kopf.

Rubik's cube?
Easy peasy for
a robot of my
calibre, reckons
Wall.E.

> *Dir* Andrew Stanton, *Pro* Jim Morris,
Screenplay Stanton and Jim Reardon, from
a story by Stanton and Pete Docter, *Pro Des*
Ralph Eggleston, *Ed* Stephen Schaffer, *M*
Thomas Newman.

Pixar Animation Studios/Walt Disney
Pictures-Buena Vista International
98 mins. USA. 2008. Rel: 18 July 2008. Cert U.

Waltz with Bashir ★ ★ ★ ★

This heartfelt film by Ari Folman investigates
his own experience in blocking out for years
his involvement in the Lebanon War and his
presence during the 1982 Sabra and Shatala
massacre when innocents died *en masse*
mistaken for Palestinian combat fighters.
Presented as an animated feature, it lacks
for us the novelty of such a technique being
applied to serious contemporary subject-
matter (c.f. *Persepolis*, 2007) and I found
the technique remarkable but sometimes
distancing. Many are, however, overwhelmed
by it and this is certainly a work of art to be
taken seriously. MS

> With Ori Sivan, Ronny Dayag, Shmuel
Frenkel, Professor Zahava Solomon.
> *Dir* and *Written by* Ari Folman, *Pro* Folman,

Serge Lalou, Yael Nahlieli and others, *Art
Dir* David Polonsky, *Ed* Nili Feller, *M* Max
Richter, *Animation* Bridgit Folman Film Gang,
Animation Dir Yoni Goodman.

Bridgit Folman Film Gang/Les Films d'ici/
Razor Films/Arte France etc.-Artificial Eye
Film Company.
90 mins. Israel/France/Germany/USA/Japan/
Finland/Switzerland/Belgium/Australia.
2008. Rel: 21 Nov 2008. Cert 18.

The Warlords ★ ★ ★ ½

General Pang miraculously survives from a
brutal war during the Taiping Rebellion in
China in the late 19th century but falls into
the hands of two bandits Zhao Er-Hu and
Jiang Wu-Yang . These three men become
blood brothers and join forces in their fight
against the corrupt Qing dynasty in order
to bring peace to the land. This epic looks
absolutely stunning and boasts strikingly rich
performances and amazing battle sequences
but its overcomplicated plot with its many
twists and turns is often too confusing
(Original title: *Tau Ming Chong*). GS

> Bao-ming Gu, Xiaodong Guo, Dehua Liu,
Lian Jieli, Wu Jincheng.

Dir Peter Chan and Wai Man-yip, *Pro* Chan and Andre Morgan, *Screenplay* Tim Nam-chun, Junli Guo, Lan Xu etc *Ph* Arthur Wong, *Pro Des* Chung Man-yee, *Ed* Wenders Li and Chris Blunden, *M* Kwong Wing-chan, Peter Kam and Leon Ko, *Cos* Yee Chung-man, Jessie Dai and Lee Pik-kwan.

Warner China Film HG Corporation/China Film Group/Media Asia Films/Applause Pictures-Metrodome Distribution.
110 mins. China/Hong Kong. 2007.
Rel: 7 Nov 2008. Cert 15.

Watchmen ★★★

Moore and Gibbons' classic deconstruction of the superhero genre finally reaches the screen, after a 23-year gestation period. Granted, this isn't the turkey which it might have been. It's quite good in parts... but much of the graphic novel's razor-sharp wit and narrative energy is dissipated in this overly-reverential adaptation. Flat pacing and a pedantic, geek-friendly screenplay work against the larger ambitions of the source material. Alan Moore's genius deserves better. RR

‣ Malin Akerman, Billy Crudup, Matthew Goode, Jackie Earl Haley, Jeffrey Dean Morgan, Patrick Wilson, Carla Gugino.
‣ *Dir* Zack Snyder, *Pro* Lawrence Gordon, Deborah Snyder and Lloyd Levin, *Screenplay* David Hayter and Alex Tse, based on Alan Moore's graphic novel, *Ph* Larry Fong, *Pro Des* Alex McDowell, *Ed* William Hoy, *M* Tyler Bates, *Cos* Michael Wilkinson.

Warner Bros Pictures/Paramount Pictures/ Legendary Pictures/Lawrence Gordon Productions-Paramount Pictures.
162 mins. USA. 2009. Rel: 6 Mar 2009. Cert 18.

The Wave ★★★½

The confident opening of this German film promises much as, drawing on a real-life occurrence, it looks at a school course that ended disastrously. It invites us to believe that today's youth could be led into succumbing to the appeal of a modern-day Hitler figure promising them a sense of self-worth and superiority. It's a disturbingly interesting notion, but the story becomes too schematic and contrived to carry weight.

‣ Jürgen Vogel, Frederick Lau, Jennifer Ulrich, Max Riemelt, Christiane Paul.
‣ *Dir* Dennis Gansel, *Pro* Christian Becker, *Screenplay* Gansel and PeterThorwath from a short story by William Ron Jones and based on the teleplay by Johnny Dawkins and Ron Birnbach, *Ph* Torsten Breuer, *Pro Des* Knut Loewe, *Ed* Ueli Christen, *M* Heiko Maile, *Cos* Ivana Milos.

Constantin Film/a Christian Becker production for Rat Pack Filmproduktion etc.-Momentum Pictures.
107 mins. Germany. 2008.
Rel: 19 Sept 2008. Cert 15.

Waveriders ★★★

This film about surfing is directly comparable with the superior *Steep* (q.v.) which dealt with extreme skiing. Both documentaries feature interviews, stunning visuals and an attempt to trace the history of the particular sport. But *Steep* is more informative, more detailed and more interesting for an outsider. But if surfing is your sport you're likely to enjoy this. MS

‣ With Richard Fitzgerald, Gabe Davies, Kelly Slater, Kevin Naughton, Drew Kampion.
‣ *Dir* Joel Conroy, *Pro* Margot Harkin, *Written by* Conroy and Lauren Davies, *Ph* Daniel Trapp, *Ed* Nathan Nugent and Douglas Moxon, *M Supervisor* Matthias Tode.

An Inís Films and Besom Productions co-production/Northern Ireland Screen etc.-Element Pictures Distribution.
78 mins. Ireland/UK. 2008.
Rel: 3 April 2009. Cert PG.

Wendy and Lucy ★★★★

Minimalistic filmmaking is far from easy to bring off but Kelly Reichardt is adept at it:

after *Old Joy* (2006) comes this unsentimental portrait of a woman's concern for her dog which goes missing as she passes through a small American town *en route* for a new life in Alaska. It's beautifully played, hugely atmospheric and potent as a comment on how small kindnesses matter. It may be a little film but it's eloquent about the human condition. MS

▶ Michelle Williams, Walter Dalton, Larry Fessenden, Will Oldham, Will Patton, John Robinson.
▶ *Dir* and *Ed* Kelly Reinhardt, *Pro* Neil Kopp and others, *Screenplay* Jon Raymond and Reinhardt from Raymond's short story *Train Choir*, *Ph* Sam Levy, *Pro Des* Ryan Smith, *Cos* Amanda Needham.

Oscilloscope Laboratories/a Film Science and Glass Eye Pix production-Soda Pictures.
80 mins. USA. 2008. Rel: 6 March 2009. Cert 15.

What Just Happened?
★ ★ ½

My answer to that question is that a talented cast gave themselves over to a piece unworthy of their talents. In elaborating on his memoir about life in Hollywood, Art Linson has concocted a comedy too unconvincing to bite or to enable the comedy to accommodate more serious moments effectively. Many players are poorly used but Robert De Niro does at least persuade us of a film producer's desperate attempts to hold things together in a crazy world. MS

▶ Robert De Niro, Catherine Keener, Sean Penn, John Turturro, Robin Wright Penn, Stanley Tucci, Bruce Willis, Michael Wincott, Kristen Stewart.
▶ *Dir* Barry Levinson, *Pro* Robert De Niro, Art Linson, Jane Rosenthal and Levinson, *Written by* Linson from his book *What Just Happened: Bitter Hollywood Tales from the Front Line*, *Ph* Stéphane Fontaine, *Pro Des* Stefania Cella, *Ed* Hank Corwin, *M* Marcelo Zarvos, *Cos* Ann Roth, *M* Gregory 'Smokey' Hormel and Will Oldham.

Magnolia Pictures and 2929 Productions/a Tribeca/Linson Films production etc.-Pathé Distribution.
102 mins. USA. 2007. Rel: 28 Nov 2008. Cert 15.

Who Killed Nancy? ★ ★ ★ ½

The title is somewhat misleading. The main focus here is not on who killed Nancy Spungen in the Chelsea Hotel in New York in 1978. Instead we have a documentary retelling of the story of Nancy and Sid Vicious aimed at persuading us that he was not responsible for her death. Some will find it a bit long, but if the subject matter attracts you then you will be held. MS

▶ With Steve 'Roadent' Connolly, John Holmstrom. Don Letts, Steve English, Alan Jones.
▶ *Dir* Alan G Parker, *Pro* Ben Timlett and Christine Alderson, *Ph* Nick Rutter, *Ed* Bill Jones, *Animation Pro* Nick Ray Rutter.

Ipso Facto Films/a Bill and Ben production etc.-Soda Pictures.
93 mins. UK. 2009. Rel: 6 Feb 2009. Cert 15.

Wild Child ★ ★ ½

Poppy Moore (Emma Roberts), a spoilt Paris Hilton wannabe, is sentenced for her sins to a stretch at an all-girls English school. So she sets out to be as obnoxious as possible, in order to be expelled posthaste. After a horrendous start, this formulaic compound of *Mean Girls* and *St Trinian's* warms nicely to its clichés. There's even a very fine turn from Natasha Richardson (as the sensible headmistress) and some well observed displays from the English gals. JC-W

▶ Emma Roberts Lexi Ainsworth, Vanessa Branch, Natasha Richardson, Selina Cadell, Linzey Cocker, Daisy Donovan, Nick Frost, Aidan Quinn.
▶ *Dir* Nick Moore, *Pro* Tim Bevan, Eric Fellner and Diana Phillips, *Screenplay* Lucy Dahl, *Ph* Chris Seager, *Pro Des* Eve Stewart, *Ed* Simon Cozens, *M* Michael Price, *Cos* Julia Caston.

Working Title Films/Universal Pictures/Studio Canal-United Pictures International.
98 mins. USA/UK/France. 2008.
Rel: 15 Aug 2008. Cert 12A.

The Women ★

The original film (1939) starred Joan Crawford, Norma Shearer and Joan Fontaine and this second remake was supposed to topline Julia Roberts, Sandra Bullock and Uma Thurman. In the event, Meg Ryan and company are reduced to soap operatic mannequins in a 'comedy' of gossipy women meddling in the worlds of fashion and publishing (think *Sex and the Suburbs* – without the sex). Shrill, flat and predictable, *The Women* is an ordeal. Watching it is like chewing plastic for two hours. JC-W

❯ Meg Ryan, Annette Bening, Eva Mendes, Jada Pinkett Smith, Bette Midler, Candice Bergen, Carrie Fisher, Cloris Leachman.
❯ *Dir* and *Screenplay* Diane English, from the play by Clare Boothe Luce and the 1939 screenplay by Anita Loos and Jane Murfin, *Pro* English, Mick Jagger, Bill Johnson and Victoria Pearman, *Ph* Anastas Michos, *Pro Des* Jane Musky, *Ed* Tia Nolan, *M* Mark Isham, *Cos* John A Dunn.

New Line Cinema/Picturehouse/ Inferno/Jagged Films/Shukovsky English Entertainment-Entertainment Film Distributors.
114 mins. USA. 2008. Rel: 12 Sep 2008. Cert 12A.

Wonderful Town ★★★

Wonderful is indeed the word for Aditya Assarat's filmmaking skills as displayed in this debut from Thailand. As a slow study of the growing bond between an architect and a hotel manageress in one of the communities ravaged by the 2004, it gains from fine acting and strong atmosphere. However, it never lives up to claims about being an insightful study into the effects of the tsunami and the narrative leads to an unsatisfactorily unclear conclusion. MS

❯ Supphasit Kansen, Anchalee Saisoontorn, Dul Yaambunying, Prateep Hanudomlap.
❯ *Dir* and *Written by* Aditya Assarat, *Pro* Soros Sukhum and Jetnpith Teerakulchanyut, *Ph* Umpornpol Yugala, *Pro Des* Karanyapas Khamsin, *Ed* Lee Chatametikool, *M* Zai Kuning and Koichi Shimizu, *Cos* Thanon Songsil.

A Pop Pictures production etc.-Soda Pictures.
92 mins. Thailand/Netherlands/Switzerland/ USA/Republic of Korea. 2007.
Rel: 13 March 2009. No Cert.

The World Unseen ★★★½

Following *I Can't Think Straight* (qv) Shamim Sarif brings the same warmth of feeling and the same engaging stars, Sheetal Sheth and Lisa Ray, to the telling of another lesbian tale. But, being set in South Africa in the 1950s and stressing issues of apartheid and its enforcement, this drama has a very different tone. It's heartfelt but the seriousness of the material underlines the superficiality of the writing. MS

❯ Lisa Ray, Sheetal Sheth, Parvin Dabas, Nandana Sen, Grethe Fox, David Dennis.
❯ *Dir* and *Written by* Shamim Sarif from her novel, *Pro* Hanan Kattan, *Ph* Michael Downie and Aseem Bajaj, *Pro Des* Tanya Van Tonder, *Ed* David Martin, *M* Richard Blackford, *Cos* Danielle Knox.

Enlightenment Productions/Dô Productions etc.-Enlightenment Films.
93 mins. UK/South Africa. 2008. Rel: 3 April 2009. Cert 12A.

The Wrestler ★★★

Increase this rating if you like macho movies. Mickey Rourke is as good as they say he is in the titular role of a wrestler past his prime and wrecked by a heart attack who nevertheless wants to go back into the ring, that being the only place where he feels like a man. Wrestling here is at its goriest and I couldn't for a moment sympathise with somebody wanting to return to this nasty sport (if you can call it that). Good support here and able filming, but I much prefer Darren Aronofsky's previous film *The Fountain*, imperfect but unjustly maligned. MS

▶ Mickey Rourke, Marisa Tomei, Evan Rachel Wood, Ernest Miller, Mark Margolis. Todd Barry.
▶ *Dir* Darren Aronofsky, *Pro* Scott Franklin and Aronofsky, *Written by* Robert Siegel, *Ph* Maryse Alberti, *Pro Des* Timothy Grimes, *Ed* Andrew Weisblum, *M* Clint Mansell, *Cos* Amy Westcott.

Fox Searchlight Pictures/Wild Bunch/ a Protozoa Pictures production- Optimum Releasing. 109 mins.USA/France. 2008. Rel: 16 Jan 2009. Cert 15.

X-Men Origins: Wolverine
★ ★ ★ ★

Wolverine was always the best thing in the *X-Men* movies, so it makes sense that this darker, solo spin-off adventure kicks some serious comic book ass, the character's best screen outing to date and a perfect companion piece to *X-2*. More for fans than casual observers, and loaded with lesser-known X-types, it delves into Logan's

murky past and focuses most closely on his relationship with feral half-brother Sabretooth, ferociously played by Liev Schreiber, every bit Hugh Jackman's equal. MJ

▶ Hugh Jackman, Liev Schreiber, Danny Huston, Will i Am, Lynn Collins, Kevin Durand, Dominic Monaghan.
▶ *Dir* Gavin Hood, *Pro* Jackman, John Palermo, Ralph Winter and Lauren Shuler Donner, *Screenplay* David Benioff and Skip Woods, *Ph* Donald M McAlpine, *Pro Des* Barry Robison, *Ed* Nicolas De Toth and Megan Gill *M* Harry Gregson-Williams, *Cos* Louise Mingenbach.

Twentieth Century Fox/Marvel Enterprises/ Donners' Company/Seed/Dune Entertainment etc-20th Century Fox. 107 mins. USA. 2009. Rel: 29 Apr 2008. Cert 12A.

The X-Files: I Want to Believe ★ ★ ½

Co-written and directed by series creator Chris Carter, this second feature spin-off of the paranoid horror/sci fi hybrid does little to encourage new fans to the franchise but should, at least, put a smile on the faces of longtime *X-Files* enthusiasts. The focus here

Hugh Jackman as Logan (aka Wolverine) provides the character's best cinematic embodiment in *X Men Origins: Wolverine.*

is not on aliens but on but the relationship between Mulder and Scully and, though it could have used more thrills and chills, it remains unremarkably interesting. MJ

▶ David Duchovny, Gillian Anderson, Amanda Peet, Billy Connolly, Xzibit, Adam Godley.
▶ *Dir* Chris Carter, *Pro* Carter and Frank Spotnitz, *Screenplay* Spotnitz and Carter, from *The X-Files* television series, *Ph* Bill Roe, *Pro Des* Mark Freeborn, *Ed* Richard Harris, *M* Mark Snow, *Cos* Lisa Tomczeszyn.

20th Century Fox Film Corporation/Crying Box Productions/Dune Entertainment III/ Company/Ten Thirteen Productions-20th Century Fox.
104 mins. USA/Canada. 2008. Rel: 1 Aug 2008. Cert 15.

Year One ★★½

Prehistoric men Zed (Jack Black) and Oh (Michael Cera) are banished from their village when Zed tastes the fruit from the forbidden tree. In their journey of discovery they come across Cain and Abel, Abraham and Isaac and finally to their delight they end up at Sodom and Gomorrah. The script

of Harold Ramis' silly but fun send-up of biblical films has some sporadically funny lines (Oh claims "I am a virgin by choice" and Zed replies "Not your choice") but the rest of it feels like it is written by numbers. GS

▶ Jack Black, Michael Cera, Oliver Platt, David Cross, Vinnie Jones, Hank Azaria.
▶ *Dir* Harold Ramis, *Pro* Judd Apatow and Clayton Townsend, *Screenplay* Ramis, Gene Stupnitsky and Lee Eisenberg, from a story by Ramis, *Ph* Alar Kivilo, *Pro Des* Jefferson Sage, *Ed* Craig Herring and Steve Welch, *M* Theodore Shapiro, *Cos* Gayle Anderson and Claire Sandrin.

Apatow Productions/Ocean Pictures-Sony Pictures Releasing.
97 mins. USA. 2009. Rel: 26 June 2009. Cert 15.

Yes Man ★★★

A fictional take on Danny Wallace's non-fiction book of the same name, *Yes Man* is a typically high-concept Jim Carrey vehicle about a negative guy who learns to make the most of life after being convinced to say yes to absolutely everything. Particularly for Carrey fans there's a lot to laugh at here, and an agreeably quirky romance with Zooey

David Duchovny and Gillian Anderson keep the franchise going for the second movie spin off based on the TV series in *X Files: I Want to Believe.*

Deschanel, but it's take-it-or-leave-it stuff that's in one eye and out the other. MJ

▶ Jim Carrey, Zooey Deschanel, Bradley Cooper, John Michael Higgins, Rhys Darby, Terence Stamp, Fionnula Flanagan.
▶ *Dir* Peyton Reed, *Pro* David Hayman and Richard D Zanuck, *Screenplay* Nicholas Stoller, Andrew Mogel and Jarpad Paul, from the book by Danny Wallace, *Ph* Robert Yeoman, *Pro Des* Andrew Laws, *Ed* Craig Alpert, *M* Mark Oliver Everett and Lyle Workman, *Cos* Mark Bridges.

Heyday Films/The Zanuck Company/Warner Bros Pictures/Village Roadshow Pictures-Warner Bros Pictures.
104 mins. USA/Australia. 2008. Rel: 26 Dec 2008. Cert 12A.

You Don't Mess With the Zohan ★ ★ ★

The first amusing Adam Sandler comedy since *50 First Dates*, though it's not as good as that or his other decent movie, *Happy Gilmore*, this likeable comedy tells the unlikely story of an Israeli special forces soldier who fakes his own death to pursue his dream of styling hair in New York City. Extremely silly and frequently crude with the occasional gross-out moment, it's no cure for cancer, but an enjoyable time-waster. MJ

▶ Adam Sandler, John Turturro, Emmanuelle Chriqi, Lainie Kazan, Rob Schneider, Charlotte Rae.
▶ *Dir* Dennis Dugan, *Pro* Sandler and Jack Garrard, *Screenplay* Sandler, Judd Apatow and Robert Smigel, *Ph* Michael Barrett, *Pro Des* Perry Andelin Blake, *Ed* Tom Costain, *M* Rupert Gregson-Williams, *Cos* Ellen Lutter.

Happy Madison Productions/Relativity Media-Sony Pictures Entertainment.
113 mins. USA. 2008. Rel: 15 Aug 2008. Cert 12A.

Young @ Heart ★ ★ ★ ½

Like last year's moving *We Are Together*, this is a documentary which celebrates the power

of music and does so in this instance by studying the Young @ Heart Chorus whose ages range from 75 to 93. The songs they sing at the behest of their music director Bob Cilman are examples of modern pop which may not appeal to the older audiences who, even if the portrait may be incomplete, will respond to the singers and may, on occasion, be reduced to tears. MS

▶ With Eileen Hall, Bob Cilman, Joe Benoit, Bob Salvini, Fred Knittle, Dora B Morrow.
▶ *Dir* Stephen Walker, *Pro* and *Music Videos Dir* Sally George, *Ph* Eddie Marritz, *Ed* Chris King.

Fox Searchlight Pictures/a Walker George Films production etc.-Yume Pictures.
108 mins. USA/UK. 2006/8. Rel: 17 Oct 2008. Cert PG.

The Young Victoria ★ ★ ★

Dealing with behind the scenes machinations as Queen Victoria waits to come to the throne and then with the relationship between her and Prince Albert, this is historical fare in traditional style not far removed from the approach taken in 1937 when Anna Neagle was Victoria. The screenplay by Julian Fellowes fails to build to a climax but on its own unambitious terms the film will please the right audience. MS

▶ Emily Blunt, Rupert Friend, Paul Bettany, Miranda Richardson, Jim Broadbent, Mark Strong.
▶ *Dir* Jean-Marc Vallée, *Pro* Graham King, Martin Scorsese, Tim Headington and Sarah Ferguson, *Written by* Julian Fellowes, *Ph* Hagen Bogdanski, *Pro Des* Patrice Vermette, *Ed* Jill Bilcock and Matt Garner, *M* Ilan Eshkeri, *Cos* Sandy Powell.

GK Films-Momentum Pictures.
105 mins. USA. 2008.
Rel: 6 March 2009. Cert PG.

Zack and Miri Make a Porno ★

Monroeville, Pennsylvania; today. When

roommates Zack (Seth Rogen) and Miri (Elizabeth Banks) find that they cannot afford their water bill, Zack suggests they make a porno film. After the thematically comparable *The Moguls* (which itself was forced and dispiriting), this takes the amateur porno premise down several notches. At once ruthlessly crude and schmaltzy, it takes the joy out of sex and puts the obvious into the romantic. Nauseating. JC-W

▶ Seth Rogen, Elizabeth Banks, Craig Robinson, Jason Mewes, Jeff Anderson, Traci Lords, Justin Long.
▶ *Dir, Screenplay* and *Ed* Kevin Smith, *Pro* Scott Mosier, *Ph* David Klein, *Pro Des* Robert Holtzman, *M* James L Venable and Chris Ward, *Cos* Salvador Pérez Jr.

Blue Askew/View Askew Productions/The Weinstein Company-Entertainment Film Distributors.
101 mins. USA. 2008. Rel: 14 Nov 2008. Cert 18.

Zero: An Investigation into 9/11 ★★★

How many conspiracy theories can you get into one film? Directors Franco Fracassi, Francesco Trento and Francesco Tre interview many famous people from public life such as Gore Vidal and Dario Fo as well as official investigators and the good old CIA. All have their own views about what was behind the attack on the Twin Towers. No doubt it will forever remain a subject of concern and conjecture. Take your pick from all the answers here presented. CB

▶ Dario Fo, Philip Berg, David Shayler, Amanda Keller, Gore Vidal.
▶ *Dir* Franco Fracassi, Francesco Trento and Francesco Tre, *Pro* Vanessa Barreiro, Gabriella Quio and Fulvia D'Ottavi, *Ph* Christian Di Prinzio and Marco Ricchello, *Pro Des* Giuseppe Reggio, *Ed* Annalisa Schillaci.

TDF Telemaco-MercuryMedia.
104 mins. Italy. 2008. Rel: 29 Aug 2008. Cert 12A.

La Zona ★★★

Modern day Mexico City is the focus here and the zone is the area where the rich live cut off from the rest of the city by protective walls and CCTV cameras. The drama that ensues links a rich boy with a child of the same age who has broken in. However, delayed revelations make for confused storytelling at times and the social comment that seems to be intended emerges less concretely than one would wish. MS

▶ Daniel Giménez Cacho, Carlos Bardem, Daniel Tovar, Marina de Tavira, Alan Chávez.
▶ *Dir* Rodrigo Plá, *Pro* Álvaro Longoria, *Written by* Laura Santullo based on her short story, *Ph* Emiliano Villanueva, *Art Dir* Antonio Muñohierro, *Ed* Bernat Vilaplana and Ana García, *M* Fernando Velázquez, *Cos* Malena de La Riva and Adela Cortázar.

A Morena Films and Buenaventura Producciones production etc.-Soda Pictures.
95 mins. Spain/Mexico. 2007. Rel: 17 Oct 2008. Cert 15.

Faces of the Year

by James Cameron-Wilson

GEMMA ARTERTON

Born: 12 January 1986 in Gravesend, Kent, England

Suddenly Gemma Arterton was everywhere. In a blur of publicity snapshots, she was the head girl of *St Trinian's*, the dead girl in *Quantum of Solace* and Tess in the BBC's four-hour *Tess of the D'Urbervilles*. Gemma A was also elementally English, very, very pretty and even more determined.

The daughter of a cleaner (her mother) and a welder (her father), she passed her audition to the RADA and paid her fees by working at a cosmetics counter in Covent Garden. And she was lucky. She was still at drama school when she was cast in Stephen Poliakoff's BBC/HBO drama *Capturing Mary*, playing the very young date of David Walliams. And she was still at the RADA when she played Rosaline in *Love's Labour's Lost* at the Globe Theatre in London. After graduating, she landed the *St Trinian's* gig, a high-profile remake that raked in more moolah at the UK box-office than *Atonement*. After that came the female lead in the controversial black comedy *Three and Out*, a striking cameo in Guy Ritchie's *RocknRolla*

and the role of Elizabeth Bennet in *Lost in Austen*, Granada TVs fanciful, critically celebrated spin on *Pride and Prejudice*.

Next, she was the refined MI6 agent Strawberry Fields in *Quantum of Solace* (bedded by Bond and murdered in bed) and the groupie Desiree in Richard Curtis's *The Boat That Rocked*. And the future looks no less rosy: she plays Alice Creed in the British thriller *The Disappearance of Alice Creed*, is the female lead in the $150 million fantasy *Prince of Persia: The Sands of Time* (with Jake Gyllenhaal and Ben Kingsley) and plays the priestess Io in the mythical epic *Clash of the Titans*, opposite Sam Worthington (qv). Then she's set to play Catherine Earnshaw in *Wuthering Heights* for director Peter Webber (*The Girl With a Pearl Earring*).

Oh, and for connoisseurs of the unusual, Gemma was born with six fingers on each hand. "It's my little oddity that I'm really proud of," she admits. "People are really interested but repulsed at the same time. But we could do more stuff if we had extra fingers – faster texting, faster emailing, better guitar-playing." Sadly, thanks to her mother's obstetrician, she's now down to five.

BEN BARNES

Born: 20 August 1981 in London, England

It wasn't until Ben Barnes was in Hollywood that the parts began to flood in. The irony is that they were all for British films. Having secured an agent in Los Angeles, the handsome Londoner returned to England for a giddying workload: he had a brief role in the starry *Stardust*, was the star of Suzie Halewood's well-received British drama *Bigga Than Ben* (as a thieving Muscovite) and then came the career shift.

The producers of *The Chronicles of Narnia: Prince Caspian* had spent a year searching for an actor to play the dashing Caspian in their follow-up to *The Lion, the Witch and the Wardrobe*. "I'd heard they'd been looking

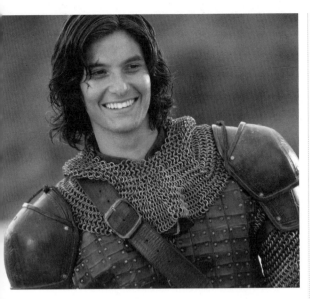

DOMINIC COOPER

Born: 2 June 1978 in Greenwich, London, England

In spite of Dominic Cooper's standout performance in Alan Bennett's thought-provoking and achingly human *The History Boys* (both the stage and film versions), nobody expected what came next. OK, so the actor next popped up as a jailbird in Rupert Wyatt's gritty and accomplished *The Escapist*, but what was unforeseen was his subsequent turn as the romantic male lead in the UK's most successful film of all time. Bronzed, bare-chested and belting out ABBA lyrics, Dominic Cooper became a household apparition in the phenomenally triumphant *Mamma Mia!*

Having trained at the London Academy of Music and Dramatic Art, Cooper found himself working at the Royal National Theatre, the Royal Sakespeare Company and the Royal Court Theatre, before landing the role of Dakin in *The History Boys* at the National. The play was a veritable hit and Cooper's edgy sexuality a selling point. The play then went on tour (to Hong Kong, New Zealand and Australia), transferred to Broadway, won the Tony Award for best play, opened in the West End and ended up as a critically acclaimed film. And each

for a year but weren't quite sure what they were looking for," confirms the actor. "They'd looked at lots of actors of different nationalities and eventually decided to go with someone British. It was very quick. I did one audition and got some feedback from Andrew [Adamson, the director] that I had delivered one of the lines with a hint of irony he hadn't heard before." The rest is box-office history: a month later Barnes was rehearsing in New Zealand and the resultant film grossed $420 million worldwide. In the meantime, Barnes has been signed for the follow-up – *The Chronicles of Narnia: The Voyage of the Dawn Treader* – and has been as busy as heck.

The son of a psychotherapist (his mother) and a professor of psychiatry (his father), Barnes elected not to follow in his parents' footsteps. Instead, he joined the boy band Hyrise. You may not have heard of them, but Hyrise were shortlisted to represent the UK in the 2004 Eurovision Song Contest (the year Britain came sixteenth). Acting quickly followed and after a couple of parts on TV, Barnes set off for Tinseltown.

Since playing Caspian he took the central part of the insouciant John Whittaker in a sprightly adaptation of Noël Coward's *Easy Virtue* – romancing the American Jessica Biel against the wishes of his disdainful mother Kristin Scott Thomas – and then landed the title role in Oliver Parker's *Dorian Gray*, opposite Colin Firth and Rebecca Hall.

time Cooper reprised the role of Dakin, the provocative schoolboy, ageing from 26 to 29.

In the interim, he snared a bit part in Neil Jordan's bold and blackly comic *Breakfast on Pluto*, had a good role in the Tom Hanks-produced *Starter for 10* and played Willoughby in the BBC serial *Sense and Sensibility*. In *Mamma Mia!* he got to sing ABBA's 'Lay All Your Love On Me' opposite Amanda Seyfried (now his girlfriend off-screen) and then became romantically entangled with Keira Knightley (on-screen) in *The Duchess*, playing the Whig prime minister-in-waiting Charles Grey. Next, he'll be seen as a ladykiller in Lone Scherfig's wildly anticipated *An Education* (having replaced Orlando Bloom at the eleventh hour) and in the American drama *Brief Interviews with Hideous Men*. Oh, and to continue his run of period dramas, he's playing the libertine James Steerforth in a TV adaptation of *David Copperfield*. Cooper has also been back at the National Theatre this year, playing opposite Helen Mirren in Racine's *Phèdre* as well as appearing in *Freefall*, Dominic Savage's TV film about the financial crisis.

MICHAEL FASSBENDER

Born: 2 April 1977 in Heidelberg, Germany
As Bobby Sands in Steve McQueen's *Hunger*, Michael Fassbender went above and beyond the call of duty. Living up to the title of the film, the German-born actor went on a starvation diet, shedding three stone from his already lean, 12-stone, six-foot physique. He was a shadow of his former self, his eyes hollowed, his skeleton barely contained beneath a pale sheath of skin and a network of veins. Production on the film – the story of the Irish Republican hunger striker – was shut down for ten weeks so that the actor could monitor his dwindling calories, living off a diet of berries, nuts and sardines. For him "it was a psychological prison," Fassbender recalls. "You don't realise how much food is on television, how much food titillation there is."

But the self-sacrifice was worth it. Fassbender won a slew of awards, including a best actor nod from the London Film Critics'

Circle and the British Independent Film Awards. Previously, he had exhibited a muscular figure in the sword-and-sandal hit *300* – as the heroic Spartan warrior Stelios – and starred in *Eden Lake*, arguably the best British thriller of 2008. But it wasn't until *Hunger* that the critics took note of his acting prowess.

The son of a German father and Northern Irish mother, Michael Fassbender was born in Heidelberg but moved to Killarney, in the Irish Republic, when he was two years old. His parents ran a successful restaurant – the West End House – and he was "pretty spoilt, food-wise, growing up." At school, he was drawn to drama and mounted a theatrical production of Quentin Tarantino's *Reservoir Dogs*. At 19, he moved to London and enrolled at the Central School of Speech and Drama. He left early to star in a touring production of *Three Sisters*, which led to a part in Steven Spielberg's HBO miniseries *Band of Brothers*. He was then Azazeal in the cult TV series *Hex*.

Since then he starred opposite Romola Garai in François Ozon's mannered, artificial *Angel* (as a tortured painter) and went on to feature prominently at the 2009 Cannes Film Festival, starring in two films in competition. He had the male lead in Andrea Arnold's *Fish Tank* – which won the Jury prize – and joined the starry ranks of *Inglourious Basterds* (as a British commando and former film critic), directed by his idol Tarantino.

Next, he'll be seen in Neil Marshall's

historical thriller *Centurion*, the Western *Jonah Hex* (with Josh Brolin and John Malkovich) and the film version of Sebastian Faulks' World War I novel *Birdsong*.

CAREY MULLIGAN
Born: 28 May 1985 in London

Seldom has so much buzz surrounded a British actress before the public had even cottoned on. True, Carey Mulligan had high-profile roles in *Bleak House* (as Ada Clare) and *Northanger Abbey* (as Isabella Thorpe) on British TV, and she played Keira Knightley's sister (Kitty Bennet) in the big-screen *Pride and Prejudice*. But in 2009 things heated up considerably. According to Harvey Weinstein she was the 'belle' of the Sundance festival, she was the romantic foil to Johnny Depp in Michael Mann's *Public Enemies* and she was seriously being touted for an Oscar. Barely had Kate Winslet compared her statuette to a shampoo bottle than American websites were positioning the 23-year-old Carey as her immediate successor for 2010.

The film that is causing all the fuss is *An Education*, in which she plays a 16-year-old Twickenham schoolgirl romanced by a man twice her age (Peter Sarsgaard). The film certainly arrives with impressive credentials, adapted by Nick Hornby from a memoir by Lynn Barber and directed by Denmark's Lone Scherfig. Mulligan's performance elicited ecstatic reviews and at Berlin got her named

as one of 2009's 'Shooting Stars'.

After all this she will be seen in the central role of *The Greatest* – opposite Pierce Brosnan and Susan Sarandon – and is in starry company in Jim Sheridan's war drama *Brothers*, appearing alongside Jake Gyllenhaal, Natalie Portman and Tobey Maguire. She will also be seen with Keira Knightley again in *Never Let Me Go* – from the novel by Kazuo Ishiguro – and is lined up to star opposite Ewan McGregor in the crime drama *The Electric Slide*.

DEV PATEL
Born: 23 April 1990 in Harrow, Middlesex, England

Can any British actor ever have accelerated so fast and so far in so little time? In a matter of months, the largely unknown teenager from Rayners Lane was seldom out of the national newspapers and, by 22 February 2009, was standing on the stage of the Kodak Theatre in Hollywood.

An unlikely candidate for international stardom, Dev Patel is gawky and geeky and has the sort of ears that would make Prince Charles feel at home. And yet, without any formal training as an actor, he has a very real talent and happened to be in exactly the right place at exactly the right moment. It was his mother who, after seeing an ad in the newspaper, put him forward for an

audition for the cult TV series *Skins* – on the day before his science exam, no less. Today he says, "I look at my performance in *Skins* now and I cringe."

In fact Dev Patel was still a pupil at Whitmore High School in Harrow when he landed the lead in Danny Boyle's *Slumdog Millionaire*. Seldom do films escape from the arts pages and thrust themselves into the headlines. But *Slumdog*, a relatively low-budget fantasy hinged on a sensational idea, leaped from obscurity to world domination. The buzz started in earnest at the London Film Festival, grew with the aid of a massive marketing campaign, swelled from word-of-mouth and then erupted in the midst of awards season.

After winning four Golden Globes, *Slumdog* accumulated eleven BAFTA nominations, ten Oscar nominations and, on that momentous day in February, skewered eight actual Oscars, including statuettes for best film and best director. Not since *Gandhi* in 1983 had a British film reaped so much Oscar glory.

Modestly, Dev has claimed that the real star of the film was the location: "Mumbai is like a character and audiences around the world can get a sense of it without spending money on a plane ticket." Punters certainly coughed up for their movie tickets and the little film that could grossed an astonishing $345 million worldwide. In the interim, Dev Patel found himself besieged by the media, glittering prizes and offers and has been romantically linked with his *Slumdog* co-star, Freida Pinto (qv). She's five years his senior and said that romancing him on screen made her feel like a paedophile. Nonetheless, she and Dev were spotted canoodling in Tel Aviv and in April Dev's mother confirmed that they were indeed an item.

Next, Dev will be seen in M Night Shyamalan's fantasy adventure *The Last Airbender*, the first segment of a $250 million trilogy.

ROBERT PATTINSON
Born: 13 May 1986 in Barnes, London, England
On the evening of Wednesday, December 3, 2008, central London's Leicester Square was gridlocked by hordes of young girls screaming their lungs out. They were there to see the arrival of Robert Pattinson at the UK premiere of *Twilight*, the film of Stephanie Meyer's cult tale of teenage angst and vampirism. The scene was reminiscent of early 1960s' Beatlemania and one needed earplugs to protect one's aural well-being. To most of the seasoned locals flogging over-priced snacks and tourist paraphernalia, star-studded premieres are a matter of course: but this was something different.

Even in an age of instant celebrity, the London-born Pattinson has risen to international idolatry spectacularly fast. "It is a bit weird," the 22-year-old concedes. "I've had a seven-year-old girl come up to me and say, 'Bite me, please!'" Pattinson was not the obvious choice to play the "impossibly beautiful" 17-year-old vampire Edward Cullen (apparently modelled on Jane Austen's Darcy) in *Twilight*. Leonardo DiCaprio was in pole position when Stephanie Meyer gave her unreserved approval for the unknown Londoner, a vote of confidence that went some way in placating the book's outraged pubescent fans. Until *Twilight*, Pattinson was best known for playing Quidditch captain Cedric Diggory in *Harry Potter and the Goblet of Fire* and *The Order of the Phoenix*. But when *Twilight* recouped its entire budget on its opening day in the US and went on to gross $380 million worldwide, Pattinson was a *bona fide* star.

Since then he's been seen as Salvador Dali in Paul Morrison's elegiac but dull *Little*

Ashes and played a struggling musician in the independent British comedy-drama *How To Be*. Although the latter failed to find a distributor in the UK, Pattinson won a best actor nod for his part at the Strasbourg Film Festival. Next, he'll reprise his role as Cullen in the *Twilight* sequel, *The Twilight Saga: New Moon*, and will star alongside Hugh Jackman and Rachel Weisz in the Western *Unbound Captives*.

FREIDA PINTO

Born: 18 October 1984 in Mumbai, India

In a matter of weeks Freida Pinto went from being practically unknown to being more famous than Shilpa Shetty. A few weeks later, she was probably the most famous Indian actress of all time. Not only is Freida breathtakingly beautiful but she was the female star of the year's most unexpected critical and commercial hit, *Slumdog Millionaire*. As she became the darling of the red tops, offers of work flooded in, including two juicy projects with Julian Schnabel and Woody Allen. Meanwhile, the former model quickly sharpened her thespian skills, enrolling for a three-month workshop with the acting guru Barry John.

Having earned herself a BA in English Literature, Freida used her exceptional looks to land a host of modelling engagements, promoting DeBeers, Škoda, Vodafone India and Wrigley's chewing gum, as well as presenting the travel show *Full Circle*. With a view to acting, she tried out for the role of Camille Montes in *Quantum of Solace*, but lost out to Olga Kurylenko, and then auditioned for *Slumdog Millionaire* as Latika, the girl from the slums who still dreams of her childhood friend, Jamal, played by Dev Patel (qv).

As the film registered 8.0 on the Richter scale, Freida was recognised for her own contribution and took home a BAFTA nomination. Next, she began work on Julian Schnabel's *Miral* in Israel, starring alongside Willem Dafoe and Hiam Abbass, and then joined Josh Brolin, Antonio Banderas, Anthony Hopkins and Naomi Watts in Woody Allen's as-yet-unnamed 'London Project.' She was also chosen as the new face of L'Oreal Paris, following in the high heels of Beyoncé, Penélope Cruz and Eva Longoria. This deal alone ensured that we were not going to forget the face of Freida Pinto any time soon.

MAYA RUDOLPH

Born: 27 July 1972 in Gainesville, Florida, USA

Maya Rudolph can do a mean impression of Freida Pinto (qv). She's also being tipped for an Oscar nomination for Sam Mendes' *Away We Go*. Oh, and she has joined the ranks of Adam Sandler, Mike Myers, Bill Murray and Tina Fey by cutting her comedic teeth on NBC's immortal comic revue *Saturday Night Live*. But for those who can remember the 1970s and the excruciatingly twee song 'Lovin' You', Maya Rudolph may be best known as the daughter of that record's vocalist, Minnie Riperton. Four years after 'Lovin' You' peaked at Number 1 in the charts, Ms Riperton died from breast cancer. Maya was just six years old.

Since then Maya has had bits parts in *Gattaca*, *As Good As It Gets*, *Duets* – with her childhood friend Gwyneth Paltrow – and *50 First Dates*, and she briefly played keyboards and sang for the New Wave rock group The Rentals. She put her vocals to good effect on *Saturday Night Live* – the revue she joined in 1999 – when she gave a blistering impersonation of Beyoncé Knowles opposite Prince. She also clocked up impressions of Oprah Winfrey, Condoleezza Rice, Paris Hilton, Liza Minnelli and her speciality,

Donatella Versace.

On film, she joined the all-star ensemble of *A Prairie Home Companion*, voiced Rapunzel on the soundtrack of *Shrek the Third* and starred opposite Luke Wilson in Mike Judge's little-seen sci-fi comedy *Idiocracy*. Then she landed the lead in *Away We Go*, a dramatic comedy about a pregnant woman who joins her partner (John Krasinski) on a trip around the USA in search of the perfect place to bring up her child. Selected to open the 63rd Edinburgh Film Festival, the film garnered superlative reviews Stateside, accumulating considerable awards buzz along the way. Then Ms Rudolph joined fellow *SNL* alumnus Adam Sandler for the ensemble comedy *Grown Ups*.

SAM WORTHINGTON

Born: 2 August 1976 in Perth, Western Australia
It's been an amazing year for Sam Worthington. Having followed in the footsteps of Arnold Schwarzenegger in *Terminator Salvation*, the 32-year-old Australian also had the lead role in James Cameron's long-awaited *Avatar*. In the former he played a man blended into a machine and in the latter was a half-man, half-alien. Even so, Worthington is all man.

A native of Perth, Western Australia, Worthington enrolled at Sydney's National Institute of Dramatic Art and after a spell in the theatre appeared in a number of Australian films. However, it was his key role as a sexually disorientated farmhand in Cate Shortland's critically lauded *Somersault* – opposite Abbie Cornish – that established his international status. He followed this with a supporting role in *The Great Raid* (which, in spite of a starry cast headed by James Franco and Joseph Fiennes, failed to find a distributor in the UK) and the lead in a local action-comedy called, er, *Fink!* More impressively, he played the title role in a modern-day production of *Macbeth* (shot in Melbourne) which The New York Times described as "brutal and thrilling", while praising the "consistently imaginative, lively performances". He then starred in the timely *Rogue*, an Aussie thriller about a particularly ill-humoured crocodile, inspired by the real-life offensives of a monster affectionately dubbed 'Sweetheart'.

Worthington was then snapped up to play the cyborg Marcus Wright in *Terminator Salvation* and stole the film from Christian Bale in an imposing display of tortured bravado. After that he took the title role in *Avatar* and was the male lead in the New York drama *Last Night*, juggling the affections of Keira Knightley and Eva Mendes. Next, he'll be seen in John Madden's thriller *The Debt*, with Helen Mirren, and plays the heroic Perseus in the big-budget epic *Clash of the Titans*, co-starring Liam Neeson and Ralph Fiennes.

The View from Eastbourne

Mansel Stimpson *takes a look at the current state of cinema in Britain.*

How was it for you, this past year? When reporting on which films have been available on release in this country, the fact that most critics in the UK are London based can always colour their outlook. While a study of what gets shown in the capital is relevant to any survey of cinema-going in Britain, a very different picture can emerge when you put yourself in the shoes of somebody living in – well, let's say Eastbourne. That's not a random choice actually since I grew up in that town in the post-war years of the late1940s when it had at least eight cinemas and even now I maintain links with it despite living in London. Today those eight cinemas are reduced to two, a multiplex (lately in the hands of UGC and now belonging to Cineworld and situated on the outskirts) and one independent town centre cinema surviving from my childhood. Built as long ago as 1920, the latter used to be the Picturedrome but is now the Curzon and it belongs to an old friend of mine, Roy Galloway, to whom I have dedicated this volume.

Many towns today rely for their film entertainment on a multiplex which, in many cases, regardless of the number of their screens, present very little that is outside of the mainstream and which consequently deal mainly with the big distributors. To keep going the Curzon, now a cinema with three screens, has to give pride of place to this kind of product. Nevertheless it does from time to time offer a one-day special or even a longer run that screens titles ignored by the local multiplex. Even more importantly, especially from my point of view, it houses an annual season of one day presentations by the Eastbourne Film Society with which I have been associated for many years. These screenings supported by its members are also open to the general public and they come in numbers that are very encouraging. With a short spring season often added, the Society's presence in Eastbourne – and it has survived only due to the Curzon being there as its venue – ensures that Eastbourne audiences have the chance to see many films that never reach comparable towns in Britain.

In last year's annual I touched on two matters that remain highly significant 12 months on. I refer to the increased number of weekly releases and to the off-puttingly high cost of cinemagoing which can encourage many – not least family groups – to view films at home on DVDs instead of in the cinemas despite the fact that big screen presentation always enhances them. In the past year the number of film releases has shown no sign of a downturn. What this means is that it is harder than ever for films that are not hyped to get sufficient press coverage to bring them to the attention of the public, and that is especially so in the case of independent and foreign movies.

It's true that you can readily check up on titles on the internet, but that requires some effort by the enquirer and some awareness of new titles. What still seems essential if a smaller film is to do business is for the newspapers to provide good coverage that takes in all the new films. Readers who are film enthusiasts will seek out these reviews from an established critic of their choice, somebody whose judgment they trust. But even a year ago this was being undermined to some extent by the fact that in a week of, say, nine releases, several of the titles would be covered in only a sentence or two due to lack of space. In the past 12 months the situation has deteriorated further with a growing tendency for some new films to be ignored altogether. As a particular and striking example of this, take *The Sunday Telegraph*. Not so long ago it employed – as did several other papers – more than one critic so that the weekly load could be shared. Now, however, it has opted for a single reviewer of new films who, as I write, covers no more than three titles each week. This leaves the others, sometimes as many as seven, unmentioned – and it goes without saying that more often than not those featured will be the bigger titles and not those needing publicity to draw any kind of an audience. It's an attitude which suggests that newspapers instead of serving their readers by providing intelligent arts coverage are more and more frequently cutting down on that

Finding the right word – Peter Capaldi and Chris Addison in the sharp political satire *In The Loop*.

at the very time when they should be fighting the competition of comments circulating on the internet by showing that their own arts coverage (and not just that of cinema) is the best available.

If one turns back to the example provided by Eastbourne one becomes aware of the extent to which the current situation is depriving audiences of works they would enjoy. The Film Society provides reaction forms to enable those present, be they members or general public, to rate a film in one of five categories. These range from 'poor' to 'excellent' and, by giving each level a higher figure as they move upwards and then dividing by the total of those returned, comparable percentage figures can be produced to show how well each film has fared (and with votes from usually well over half those present the process is a good indicator of success or failure). The 2008/09 season consisted of 11 titles, most of them films reviewed in last year's edition of this annual. Despite a somewhat disappointing response to the Norwegian feature *Reprise* (it earned a mere 59.5 per cent), the programme as a whole was remarkably popular.

Before taking on board the percentage figures that follow, it should also be borne in mind that the comments made it clear that because of limited publicity from reviewers and the short runs of some of the films in London it was frequently the case that audiences were attending films of which they had not heard previously. The public quite as much as the members were drawn in because, over the years, the Society has established a good reputation for the quality of its films. Here then are the ten remaining titles in descending order: *We Are Together* (93.0 per cent), *The Fallen Idol* (91.3 per cent), *The Italian* (88.7 per cent), *Azur and Asmar: The Princes' Quest* (88.2 per cent), *The Edge of Heaven* (85.5 per cent), *Under the Bombs* (84.8 per cent), *El Violin* (82.6 per cent), *A Mighty*

Heart (80.8 per cent), *Couscous* (79.1 per cent) and *Dan in Real Life* (75.2 per cent). All of the titles other than the reissue of *The Fallen Idol* were films new to Eastbourne and, while the majority can be defined as arthouse movies, *Dan in Real Life* starring Steve Carell was an example of a mainstream movie ignored by the multiplex.

It is particularly striking that three of these well-received films came from Soda Pictures, an admirably adventurous distributor but one which must find it increasingly difficult to survive. The touching Russian film about a boy searching for his mother (*The Italian*), the powerful Mexican drama *El Violin* with its remarkable central performance by an octogenarian making his acting debut, and the delightful and breathtakingly beautiful animated work *Azur and Asmar* were all films that suffered neglect at the box-office for the reasons I have given. Admittedly you have to add to the equation the regrettable reluctance of audiences to be adventurous. When outside of the Society's screenings the Curzon showed *In the Loop* and *The Damned United*, both of which had failed to appear at Eastbourne's multiplex, the attendances were disappointing given the high praise for the former and the stunning performance by Michael Sheen in the latter. However, given the other point mentioned (the high price of cinema tickets) you can't altogether blame the public for their lack of support, especially when they stay away from films that they know all too little about due to the reduction of press coverage. What works for the Eastbourne Film Society is their reputation which is such that it doesn't seem too much of a gamble to go to their screenings of titles that may not have previously registered.

Of course, those whose interest is chiefly centred on special effects action movies or the latest instalment of a franchise can feel that all is well in the cinema world and respond to recent encouraging figures for box-office takings as evidence that no real problems exist. But if the downgrading of coverage in the national press for the less obvious titles continues, then the future for cinemas that want to offer worthwhile experiences to a whole range of audiences may be undermined and the time may come when those distributors offering more intelligent and idiosyncratic fare will have disappeared from the scene. Even now the writing may be on the wall, and the loss for those who love the cinema would be enormous.

They Shouldn't Be In Pictures

Whatever else he did Michael Jackson was never a great star of the cinema. Many other pop and rock singers and musicians have tried to cross over into films, often with disastrous results. **Michael Darvell** *counts the empties…*

The premature death of Michael Jackson, the most successful pop music artist of his generation, brings into sharp focus the fact that he had never made much of an impression on the cinema industry. There was one single feature film, *The Wiz* in 1978, preceded by *Save the Children*, a filmed concert made for the charity in 1973, and followed by *Moonwalker*, another live concert in 1988 and, apart from many guest shots on television and in films such as *Men in Black II* (2002) and *Miss Cast Away* (2004) and appearing in music videos directed by John Landis (*Thriller*, 1983) and Martin Scorsese (*Bad*, 1987) well… er, that's all, or almost all. In 2009 he appeared in *Life on the Road with Mr & Mrs Brown*, a documentary on singers James Brown and his wife Tomi which, at time of writing, has yet to be released. The film also features David Carradine, who died three weeks before Michael Jackson.

There was another Michael Jackson film, *Captain EO*, a 3D space opera that was featured in Disneyland theme parks around the world between 1986 and 1998. It had impeccable credentials: producer George Lucas, director Francis Ford Coppola, music by James (*Titanic*) Horner, a couple of songs by Michael Jackson who played the eponymous hero, and a co-star in Anjelica Huston as the Witch Queen. It cost $30 million for a running time of just 17 minutes which, on a cost per minute basis, makes it the most expensive film ever made, working out at $1.76 million per minute.

Another short (38-minute) film, *Ghosts*, made in 1997, had Jackson playing five characters including The Maestro, a magician who runs foul of the people of Normal Valley who thinks he's too weird for their community. Written and directed by special effects and make-up guru Stan Winston, it was based on an idea by Stephen King and was initially released with the Stephen King horror film *Thinner*. And that really was the total film output while Michael Jackson was alive. After his death the reference to him in Sacha Baron Cohen's *Brüno* was excised, presumably on grounds of taste.

However, by the time you read this there will be another Michael Jackson film to see, namely Columbia Pictures' *This Is It*, a compilation of rehearsal and pre-recorded footage of what was to have been a series of live concerts by Jackson at The O2 arena (formerly known as the Millennium Dome) in London's north Greenwich. Planned before Jackson's untimely death, the concerts were going to be a way of making money for the apparently cash-strapped music star. But it was not to be. However, now that he is no longer with us and, considering the way he died, there may well be a biopic on the enigma that was Michael Jackson. New stories appear on a daily basis about him, so there's probably gold in them thar tills just waiting to be cashed in.

If Elvis Presley starred in over 30 feature films, how can we explain the lack of movie appearances by Michael Jackson apart, that is, from his music videos? And how come Jackson was never the star of any film except those comprising mainly his performance footage? It is likely that, just as Presley was around too soon for the MTV music video explosion, Michael Jackson came too late to cash in on the Hollywood film industry. Anyway he preferred to do his own thing rather than end up as Presley eventually did, appearing in routine potboilers that only his most ardent of fans could appreciate. Having split from his family, Jackson preferred to go his own way, whereas Presley, under the guidance and the thumb of Colonel Tom Parker just did as he was told. He had the talent but not the nous to exploit it in the best possible ways.

In the days before MTV the only way a singer could capture a worldwide audience was to make films and, since Elvis hardly ever appeared outside of the US (Canada being the only exception) the movies were a replacement for the real thing. From *Love Me Tender* in 1956 to *Change of Habit* in 1969, Elvis made 31 features at a rate or two or three a year, a punishing schedule for any artist. However, as awful as most of the films latterly became, they

Michael Jackson

did make money at the box office and all spawned lucrative album sales. Of course, since his death aged 42, at an even younger age than Jackson, the King of Rock 'n' Roll, still remains a nice little earner, not only for the Presley estate but also for the industry of look- and soundalikes that has burgeoned ever since. Maybe this will also be the fate of Michael Jackson, the 50-year-old boy King

of Pop who died on 25 June, 2009. Remember, you are never ever very far away from a Wacko Jacko impersonator...

What of others in the music biz who tested the movie waters? Bette Midler is probably the most accomplished case of a contemporary singer turned actress who has managed to pursue both careers with equal success. Some of her movies have not been of the best quality but with titles such as *The Rose*, *Down and Out in Beverly Hills*, *Beaches*, *Stella*, *Gypsy* and *The First Wives Club* to her name, she has nothing to be ashamed of, and her talents are such that she can play either comic or dramatic roles with equal assurance.

David Bowie has had a not inconsiderable movie career, from *The Man Who Fell to Earth* through *The Hunger*, *Merry Christmas Mr Lawrence*, *Absolute Beginners*, *Labyrinth* and *The Last Temptation of Christ* to the more recent *The Prestige* and *August* (unreleased in the UK). Likewise Sting began well in *Quadrophenia* and *Brimstone and Treacle*, but then there was *Dune* and *Plenty* etc. Jon Bon Jovi has appeared extensively on film from *Young Guns II* in 1990, as well on TV in *Sex and the City*, *Ally McBeal*, *The West Wing* etc. Roger Daltrey was in Ken Russell's *Tommy* and *Lisztomania* and later graced *McVicar* and *Buddy's Song*, both of which he also produced. Other appearances include playing Rodney Marsh in a film about George Best and TV shots in *Highlander*, *The Bill* and *CSI* etc. He is also the producer of a new film about Keith Moon.

But what of major artists who jumped in deep and nearly drowned in the process? Despite her success in music and dance, Madonna's film career has been patchy, to say the least. She can go from a successful mainstream debut in *Desperately Seeking Susan* to an absolute turkey, *Shanghai Surprise*, with husband Sean Penn, then do another couple of no-hopers, *Who's That Girl* (with John Mills) and *Bloodhounds of Broadway*. She was well received in *Dick Tracy* and did a cameo for Woody Allen in *Shadows and Fog*, while the baseball comedy *A League of Their Own*, with Tom Hanks in 1992, was a commercial hit. However, the following year came the flop that was *Body of Evidence*, a would-be sexy thriller and, although she personally fared better in Abel Ferrara's *Dangerous Games* (*Snake Eyes* in the UK), the film went straight to video.

After more guest appearances Madonna finally got to play Eva Perón in Alan Parker's *Evita*, the musical by Andrew Lloyd Webber and Tim Rice, for which she won a Best Actress Golden Globe Award. This is likely to be the apex of her film appearances. There are two dozen films in which Madonna was slated to appear but was either replaced or the films never got made. These include *The Fabulous Baker Boys* and *Batman Returns* in which both parts went to Michelle Pfeiffer. Of course acting is just one string to her professional bow. Her career quiver also includes singer-songwriter, record producer, dancer, author, film producer-director, fashion designer and entrepreneur. We await further film developments but won't be holding our breath.

Then there's Mick Jagger… In 1968 he made a promising debut in *Performance*, Nicolas Roeg's first feature which he co-directed with Donald Cammell. But then Jagger played *Ned Kelly* in Tony Richardson's film and more movie offers seem not to have been forthcoming. Apart from The Rolling Stones' performance films, Jagger had to wait a while for further acting roles in *Freejack* (1992), *Bent* (1997) and *The Man from Elysian Fields* (2001). However, he did become a film producer on *Enigma* (1999), the story of wartime codebreaking at Bletchley Park, and for the recent remake of *The Women*, which was not a success. He also contributed

Annette Benning does some multi-tasking in *The Women*, a poor remake of George Cukor's original sparkling comedy of divorce seen from the distaff side.

Steve Martin wonders why *The Pink Panther 2* is not as funny as the original.

music to the remake of *Alfie* with Jude Law.

Bob Dylan has had a fairly short feature film career although his music has been used on the soundtracks of umpteen movies. D A Pennebaker filmed a documentary about the singer in 1967, *Don't Look Back*, but, apart from other documentaries and performance films, features for Bob have been sparse: Sam Peckinpah's *Pat Garrett and Billy the Kid* in 1973, *Hearts of Fire* in 1987, an uncredited part in Dennis Hopper's *Catchfire* in 1990, *Paradise Cove* in 1999, and *Masked and Anonymous* in 2003, the last about a singer facing failure in a script co-written by Dylan. He also co-wrote (with Sam Shepard) and directed, edited and appeared in *Renaldo and Clara*, an epic 1978 concert/documentary which originally ran for four and a half hours. And his latest project? He may become the new voice of sat-nav!

Bruce Springsteen, like Bob Dylan, has seen his music used on many film soundtracks including *Texasville*, *Dead Man Walking*, *Jerry McGuire*, *Lawn Dogs*, *The Wedding Singer*, *Jersey Girl*, *Running with Scissors*, *The Heartbreak Kid*, *The Wrestler* and *High Fidelity*. In the last one, Stephen Frears' film based on Nick Hornby's novel, Springsteen also had a cameo role as himself. He also appears as

himself in the forthcoming *The People Speak* based on Howard Zinn's book *A People's History of the United States*. Beyoncé Knowles divides her time successfully between music, writing and acting in a mixed bunch of films such as *Austin Powers in Goldmember*, *The Pink Panther*, *Dreamgirls*, *Cadillac Records* and the recent *Obsessed*. On the other hand, The Spice Girls came and went in their one and only film, *Spice World*. Boy, was that a relief! David Essex's career has skilfully mixed singing and song-writing with acting on stage (*Godspell*, *Evita*, *Mutiny*) and in films including *That'll Be the Day*, *Stardust*, *Silver Dream Racer* which were written for him. The latest news is that Liam Gallagher, formerly of Oasis, will appear with DJ Guru Josh in *Powder*, a film of Kevin Sampson's novel about a rock band who get into sex and drugs – that sounds familiar. But what happened to Liam's previous (2005) debut playing a gangland boss with Robert Carlyle in *The Apprentice*? Nothing, yet.

In their day The Beatles collectively had the right idea and only appeared in films tailor-made for them, such as *A Hard Day's Night*, *Help!*, *Yellow Submarine* and *Let It Be*. However, they also had separate film careers of a sort. John Lennon appeared in Richard Lester's *How I Won the War* and Peter Whitehead's *Fire in the Water*, as well as the many shorts he made with Yoko Ono. Paul made a documentary called *Rockshow* and also played himself in a fictional documentary, *Give My Regards to Broad Street* with, among others, his wife Linda, Leslie Sarony, Ralph Richardson and Ringo. Now Ringo made many features including *Candy*, *The Magic Christian*, *200 Motels*, with Frank Zappa, *Son of Dracula*, which he also co-produced, Ken Russell's *Lisztomania* and Mae West's last film, *Sextette*, before becoming the voice of Thomas the Tank Engine.

Of the four Beatles, however, it was George Harrison who contributed most to the movie industry. He set up Handmade Films without which we would never have seen *Monty Python's Life of Brian*, *The Long Good Friday*, *Time Bandits*, *Privates on Parade*, *The Missionary*, *A Private Function*, *Mona Lisa*, *Withnail and I*, *How to Get Ahead in Advertising* and *Nuns on the Run* etc. Without him too we might never have been subjected to Madonna in *Shanghai Surprise*, but then, as you can see from many of the films listed here, nobody's that perfect.

The International Scene

Mansel Stimpson *reports on the latest crop of foreign language features.*

With so many films being released these days, it should come as no surprise that in the period under review foreign language works have been arriving in London at the rate of more than one a week – and that is without taking into account the specialised items from Bollywood. In so far as that provides the opportunity to see films from an enormously wide range of countries, it can only be good news, but, as is also the case with English language releases, the extra numbers have resulted in quite a lot of duds appearing alongside works of quality. The sheer quantity means that this survey can only pick out key titles and comment on trends while leaving it to our review section to provide comprehensive coverage on world cinema as reflected by movies distributed in the United Kingdom during the 12 months to the end of June 2009.

It could well be that the gap between so-called 'art-house films' and the mainstream is closing. French films have long been the most popular with those British audiences who enjoy foreign movies and, following on from the earlier box-office success of such films as the Piaf biopic *La Vie en Rose* and the thriller *Tell No One* we have this year had an increased number of French works aimed, successfully or not, at a broad appeal. Such films include family dramas in all shapes and sizes (*Anything for Her*, *The Mark of an Angel*, *Let's Talk about the Rain*, *Summer Hours* and, most notably in terms of box-office, *I've Loved You So Long*), rural tales (*The Grocer's Son*, *Conversations with my Gardener*), Parisian pieces (both *Paris* and *Paris 36*) and even one set in London (*Mes Amis, Mes Amours*). If *The Girl Cut in Two* from New Wave veteran Claude Chabrol just about fits in here, the most obvious example of imported commercial mainstream fare was to be found in the spy parody *OSS 117: Cairo Nest of Spies* which was as much a spoof of the James Bond movies as of anything more French-based.

But it's not just French cinema that competes in popular genres: we've had Second World War exploits in Denmark (*Flame & Citron*) and in Norway (*Max Manus*), real-life crime from Italy (*Gomorrah*), a big action movie from Asia in John Woo's *Red Cliff*,

Tony Leung Chiu Wai in John Woo's lavish *Red Cliff*.

A scene from Ari Folman's remarkable *Waltz with Bashir*.

horror from the French director Pascal Laugier (*Martyrs*), police dramas from Iceland and Korea (*Jar City* and *The Chaser* respectively) and from Spain we even had what was virtually a remake of Agatha Christie's *Ten Little Indians* in *Fermat's Room*. However, when it comes to the best films in this category I would not hesitate over nominating the Swedish/Norwegian co-production *Let The Right One In*, already regarded a classic horror yarn, and Mexico's *Rudi & Cursi* which, aimed fairly and squarely at a young macho audience, carried out its aims with absolute assurance.

At the opposite extreme, we have had a goodly number of pieces that could be described as examples of avant-garde cinema. You can guarantee that any work in this category will bore some people but, if personal taste is very much involved here (I myself could not relate to José Luis Guerín's *In the City of Sylvia* which was highly praised by some), the variety of what has been on offer is notable. The one that I personally rated most highly is the minimalistic *Lake Tahoe* from Mexico, but I liked also another work from that country which experimented with static shots, *Año uña*, while Russia's *The Banishment* despite weaknesses contained such remarkable scenes

that I felt it was underestimated by many. Other works in this category include Béla Tarr's *The Man from London*, Abbas Kiarostami's *Shirin*, Alexander Sokurov's *Alexandra* and *Belle toujours*, that remarkable footnote to Buñuel's *Belle de Jour* made by the Portuguese director Manoel de Oliveira at the age of 97.

Plenty of other titles emerged over the 12 months which were neither avant-garde nor designedly popular in their slant, but a number of them are among the films that I consider overpraised. In this category I would put such works as *A Christmas Tale* from France and *Tony Manero* set in Santiago de Chile, while both the Dardennes brothers (with *The Silence of Lorna*) and Nuri Bilge Ceylan (with *Three Monkeys*) disappointed me if not necessarily others. As for *The Baader-Meinhof Complex*, it was less interesting than the earlier feature *Stammheim* which dealt with the same subject matter. But the film which stands out as the most overrated is one that is far better than any of the others just mentioned and that is *The Class*. It does so because for most critics it was *the* French film of the year. It was indeed brilliant as an example of a drama acted so naturalistically that it could pass as a documentary, but I do

Hatice Aslan and Yavuz Bingol in the Turkish drama
Three Monkeys.

feel that it was far, far too long. In contrast, even if its ending seemed contrived, there was a sad lack of recognition in many quarters for a film of stunning visual beauty, *Delta* from Hungary's Kornel Mundruczó.

But to conclude this survey of key releases I would prefer to turn to the real achievements, some adequately acclaimed but some not. The outstanding documentary of the year was French: Raymond Depardon's wonderful human document *Modern Life* recording the lives of farmers in the Cevennes and surely destined to become a vital historical record of a way of life that is passing. No less distinguished was a film that firmly puts in their place other recent dramas recreating events from the Second World War: Andrzej Wajda's *Katy*. It deals with the genocide that took place in Poland in 1940 and with the attempt by the Russians to distort history by putting the blame on the Germans. This is a work fully worthy of the occasion, a memorial to a tragedy that is at the heart of Poland's history in the 20th century.

If both *Modern Life* and *Katy* are films in a traditional mode, there were others more innovative that also stood out. I have already mentioned the haunting *Lake Tahoe*, an outstanding example of minimalism, and, if not quite a work of the avant-garde, the stylised political drama *Il Divo* was the best Italian film of the year, one that in portraying the career of Giulio Andreotti brought a new look and a fresh approach to cinema's treatment of politics. In addition in the contribution by Toni Servillo it gave us the year's best performance by an actor. Innovative in another way was the remarkable *Waltz with Bashir* which, like last year's *Persepolis*, used animation to treat serious issues while also developing new ways of presenting testimonies about war and its traumas. I have already referred

above to two outstanding pieces in a popular vein, *Let The Right One In* and *Rudo & Cursi*, while *The Fox and the Child*, a unique blend of nature film and childhood memoir, proved that *March of the Penguins* (2005) was not a one-off for director Luc Jacquet.

The final set of titles deserving of special mention are so varied that they again underline the range of what we have been seeing from around the world. *Lemon Tree* from the Israeli director Eran Riklis is worth remembering for the star quality of Hiam Abbass (also seen to good effect in *The Visitor*) as well as for the breadth of sympathy it exhibits towards those caught up in the conflict between Israel and Palestine. The exquisite *Sakuran* from Japan treated its story of an 18th century courtesan in such high style that you could call it camp, while the underestimated cartoon film *Fear(s) of the Dark* used contributions from several filmmakers to take us memorably into an animated world of dreams and nightmares.

Outside England (and even in England if newspaper reports count), the cinematic sensation of the year was the shock created at the Cannes Film Festival by Lars von Trier's *Antichrist*, although its arrival in our own cinemas uncut fell just outside the period of this survey. Meanwhile we had seen Ulrich Seidl's *Import Export* with its critical view of modern life in Austria, Ukraine and Slovakia as it linked explicit sex scenes with sympathy for exploited women. Equally honest and frank was *Before I Forget* by Jacques Nolot portraying the lives of older homosexual men in Paris. Last and far from least – although some reviews might not have suggested it – we had this year what may well be the last film from Eric Rohmer made in 2006 when he was 95. *The Romance of Astrea and Celadon* based on an early 17th century novel by Honoré d'Urfé is quintessentially French. Nevertheless, while telling the stylised tale of a troubled love that features shepherds, druids and nymphs, it also evokes thoughts of works by Shakespeare such as *The Winter's Tale* and *As You Like It*. Rohmer's purity of approach to this Arcadian world makes it seem timeless and wholly individual, while at the same time the philosophy of love expounded in it is something that is inextricably part of French culture. If this is Rohmer's last film, it is not an unworthy one: it could be an acquired taste, but a great filmmaker here remains wholly true to himself while creating a film unlike any other. It's surprises like this that keep alive one's faith in cinema.

A New Set of Dreams?

Kiran P Joshi *looks at both the beginnings and the re-birth of Indian cinema.*

Slumdog Millionaire

Look around. Bollywood is everywhere: *Slumdog Millionaire* sweeps the boards at the Oscars. A R Rahman, the Mozart of Madras, scores a double Oscar whammy, while Jai Ho tops the charts. Shilpa Shetty leaves the *Big Brother* house a national hero and Bollywood beauty Aishwarya Rai graces the cover of *Time* magazine, in between appearing on *The Oprah Winfrey Show* and treading the red carpet at Cannes with her *Pink Panther* co-stars. Meanwhile, Hollywood stars from Sylvester Stallone and Denise Richards to Ben Stiller are queuing up to star in the next Bollywood extravaganza. While *Lagaan* (2001) and *Devdas* (2002) found a fan in Beyoncé, Kylie Minogue is the latest music export to shimmy eastwards, with Shakira close on her vertiginous heels. Today, Indian superstars stand shoulder to shoulder with Hollywood heroes at London's famed Madame

Tussauds. Bollywood has even found a home in that bastion of Britishness, the BBC Proms.

In 2010, Bollywood is ubiquitous and everyone wants a piece of the action. The world is finally sitting up and taking notice of the Mumbai-based industry that has been making movies for 114 years. A melee of dance and fantasy, melodrama and music, romance and retro chic, festooned in glorious Technicolor and endless song, Bollywood has gone from kitsch to cool, and is today a globally recognised industry. Almost 1,000 films are produced in India every year, in all the languages of the country. Approximately 300 of these are a product of the Mumbai-based Bollywood industry. The Indian film industry has an estimated annual turnover of Rs. 60 billion (approximately US$1.33 billion) and provides employment to more than six million people.

With markets in 90 countries, Bollywood films reach nearly 3.6 billion people worldwide, captivating audiences in Asia, the Middle East, Russia, the UK, North America and the Caribbean.

But Bollywood is so much more. It has prompted parliamentary debate, challenging and shattering archaic conventions. It has created cultural icons, sparked global fashion trends, and altered perceptions of beauty along the way. It has infused itself imperceptibly into the framework of Indian society. In India, it is the life blood of the people. Abroad, it has fostered a sense of cultural identity amongst a vagrant immigrant community. It has been the endless focus of controversy and yet has promoted unity in an age of religious discord and social divide. It has the power to turn mere mortals into demigods and for those without hope it affords a rare opportunity to dream. It has spawned a new generation of all-dancing, all-singing, everyday superheroes. At times lauded, once derided, and presently celebrated the world over, the journey of Indian cinema has been a tumultuous one.

Cinema first came to India over a century ago, when the Lumière Brothers held the first showing of six silents in Bombay in 1896. Attending the Lumière presentation was a photographer named Harischandra Sakharam Bhatwadekar, affectionately known as Save Dada. In 1897 he made two short films which were publicly exhibited in 1899 using Edison's projecting Kinetoscope. While Save Dada had set the wheels in motion, Dhundiraj Govind Phalke (1870-1944) better known as Dadasaheb Phalke, is considered the father of Indian cinema with the first feature *Raja Harishchandra*. Inspired by the life of Christ, the full-length story film was shown in 1913 to widespread acclaim. Phalke followed this with a series of mythological films, among them *Lanka Dahan* (1917) which went on to become India's first box office hit. Later, as Al Jolson's *The Jazz Singer* (1927) introduced audiences to the magic of moving pictures with sound, India followed suit in 1931 with the release of *Alam Ara*, the first Indian talkie produced by the Imperial Film Company. The film also featured seven songs. Henceforth, music was to become one of the most defining features of popular Indian cinema.

The 1930s were dominated by films portraying social unrest such as V Shantaram's *Amar Jyoti* (1936), the first Indian film to be screened at an international film festival (Venice). In the aftermath of Independence the late 1940s, '50s and '60s were regarded as the golden age of Indian cinema. Drawing on the experiences of life in pre- and post-Independence India, the films of Raj Kapoor and Guru Dutt reflected the social ills of the newly developing state and in doing so captured the mood of a generation. Invested with pathos and empathy for the human condition, Raj Kapoor's

Early days for all – Soumitra Chatterjee and Sharmila Tagore in Satyajit Ray's *The World of Apu* (1959), a true classic of Indian cinema.

Shree 420 (1955), Guru Dutt's *Pyassa* (1957) and Mehboob Khan's *Mother India* (1957) resonated with an audience still reeling from the effects of famine, wars, a fascist regime and the struggle for freedom.

It was during this time that director Satyajit Ray came to prominence. Ray's films *Pather Panchali* (1955), *Aparajito* (1956) and *Apur Sansar* (1959) garnered international acclaim. Scorsese and Spielberg cite Ray as one of their greatest cinematic influences, and indeed, he is regarded by many as one of the most prolific directors of all time. He was awarded a Lifetime Achievement Oscar in 1992, and his Apu Trilogy is ranked by *Time* magazine and others among the 100 greatest films ever made.

Over the next 60 years, Bollywood films would evolve into several classic genres: social protest films such as *Pyassa*; historical epics like *Mughal-e-azam* (1960), the most expensive film of its time which took ten years to make; the curry western, epitomised by *Sholay* (1975); the courtesan film, such as *Pakeezah* (1972), the mythological movie, represented by *Jai Santoshi Maa* (1975) and the perennial masala potboiler. With them came a new triumvirate of superstars. Dharmendra, Jeetendra and Rajesh Khanna were the screen idols for a new generation. The masala film emerged as a panacea for the travails of real life, combining melodrama and action with music. By the 1970s, Hindi film began to combine all genres into a single movie, with song and dance firmly at the heart of the narrative. Another landmark occurred with the release of Ramesh Sippy's *Sholay*, the first Indian movie produced in 70mm with stereophonic sound. A groundbreaking film, it ran for five years to full houses, ushering in the era of the angry man. Reflecting the era of industrialisation and transition, seminal films in Indian history such as *Sholay* and *Deewar* (1975) were to establish Amitabh Bachchan as an unparalleled icon and an unstoppable force in Indian cinema.

In the late 1980s and '90s Indian cinema halls were refurbished and reclaimed by

Bollywood stars Kajol and Shahrukh Khan.

family audiences and Bollywood experienced an unprecedented revival. Musical love stories were back in vogue and with them came a new brand of star in the form of the 'chocolate box' hero. In a throwback to the 1950s the focus returned to lyricism, melody and heartfelt emotion. With the popularity of the audio cassette, music had the power to propel a film into the mind of the audience. Films such as *Qayamat Se Qayamat Tak* (1988), *Tezaab* (1988) and *Maine Pyar Kiya* (1989) were typical of films of the era which achieved popularity on the back of their music.

A generation of young stars emerged who would dominate cinema in the 1990s. Madhuri Dixit, Juhi Chawla, Aamir Khan, Salman Khan and Shah Rukh Khan led the charge for the new teen idols on the block. Reacting to the excesses of the 1980s, the films were wholesome musical dramas designed to cater to the delicate sensibilities of Indians and allowing families to watch films together once more. With fourteen songs, a domestic story at its core, no villain and the mantra 'I love my family' reverberating endlessly throughout, Rajshri's *Hum Aapke Hain Kaun* (1994), went on to become the highest-grossing Indian film of all time, simultaneously bringing Bollywood back to the people.

With his subversive roles in *Baazigar* (1993) and *Darr* (1993) Shah Rukh Khan made a strong impact on audiences, but it was *Dilwale Dulhania Le Jayenge* (1995) that bolstered this more controversial genre further and created a new superstar of Indian cinema. With exotic Swiss locales, lyrical love songs and a strategy to appeal to the affluent but culture-starved audiences, Yash Raj films awakened a new generation to the wonder of Bollywood. A later partnership with director Karan Johar saw Shah Rukh Khan preside over the box office with a succession of films focused on the experiences of non-resident Indians. Multi-star casts, lavish settings and infectious music were intrinsic to them all, as was a title beginning with K, a testament to Johar's faith in numerology. *Kuch Kuch Hota Hai* (1998)), *Kabhie Khushi Khabhie Gham* (2001), *Kal Ho Na Ho* (2003), and *Kabhie Alvida Na Kehna* (2006) lured audiences back.

The 1990s also saw a surge in the national popularity of Tamil cinema, as films directed by Mani Ratnam captured India's imagination. Politically charged films, such as *Roja* (1992) and *Bombay* (1995), offered the intellectual elite an alternative to formula-driven Bollywood love stories with a new sound to transform the tenor of Bollywood – the music of A R Rahman, perhaps India's greatest export, which would leave an indelible print on world cinema.

Reflecting the darker side of modern life in the late 1990s, a grittier 'parallel cinema' came to the fore, spurred on by the critical and commercial success of *Satya* (1998), a low-budget film based on the Mumbai underworld. The film's success led to the emergence of a distinct genre known as 'Mumbai Noir', urban films reflecting social problems and corruption. Ram Gopal Varma's *Company* (2002) and Anurag Kashyap's *Black Friday* (2004) followed, while Madhur Bandarker found his niche in *Corporate* (2006) and *Fashion* (2009) which exposed the seamy underbelly of Mumbai life.

Modern Indian cinema has diversified into several separate camps – the big-budget, all-star movies, the parallel branch of cinema upholding artistic standards, and the small independent cinema which addresses everyday issues. And while Indian audiences are increasingly discerning, there is room for everything, be it *Lagaan* (2001), the Oscar nominated story of tax and cricket, Dostana's gay comedy, *Love Aaj Kal* (2009) with its contemporary take on romance, the gritty realism of *New York* (2009), *Kambakkht Ishq* (2009) with comic turns for the masses, the fantastic world of *Aladin* (2009) or the rambunctious homage to Bollywood, *Om Shanti Om* (2007).

The world of international cinema has bowed to the box office clout of Bollywood. Bolstered by the 'Slumdog Effect', the iconic Indian film industry has international movie stars, directors and producers vying to be a part of the new empire. Hollywood star Ben Stiller is the latest conscript to Bollywood. "Everyone is aware of Bollywood," says Stiller. "There is so much drama, music and dance in Indian films. It's amazing!" And, in a landmark collaboration, Indian billionaire Anil Ambani's Reliance group has pledged $325 million to finance six feature film projects, which may include a Bollywood-style movie for Steven Spielberg's DreamWorks, as well as forging production agreements with George Clooney and Julia Roberts' production houses. Spielberg hailed the arrangement as a "visionary step", saying that it gives his company "a new set of dreams to work towards".

Look around. Bollywood is everywhere. It is a cultural phenomenon, it is the cinema of India. It is Bollywood and it is not to be underestimated.

Awards and Festivals

The 81st American Academy of Motion Picture Arts and Sciences Awards ('The Oscars') and Nominations for 2008, Kodak Theatre, Los Angeles, 22 February 2009

▷ **Best Film**: *Slumdog Millionaire*; **Nominations:** *The Curious Case of Benjamin Button*; *Frost/Nixon*; *Milk*; *The Reader*

▷ **Best Director**: Danny Boyle for *Slumdog Millionaire*; Nominations: David Fincher for *The Curious Case of Benjamin Button*; Ron Howard for *Frost/Nixon*; Gus Van Sant for *Milk*; Stephen Daldry for *The Reader*

▷ **Best Actor:** Sean Penn for Milk; Nominations: Richard Jenkins for *The Visitor*; Frank Langella for *Frost/Nixon*; Brad Pitt, for *The Curious Case of Benjamin Button*; Mickey Rourke for *The Wrestler*

▷ **Best Actress**: Kate Winslet for *The Reader*; **Nominations:** Anne Hathaway for *Rachel Getting Married*; Angelina Jolie for *Changeling*; Melissa Leo for *Frozen River*; Meryl Streep for *Doubt*

▷ **Best Supporting Actor**: Heath Ledger for *The Dark Knight*; **Nominations:** Josh Brolin for *Milk*; Robert Downey Jr. for *Tropic Thunder*; Philip Seymour Hoffman for *Doub*; Michael Shannon for *Revolutionary Road*

▷ **Best Supporting Actress**: Penélope Cruz for *Vicky Cristina Barcelona*; **Nominations:** Amy Adams for *Doubt*; Viola Davis for *Doubt*; Taraji P. Henson for *The Curious Case of Benjamin Button*; Marisa Tomei for *The Wrestler*

▷ **Best Animated Feature**: Andrew Stanton for *Wall.E*; **Nominations:** Chris Williams and Byron Howard for *Bolt*; John Stevenson and Mark Osborne for *Kung Fu Panda*

▷ **Best Original Screenplay**: Dustin Lance Black for *Milk*; **Nominations:** Courtney Hunt for *Frozen River*; Mike Leigh for *Happy-Go-Lucky*; Martin McDonagh for *In Bruges*; Andrew Stanton, Jim Reardon, Pete Docter for *Wall.E*

▷ **Best Adapted Screenplay**: Simon Beaufoy for *Slumdog Millionaire*; **Nominations:** Eric Roth and Robin Swicord for *The Curious Case of Benjamin Button*; John Patrick Shanley for *Doubt*; Peter Morgan for *Frost/Nixon*; David Hare for *The Reader*

▷ **Best Cinematography**: Anthony Dod Mantle for *Slumdog Millionaire*; Nominations: Tom Stern for Changeling; Claudio Miranda for *The Curious Case of Benjamin Button*; Wally Pfister for *The Dark Knight*; Chris Menges and Roger Deakins for *The Reader*

▷ **Best Editing**: Chris Dickens for *Slumdog Millionaire*; **Nominations:** Kirk Baxter and Angus Wall for *The Curious Case of Benjamin Button*; Lee Smith for *The Dark Knight*; Mike Hill and Dan Hanley for *Frost/Nixon*; Elliot Graham for *Milk*

▷ **Best Original Score**: A.R. Rahman for *Slumdog Millionaire*; **Nominations:** Alexandre Desplat for *The Curious Case of Benjamin Button*; James Newton Howard for *Defiance*; Danny Elfman for *Milk*; Thomas Newman for *Wall.E*

▷ **Best Original Song**: by A.R. Rahman and Gulzar for 'Jai Ho' from *Slumdog Millionaire*; **Nominations:** Peter Gabriel and Thomas Newman for 'Down to Earth' from *Wall.E*; A.R. Rahman and Maya Arulpragasam for 'Saya' from *Slumdog Millionaire*

▷ **Best Costume Design**: Michael O'Connor for *The Duchess*; **Nominations:** Catherine Martin for *Australia*; Jacqueline West for *The Curious Case of Benjamin Button*; Danny Glicker for *Milk*; Albert Wolsky for *Revolutionary Road*

▷ **Best Art Direction**: Donald Graham Burt, Victor J. Zolfo for *The Curious Case of Benjamin Button*; **Nominations:** James J. Murakami and Gary Fettis for *Changeling*; Peter Lando and Nathan Crowley for *The Dark Knight*; Michael Carlin and Rebecca Alleway for *The Duchess*; : Kristi Zea and Debra Schutt for *Revolutionary Road*

▷ **Best Sound Editing**: Richard King for *The Dark Knight*; **Nominations:** Frank Eulner and Christopher Boyes for *Iron Man*; Glenn Freemantle and Tom Sayers for *Slumdog Millionaire*; Ben Burtt and Matthew Wood for *Wall.E*; Wylie Stateman for *Wanted*

▷ **Best Sound Mixing**: Ian Tapp, Richard Pryke and Resul Pookutty for *Slumdog Millionaire*; **Nominations:** David Parker, Michael Semanick, Ren Klyce and Mark Weingarten for *The Curious Case of Benjamin Button*; Lora Hirschberg, Gary Rizzo and Ed Novick for *The Dark Knight*; Tom Myers, Michael Semanick and Ben Burtt for *Wall.E*; Chris Jenkins, Frank A. Montaño and Petr Forejt for *Wanted*

▷ **Best Makeup**: Greg Cannom for *The Curious Case of Benjamin*

Button; **Nominations:** John Caglione, Jr. and Conor O'Sullivan for *The Dark Knight*; Mike Elizalde and Thom Floutz for *Hellboy II: The Golden Army*

▷ **Best Visual Effects:** Eric Barba, Steve Preeg, Burt Dalton and Craig Barron for *The Curious Case of Benjamin Button*; **Nominations:** John Nelson, Ben Snow, Dan Sudick and Shane Mahan for *Iron Man*; Nick Davis, Chris Corbould, Tim Webber and Paul Franklin for *The Dark Knight*

▷ **Best Animated Short Film:** Kunio Kato for *La Maison en Petits Cubes*; **Nominations:** Konstantin Bronzit for *Lavatory – Lovestory*; Emud Mokhberi and Thierry Marchand for *Oktapodi*; Doug Sweetland for *Presto*; Alan Smith and Adam Foulkes for *This Way Up*

▷ **Best Live Action Short Film:** Jochen Alexander Freydank for *Spielzeugland (Toyland)*; **Nominations:** Reto Caffi for *Auf der Strecke (On the Line)*; Elizabeth Marre and Olivier Pont for *Manon on the Asphalt*; Steph Green and Tamara Anghie for *New Boy*; Tivi Magnusson and Dorte Høgh for *The Pig*

▷ **Best Documentary Feature:** James Marsh and Simon Chinn for *Man on Wire*; **Nominations:** Ellen Kuras and Thavisouk Phrasavath for *The Betrayal*; Werner Herzog and Henry Kaiser for *Encounters at the End of the World*; Scott Hamilton Kennedy for *The Garden*; Tia Lessin and Carl Deal for *Trouble the Water*

▷ **Best Documentary Short:** Megan Mylan for *Smile Pinki*; **Nominations:** Steven Okazaki for *The Conscience of Nhem En*; Irene Taylor Brodsky and Tom Grant for *The Final Inch*; Adam Pertofsky and Margaret Hyde for *The Witness – From the Balcony of Room 306*

▷ **Best Foreign Language Film:** *Departures* (Japan); **Nominations:** *The Baader Meinhof Complex*

(Germany); *The Class* (France); *Revanche* (Austria); *Waltz with Bashir* (Israel)

▷ **Honorary Award:** Robert Boyle

Ninth American Film Institute Awards: 9 January 2009, Four Seasons Hotel, Los Angeles

AFI Movies of the Year: Official Selections

▷ *The Curious Case of Benjamin Button*
▷ *The Dark Knight*
▷ *Frost/Nixon*
▷ *Frozen River*
▷ *Gran Torino*
▷ *Iron Man*
▷ *Milk*
▷ *Wall.E*
▷ *Wendy and Lucy*
▷ *The Wrestler*

The 50th Australian Film Institute Awards: 5-6 December 2008

▷ **Best Film:** *The Black Balloon*
▷ **Best Actor:** William McInnes for *Unfinished Sky*
▷ **Best Actress:** Monic Hendrickx for *Unfinished Sky*
▷ **Best Supporting Actor:** Luke Ford for *The Black Balloon*
▷ **Best Supporting Actress:** Toni Collette for *The Black Balloon*
▷ **Best Director:** Elissa Down for *The Black Balloon*
▷ **Best Original Screenplay:** Elissa Down and Jimmy the Exploder for *The Black Balloon*
▷ **Best Screenplay Adaptation:** Peter Duncan for *Unfinished Sky*
▷ **Best Cinematography:** Robert Humphreys for *Unfinished Sky*
▷ **Best Editing:** Veronika Jenet for *The Black Balloon*
▷ **Best Music:** Antony Partos for

Unfinished Sky
▷ **Best Production Design:** Gemma Jackson for *Death Defying Acts*
▷ **Best Costumes:** Cappi Ireland for *The Tender Hook*
▷ **Best Sound:** Andrew Plain, Annie Breslin & Will Ward **for** *Unfinished Sky*
▷ **Australia's Favourite Film:** *The Castle*
▷ **Best Documentary:** Craig Griffin and Michael Lynch for *Not Quite Hollywood*
▷ **Best Direction in a Documentary:** Ian Darling and Sascha Ettinger Epstein for *The Oasis*
▷ **Best Short Fiction Film:** Stuart Parkyn and Julius Avery for *Jerrycan*
▷ **Best Screenplay for a Short Fiction Film:** Rene Hernandez for *The Ground Beneath*
▷ **Outstanding Achievement in Short Film Screen Craft:** Xanthe Highfield (Production Design) for *fOUR*
▷ **AFI Award for Best Cinematography in a Documentary:** Andrew Commis & Rachel Landers for *A Northern Town*.
▷ **Best Editing on a Documentary:** Sally Fryer for *The Oasis*
▷ **Best Short Animation:** Steve Baker and Damon Escott for *Dog With Electric Collar*
▷ **AFI International Aware for Best Actor:** Heath Ledger for *The Dark Knight*
▷ **AFI International Aware for Best Actress:** Cate Blanchett for *Elizabeth: The Golden Age*
▷ **Young Actor Award:** Danielle Catanzariti for *Hey, Hey, It's Esther Blueburger*
▷ **Byron Kennedy Award:** Chris Lilley for *Summer Heights High*
▷ **Reader's Choice Award:** Hugh Jackman for *Australia*

The 59th Berlin International Film Festival: 14 February 2009

Golden Bear for Best Film: Claudia Llos for *La teta asustada / The Milk of Sorrow* (Peru)

Silver Bear, Grand Jury Prize (shared): Maren Ade for *Alle Anderen / Everyone Else* (Germany) and Adrián Biniez for *Gigante* (Uruguay / Argentina**)**

Silver Bear, Best Director: Asghar Farhadi for *About Elly* (Iran)

Silver Bear, Best Actor: Sotigui Kouyate for *London River*

Silver Bear, Best Actress: Birgit Minichmayr for *Everyone Else*

Silver Bear, Best Screenplay: Oren Moverman and Alessandro Camon for *The Messenger* by Oren Moverman

Silver Bear for Individual Artistic Contribution: Gábor Erdély and Tamás Székely for the Sound Design of *Katalin Varga*

Alfred Bauer Prize: Adrián Biniez for *Gigante* and Andrzej Wajda for *Tatarak (Sweet Rush)*

Honorary Golden Bear: Maurice Jarre

The Best First Feature Award: Adrián Biniez for *Gigante*

Special Mention: Fredrik Edfeldt for *Flickan (The Girl)*

Golden Bear for Best Short Film: David O'Reilly for *Please Say Something*

Silver Bear for Best Short Film: Daniel Elliott for *Jade*

DAAD Short Film Prize: Susana Barriga for *The Illusion*

Glass Bear for Best Feature Film: Philippe Falardeau for *C'est pas moi, je le jure! (It's Not Me, I Swear!)*

Glass Bear for Best Feature Film: David Lee Miller for *My Suicide*

Glass Bear Special Mention for a Feature Film: Lotte Svendsen for *Max Pinlig (Max Embarrassing)*

Glass Bear for Best Short Film: Bair Dyshenov for *Ulybka Buddy (Buddha's smile)*

Glass Bear for Best Short

Film: Adam Strange for *Aphrodite's Farm*

Glass Bear Special Mention for a Short Film: Anne Sewitsky for *Oh, My God!*

Glass Bear Special Mention for a Short Film: David Aronowitsch and Hanna Heilborn for *Slavary*

Berlinale Short Film Nominee for the European Film Awards 2009: Lola Randl for *Die Leiden des Herrn Karpf. Der Geburtstag*

Special Mentions: Leila Albayaty for *VU* and Christoph Girardet and Matthias Müller for *Contre-jour*

Berlinale Camera: Claude Chabro; Günter Rohrbach; Manoel de Oliveira

Ecumenical Jury Prizes:

Competition: Annette K. Ohleson for *Lille Soldat*

Special Mention: Rachid Bouchareb for *London River* and Richard Loncraine for *My One and Only*

Grand Prix for the best feature: Philippe Falardeau for *C'est pas moi, je le jure! (It's Not Me, I Swear!)*

Special Mention: Fredrik Edfeldt for *Flickan (The Girl)*

Special Prize for Best Short Film: Anne Sewitsky for *Oh, My God!*

Special Mention: *Julius Avery for Jerrycan*

Panorama: *Philippe Lioret for Welcome*

Forum: *So Yong Kim for Treeless Mountain*

FIPRESCI Prizes:

Competition: Claudia Llosa for *La teta asustada (The Milk Of Sorrow)*

Panorama: Rune Denstad Langlo for *Nord (North)*

Forum: Sono Sion for *Ai no mukidashi (Love Exposure)*

German Arthouse Cinemas

Guild: Hans-Christian Schmid for *Storm*

CICAE (international confederation of art cinemas):

Panorama: Roberto Castón for *Ander*

Forum: Radu Jude for *Cea mai fericita fata din lume (The Happiest Girl in the World)*

Teddy Bear Award, Best Feature: Julián Hernández for *Rabioso sol, rabioso cielo (Raging Sun, Raging Sky)*

Teddy Bear Award, Best Documentary: John Greyson for *Fig Trees*

Teddy Bear Award, Short: Barbara Hammer for *A Horse Is Not A Metaphor*

Dialogue en perspective: Anna Deutsch for *Gitti*

Special Mention: Michael Koch for *Polar*

Actor's Award: *Franziska Petri for Für Miriam (For Miriam) and Jacob Matschenzfor Fliegen (Fly)*

Caligari Film Prize: Sono Sion for *Ai no mukidashi (Love Exposure)*

NETPAC Prize (tie): Cong Feng for *Ma dai fu de zhen suo (Doctor Ma's Country Clinic)* and Lee Suk-Gyung for *Eoddeon gaien nal (The Day After)*

Amnesty International Film Prize: Hans-Christian Schmid for *Storm*

Femina Film Prize: Silke Fischer for Production Design in *Alle Anderen (Everyone else)*

Label Europa Cinemas Prizes (tie): Rune Denstad Langlo for *Nord (North)* and Philippe Lioret for *Welcome*

Readers Juries And Audience Awards: *Berliner Morgenpost*

Readers' Prize: Hans-Christian Schmid for *Storm*

ELSE Siegessäule Reader's Choice Award: Yun Suh for *City Of Borders*

Tagesspiegel Readers' Prize: Reha Erdem for *Hayat var (My Only Sunshine)*

Penélope Cruz in *Vicky Cristina Barcelona*.

⟩**Volkswagen Score Competition Award**: Atanas Valkov

⟩ *Berlin Today* **Award**: Supriyo Sen for *Wagah*

⟩**Peace Film Prize**: Oren Moverman for *The Messenger*

⟩**Panorama Audience Award**: Mike Bonanno, Andy Bichlbaum and Kurt Engfehrfor for *The Yes Men Fix The World*

⟩**Golden Bear Jury**: Tilda Swinton (president), Wayne Wang, Isabel Coixet, Christoph Schlingensief, Alice Waters, Gaston Kabore, Henning Mankell

The 2009 British Academy of Film and Television Arts Awards ('BAFTAs'), Royal Opera House, Covent Garden, London, 8 February 2009

⟩**Best Film**: *Slumdog Millionaire*

⟩**Alexander Korda Award for Best British Film**: *Man on Wire*

⟩**David Lean Award for Direction**: Danny Boyle for *Slumdog Millionaire*

⟩**Best Original Screenplay**: Martin McDonagh for *In Bruges*

⟩**Best Adapted Screenplay**: Simon Beaufoy for *Slumdog Millionaire*

⟩**Best Actor**: Mickey Rourke for *The Wrestler*

⟩**Best Actress**: Kate Winslet for *The Reader*

⟩**Best Supporting Actor**: Heath Ledger for *The Dark Knight*

⟩**Best Supporting Actress**: Penélope Cruz for *Vicky Cristina Barcelona*

⟩**Best Cinematography**: Anthony Dod Mantle for *Slumdog Millionaire*

⟩**Best Production Design**: Donald Graham Burt and Victor J. Zolfo for *The Curious Case of Benjamin Button*

⟩**Best Editing**: Chris Dickens for *Slumdog Millionaire*

⟩**Anthony Asquith Award for Film Music**: A. R. Rahman for *Slumdog Millionaire*

⟩**Best Costumes**: Michael O'Connor for *The Duchess*

⟩**Best Sound**: Glenn Freemantle, Resul Pookutty, Richard Pryke, Tom Sayers and Ian Tapp for *Slumdog Millionaire*

⟩**Best Special Visual Effects**: Eric Barba, Craig Barron, Nathan McGuinness and Edson Williams for *The Curious Case of Benjamin Button*

⟩**Best Make Up/Hair**: Jean Black, Colleen Callaghan for *The Curious Case of Benjamin Button*

⟩**Best Non-English Language Film**: Yves Marmion, Philippe Claudel for *I've Loved You So Long*

⟩**Best Short Film**: Stewart le Maréchal and Esther May Campbell for *September*

⟩**Best Animated Film**: Andrew Stanton for *Wall.E*

⟩**Best Short Animated Film**: Steve Pegram, Nick Park and Bob Baker for *Wallace and Gromit: A Matter of Loaf and Death*

⟩**Carl Foreman Award for the Most Promising Newcomer**: Steve McQueen for *Hunger*

⟩**The Orange Rising Star Award**: Noel Clarke

⟩**BAFTA Fellowship**: Terry Gilliam

⟩**Michael Balcon Award**

for Outstanding British Contribution to Cinema: Pinewood Studios and Shepperton Studios

The 29th Canadian Film Awards ('Genies'), Toronto, 4 April 2009

➤**Best Film**: Niv Fichman, Francis Damberger, Paul Gross and Frank Siracusa for *Passchendaele*
➤**Best Director**: Benoit Pilon for *Ce qu'il faut pour vivre / The Necessities of Life*
➤**Best Actor**: Natar Ungalaaq for *Ce qu'il faut pour vivre / The Necessities of Life*
➤**Best Actress**: Ellen Burstyn for *The Stone Angel*
➤**Best Supporting Actor**: Callum Keith Rennie for *Normal*
➤**Best Supporting Actress**: Kristin Booth for *Young People Fucking*
➤**Best Original Screenplay**: Bernard Émond for *Ce qu'il faut pour vivre / The Necessities of Life*
➤**Best Adapted Screenplay**: Marie-Sissi Labrèche and Lyne Charlebois for *Borderline*
➤**Best Cinematography**: Gregory Middleton for *Fugitive Pieces*
➤**Best Art Direction/ Production Design**: Carol Spier and Janice Blackie-Goodine for *Passchendaele*
➤**Best Art Direction/Costume Design**: Wendy Partridge for *Passchendaele*
➤**Best Music (Original Score)**: John McCarthy for *The Stone Angel*
➤**Best Music (Original Song)**: Dr Shiva for 'Amal Rahi Nagufta'
➤**Best Editing:** Richard Comeau for *Ce qu'il faut pour vivre / The Necessities of Life*
➤**Best Overall Sound**: Lou Solakofski, Garrell Clark, Steve Foster and Don White for *Passchendaele*
➤**Best Sound Editing**: Jane Tattersall, Kevin Banks, Barry Gilmore, Andy Malcolm, Dave Rose for *Passchendaele*
➤**Best Documentary**: Yung Chang, Mila Aung-Thwin, John Christou and Germaine Ying-Gee Wong for *Up The Yangtze*
➤**Best Live-Action Short**: Denis Villeneuve and Phoebe Greenberg for *Next Floor*
➤**Best Animated Short**: Claude Cloutier and Marcel Jean for *Sleeping Betty*
➤**The Golden Reel Award:** Niv Fichman, Francis Damberger, Paul Gross, Frank Siracusa for *Passchendaele*
➤**Claude Jutra Award:** Yves-Christian Fournier for *Tout Est Parfait / Everything Is Fine*
➤**Special Award For Outstanding Achievement In Make-Up Design:** Adrien Morot, Réjean Goderre, Marie-France Guy, Bruno Gatien and Nathalie Trépanier for *Cruising Bar 2*

The 59th Cannes Film Festival Awards, 17-28 May 2009

➤**Palme d'Or for Best Film**: Michael Haneke for *Das Weisse Band (The White Ribbon)*
➤**Grand Prix du Jury**: Jacques Audiard for *Un Prophète (A Prophet)*
➤**Lifetime achievement award for his work and exceptional contribution to the history of cinema**: Alain Resnais for *Les Herbes Folles (Wild Grass)*
➤**Best Actor**: Christoph Waltz for *Inglourious Basterds*
➤**Best Actress**: Charlotte Gainsbourg for *Antichrist*
➤**Best Director**: Brillante Mendoza for *Kinatay*
➤**Best Screenplay**: Lou Ye for *Chun Feng Chen Zui De Ye Wan (Spring Fever)*
➤**Palme d'Or for Best Short**: João Salaviza for *Arena*
➤**Short Film Special Distinction:** Louis Sutherland and Mark Albiston for *The Six Dollar Fifty Man*
➤**Vulcain Technical Prize**: Isabel Coixet for *C.S.T. Map of The Sounds Of Tokyo*
➤**Prix du Jury** (ex-aequo): Andrea Arnold for *Fish Tank* and Chan-Wook Park for *Bak-Jwi (Thirst)*
➤**Caméra d'or:** Warwick Thornton for *Samson And Delilah*
➤**Camera d'Or – Special Distinction:** Scandar Copti and Yaron Shani for *Ajami*
➤**Une Certain Regard: Awards Cinéfondation**
➤**First Prize:** Zuzana Kirchnerová-Špidlová for *Bába*
➤**Second Prize**: Song Fang for *Goodbye*
➤**Third Prize (ex-aequo):** Yaelle Kayam for *Diploma* and Jo Sung-Hee *Don't Step Out Of The House*
➤**Prix Un Certain Regard – Fondation Gan pour le Cinéma:** Yorgos Lanthimos for *Kynodontas (Dogtooth)*
➤**Une Certain Regard Special Jury Prize**: Corneliu Porumboiu for *Politist, Adjectiv (Police, Adjective)*
➤**Un Certain Regard Special Jury Prize(ex-aequo):** Bahman Ghobadi for *Kasi Az Gorbehaye Irani Khabar Nadareh (No One Knows About Persian Cats)* and Mia Hansen-Løve for *Le Père De Mes Enfants (Father Of My Children)*

➤*Juries: Feature Films Jury: President of the Jury:* **Isabelle Huppert, president**
➤*Members of the Jury: Asia Argento, Nuri Bilge Ceylan, Lee Chang-Dong, James Gray, Hanif Kureishi, Shu Qi, Robin Wright Penn*

➤*Cinefondation and Short Films*

Tony Servillo in *Il Divo*.

Jury: President of the Jury: John Boorman
Members of the Jury: Bertrand Bonello, Ferid Boughedir, Leonor Silveira, Zhang Ziyi

▶ *Un Certain Regard Jury: President Of The Jury: Paolo Sorrentino; Members Of The Jury: Uma Da Cunha, Julie Gayet, Piers Handling, Marit Kapla*

Camera D'or Jury: President Of The Jury: Roschdy Zem; Members Of The Jury: Diane Baratier ,Olivier Chiavassa, Sandrine Ray, Charles Tesson, Edouard Waintrop

53rd David Di Donatello Academy Awards ('The Davids'), Rome, 16 April 2009

▶ **Best Film**: *Gomorrah*
▶ **Best Director**: Matteo Garrone for *Gomorrah*
▶ **Best New Director**: Gianni Di Gregoriofor *Table of August*
▶ **Best Screenplay**: Maurizio

Braucci, Ugo Chiti, Gianni Di Gregorio, Matteo Garrone, Massimo Gaudioso and Roberto Saviano for *Gomorrah*
▶ **Best Producer**: Domenico Procacci for *Gomorrah*
▶ **Best Actor**: Toni Servillo for *Il Divo*
▶ **Best Actress**: Alba Rohrwacher for *Il Papa 'Di Giovanna*
▶ **Best Supporting Actor**: Giuseppe Battiston for *Non Pensarci*
▶ **Best Supporting Actress**: Piera Degli Esposti for *Il Divo*
▶ **Best Cinematography**: Luca Bigazzi for *Il Divo*
▶ **Best Music**: Teho Teardo for *Il Divo*
▶ **Best Original Song**: Robert Del Naja, Neil Davidge, Euan Dickinson, Robert Del Naja and Neil Davidge for 'Herculaneum' from *Gomorrah*
▶ **Best Production Design**: Francesco Frigeri for *The Demons of Saint Petersburg*
▶ **Best Costume Design**: Elisabetta Montaldo for *The Demons of Saint Petersburg*
▶ **Best Makeup:** Vittorio Sodano for *The Demons of Saint Petersburg*

▶ **Best Hairdressing:** Aldo Signoretti for *Il Divo*
▶ **Best Editing**: Marco Spoletini for *Gomorrah*
▶ **Best Sound**: Maricetta Lombardo for *Gomorrah*
▶ **Best Visual Effects**: Nicola Sganga and Rodolfo Migliaro for *Il Divo*
▶ **Best Documentary Feature**: Daniele Gaglianone for *Rate Nece Biti (War There Will Be')*
▶ **Best Short**: Paolo Zucca for *Referee*
▶ **Best European Union Film:** *Danny Boyle for Slumdog Millionaire*
▶ **Best Foreign Film**: Clint Eastwood for *Gran Torino*
▶ **Young David**: Giulio Manfredonia for *It Can Do*
▶ **Special Awards**: Christian De Sica, Virna Lisi, Fulvio Lucisano, Paolo Villaggio

The 34th Deauville Festival of American Cinema, 14 September 2008

▶ **Grand Prix For Best Film**: Tom McCarthy for *The Visitor*

Awards and Festivals

> **Jury Prize**:
Lance Hammer for *Ballast*
> **International Critics Award**:
Damian Harris for *Gardens of The Night*
> **Most Promising Newcomer Award:** Lance Hammer for *Ballast*
> **Michel D'Ornano Prize**:
Jean-Stéphane Sauvaire for **Johnny Mad Dog**

The 21st European Film Awards ('The Felixes'), Copenhagen, Denmark, 6 December 2008

> **Best European Film**: *Gomorra*
> **Best European Director**:
Matteo Garrone for *Gomorrah*
> **Best European Actor**:
Toni Servillo for *Il Divo*
> **Best European Actress**: Kristin Scott Thomas for *Il y a longtemps que je t'aime*
> **Best European Screenplay**:
Maurizio Braucci, Ugo Chiti, Gianni Di Gregorio, Matteo Garrone, Massimo Gaudioso and Roberto Saviano for *Gomorrah*
> **Best European Cinematographer**:
Marco Onorato for *Gomorrah*
> **Best European Music**:
Max Richter for *Vals Im Bashir*
> **Prix d'Excellence**:
Magdalena Biedrzycka for *Katyn* (costume design)
> **Outstanding European Achievement in World Cinema:** Søren Kragh-Jacobsen, Kristian Levring, Lars von Trier, Thomas Vinterberg (the Dogma founders).
> **European Film Academy Lifetime Achievement Award**:
Judi Dench
> **Discovery of the Year (Fassbinder Award):** Steve McQueen for *Hunger*
> **Critics Award, FIPRESCI Prize**:
Abdel Kechiche for *La graine et le mulet*

> **Documentary, Prix Arte**:
Helena Trestikova for *René*
> **Short Film, Prix UIP**:
Darren Thornton for *Frankie*
> **The Jameson People's Choice Awards**: David Yates for *Harry Potter and the Order of the Phoenix*

The Golden Raspberries ('The Razzies'): 21 February 2009 at the Barnsdall Gallery Theatre, Hollywood

> **Worst Picture:** *The Love Guru*
> **Worst Actor:** Mike Myers in *The Love Guru*
> **Worst Actress:** Paris Hilton in *The Hottie and the Nottie*
> **Worst Supporting Actor**:
Pierce Brosnan in *Mamma Mia!*
> **Worst Supporting Actress**:
Paris Hilton in *Repo! The Genetic Opera*
> **Worst Director:** Uwe Boll for *1968 Tunnel Rats*, *In the Name of the King: A Dungeon Siege Tale*, and *Postal*
> **Worst Screenplay**:
Mike Myers and Graham Gordy for *The Love Guru*
> **Worst Career Achievement:**
Uwe Boll ('Germany's answer to Ed Wood')
> **Worst Remake or Sequel**:
Indiana Jones and the Kingdom of the Crystal Skull
> **Worst Screen Couple**: Paris Hilton and either Christine Lakin or Joel David Moore in *The Hottie and the Nottie*

The 66th Hollywood Foreign Press Association ('Golden Globes') Awards, 11 January 2009

> **Cecil B DeMille Award**:
Steven Spielberg
> **Best Motion Picture – Drama**:
Slumdog Millionaire

> **Best Motion Picture – Musical or Comedy**:
Vicky Cristina Barcelona
> **Best Director**:
Danny Boyle for *Slumdog Millionaire*
> **Best Performance by an Actor for a Motion Picture – Drama**: Mickey Rourke for *The Wrestler*
> **Best Performance by an Actress for a Motion Picture – Drama**: Kate Winslet for *Revolutionary Road*
> **Best Performance by an Actor for a Motion Picture – Comedy/Musical**:
Colin Farrell for *In Bruges*
> **Best Performance by an Actress for a Motion Picture**:
Sally Hawkins for *Happy-Go-Lucky*
> **Best Performance by an Actor for a Supporting Role**:
Heath Ledger for *The Dark Knight*
> **Best Performance by an Actress for a Supporting Role – Motion Picture**:
Kate Winslet for *The Reader*
> **Best Foreign Language Film**:
Waltz With Bashir
> **Best Screenplay**: Simon Beaufoy for *Slumdog Millionaire*
> **Best Original Score**: A. R. Rahman for *Slumdog Millionaire*
> **Best Original Song**: Bruce Springsteen for 'The Wrestler' from *The Wrestler*

The 29th London Film Critic's Circle Awards, The Grosvenor House Hotel, London, 4 February 2009

> **Best Film**:
Darren Aronofsky *for The Wrestler*
> **Attenborough Film of the Year (Best British Film)**: Danny Boyle for *Slumdog Millionaire*
> **Best Actor**:
Mickey Rourke for *The Wrestler*
> **Best Actress**: Kate Winslet for *The Reader* and *Revolutionary Road*

Michael Fassbender in *Hunger*.

⯈ **Best Director**: David Fincher for *The Curious Case of Benjamin Button*

⯈ **Best Screenwriter**: Simon Beaufoy for *Slumdog Millionaire*

⯈ **Best British Director**: Danny Boyle for *Slumdog Millionaire*

⯈ **Best British Actor**: Michael Fassbender for *Hunger*

⯈ **Best British Actress**: Kristin Scott-Thomas for *I've Loved You So Long*

⯈ **Best British Supporting Actor**: Eddie Marsan for *Happy-Go-Lucky*

⯈ **Best British Supporting Actress**: Tilda Swinton for *The Curious Case of Benjamin Button*

⯈ **NSPCC Award: Young British Performance of the Year:** Thomas Turgoose for *Somers Town* and *Eden Lake*

⯈ **Best British Newcomer**: Steve McQueen for *Hunger*

⯈ **Best Foreign Language Film**: Ari Folman for *Waltz With Bashir*

⯈ **Dilys Powell Award**: Dame Judi Dench

The Los Angeles Film Critics' Association Awards, InterContinental Hotel, Los Angeles, 12 January 2009

⯈ **Best Picture**: *Wall.E*

⯈ **Best Actor**: Sean Penn for *Milk*

v**Best Actress**: Sally Hawkins for *Happy-Go-Lucky*

⯈ **Best Supporting Actor:** Heath Ledger for *The Dark Knight*

⯈ **Best Supporting Actress**: Penélope Cruz for *Vicky Cristina Barcelona* and *Elegy*

⯈ **Best Director**: Danny Boyle for *Slumdog Millionaire*

⯈ **Best Screenplay**: Mike Leigh for *Happy-Go-Lucky*

⯈ **Best Foreign Film**: Zhang Ke Jia for *Sanxia haoren*

⯈ **Best Documentary**: James Marsh for *Man on Wire*

⯈ **Best Cinematography:** Nelson Yu Lik-wai for *Sanxia haoren*

⯈ **Best Production Design**: Mark Friedberg for *Synecdoche, New York*

⯈ **New Generation Award**: Steve McQueen for *Hunger*

⯈ **Best Animation**: Ari Folman for *Vals Im Bashir*

⯈ **Career Achievement Award**: John Calley

⯈ **Independent/Experimental Film and Video Award:** James Benning for *RR* and *Casting a Glance*

18th MTV Movie Awards, Gibson Amphitheatre, Universal City, California, 31 May 2009

⯈ **Best Movie**: *Twilight*

⯈ **Best Actress**: Kristen Stewart for *Twilight*

⯈ **Best Actor**: Zac Efron for *High School Musical 3: Senior Year*

⯈ **Best Comedic Performance**: Jim Carrey for *Yes Man*

⯈ **Best Breakthrough Performance (female)**: Ashley Tisdale for *High School Musical 3: Senior Year*

⯈ **Best Breakthrough Performance (male)**: Robert Pattinson for *Twilight*

⯈ **Best Villain**: Heath Ledger for *The Dark Knight*

⯈ **Best Song**: Miley Cyrus for 'The Climb' from *Hannah Montana: The Movie*

⯈ **Best Fight**: Robert Pattinson vs.

Cam Gigandet from *Twilight*

> **Best Kiss**: Kristen Stewart and Robert Pattinson from *Twilight*
> **Best WTF Moment**: Amy Poehler from *Baby Mama* ('Peeing in the Sink')
> **MTV Generation Award**: Ben Stiller

The 80th National Board of Review of Motion Picture Awards, New York, 4 December 2008

> **Best Film**: *Slumdog Millionaire*
> **Best Actor**: Clint Eastwood for *Gran Torino*
> **Best Actress**: Anne Hathaway for *Rachel Getting Married*
> **Best Supporting Actor**: Josh Brolin for Milk
> **Best Supporting Actress**: Penelope Cruz for *Vicky Cristina Barcelona*
> **Best Director**: David Fincher for *The Curious Case of Benjamin Button*
> **Best Adapted Screenplay (tie)**: Simon Beaufoy for *Slumdog Millionaire* and Eric Roth for *The Curious Case of Benjamin Button*
> **Best Original Screenplay**: Nick Schenk for *Gran Torino*
> **Best Adapted Screenplay: Spotlight Award**: Melissa Leo for *Frozen River* and Richard Jenkins for *The Visitor*
> **Best Ensemble Cast**: *Doubt*
> **Best Foreign Language Film**: *Mongol*
> **Best Animated Feature**: *Wall.E*
> **Best Documentary**: *Man on Wire*
> **Breakthrough Performances (Actor)**: Dev Pate for *Slumdog Millionaire*
> **Breakthrough Performances (Actress)**: Viola Davis for *Doubt*
> **Best Directorial Debut**: Courtney Hunt for *Frozen River*
> **William K Everson Award for Film History**: Molly Haskell and

Andrew Sarris

> **Special Recognition of Films that Reflect the Freedom of Expression**: *Trumbo*
> **Top 10 Films of 2008 in Alphabetical Order**
> *Burn After Reading*
> *Changeling*
> *The Curious Case of Benjamin Button*
> *The Dark Knight*
> *Defiance*
> *Frost/Nixon*
> *Gran Torino*
> *Milk*
> *Wall.E*
> *The Wrestler*
> **Top 5 Foreign Language Films**
> *The Edge of Heaven*
> *Let the Right One In*
> *Roman De Gare*
> *A Secret*
> *Waltz with Bashir*
> **Top 5 Documentaries**
> *American Teen*
> *The Betrayal*
> *Dear Zachary*
> *Encounters at the End of the World*
> *Roman Polanski: Wanted and Desired*
> **Top Independent Films of 2008**
> *Frozen River*
> *In Bruges*
> *In Search of a Midnight Kiss*
> *Mr Foe*
> *Rachel Getting Married*
> *Snow Angels*
> *Son of Rambow*
> *Wendy and Lucy*
> *Vicky Cristina Barcelona*
> *The Visitor*

The 43rd National Society of Film Critics' Awards, New York, 7 January 2009

> **Best Film**: Ari Folman for *Waltz with Bashir*
> **Best Actor**: Sean Penn for *Milk*
> **Best Actress**: Sally Hawkins for

Happy-Go-Lucky

> **Best Director**: Mike Leigh for *Happy-Go-Lucky*
> **Best Supporting Actor**: Eddie Marsan for *Happy-Go-Lucky*
> **Best Supporting Actress**: Hanna Schygulla for *The Edge of Heaven*
> **Best Screenplay**: Mike Leigh for *Happy-Go-Lucky*
> **Best Cinematography**: Anthony Dod Mantle for *Slumdog Millionaire*
> **Best Experimental Film**: Ken Jacobs for *Razzle Dazzle*
> **Best Non-Fiction Film**: James Marsh for *Man on Wire*
> **Film Heritage Awards**:
> **Special Award**: The Criterion Collection for finally making Samuel Fuller's suppressed *White Dog* available to a wide American audience via DVD release.
> **Special Award**: *The Exiles* Kent Mackenzie's realistic 1961 independent film about Native Americans in Los Angeles. (Restored by Ross Lipman of the UCLA Television and Film Archives and distributed by Milestone.)
> **Special Award**: Flicker Alley for releasing DVD collections of rare early U.S. and foreign silent films.
> **Special Award**: Twentieth Century Fox Home Entertainment for its DVD set *Murnau, Borzage and Fox*.

The 74th New York Film Critics' Circle Awards, Strata, New York City, 3 January 2009

> **Best Film**: *Milk*
> **Best Actor**: Sean Penn for *Milk*
> **Best Actress**: Sally Hawkins for *Happy-Go-Lucky*
> **Best Supporting Actor**: Josh Brolin for *Milk*
> **Best Supporting Actress**: Penelope Cruz for *Vicky Cristina*

Barcelona
> **Best Director**:
Mike Leigh for *Happy-Go-Lucky*
> **Best Screenplay**: Jenny Lumet
for *Rachel Getting Married*
> **Best Cinematographer**:
Anthony Dod Mantle for
Slumdog Millionaire
> **Best Foreign Film**: *4 Months,
3 Weeks and 2 Days (4 luni, 3
saptamani si 2 zile)* (Romania)
> **Best Nonfiction Film**:
Man on Wire
> **Best Animated Film**: *Wall.E*
> **Best First Feature**: Courtney
Hunt for *Frozen River*

The 26th Sundance Film Festival, Park City, Utah, January 2009

> **Grand Jury Prize –
Documentary**: *We Live in Public*
> **Grand Jury Prize – Dramatic**:
*Precious: Based on the Novel Push by
Sapphire*
> **Grand Jury Prize – World
Cinema Dramatic**:
The Maid (La Nana)
> **Grand Jury Prize – World
Cinema Documentary**:
Rough Aunties
> **Audience Award – Documentary**:
The Cove
> **Audience Award – Dramatic**:
Push: Based on a Novel by Sapphire
> **World Cinema Audience
Award – Documentary**:
Afghan Star
> **World Cinema Audience
Award – Dramatic**: *An Education*
> **Documentary Directing
Award**: Natalia Almada for
El General
> **Dramatic Directing Award**:
Cary Joji Fukunaga for *Sin Nombre*
> **World Cinema Directing
Award – Dramatic**: Oliver
Hirschbiegel for *Five Minutes of
Heaven*

> **World Cinema Directing
Award – Documentary**: Havana
Marking for *Afghan Star*
> **Excellence in Cinematography
Award – Dramatic**: Bob Richman
for *The September Issue*
> **Excellence in Cinematography
Award – Dramatic**: Adriano
Goldman for *Sin Nombre*
> **World Cinema
Cinematography Award –
Documentary**: John De Borman
for *An Education*
> **World Cinema
Cinematography Award –
Dramatic**: John Maringouin for
Big River Man
> **Documentary Film Editing**:
Karen Schmeer for *Sergio*
> **World Cinema Documentary
Editing Award**: Janus Billeskov
Jansen and Thomas Papapetros *for
Burma VJ*
> **Waldo Salt Screenwriting
Award – Dramatic**: Nicholas
Jasenovec and Charlyne Yi for *Paper
Heart*
> **World Cinema Screenwriting
Award**: Guy Hibbert for *Five
Minutes of Heaven*
> **Special Jury Prize for
Originality – World Cinema
Drama**: *Louise-Michel*
> **Special Jury Prize – World
Cinema Documentary**:
Tibet in Song
> **Special Jury Prize for Acting –
World Cinema**: Catalina Saavedra
for *The Maid (La Nana)*
> **Special Jury Prize – U.S.
Documentary**: *Good Hair*
> **Special Jury Prize for Spirit of
Independence**: *Humpday*
> **Special Jury Prize for Acting**:
Mo'Nique for *Precious: Based on the
Novel Push by Sapphire*
> **Jury Prize – U.S. Short
Filmmaking**: *Short Term 12*
> **Jury Prize – International
Short Filmmaking**: *Lies*
> **2009 Alfred P. Sloan Prize**:

Adam

Dramatic Jury
*Virginia Madsen, Scott McGehee,
Maud Nadler, Mike White, Boaz
Yakin*

Documentary Jury
*Patrick Creadon, Carl Deal, Andrea
Meditch, Sam Pollard, Marina
Zenovich*

World Dramatic Jury
*Colin Brown, Christine Jeffs,
Vibeke Windelov*

World Documentary Jury
*Gillian Armstrong, Thom Powers,
Hubert Sauper*

Shorts Jury
*Gerardo Naranjo, Lou Taylor Pucci,
Sharon Swart*

Alfred P. Sloan Jury
*Fran Bagenal, Rodney Brooks,
Ray Gesteland, Jeffrey Nachmanoff,
Alex Rivera*

In Memoriam
July 2008 - June 2009
by Jonathan Rigby

Given the hundreds of film personalities who died during the period under review, the following selection of just 50 must remain a purely personal one. Pressure of space has excluded from the main entries a number of important people, some 60 of whom are noted in parentheses to the main entries. And nearly 150 others are listed in the month-by-month round-up at the end.

Edie Adams

Terence Alexander

EDIE ADAMS

Born: 16 April 1927, Kingston, Pennsylvania, USA.
Died: 15 October 2008, Los Angeles, California, USA.

Broadway star Edie Adams made her film debut, in a delightful performance as Fred MacMurray's worldly-wise secretary, in *The Apartment* (1960). Her vivacious comic personality then became a guarantee of quality for some five years, during which she played opposite Rock Hudson in *Lover Come Back*, Bob Hope in *Call Me Bwana*, Steve McQueen in *Love with the Proper Stranger*, Jack Lemmon in *Under the Yum Yum Tree* and Rex Harrison in *The Honeypot*.

TERENCE ALEXANDER

Born: 11 March 1923, London, England.
Died: 28 May 2009, London, England.

The kind of urbane gentleman-actor once so prevalent in British cinema, Terence Alexander claimed only to have started making decent money during his ten-year stint in the 1980s TV series *Bergerac*. Prior to that, his suave and sometimes slightly shifty charm was featured in *The One That Got Away* (1957), *The League of Gentlemen* (1960), *Carry On Regardless* (1961), *Bitter Harvest* (1963), *The Intelligence Men* (1965), *Only When I Larf* (1967), *Waterloo* (1969) and *The Day of the Jackal* (1973).

➤ Several other well-known British character actors died in the period under review, among them **Elizabeth Spriggs** and **Hugh Lloyd** (both in July), **Terence Rigby** (August), **William Fox** (September), **Peter Copley** and

Sam Bottoms

Eileen Herlie (both in October), **Laurence Payne** (February) and **John Cater** (March).

KEN ANNAKIN

Born: 10 August 1914, Beverley, Yorkshire, England.
Died: 22 April 2009, Beverly Hills, California, USA.

Director Ken Annakin had an immediate hit with his first feature, *Holiday Camp* (1947). He then alternated such films as *Hotel Sahara* (1951) and *Across the Bridge* (1957) with Disney projects like *The Sword and the Rose* (1953) and *Swiss Family Robinson* (1960). Latterly, sprawling war epics (eg, *The Longest Day*, 1962) and equally sprawling international farces (eg, *Monte Carlo or Bust!*, 1969) rubbed shoulders with smaller (and generally more effective) pictures like *The Informers* (1963) and *Paper Tiger* (1975).

▶ Other directors who died during the year include the multi-award-winning Cuban filmmaker **Humberto Solás** (September), among whose films are *Lucía* (1968) and *Cecilia* (1982), former Hollywood ad man **Howard Zieff** (February), who directed *Slither* (1973), *Private Benjamin* (1980) and *My Girl* (1991), and **Salvatore Samperi** (March), writer-director of such provocative Italian hits as *Malizia* (1973) and *Ernesto* (1979).

CLAUDE BERRI

Born: 1 July 1934, Paris, France.
Died: 12 January 2009, Paris, France.

Hailed by French premier Nicolas Sarkozy as "the most legendary figure in French cinema," Claude Berri certainly staked a claim to that title with his lushly pastoral Pagnol adaptations *Jean de Florette* and *Manon des sources* (both 1986). Starting out as an actor, he won an Oscar for his first film as director, the short *Le Poulet* (1965). As producer he was responsible for *Taking Off* (1971), *Tess* (1979), *La petite voleuse* (1988) and *La Reine Margot* (1994), among others, while his other directing projects included *Sex-Shop* (1972), *Germinal* (1993) and *Lucie Aubrac* (1997).

BETSY BLAIR

Born: 11 December 1923, Cliffside Park, New Jersey, USA.
Died: 13 March 2009, London, England.

Though her screen opportunities were limited by her left-wing politics, Betsy Blair gained an Oscar nomination – and won a BAFTA – for her role in *Marty* (1955), thereafter pursuing a picaresque career path that encompassed France (*Rencontre à Paris*, 1956), Spain (*Calle Mayor*, 1956), Italy (Antonioni's *Il grido*, 1957) and England (*All Night Long*, 1962). Formerly married to Gene Kelly, in the UK she married director Karel Reisz and thereafter made only sporadic appearances, notably in *Descente aux enfers* (1986) and *Betrayed* (1988).

SAM BOTTOMS

Born: 17 October 1955, Santa Barbara, California, USA.
Died: 16 December 2008, Los Angeles, California, USA.

Sam Bottoms got his start through director Peter Bogdanovich, who cast him opposite his elder brother Timothy in *The Last Picture Show* (1971). He subsequently appeared in Clint Eastwood's *The Outlaw Josey Wales* and in 1976, aged 20, began a gruelling 18-month stint in the Philippines, filming Francis Coppola's *Apocalypse Now*. There were rematches with Eastwood and Coppola in *Bronco Billy* and *Gardens of Stone* respectively, and Bottoms' last films included *Seabiscuit* and *SherryBaby*.

Kathleen Byron

David Carradine

IRVING BRECHER

Born: 17 January 1914, The Bronx,
New York City, New York, USA.
Died: 17 November 2008, Los Angeles,
California, USA.

Starting out as gag writer for Milton Berle,
Irving Brecher graduated to script doctor
on *The Wizard of Oz* (1939) – and called his
posthumously published autobiography *The
Wicked Wit of the West*. He wrote two Marx
Brothers scripts, *At the Circus* (1939) and *Go
West* (1940), and shared an Oscar for *Meet Me in
St Louis* (1944). In addition, he created the radio
classic *The Life of Riley*, directed three feature
films, and wound up his writing career with
Bye Bye Birdie in 1963.

➤ Two other writers of enduring Hollywood
classics died in November: **Arthur A Ross**,
who wrote *Creature from the Black Lagoon* (1954),
The Great Race (1965) and *Brubaker* (1980), and
John Michael Hayes, best known for writing
Rear Window (1954) and three other Hitchcock
titles in the same period.

KATHLEEN BYRON

Born: 11 January 1921, London, England.
Died: 18 January 2009, Northwood, Middlesex,
England.

Grievously wasted in British cinema, Kathleen
Byron nevertheless became a cult figure through
her startling performance as the erotomaniac
nun, Sister Ruth, in *Black Narcissus* (1947). Also
for Powell and Pressburger, she appeared in *A
Matter of Life and Death* (1946) and *The Small
Back Room* (1949). After a trip to Hollywood for
Young Bess (1953), she was mainly occupied with
'B' pictures and television. Latterly, however, she
enjoyed cameos in *Emma* (1995), *Saving Private
Ryan* and *Les Misérables* (both 1998).

JACK CARDIFF

Born: 18 September 1914,
Great Yarmouth, Norfolk, England.
Died: 22 April 2009, Ely, Cambridgeshire, England.

A child actor during the silent era, Jack
Cardiff later won an Academy Award as
cinematographer of *Black Narcissus* (1947),
was nominated for another as director of *Sons
and Lovers* (1960), and picked up a final –
honorary – Oscar in 2001. Indisputably one of
Britain's most inspired lighting cameramen, his
incandescent touch was evident in such films
as *Caesar and Cleopatra* (1945), *The Red Shoes*
(1948), *The African Queen* (1951), *The Prince and
the Showgirl* (1957) and *Death On the Nile* (1978).
His other pictures as director included *Intent to
Kill* (1958), *The Long Ships* (1964) and *Girl on a
Motorcycle* (1968).

DAVID CARRADINE

Born: 8 December 1936, Los Angeles, California, USA.
Died: 3 June 2009, Bangkok, Thailand.

Breaking through to stardom in the TV hit *Kung Fu* (1972-75), David Carradine subsequently starred in the cult film *Death Race 2000* (1975) and played Woody Guthrie in *Bound for Glory* (1976). He also worked with Ingmar Bergman on *The Serpent's Egg* (1977) and played opposite his brothers Keith and Robert in *The Long Riders* (1980). A millennial return to high-profile status came courtesy of Quentin Tarantino, for whom Carradine played the eponymous Bill in both 'vols' of *Kill Bill*.

MARILYN CHAMBERS

Born: 22 April 1952, Providence, Rhode Island, USA.
Died: 12 April 2009, Santa Clarita, California, USA.

Made famous by the early 1970s' vogue for porn chic, Marilyn Chambers' hardcore notoriety was founded on *Behind the Green Door* (1972). Other lascivious landmarks ranged from *Resurrection of Eve* (1973) to *Insatiable* (1980), together with a semi-documentary waggishly entitled *Inside Marilyn Chambers* (1975). In the meantime, she was exceptional in her only notable mainstream role, playing the doomed carrier of a vampiric plague in David Cronenberg's *Rabid* (1977).

MICHAEL CRICHTON

Born: 23 October 1942, Chicago, Illinois, USA.
Died: 4 November 2008, Los Angeles, California, USA.

Dubbed 'the Hit Man' by *Time* magazine, bestselling novelist Michael Crichton was also the prime mover behind the hit NBC series *ER* (1994-2009). Among the films adapted from his novels are *The Andromeda Strain* (1971), *The Terminal Man* (1973), *Jurassic Park*, *Rising Sun* (both 1993), *Congo* (1995) and *Sphere* (1998). In addition, he directed the film of *The First Great Train Robbery* (1979) himself, as well as directing his original screenplay *Westworld* (1973). Further hit films bearing his name include *Coma* (1978) and *Twister* (1996).

▶ Other novelist-screenwriters who died this year include **Donald E Westlake** (December), best known for *Point Blank* (1967) and *The Stepfather* (1987), **John Mortimer** (January), whose films include *Bunny Lake is Missing* (1965) and *John and Mary* (1969), and **Alan Hackney** (May), writer of *I'm All Right, Jack* (1959) and *You Must Be Joking!* (1965). Playwright **Robert Anderson**, among whose film credits are *Tea and Sympathy* (1956), *The Sand Pebbles* (1966) and *I Never Sang for My Father* (1970), also died in May.

GERARD DAMIANO

Born: 4 August 1928, The Bronx, New York City, New York, USA.
Died: 25 October 2008, Fort Myers, Florida, USA.

Former hairdresser Gerard Damiano became the focus of worldwide controversy with the rough-edged but epoch-making *Deep Throat*. The film's six-day shoot reportedly cost $22,000; released in June 1972, it went on to earn, according to some estimates, $600 million. Damiano's status as a hardcore auteur was confirmed by *The Devil in Miss Jones* (1973), *Memories Within Miss Aggie* (1974) and *The Story of Joanna* (1975), after which he continued in similar vein for another 20 years.

MARPESSA DAWN

Born: 3 January 1934, Pittsburgh, Pennsylvania, USA.
Died: 25 August 2008, Paris, France.

In her teens, the exotic beauty Marpessa Dawn moved to England, where she appeared in an *Armchair Theatre* episode and was fed to a carnivorous tree in *Womaneater* (1957). Moving to France, she married director Marcel Camus and went with him to Rio de Janeiro, where she starred as the doomed Eurydice in Camus' 1959 art-house classic *Orfeu negro* (Black Orpheus). Despite a role in Dusan Makavejev's controversial *Sweet Movie* in 1974, nothing in Dawn's subsequent career lived up to this Brazilian highpoint.

▶ Dawn's handsome Orpheus in *Orfeu negro*, Brazilian footballer and actor **Breno Mello**, predeceased her by a mere six weeks, in July. Other Brazilian actors who died this year include **Dercy Gonçalves** (also July), 101-year-old star of numerous indigenous comedies, and **Fernando Torres** (September), who was best known internationally for *Kiss of the Spider Woman* (1985).

Farrah Fawcett

Nina Foch

DOM DeLUISE

Born: 1 August 1933, Brooklyn,
New York City, New York, USA.
Died: 4 May 2009, Santa Monica, California, USA.

Rotund comic star Dom DeLuise made his screen debut in the nuclear thriller *Fail-Safe* (1964) but found his niche in the films of writer-director Mel Brooks, among them *Blazing Saddles* (1974), *Silent Movie* (1976), *History of the World: Part I* (1981) and *Robin Hood: Men in Tights* (1993). He was also a regular on Dean Martin's 1960s TV show,
a frequent Burt Reynolds co-star and the author of several cook books.

▶ Another Burt Reynolds co-star, country & western singer and *Smokey and the Bandit* regular **Jerry Reed**, died in September. Further US character actors who passed away this year include comedian **Bernie Mac** (August), **Robert Prosky**, **Bernie Hamilton** and **Majel Barrett-Roddenberry** (all in December), **Pat Hingle** (January) and **Harve Presnell** (June).

GUILLAUME DEPARDIEU

Born: 7 April 1971, Paris, France.
Died: 13 October 2008, Garches, France.

Guillaume Depardieu had his first major role in *Tous les matins du monde* (1991), where the character's older self was played by his father Gérard, with whom Guillaume had a famously turbulent relationship. The younger Depardieu then won a César for Pierre Salvadori's *Les Apprentis* (1995), subsequently appearing in … *Comme elle respire* (1998) and *Les Marchands de sable* (2000) for the same director. He also gave strong performances for Leos Carax (*Pola X*, 1998) and Jacques Rivette (*Ne touchez pas la hache*, 2007).

FARRAH FAWCETT

Born: 2 February 1947, Corpus Christi, Texas, USA.
Died: 25 June 2009, Santa Monica, California, USA.

Prior to becoming one of the iconic faces of the late 1970s in the first series of *Charlie's Angels*, Farrah Fawcett had made minor waves in *Myra Breckinridge* and *Logan's Run*; after it, she struggled for serious acceptance in misfires like *Sunburn* and *Saturn 3*. More hard-hitting roles in the 1980s (eg, *The Burning Bed* and *Extremities*) were followed by such millennial titles as *Dr T and the Women* (2000) and *The Cookout* (2004).

NINA FOCH

Born: 20 April 1924, Leiden, Zuid-Holland, Netherlands.
Died: 5 December 2008, Los Angeles, California, USA.

Cool and elegant Nina Foch excelled in such noir Columbia classics as *My Name is Julia*

Beverly Garland

The dazzling Marie Glory made her screen debut in *Le Miracle des loups* (1924) and four years later starred in the Marcel l'Herbier classic *L'Argent*. She moved into talking pictures with *Le Roi de Paris* (1930) and later made *The King of Paris* (not a remake) in the UK; she also starred in the French version of Noël Coward's *Private Lives*, *Les Amants terribles*. Her best-known role in later years was Brigitte Bardot's mother-in-law in *Et Dieu … créa la femme* (1956).

ISAAC HAYES

Born: 20 August 1942, Covington, Tennessee, USA.
Died: 10 August 2008, Memphis, Tennessee, USA.

Helping to craft the Memphis Sound for the iconic Stax label, songwriter Isaac Hayes went on to become a bejewelled funk superstar in his own right. His epoch-making score for *Shaft* (1971) brought him an Oscar and two Grammy awards. Having starred in the Blaxploitation classic *Truck Turner* (1974), he appeared in, among others, *Escape from New York* (1981), *I'm Gonna Git You Sucka* (1988) and *Hustle & Flow* (2005), as well as supplying the voice of Chef in *South Park* (1997-2005).

▷ Just as Hayes was a crucial component of Stax, so **Norman Whitfield**, who died in September, was a legendary mainstay of Motown. In 1977 his hit-laden soundtrack for *Car Wash* earned him a Grammy award.

FERNANDO HILBECK

Born: 7 July 1933, Madrid, Spain.
Died: 25 April 2009, Madrid, Spain.

As well as numerous Spaghetti Westerns, Anglo-Spanish character actor Fernando Hilbeck appeared in Orson Welles' *Chimes at Midnight* (1966) and the very early Dustin Hoffman vehicle *Un dollaro per 7 vigliacchi* (Madigan's Millions, 1967). Later credits included Paul Verhoeven's *Flesh + Blood* (1985) and the BBC mini-series *Nostromo* (1996). In the meantime, his gaunt features and soulful eyes made the chief zombie in *No profanar el sueño de los muertos* (The Living Dead at Manchester Morgue, 1974) resemble an El Greco martyr.

▷ Of other European genre actors, **Harald Heide-Steen Jr** (comic regular in Norway's

Ross (1945), *The Dark Past* (1948) and *Johnny Allegro* (1949). Moving to Metro, she played opposite Gene Kelly in *An American in Paris* (1951), was Marie Antoinette in *Scaramouche* (1952) and gained an Oscar nomination for *Executive Suite* (1954). Much TV followed, plus a distinguished second career as a drama teacher. A septuagenarian comeback included roles in *Sliver* (1993), *Hush* (1998) and *How to Deal* (2003).

BEVERLY GARLAND

Born: 17 October 1926, Santa Cruz, California, USA.
Died: 5 December 2008, Hollywood Hills, California, USA.

Beverly Garland began her film career in the classic noir *D.O.A.* (1950) and soon became undisputed Queen of 1950s 'B' movies, including five for director Roger Corman. Among these, she battled a giant fanged cucumber in *It Conquered the World* and enjoyed a rough-house role as a female sheriff in *Gunslinger* (both 1956). Rewarding latterday credits included two mothers: Tuesday Weld's in *Pretty Poison* (1968) and Michael Douglas' in *It's My Turn* (1980).

MARIE GLORY

Born: 3 March 1905, Mortagne-au-Perche, Normandy, France.
Died: 24 January 2009, Cannes, France.

Van Johnson

Edward Judd

'Olsenbanden' films of the 1970s and 80s) died in July. **Eva Pflug** – star of the first Edgar Wallace 'krimi', *Der Frosch mit der Maske* (1959), and Germany's hit *Space Patrol* TV series – died in August, and Russian-born beauty **Evelyne Kraft**, glamorous centrepiece of exploitation titles like *Paris Sex Murders* and *Lady Dracula*, in January.

MAURICE JARRE

Born: 13 September 1924, Lyon, Rhône, France.
Died: 28 March 2009, Malibu, California, USA.

Among composer Maurice Jarre's first film commissions were Georges Franju's *Les Yeux sans visage* (1959) and *Judex* (1963). Having made a smooth transition to English-speaking films with *Crack in the Mirror* (1960) and *The Longest Day* (1962), Jarre's work for David Lean brought him three Oscars – for *Lawrence of Arabia* (1962), *Doctor Zhivago* (1965) and *A Passage to India* (1984). His other scores numbered more than 150 and included *Isadora*, *The Damned*, *Plaza Suite*, *The Last Tycoon*, *Witness*, *Fatal Attraction*, *Ghost* and *Sunshine*.

CHARLES H JOFFE

Born: 16 July 1929, Brooklyn, New York City, New York, USA.
Died: 9 July 2008, Los Angeles, California, USA.

As a talent agent, Charles H Joffe was crucial

to the careers of such US comedians as Lenny Bruce and Robin Williams. With his business partner Jack Rollins, he ensured that Woody Allen directed as well as starred in *Take the Money and Run* (1969). Thereafter, Joffe was producer on nearly all of Allen's output, taking in *Annie Hall* (1977, which won the Best Picture Oscar) and *Hannah and Her Sisters* (1986) – right up to *Whatever Works* in 2008.

➤ Other producers who passed away in the year under review were **Mark Shivas** (October), whose credits include *A Private Function* (1984), *The Witches* (1990) and *Hideous Kinky* (1998), **Christian Fechner** (November), producer of *Camille Claudel* (1988), *Les Amants du Pont-Neuf* (1991) and *La Fille sur le pont* (1999), **B R Chopra** (November), a key figure in the development of Bollywood whose titles range across nearly 60 years, from *Afsana* (1951) to *Bhoothnath* (2008), and **Simon Channing Williams** (April), whose work with Mike Leigh yielded such titles as *High Hopes* (1988), *Naked* (1993) and *Vera Drake* (2004).

VAN JOHNSON

Born: 25 August 1916, Newport, Rhode Island, USA.
Died: 12 December 2008, Nyack, New York, USA.

After the success of *A Guy Named Joe* in 1943, Van Johnson's All-American charm made him a big wartime draw in frothy Metro musical-comedies, together with grittier war dramas like *Thirty Seconds over Tokyo* (1944) and *Battleground* (1949). In the following decade he added *The Caine Mutiny*, *The End of the Affair* and *23 Paces to Baker Street* to his CV. Later, he was chiefly occupied with continental exploitation films but made an exception for Woody Allen's *The Purple Rose of Cairo* (1985).

EDWARD JUDD

Born: 4 October 1932, Shanghai, China.
Died: 24 February 2009, Mitcham, Surrey, England.

Edward Judd got his big break in the prophetic SF classic *The Day the Earth Caught Fire* (1961), after which he secured the lead in *First Men in the Moon* (1964). His position as a sturdy stalwart of British SF and fantasy was bolstered further by roles in *Invasion*, *Island of Terror* and *The Vengeance of She*. But stories of his 'difficult' behaviour made casting directors steer clear. By 2004, his eclipse was so total that the *Equity Journal* announced his death five years too soon.

FRANCES KAVANAUGH

Born: 5 February 1915, Dallas, Texas, USA.
Died: 23 January 2009, Encino, California, USA.

Popularly known as 'The Cowgirl of the Typewriter', Frances Kavanaugh wrote the screenplays of some 30-odd 'B' Westerns of the 1940s and was script doctor on plenty of others. The vast majority of her output was for Poverty Row studios Monogram and PRC, sporting titles like *Dynamite Canyon*, *Blazing Guns*, *Tumbleweed Trail* and *Colorado Serenade*, and among the stars she wrote for were Ken Maynard, Bob Steele, Al 'Lash' LaRue and 'Singing Cowboy' Eddie Dean. She retired from showbusiness in the mid-1950s.

▶ A further Singing Cowboy, **Monte Hale** – who had a brief but prolific run at Republic, starting with *Home on the Range* in 1946 – died in March. Yet another veteran of 'B' Westerns, **Gale Storm**, starred in dozens of films for Monogram, Republic and Universal before graduating to the classic 1950s sitcom *The Gale Storm Show*; she died in June. Western and action stars of the 1950s and 60s who passed away in 2009 included **Philip Carey** (February) and **Jody McCrea** (April).

Patrick McGoohan

EVELYN KEYES

Born: 20 November 1916, Port Arthur, Texas, USA.
Died: 4 July 2008, Montecito, California, USA.

Referring to her role in *Gone With the Wind* (1939), Evelyn Keyes called her 1977 autobiography *Scarlett O'Hara's Younger Sister*. Brought into pictures by Cecil B DeMille, she numbered among her co-stars Robert Montgomery (*Here Comes Mr Jordan*, 1941), Dick Powell (*Johnny O'Clock*, 1947) and David Niven (*Enchantment*, 1948). She also scored a big personal success in *The Jolson Story* (1946). But, after roles in *The Prowler* (1951) and *The Seven Year Itch* (1955), she effectively retired from the screen.

PATRICK McGOOHAN

Born: 19 March 1928, Astoria, Queens, New York City, New York, USA.
Died: 13 January 2009, Santa Monica, California, USA.

Charismatic Irish actor Patrick McGoohan won enduring fame as the star of *Danger Man* (1960-67) and the self-devised Kafkaesque enigma *The Prisoner* (1967-68). He also turned down the role of James Bond, instead making a major impact in such films as *Hell Drivers* (1958) and *Ice Station Zebra* (1968). As well as directing an offbeat *Othello* adaptation (*Catch My Soul*, 1973), he won further plaudits for his roles (generally villainous) in *Escape from Alcatraz* (1978), *Scanners* (1980) and *Braveheart* (1995).

Paul Newman

RICARDO MONTALBÁN

Born: 25 November 1920, Mexico City, Mexico.
Died: 14 January 2009, Los Angeles, California, USA.

In addition to paying his dues as a smouldering Latin lover opposite Hollywood stars like Cyd Charisse, Esther Williams and Lana Turner, Ricardo Montalbán landed more rewarding roles in such films as *Border Incident*, *Battleground* (both 1949) and *Across the Wide Missouri* (1951). Later he became a Tony award winner on Broadway and in 1982 enjoyed his most famous and full-blooded film role, acting up a storm in *Star Trek II: The Wrath of Khan*.

▶ Also featured in *Across the Wide Missouri* was **María Elena Marqués**, who was a star in Mexico for some 40 years, particularly for her lead role in *La perla* (1947); she died in November.

ROBERT MULLIGAN

Born: 23 August 1925, The Bronx, New York City, New York, USA.
Died: 20 December 2008, Lyme, Connecticut, USA.

Having graduated from TV to film with *Fear Strikes Out* (1957), director Robert Mulligan crafted an enduring classic in *To Kill a Mockingbird* (1962), which remains an exemplar of his sincere and compassionate style. It was

followed by such rewarding titles as *Love With the Proper Stranger* (1963) and *Baby, the Rain Must Fall* (1964), after which he scored a colossal hit with the sentimental *Summer of '42* (1971). His later films made less impact, though his last, *The Man in the Moon* (1991), was characteristically sensitive and bittersweet.

▶ The Oscar-winning screenplay for *To Kill a Mockingbird* was the work of **Horton Foote**, who died in March and also wrote *Hurry Sundown* (1967) and *The Trip to Bountiful* (1985). Foote's fellow screenwriter **Millard Kaufman** died the same month, his credits ranging from *Bad Day at Black Rock* (1955) and *Raintree County* (1957) to *Never So Few* (1959).

PAUL NEWMAN

Born: 26 January 1925, Shaker Heights, Ohio, USA.
Died: 26 September 2008, Westport, Connecticut, USA.

Perhaps the greatest of all postwar Hollywood stars, and America's most generous philanthropist to boot, Paul Newman recovered from a singularly catastrophic film debut in *The Silver Chalice* (1954) with striking late-1950s performances in *Somebody Up There Likes Me*, *The Left Handed Gun* and *Cat on a Hot Tin Roof*. In Robert Rossen's *The Hustler* (1961), he achieved a new complexity as compromised pool player 'Fast Eddie' Felsen, though an Oscar for the role was withheld until he reprised it 25 years later in Martin Scorsese's *The Color of Money*. His parade of iconic 1960s anti-heroes – *Hud*, *Harper*, *Hombre*, *Cool Hand Luke* – culminated in *Butch Cassidy and the Sundance Kid* (1969) and a move into direction with *Rachel, Rachel* (1968). He subsequently starred in 1970s blockbusters *The Sting* and *The Towering Inferno*, then added to a long list of Oscar nominations with *The Verdict* (1982), *Nobody's Fool* (1994) and *Road to Perdition* (2002).

ANITA PAGE

Born: 4 August 1910, Flushing, New York, USA.
Died: 6 September 2008, Van Nuys, California, USA.

The last surviving star of American silent pictures, Anita Page rocketed to fame alongside Joan Crawford in the 1928 smash *Our Dancing Daughters*. She subsequently co-starred with

Lon Chaney in *While the City Sleeps* and made a triumphant transition to sound in *The Broadway Melody*. But an embarrassing flood of fan mail from Benito Mussolini, together with her unwillingness to sleep with the top brass at M-G-M, terminated her career at the early age of 23. Sixty years later, she made a surprising comeback in several indie horror flicks.

MICHAEL PATE

Born: 26 February 1920, Drummoyne, New South Wales, Australia.
Died: 1 September 2008, Sydney, New South Wales, Australia.

Michael Pate's film career began and ended in his native Australia. In the meantime he went to Hollywood, where his saturnine looks were well exploited in such films as *Hondo* (1953), *The Oklahoman* (1957), *Curse of the Undead* (as a vampire gunslinger, 1959), and *Major Dundee* (1965), plus a slew of television. Back in Australia, he starred in the Network Ten series *Matlock Police* and was writer-producer of *The Mango Tree* (1977) and *Tim* (1979), also directing the latter.

TULLIO PINELLI

Born: 24 June 1908, Turin, Piedmont, Italy.
Died: 7 March 2009, Rome, Italy.

Having won a contract with Rome's biggest film company, Lux, playwright Tullio Pinelli met Federico Fellini, whose first nine films as a director Pinelli would co-write. These included *I vitelloni* (1953), *La strada* (1954), *Le notti di Cabiria* (1957), *La dolce vita* (1959), *8½* (1963) and *Giulietta degli spiriti* (1965), all but two of which brought Pinelli Oscar nominations. After working for directors like Alberto Lattuada and Liliana Cavani, Pinelli was recalled into the Fellini fold for *Ginger e Fred* (1985) and *La voce del luna* (1990).

▷ Two other Italian screenwriters, **Marcello Fondato** and **Ennio de Concini**, died within a week of each other in November. Both were best known for their collaborations with horror maestro Mario Bava: Fondato on *I tre volti della paura* (1963) and *Sei donne per l'assassino* (1964), and de Concini on *La maschera del demonio* (1960) and *La ragazza che sapeva troppo* (1963).

Harold Pinter

HAROLD PINTER

Born: 10 October 1930, Hackney, London, England.
Died: 24 December 2008, London, England.

Arguably the greatest of all postwar British playwrights, Harold Pinter was awarded the Nobel Prize for Literature in 2005. He also made a major impact on cinema, most memorably in his collaboration with director Joseph Losey on *The Servant* (1964), *Accident* (1967) and *The Go-Between* (1971). His own broodingly sinister dramas formed the basis of *The Caretaker* (1964), *The Birthday Party* (1968), *The Homecoming* (1973) and *Betrayal* (1982), while his artful adaptations of other writers' work included *The Pumpkin Eater* (1964), *The Quiller Memorandum* (1966), *The Last Tycoon* (1976), *The French Lieutenant's Woman* (1981), *The Comfort of Strangers* (1991) and *Sleuth* (2007). And, having started out as an actor, in later years he resurrected this sideline in such films as *Mojo* (1997), *Mansfield Park* (1999) and *The Tailor of Panama* (2001).

EDMUND PURDOM

Born: 19 December 1924, Welwyn Garden City, Hertfordshire, England.
Died: 1 January 2009, Rome, Italy.

The highlights of Edmund Purdom's brief Hollywood career involved substituting for Mario Lanza in *The Student Prince* and Marlon Brando

Natasha Richardson

Peter Rogers

in *The Egyptian* (both 1954). The latter was an expensive fiasco, as was Purdom's next, *The Prodigal* (1955), whereupon he began a long career in Italian exploitation films. There were periodic returns to the UK, yielding roles in *The Beauty Jungle* and *The Comedy Man* (both 1964), plus a stint as director-star of the notorious British slasher *Don't Open 'Til Christmas* (1984).

ROBERT QUARRY

Born: 3 November 1925,
Santa Rosa, California, USA.
Died: 20 February 2009,
Woodland Hills, California, USA.

Having struggled to make an impression in earlier films, Robert Quarry was a memorably sardonic bloodsucker in the 1970 sleeper hit *Count Yorga Vampire*. As well as a Yorga sequel, he also starred for AIP in the exotic shockers *The Deathmaster* and *Sugar Hill* and went to England to appear in *Dr Phibes Rises Again* and *Madhouse*. After his career was derailed by a car accident and a severe mugging, he was given numerous latterday roles by fringe filmmaker Fred Olen Ray.

➤ Another significant AIP name from the early 1970s was screenwriter **Christopher Wicking** (*Scream and Scream Again* and – for Hammer – *To the Devil a Daughter*), who died in October. **Chris Bryant**, co-writer of *Don't Look Now*

(1973) and *The Awakening* 1980), died later the same month. Another horror name, **Harry Spalding** (aka Henry Cross) – who wrote *Curse of the Fly* (1964) and *The Watcher in the Woods* (1980), among others – died in July. Finally, **Forrest J Ackerman** – 'Mr Science Fiction', longtime editor of *Famous Monsters of Filmland* and occasional actor – passed away in December.

JANE RANDOLPH

Born: 30 October 1915, Youngstown, Ohio, USA.
Died: 4 May 2009, Gstaad, Switzerland.

At RKO in the 1940s, Jane Randolph was a worldly-wise presence in both *The Falcon's Brother* and *The Falcon Strikes Back*, bringing the same quality to *Cat People* (in which she's stalked by a shadowy panther in two unforgettably queasy sequences) and its fey semi-sequel *The Curse of the Cat People*. Going freelance, she played a smouldering beautician in the noir classic *Railroaded!* and a pert insurance investigator in *Abbott and Costello Meet Frankenstein*, after which she retired to Spain.

➤ Other Hollywood leading ladies of the 1940s were **June Vincent**, who died in November and starred in *Black Angel* (1946) and *The Creeper* (1948), and **Susanna Foster**, the soprano star of Universal's 1943 *Phantom of the Opera* remake, who died in January.

NATASHA RICHARDSON

Born: 11 May 1963, London, England.
Died: 18 March 2009, New York City, New York, USA.

Making an impact in the lurid *Gothic* (1986) and the sensitive *A Month in the Country* (1987), Natasha Richardson was then cast by director Paul Schrader in the title role of *Patty Hearst* (1988). Further Hollywood projects followed – *The Handmaid's Tale*, *The Comfort of Strangers* (both 1990, the latter for Schrader again) and *Nell* (1994) – but Richardson's chief preoccupation was a successful conquest of Broadway. Sporadic latterday film appearances included the 2005 titles *The White Countess* and (as both star and executive producer) *Asylum*.

PETER ROGERS

Born: 20 February 1914, Rochester, Kent, England.
Died: 14 April 2009, Gerrards Cross, Buckinghamshire, England.

Having been associate producer to his wife Betty Box on several minor postwar comedies, Peter Rogers became fully fledged producer on, among others, *You Know What Sailors Are* (1954) and *Time Lock* (1957). In the early 1970s, he added *Assault*, *Revenge* and *All Coppers Are...* to his CV. All these, however, were overshadowed by the 30-strong comedy series initiated by *Carry On Sergeant* in 1958. Among Rogers' other credits were such quasi-Carry Ons as *Nurse on Wheels* (1963) and *The Big Job* (1965).

➤ As well as 'Mr Carry On' himself, three of the series' regulars also departed this year – **Jack Douglas** (who died in December and was in *Matron*, *Abroad*, *Girls*, *Dick*, *Behind*, *England*, *Emmannuelle* and *Columbus*), **Dilys Laye** (February; *Cruising*, *Spying*, *Doctor* and *Camping*), and **Wendy Richard** (February; *Matron* and *Girls*).

ANN SAVAGE

Born: 19 February 1921, Columbia, South Carolina, USA.
Died: 25 December 2008, Hollywood, California, USA.

Ann Savage's signature role was the predatory Vera, a world-class femme fatale in Edgar Ulmer's six-day PRC wonder *Detour* (1945). Before it, a Columbia contract had yielded three films with her *Detour* co-star Tom Neal, whom she disliked. After it, she was in such titles as *Scared Stiff* (1945) and *Satan's Cradle* (1949) before a brief career in television. In 2007 she made a remarkable comeback in Guy Maddin's *My Winnipeg*, playing the director's mink-swathed mom.

SONJA SAVIĆ

Born: 15 September 1961, Čačak, Serbia, Yugoslavia.
Died: 23 September 2008, Belgrade, Serbia.

Cult Serbian star Sonja Savić became famous, aged 16, in the 1977 comedy *Leptirov oblak* (Butterfly Cloud). She subsequently won festival awards for *Secerna vodica* (Sugar Water, 1983), *Zivot je lep* (Life is Beautiful, 1985) and *Kruh in mleko* (Bread and Milk, 2001). In her own estimate her most demanding role was in *Braca po materi* (Maternal Brothers, 1988), while her only international project was *The Dark Side of the Sun* (also 1988), with a young Brad Pitt.

➤ Other notable European actors who died this year include **Marisa Merlini** (July), who starred in the Italian postwar smash *Pane, amore e fantasia* (1953), and **Annie-Marie Blanc** (February), who played the lead in the Swiss wartime classic *Gilberte de Courgenay* (1941). From Germany, **Karl Michael Vogler** (June) was best known as Field Marshal Rommel in *Patton* (1970). And Russian cinema lost two major figures – **Nonna Mordyukova** (July) and **Oleg Yankovsky** (May). The former was made famous by *Molodaya gvardiya* (1948), the latter was best known for Andrei Tarkovsky's *Zerkalo* (1975) and *Nostalghia* (1983); both were named People's Artists of the USSR (in 1974 and 1991 respectively).

CHARLES H SCHNEER

Born: 5 May 1920, Norfolk, Virginia, USA.
Died: 21 January 2009, Boca Raton, Florida, USA.

The name of producer Charles H Schneer, coupled with that of special effects wizard Ray Harryhausen, spelt movie magic to several generations of budding filmgoers. The two men collaborated first on 1950s SF classics like *It Came from Beneath the Sea* and *20 Million Miles to Earth*, afterwards graduating to mythological fantasies *The 7th Voyage of Sinbad* (1958) and *Jason and the Argonauts* (1963). Other projects included *The Valley of Gwangi* (1969), two 1970s Sinbad sequels, and – their last – *Clash of the Titans* (1981).

RON SILVER
Born: 2 July 1946, New York City, New York, USA.
Died: 15 March 2009, New York City, New York, USA.

Between the iconic television series *Rhoda* (1975-78) and *The West Wing* (2001-06), Tony award winner Ron Silver enjoyed several eye-catching film roles, from *The Entity* (1981) and *Silkwood* (1983) to *Blue Steel* (1989) and *Ali* (2001). His most notable role was probably Claus von Bulow's defence lawyer in *Reversal of Fortune* (1990). Well known as a liberal activist, his political sympathies took a pronounced rightward turn in his final years.

GREG SMITH
Born: 4 November 1939, London, England.
Died: 19 February 2009, London, England.

Late in his career, producer Greg Smith's name was attached to such distinguished items as *Twelfth Night* (1996) and *Agnes Browne* (1999). He was also behind the film version of *Dad's Army*, a Spike Milligan biopic and the 1978 remake of *The 39 Steps*. But he will remain best remembered for his pivotal role in the astonishing success of British sex comedies during the 1970s, in particular the money-spinning Columbia-backed series initiated by *Confessions of a Window Cleaner* (1974).

CHARLES TINGWELL
Born: 3 January 1923, Coogee, Australia.
Died: 15 May 2009, Melbourne, Australia.

'Bud' Tingwell began his career in Australian films and in 1952 went to Hollywood for *The Desert Rats*. During a 17-year stint in England, he starred in the ATV soap *Emergency – Ward 10*, all four of M-G-M's Miss Marple films and Hammer's *Dracula Prince of Darkness* (1965). In 1973 he returned to his homeland, and 26 years later was awarded the Order of Australia. He enjoyed an Indian summer in a host of distinguished Australian films, notably *The Castle*, *Innocence*, *Irresistible* and *Jindabyne*.

REG VARNEY
Born: 11 July 1916, Canning Town, London, England.
Died: 16 November 2008, Budleigh Salterton, Devon, England.

East End comic Reg Varney achieved fame in various TV sitcoms – *The Rag Trade*, *Beggar My Neighbour* and, pre-eminently, *On the Buses* (1969-73). The first of these gained him showy roles in *Joey Boy* (1965) and *The Great St Trinian's Train Robbery* (1966); the third sired a same-titled cinema spin-off that became Britain's biggest moneymaker of 1971 and itself sired two sequels. Two more off-beat Varney vehicles followed in 1972 – *Go For a Take* and *The Best Pair of Legs in the Business*.

COY WATSON JR
Born: 16 November 1912, Los Angeles, California, USA.
Died: 14 March 2009, Alpine, California, USA.

Coy Watson first appeared on film, aged nine months, in *The Price of Silence* for the Selig studio. His father was a Mack Sennett employee and occasional member of the Keystone Kops, and in due course Coy became known as the Keystone Kid. He worked with such 1920s superstars as Lon Chaney, Marion Davies, 'Fatty' Arbuckle and John Barrymore, and in the meantime all eight of his siblings also turned to acting. He retired aged 18 and became a noted news photographer.

➤ Coy's younger brother **Delmar Watson**, who also exchanged the role of child star for news photographer, predeceased Coy by five months, in October. He was one of several actors associated with the vintage Our Gang comedies who died this year. Among them were **Bobby Mallon** and **Buddy McDonald** (both in September), **Henry 'Spike' Lee** (November) and **Shirley Jean Rickert** (February).

JAMES WHITMORE
Born: 1 October 1921, White Plains, New York, USA.
Died: 6 February 2009, Malibu, California, USA.

James Whitmore won a Golden Globe for his second film, *Battleground* (1949). Thereafter his M-G-M contract yielded roles in *The Asphalt Jungle* (1950) and *Kiss Me Kate* (1953), while a spell at Warner Bros involved a heroic stand against giant ants in *Them!* (1954). Other major titles include *Crime in the Streets* (1956), *Black Like Me* (1964) and *Chato's Land* (1972), plus an Oscar nomination for *Give 'em Hell, Harry!* (1975) and a touching performance as the prison librarian in *The Shawshank Redemption* (1994).

The following people also died during the period under review...

July 2008 – director Bruce Conner; producer Lata Ryan; writer-producer Luther Davis; editor James Heckert; make-up artist Benôit Lestang; singer Jo Stafford; actor-writer Peter Coke.

August 2008 – director-cinematographer Leonard Hirschfield; producer Howard Minsky; screenwriters Leopoldo Serran and Ted Mosel; cinematographers Robert Jessup and Tomislav Pinter; art directors Vlastimir Gavrik and José Duarte; composers Tadashi Hattori and Eldon Rathburn; actor-director Jud Taylor; actors Gertan Klauber, George Furth, and Roberta Collins.

September 2008 – directors Florestano Vancini, David (Hugh) Jones and Jun Ichikawa; cinematographers Julio Madruga and Jeri Sopanen; editor Anne Sarraute; stuntwoman Alice Van; actor-director Miguel Corcega; actor John Matshikiza.

October 2008 – director Servando González; producers John Daly and Gianluigi Braschi; composer Neal Hefti; actor-director Per Sjostrand; actor-choreographer Peter Gordeno; actor-singer Mae Mercer; actor-comedian Rudy Ray Moore; actors Robert Arthur, House Peters Jr, Kim Chan, Vija Artmane, Ken Ogata, Françoise Seigner, Suzzanna, John Ringham, Estelle Reiner, and Roy Stewart.

November 2008 – directors Stanislaw Rózewicz and Charles Matton; director-cinematographer Georges Dufaux; screenwriter Robert Schlitt; editor Keiichi Uraoka; make-up artist Charles Schram; actors Marcelle Derrien, Michael Higgins, Michael Hinz, Fong Lung, Jan Machulski, and De'Angelo Wilson.

December 2008 – director Bob Spiers; director-writer Gerard Lauzier; screenwriter Dale Wasserman; cinematographer Alain Renoir; composer Derek Wadsworth; Burlesque legend Bettie Page; actor-singer Eartha Kitt; actors Paul Benedict, James Bree, Horst Tappert, Kathy Staff, and Kwang-Jung Park.

January 2009 – directors Alvin Ganzer and Tapan Sinha; producers Ned Tanen, Jacques Bar and Leo Fuchs; Z-movie maestro Ray Dennis Steckler; writer-director François Villiers; producers Arthur A Jacobs and Georges Cravenne; screenwriters Johannes Mario Simmel and Mickell Novak Seltzer; composer Angela Morley (aka Wally Stott); actor-stuntman Gerry Crampton; actor-singer Olga San Juan; actors Russ Conway and André Badin.

February 2009 – producers Peter Shepherd and Hercules Bellville; writer-director Francis Marischka; screenwriter Hugh Leonard; cinematographer Josef Vanis; art director Linwood Taylor; actor-director Dana Vavrova; actors Jean Martin, Susan Walsh, Claude Nollier, Oreste Lionello, Frank Gallacher, and Roland LeSaffre.

March 2009 – writer-director-actor Ronald Tavel; actor-director Åke Lindman; producer Robert Haggiag; former UA executive Stephen Bach; screenwriter Laura Toscano; cinematographer Danny Betterman; actors Sydney Chaplin, Anna Manahan, Minoru Ohki, John Franklyn-Robbins, Altovise Davis, and Terence Edmond.

April 2009 – director Lee Madden; novelist J G Ballard; actor-director Feroz Khan; actors Louis Perryman, Maxine Cooper, Jane Bryan, Tita Muñoz, Lesley Gilb, and Bea Arthur.

May 2009 – director-producer-writer Marc Rocco; producer Mort Abrahams; showbiz legend Danny La Rue; actors Fred Delmare, Fritz Muliar, Monica Bleibtreu, Lucy Gordon, Simon Oates and Barbara Rudnik.

June 2009 – director Bob Bell; director-cinematographer Peter Newbrook; screenwriter Ric Hardman; set decorator Hugh Scaife; showbiz superstar Michael Jackson; actors Dorothy Layton, Jo Anna March, Shih Kien, Mary Howard, and Jan Rubes.

Index

Index

The Wave 155
Waveriders 155
Wendy and Lucy 155
What Just Happened? 156
Who Killed Nancy? 156
Wild Child 156
The Women 157
Wonderful Town 157
The World Unseen 157
The Wrestler 157

X-Men Origins: Wolverine 12,158
The X-Files: I Want to Believe 158

Year One 159
Yes Man 159
You Don't Mess With the Zohan 160
Young @ Heart 160
The Young Victoria 160

Zack and Miri Make a Porno 161
Zero: An Investigation into 9/11 161

La Zona 161

ACTORS, DIRECTORS AND WRITERS

Affleck, Ben 135
Auteuil, Daniel 44

Baldwin, Alec 98, 107
Bale, Christian 13, 141, 142, 168
Basinger, Kim 37
Bates, Kathy 40, 48, 111, 155
Bening, Annette 157
Binoche, Juliette 115, 130, 137
Black, Jack 159
Blanchett, Cate 47
Bonham Carter, Helena 142
Boyle, Danny 131, 166
Branagh, Kenneth 31, 151, 152
Brody, Adrien 37
Brolin, Josh 104, 153
Brosnan, Pierce 99, 101, 165
Brown, Dan 18

Cage, Nicolas 23, 24, 90
Caine, Michael 48, 64, 87
Carrey, Jim 13, 149, 159
Chabrol, Claude 71, 175
Chan, Jackie 65, 91
Claudel, Philippe 87
Clooney, George 13, 36, 181
Coen, Joel 36
Coen, Ethan 36
Crowe, Russell 31, 32, 130, 135, 141
Cruise, Tom 145, 151
Cusack, John 44, 83
Craig, Daniel 13, 50, 51, 118, 1119
Crump, James 28
Cruz, Penélope 57, 152, 167
Curtis, Jamie Lee 27, 111
Curtis, Richard 31, 103, 131, 162
Cusack, Joan 44
Cyrus, Miley 77

Damon, Matt 39, 134, 148
Davies, Terence 26, 108, 133
del Toro, Benico 39, 126
Deneuve, Catherine 26, 42

De Niro, Robert 123, 124, 156
Demme, Jonathan 88, 121
Depardieu, Gérard 22
DiCaprio, Leonardo 31, 32, 122, 123, 166
Diaz, Cameron 107, 108
Diesel, Vin 13, 22, 60
Douglas, Michael 71, 1198
Downey, Robert Jr 13, 145, 146

Eastwood, Clint 74
Efron, Zac 13, 14, 79, 80

Fassbender, Michael 17, 56, 81, 164
Fiennes, Ralph 28, 121, 168
Fincher, David 47
Firth, Colin 44, 57, 67, 69, 99, 142, 163
Fraser, Brendan 85, 88, 106
Frears, Stephen 40, 174
Freeman, Morgan 48

Garai, Romola 17, 164
Giamatti, Paul 55

Hanks, Tom 13, 42, 164,173
Harlin, Renny 14
Harrelson, Woody 66
Harris, Ed 20
Hatcher, Teri 45
Hathaway, Anne 34, 69, 121, 134
Hoffman, Dustin 91, 92, 93, 104, 140, 197
Hoffman, Philip Seymour 31, 53, 139
Hopper, Dennis 39, 111, 139, 174
Howard, Ron 18, 39, 67
Hudson, Kate 34, 107
Huston, Angelica 34, 41

Ifans, Rhys 31
Irons, Jeremy 20, 116

Jackman, Hugh 20, 21, 158, 167
Jackson, Samuel L 92, 133
Jolie, Angelina 38, 39, 91

Kapoor, Anil 131
Kidman, Nicole 7, 20, 21
Kingsley, Ben 57, 62, 98, 153, 162
Knightley, Keira 5, 55, 164, 165

Ledger, Heath 48
Levinson, Barry 156
Luhrmann, Baz 20, 21

McDormand, Frances 36, 104
McGregor, Ewan 18, 85, 165
McQueen, Steve 81, 164, 192
Malkovich, John 36, 167
Mamet, David 122
Martin, Steve 22, 144, 174
Mendes, Sam 123, 167
Miller, Frank 133
Moore, Demi 64
Moore, Julianne 29, 127
Mortensen, Viggo 20, 72, 73
Murphy, Eddie 102
Murray, Bill 42, 69, 97, 167
Myers, Mike 98, 167

Neill, Sam 17, 49
Nighy, Bill 31, 150, 151, 152
Nolan, Christopher 48

Nolot, Jacques 25, 177

Oldman, Gary 149
Owen, Clive 55, 86
Ozon, François 17, 164

Pacino, Al 16, 123, 124
Palahniuk, Chuck 41
Paltrow, Gwyneth 148, 167
Parker, Alan 173
Patel, Dev 11, 131, 165, 166
Perry, Matthew 14, 112
Pfeiffer, Michelle 40, 173
Phoenix, Joaquin 148
Pitt, Brad 36, 47, 148, 203
Postlethwaite, Pete 16

Quaid, Dennis 59

Rampling, Charlotte 17, 22, 54
Reeves, Keanu 49
Reilly, Kelly 56, 117, 118
Reynolds, Burt 36, 196
Roache, Linus 26
Robbins, Tim 42
Roberts, Julia 157, 181
Roeg, Nicolas 108, 117, 118, 173
Rourke, Mickey 157, 158
Ruffalo, Mark 29

Sandler, Adam 13, 25, 81, 116, 160, 167
Scott, Ridley 31, 32
Scott Thomas, Kristin 44, 56, 87, 163
Servillo, Toni 52, 72, 177
Sheen, Michael 47, 67, 150, 170
Singer, Bryan 151, 152
Smith, Will 75, 76, 102, 128
Soderbergh, Steven 39
Softley, Ian 85
Sokurov, Alexander 16, 176
Stiller, Ben 13, 109, 145, 146, 178, 181
Stone, Oliver 153
Streep, Meryl 13, 53, 99
Swinton, Tilda 36, 47, 89, 100

Tandan, Loveleen 131
Theron, Charlize 37, 76
Thurman, Uma 95, 157
Travolta, John 13, 32, 143

Vang, Bee 74
Van Sant, Gus 104

Weaver, Sigourney 22, 71, 153
Williams, Robin 109. 198
Wilkinson, Tom 55, 125, 152
Winslet, Kate 121, 122

Yeoh, Michele 22, 61, 106

Zellweger, Renée 20, 106, 108, 109